MW01008624

A
NERVOUS
STATE

A

NERVOUS

STATE

Violence, Remedies, and Reverie
in Colonial Congo

NANCY ROSE HUNT

Duke University Press | Durham and London | 2016

© 2016 Duke University Press
All rights reserved
Printed in the United States of America on acid-free paper ∞
Designed by Heather Hensley
Typeset in Minion Pro and Trade Gothic by Copperline

Library of Congress Cataloging-in-Publication Data
Hunt, Nancy Rose, author.
A nervous state : violence, remedies, and reverie in colonial Congo /
Nancy Rose Hunt.
pages cm
Includes bibliographical references and index.
ISBN 978-0-8223-5946-3 (hardcover : alk. paper)
ISBN 978-0-8223-5965-4 (pbk. : alk. paper)
ISBN 978-0-8223-7524-1 (e-book)
1. Belgium—Colonies—Congo (Democratic Republic)—Social conditions.
2. Medicine—Colonies—Belgium—History. 3. Congo (Democratic
Republic)—History—1908–1960. I. Title.
DT657.H86 2016
967.51'024—dc23
2015024233

Cover art: Group photograph of the Bolenge hospital staff, 1924. Courtesy
of Disciples of Christ Historical Society, Nashville, Tennessee.

Duke University Press gratefully acknowledges the support
of the University of Michigan, which provided funds toward
the publication of this book.

Ina Rose
Ina Rose sat on a tack
Ina Rose

For my dear mother, in loving memory

CONTENTS

ABBREVIATIONS

AA	Archives Africaines, Brussels
AAeq	*Annales Aequatoria*
AE	Affaires étrangères
AI	Affaires indigènes
AIMO	Affaires Indigènes et Main d'Oeuvre
AT	adminisrateur territorial
BBOM	*Biographie Belge d'Outre-Mer*
BCB	*Biographie Coloniale Belge*
CARD	Colonie Agricole pour des Relégués Dangereux
CDD	commissaire du district
DCHS	Disciples of Christ Historical Society, Nashville
FBEI	Fonds du Bien Etre Indigène
GG	gouverneur général
HCB	Huileries du Congo Belge
LSE	London School of Economics
MRAC	Musée Royal de l'Afrique Centrale, Tervuren
NGO	nongovernmental organization
RA/CB	Rapports Annuels, Congo Belge
ROM	Royal Ontario Museum, Toronto
SAB	Societé Anonyme Belge pour le Commerce du Haut Congo
SAMI	Service d'Assistance Médicale Indigène

SECLI	Societé Equatoriale Congolaise Lulonga Ikelemba
SPA	Service du personnel d'Afrique
UAC	United Africa Company
VGG	vice-gouverneur général

ACKNOWLEDGMENTS

This book began as if on a whim. Many journeys and friendships followed.

A startling archival discovery when delving into missionary papers in Bamanya, Zaire, enabled a research chase a dozen years later. I learned about an intriguing colonial planter whose interests mixed up Heinrich Heine, enemas, and this Belgian's performative experiments in increasing the low birth rate near Ingende.[1] Just when it became clear that my pursuit risked becoming narrowly medical, too biographical, and shallow in time, the Archives Africaines in Brussels opened some seven new kilometers of records from the governor general's offices in ex-Léopoldville. During a splendid year at the Netherlands Institute for Advanced Study (NIAS) in Wassenaar, I began to explore their wealth: notably some interrogation records from Equateur. I remain grateful to NIAS for the helpful colleagues, many North Sea walks, and help comprehending Dutch texts, as I sorted out diverse Charles Lodewyckx and Flemish strands that year.

When I began deepening this history, exploring harm in and beyond the Free State years, this planter figure became minor, unable to keep up with the new questions, bulging and fitful these. As repetition in insurgency over a *longue durée* suggested intricate narrative lines about colonial policing and poetic imaginations, I decided to separate out the biographical story for another day.

There were many ethnographic, field and archival visits along the way. A major blessing and turning point came in 2007 with a Fulbright fellowship in Kinshasa. Thanks for this magnificent intellectual year go first and foremost to *mon frère*, Professor Sabakinu Kivilu. I made several trips into the field, the most wonderful on back streams seeking traces of Maria N'koi. Another special journey came due to the generosity of the talented, charismatic Flemish primatologist and bonobo expert, Jef Dupain, now of the American Wildlife Foundation. From his base in Kinshasa, he invited me to travel with him and potential funders to observe the fascinating work of his ecotouristic nongovernmental organization in the Lomako forest, near former Abir sites as well as Befale and Ekafera.

All my historian colleagues at the University of Kinshasa made this year stimulating and pleasant, notably Jean-Marie Mutamba Makombo, Sindani Kiangu, Jérome Mumbanza mwa Balele, Isidore Ndaywel è Nziem, and Noel Obotela. Other precious guides, aides, and comrades in Kinshasa included Mama Pauline, Tuna, Nzolani, and Papa Mfumu'eto the 1st. I am especially grateful to Emery Kalema, superb student and research assistant, for the beautiful, exacting transcription and translation work. Without all of my graduate students in Kinshasa, my trip to Maria N'koi's world would never have happened. First, we interpreted the Jadot and Collignon texts and later the field findings. I am grateful for so many ideas and favors extended from fellow travelers Jean Ibola (in 2001) and Philippe Ibaka, as well as from Anne Marie Akwety, Antoine Yok Bakwey, Nephtali Fofolo, Aimé-Willy Kaba, Pitshou Lumbu, Charlotte Olela, and Jean-Baptiste Wolopio.

Charles Lonkama was a marvelous, astute guide on that Maria N'koi journey. I thank him and everyone along the way in Besefe, Ikanga, and Bokatola, notably Mboto Y'Ofaya, David Ikeke, Thomas Ndio, Dieudonné Bosembu, Nzampenda Lokamba, Bekolo Lokombo, Booto, and Eloliin Ikanga. Indefatigable and generous in sharing memories and archives was Antoine Sonzolo Efoloko in Mbandaka. Not to be forgotten were the precious, spirited interventions about Zebola, Yebola, and Maria N'koi from the Ekonda researcher, then supervising oral traditions at Kinshasa's national museum, Papa Martin Biolo Mbula. I thank them all.

Mama Ekila and her family, notably Jean Fodderie and Albert Fodderie, shared invaluable memories. They also teased, welcomed, and offered brilliant, concrete forms of help from Ekila restaurants in Brussels and Kinshasa and Fodderie quarters and ex-quarters in Mbandaka and beyond. I thank them as I do the skilled, thoughtful demographer Anatole Romaniuk, who welcomed me to Ottawa more than once, generously sharing ideas, memories and archives with me.

A Nervous State would not *be* and would not be the *same* without Ann Stoler's generosity and discerning mind and sensibilities. Her wisdom, friendship, and invitations, professional and into her warm, loving home, steered me back to laptop screens with fresh ideas more than once. In particular, her remaking of *debris* as *ruination* arrived just before I left for Congo in 2007. It inspired my essay, "An Acoustic Register," about perceiving and narrating violence that came to anchor this book. At a much later stage, Todd Meyers deepened my understandings of Canguilhem and of Detroit. He listened, read, and suggested more to read, and his friendship made a lovely difference in the final stages of writing. When Jan Vansina phones often, it is a sign that one best hurry and soon. This generous, wise guide of long date persisted, shared, and fortified, and in Madison at a crucial stage, he lifted some of his own Equateur archive-on-loan into my car trunk.

Steve Feierman read and read again. Ever loyal, he also wrote for me again and again. Mostly, he advised brilliantly at several junctures while opening doors to intellectual worlds. Steve and I organized the first meeting of the fluid "Body/Antibody" alliance that met several times after African Studies meetings for camraderie and critique. It deepened wonderful intellectual friendships with Murray Last, Julie Livingston, David Schoenbrun, Lynn Thomas, and Sinfree Makoni too—splendid readers, interlocutors, wits, all.

That Steve and Julie invited me to join their African health cluster meant a year at the unmatched Wissenschaftskolleg. In Berlin, I tested and refined *A Nervous State*'s first draft and core concepts. I remain grateful to Luca Guiliani and his extraordinary staff for this bounteous year among wonderful, smart, and diverse souls. Special thanks for insights and amities go to Kamran Ali, Bruce Campbell, Dieter Ebert, Petra Gehring, Albrecht Koschorke (especially for his "Figures/Figurations of the Third"), Birgit Meyer, Iruka Okeke, Tanja Petrovic, Ilma Rakusa, Karl Schlögel, and Jojada Verrips (who helped me grasp the complex layers of a Flemish-Dutch text).

Congolese studies is a very special mesh of serious, creative, urgent intellectual workers who value rich, invigorating, and often quirky hedonisitic forms of exchange. In addition to many kindred spirits in Kinshasa and Mbandaka, I thank those in the North. Johan Lagae welcomed me to his home in Ghent again and again, while sharing with me his impeccable work, original ideas, and a conference co-organized in Kinshasa with Sabakinu. Jean-Luc Vellut listened and shared in all kinds of ways before my diverse research pursuits, including some archival notes from 1983. He answered countless questions, forwarded precious elements, gave us all the gift of his formidable work, and examined the maps with a critical eye. Filip De Boeck, ever creative and inspiring, shared and shared again. Joe Trapido showed up, and I am glad he did. Joshua Walker's helpful comments on the Maria N'koi chapter were perceptive, spot on. Bob White shared his work, enthusiasm, and contacts. He helped me come to meet the very special Ellen Corin and Gilles Bibeau in Montreal, a beautiful encounter at their home for which I remain most grateful. Kristien Greenen made Kinshasa infinitely more interesting and warm. Always pointing me in new directions, she also helped secure access to a photograph in speed time. Andreas Eckert, ever the hedonist, joined (and helped fund) the Congolese fold for a few days in 2011, joining with me and our doctoral students from Humboldt and Michigan so their work in Congolese history would benefit from serious criticism in a workshop at the Wiko in Berlin. I also thank Dominic Pistor, Lys Alcayna-Stevens, Césarine Bolya, Nichole Bridges, Tatiana Carayannis, Pierre Halen, Adam Hochschild, Bogumil Jewsiewicki, Mbala Nkanga, Katrien Pype, and Zoe Strother for sharing work and their ideas, energy, scholarship, and generosity.

Several scholars played critical roles as readers, critics, guides, friends, and referees. I especially thank Megan Vaughan, Jean Comaroff, Peter Geschiere, and Luise White. Veena Das read, intervened, and listened in Baltimore. Paul Landau sent his marvelous book through the mail. As part of a large network of historians and anthropologists of medicine in Africa, several members read work, issued invitations, critiqued chapters, and kept life and thinking fun. I am grateful to Wenzel Geissler, Kris Peterson, and Catherine Burns. Guillaume Lachenal and Vinh-Kim Nguyen, generous friends and kindred scholars of francophone Africa, paved the way toward a wonderful year in Paris. Vinh-Kim has welcomed me into homes in Montreal, Abidjan, and beyond for over a decade, and at many junctures he made academic life what it should be: warm, delightful, and acutely interesting, spilling into friendship while opening doors.

As this book went to press, I arrived as a Eurias fellow at the Institut d'études avancées in Paris, from where I had the pleasure of navigating some of this city's many scholarly and African worlds. I warmly thank Gretty Mirdal and her wonderful staff as well as the other fellows for this year. Very special thanks go to Marie-Thérèse Cerf for valuing my work and archive in Congolese comic arts and pointing the way, along with Bob White, to their recognition.

Michigan's Department of History has been an extraordinary intellectual home. I have found some of my most wonderful, astute colleagues and friends from throughout the world among historians and anthropologists in Ann Arbor. Special thanks for acts of kindness, rigor, and merriment go to some of my oldest and dearest friends: Katheen Canning, David William Cohen, Fred Cooper, Rudolph Mrázek, and Helmut Puff. I am grateful to all my colleagues for their work and our intellectual collaborations. For friendship, critical comments, smarts, and camaraderie, I especially thank Kathryn Babayan and Melanie Tanielian (for the swimming); Geoff Eley for the excellent comentoring;

Joel Howell, Marty Pernick, Liz Roberts, and Alex Stern for the solidarity; and for good deeds, warmth, and decency, John Carson, Dario Gaggio, Will Glover, Paul Johnson, Mary Kelley, Farina Mir, Gina Morantz-Sanchez, Rachel Neis, Doug Northrup, Minnie Sinha, and Scott Spector. I have been blessed to have an appointment in the medical school and benefited enormously from Michigan's unparalleled Joint Anthropology and History Program as well as its STS and African Studies programs. Tim Johnson was the best boss I ever had: thank you. I also am very grateful to my comrades current and past in African history and African studies for making our intellectual lives so interesting; Adam Ashforth, Mamadou Diouf, Rebecca Hardin, Mike McGovern, Kelly Askew, Frieda Ekotto, Simon Gikandi, Gabrielle Hecht, Judy Irvine, Derek Peterson, Howard Stein, and Butch Ware are among them.

Many colleagues and friends invited or welcomed me to present my work as lectures, workshop talks, and conference presentations. Some critiqued or helped it appear in print. I am grateful to Vincenne Adams, David Arnold, Charles Becker, Florence Bernault, Sanjoy Bhattacharya, Doris Bonnet, Geert Castryck, R. Lane Clark, Jean Comaroff, John Comaroff, Barbara Duden, Jean-Paul Gaudrillère, Tamara Giles-Vernick, Jon Glassman, Rob Gordon, Jane Guyer, Clara Han, Bob Harms, Patrick Harries, Patricia Hayes, Sarah Hodges, Marcia Inhorn, Neil Kodesh, Gesine Kruger, Guillaume Lachenal, Paul Landau, Pier Larson, Anne Lovell, Greg Mann, Phyllis Martin, Assitou Mbodj, Vinh-Kim Nguyen, Randall Packard, John Parker, Katrien Pype and her fabulous Congo Research Network, Ciraj Rasool, Richard Rottenburg, David Schoenbrun, Lyn Schumaker, Bonnie Smith, Dan Smith, Arno Sonderegger, Lynn Thomas, Mark Thurner, Helen Tilley, Lenny Urena, Wim van Binsbergen, Boris Wastiau, and Claire Wendland.

I presented parts of this work many times. Wonderful and rare was the Parisian African venue, the "intelligent" Pitch Me bar, as part of a *Politique Africaine* evening organized by Guillaume Lachenal and Assitou Mbodj with RFI's Sonia Rolley and Editions Karthala's Xavier Audrain. I am also grateful for invitations to present work at the Working Group on Anthropology and Population, Brown University; History and Philosophy of Science, Cambridge University; the 2011 Dahlem Koferenzen, Berlin; Ecole des Hautes Etudes, Paris; Ghent University; Harvard African Studies Workshop; African Studies, Indiana University; Institut Français de Recherche pour le Développement en Coopération; International Women's University; Anthropology, and History of Science, Medicine & Technology, Johns Hopkins University; Katholieke Universiteit Leuven; KEMRI/Wellcome Trust Programme, Kilifi, Kenya; London School of Hygiene and Tropical Medicine; Max Planck Institute for the History of Emotions, Berlin; the Max Planck German-American Social Sciences Symposium; Anthropology, The New School; Nordic Cultural Fund, Helsinki; History, Northwestern University; Past & Present and Anglo-American Conference, London; Re:Work, Berlin; Royal Museum of Central Africa; Institut für Geschichte, Swiss Federal Institute of Technology; University of Amsterdam; University of Basel; Anthropology, History and Social Medicine, University of California, San Francisco; African Studies Workshop, University of Chicago; University of Hannover; Area Studies Centre, University of Leipzig; Body/Body Politics Seminar, University of Maryland; University of Nairobi; Wellcome Unit for the History of Medicine, University of Oxford; School of Medicine and Humanities, University of Puerto Rico; Institut für Afrikawissenschaften, University of Vienna; History, University of Washington; History, University of Western Cape; African Studies, University of Wisconsin-Madison, Centre of Global Health Histories, University of York; and African Studies, Yale University.

I learned enormously from three doctoral students now all producing fascinating, sparkling work in the ethnographic history of Congo: Isabelle de Rezende, Pedro Monaville, and Jonathan Shaw. Michigan blessed me with many doctoral advisees whose work has inspired and made life interesting: Tara Diener, Andrew Ivaska, Sara Katz, Shana Melnysyn, Nana Qauarshie, Eric Stein, and Edgar Taylor. I also appreciated learning from Apollo Amoko, Andrew Cavin, Robyn d'Avignon, Brady G'sell, Menan Jangu, Cyrius Khumalo, Marti Lybeck, Clapperton Mavhunga, Edward Murphy, Vanessa Noble, Emma Park, Ashley Rockenbach, Lenny Urena, and in Kinshasa, from Mbul Imuan'l Kwete.

Many more lent a hand. Jake Coolidge is a gifted cartographer whose fine research and design work are featured here. I am profoundly grateful to Anneke Prins, a scholar of Dutch medieval texts, who delighted in producing a gorgeous translation from Flemish of Boelaert's first Lianja variant for me. Grey Osterud offered invaluable suggestions about one version of the manuscript. Pedro Monaville shared with me his splendid work on postal politics, his interview with Justin Bomboko, and his understanding of Mongo stereotypes. Marti Lybeck did a marvelous translation of some Paul Schebesta passages for me. Isabelle de Rezende translated a key song. I am indebted to Vincent Kenis, formidable Congolese music historian, collector, and curator, for designing the Loningisa photomontage and permitting its publication here. From Kinshasa, Léon Tsambu sent me Bowane clues. In Madison, Philip Janzen and Nicole Eggers helped locate a precious archival letter. John and Sue McNee were dear, generous hosts more than once while I did research in Ottawa and Brussels.

Tristine Smart has been a most loyal and skilled research assistant for many years. She read every word many times with an astute mind and canny eye, maintaining consistency and precision in all kinds of matters bibliographic and stylistic, in addition to sorting out copyright, securing permissions, and doing precious research. I am deeply grateful for her generosity, smarts, good sense, and dedication. Faith Cole, Alyssa Meller, and indexer Eileen Quam were fine last minute additions to the endeavor.

Perhaps no one helped me more than the remarkable historian and archivist Honoré Vinck who I first met during that Bamanya archival discovery in 1989. Father Vinck has been generously providing me with contextual information and primary source evidence ever since, including translations and photographs. Many other archivists, librarians, curators, and image warehouses offered precious help, either when I did research in their repositories or through replying to queries about copyright, permissions, and image reproduction. I extend my deep thanks to staff at the Archives Africaines, Brussels, especially Pierre Dondoy; the Royal Museum of Central Africa, Tervuren, notably director Guido Gryseels and his staff (especially Sabine Cornelis, Francoise Morimont, Patricia Van Schuylenburgh, Boris Wastiau); Prof. Dr. Joachim Piepke, Director, Anthropos Institute, Sankt Augustin, Germany; Paul Bettens, Société Royale Belge de Géographie; Jakub Sobik and David Assersohn, Anti-Slavery International, London; Nicola Woods, Rights and Reproductions Coordinator, and curators, Royal Ontario Museum, Toronto; Sarah Harwell and Elaine Philpott, archivists, Disciples of Christ Historical Society, Nashville; London School of Economics Archives; Lucy McCann, Bodleian Library of Commonwealth & African Studies, Rhodes House, Oxford; archivists, the Regions Beyond Missionary Union Archive, University of Edinburgh; the Library of Congress Manuscript Division, Washington, DC; University of Chicago Special Collections; and University of Wisconsin-Madison Memorial Library Special Collections. Their kind assistance is gratefully acknowledged. I also thank Olivier Cruciata, UK Development Manager, for enabling publication of an image from Studio Harcourt Paris, known since 1934 for its distinctive lighting and celebrity photographs.

As a friend, Ken Wissoker has been there almost the longest, since 1977 to be exact. The long tale of savvy, superb taste, guidance, and generosity, now as my editor, continues. Due to Ken, Duke University Press is a special institution with a marvelous sense of design. I am also grateful to Duke's Susan Albury, Jade Brooks, Michael McCullough, Bonnie Perkel, Christine Riggio, and Christopher Robinson.

Terrific, loyal friends helped out with favors and affection, their goodwill spilling into intellectual advice, practical help, and festivity. Patricia Hayes made sure I walked seasides while my work received a critical airing, more than once, in her splendid Western Cape milieu. Gesine Kruger welcomed in Zurich and Hanover. Phyllis Martin brilliantly advised and shared. Richard Eaton, Miranda Johnson, and Laura McCloskey are amazing scholars and dear friends. Gretchen Elsner-Somer believes in walking. So we did. Anne Bogat untangled and insisted on wonderful food. Dani Frank listened, pointed the way, and handed me spare keys. Marie Lechat introduced me to her distinguished father, Michel Lechat, and he told me Graham Greene stories, clarified, and encouraged. Judith and Ernie Simon welcomed me over and over again. Jacques Milesi shared Paris with me.

Sarah Schulman called me again and again when cancer made its journey. Vinh-Kim made me buy a killer coat in Montreal to mark an ending to a medicalization endured. Others saw me through these days in practical ways, especially the ever generous and dear Kathleen Canning, Jayati Lal, and my family.

My dear father Fraser, sisters Jeannie and Katie, brother Bill, and cousins McNee of Toronto and Ottawa teased. Everyone came together resoundingly in 2007 and again since for a very big birthday on a distinguished lawn in the Berskshires. As individuals and pairs, they listened, welcomed, and shared, while Fraser kept us alert, insisting on concerts, exhibits, backroads, and other pleasures in his world and beyond.

Thank you, truly, one and all.

The Belgian colonial state was born from nervousness, and Congo became a nervous state.

There are many ways to enter into a history of Congo's Equateur, once the vortex of a ghastly rubber regime in King Leopold II's Free State colony, unhinged by terrible war, scandal, and "atrocities."[1] Cut-off human hands, rape, and war were not uncommon in the 1890s and 1990s. Yet to again seek narrative entry through "The horror! The horror!"[2] would unleash *catastrophe logic* and efface much else. This book pursues a different reading of the past, by attending to perceptions, moods, and capacities to wonder and move. Generational nicknames in women's dance songs from the 1930s are helpful clues. They divided elders who experienced abuse and grueling rubber taxes from a younger Equateur generation, consuming through francs. A violent economy (operating through payments in kind) marked seniors with brutality and death, while the youthful singers understood that money in coin was fashioning their desires.[3] Money time went with distraction, many lovers, and few or no children, their songs suggest. This sardonic consciousness is a fitting beginning here, since Equateur, once an atrocious milieu, bred perceptions of reproductive mayhem and the pursuit of pleasure for decades to come.

Were bodies "imprinted by history" in this Congolese region? Michel Foucault's words offer up an important interpretive challenge, although this book seeks to reshape their weight. When explaining *genealogy*,

Foucault wrote of "a body totally imprinted by history" and the "stigmata of past experience," too.[4] Wary of imperial and degenerationist tropes like stigmata and "racial suicide,"[5] this book questions any *total* colonial marking of bodies and imaginations. Colonial numeracy[6] in Equateur became stark, repetitive, and fixated on childlessness. Consequently, how reproductive disruption remade lives and horizons is a part of this undertaking.

The event and structure of violence, their duration and reproduction across generations—through bodies, imaginations, and intellects—underlie this exploration. Georges Canguilhem defined health as "a certain latitude a certain play." I historicize *latitude* within a *shrunken milieu*, drawing on Canguilhem to do so.[7] The first idea embraces motion, plasticity, maneuvering, and will. *Shrunken* suggests loss, emaciation, and constraint. *Ruination* is valuable for discerning the duration of duress.[8] Congolese produced intense trafficking in stories and yearning, however, suggesting a capacious range in artifice, secrecy, and distraction. Combing for the withered *and* for plasticity helps shake loose the aleatory *amid* harm.

Not Aftermath

A Nervous State is situated in southern Equateur, a humid expanse of marshy, equatorial forest stretching from ex-Coquilhatville (Mbandaka), north to Basankusu, west to Boende, and south of the Ruki toward Bokatola, sometimes beyond to Inongo (see map 1.1). It is a wide region, where many speaking languages close to Lomongo have long lived. Equateur became part of King Leopold's notorious Congo Free State from its emergence in 1885. The ambitious Belgian monarch secured his anomalous colony, almost a personal possession, through cunning machinations, notably at the Berlin Conference of 1884–85, which set the terms of partition for Africa.

In Equateur, conquest and concessionary politics combined with forced extraction of wild-growing rubber. From the 1890s, the results were nasty, shocking, with punitive forms of coerced labor, jailing wives as hostages, and severing human hands and feet from dead and sometimes live bodies. Graphic mutilation photographs produced horrified public attention, with moral indignation ricocheting around the globe. Ever since, these "Congo atrocities" have been generalized, often wrongly, to all corners of the immense colonial state.

Contemporary investigation focused on the same region at the crux of this history.[9] Travelers, missionaries, journalists, the British Consul, and the king's own commissioners easily journeyed by steamboat up the Congo and along its tributaries, the Ruki, Busira, Tshuapa, Maringa, Lopori, and Lulonga rivers. So it was that the brutalities of this key rubber-producing zone became so well known. From the moment the first photographs of mutilated youth appeared, they became ammunition in the growing propaganda war against Leopold's Congo. Humanitarian critics included the sensitive, observant Irishman British Consul Roger Casement,[10] the relentless British publicist E. D. Morel, scores of evangelicals, and some prominent public figures like the novelist Mark Twain.

As spectacular violence congealed as *event*, the process included—in Joseph Conrad's brilliant words "fascination" before "abomination." Congo's violence remains iconic and spectral in public consciousness today, though more through the still-circulating mutilation photographs than through Conrad's perceptive *Heart of Darkness*.[11] The history of Congo "atrocities" again reached wide audiences through the success of Adam Hochschild's riveting *King Leopold's Ghost*, published in 1998. It movingly dramatizes terrible violence and humanitarian rescue through a strong pair: the duplicitous scoundrel of a king and the indefatigable, heroic propagandist Morel.[12]

A Nervous State aims for no heroes, no villains, and little haunting.[13] Seeking to move historical imaginations beyond horror and humanitarianism, it sets Free State violence within this pivotal region's long duration of grim, predatory raiding. Second, it asks about *afterward*. Seeking a range of sequels up through Belgian Congo's final decade—the 1950s—numerous *afterlives* emerge as quite distinct from a single *aftermath*. The distinction is decisive, just as Nietzsche's concept, an "excess of history," forces grappling with distortions arising from a lopsided, teeming fixation with a past.[14]

Postcolonial witnessing of a past abomination remains vexed. Michael Taussig and Edward Said turned to Leopold's Congo in recent years, rereading Conrad and Casement with a careful urgency. With Hochschild's valuable treatment among others, and Hannah Arendt's critical insights abetting, scholars have spawned a new fashion: reading imperial violence as "genocide."[15] The Free State has been rescripted as a—or the—worst example. Such scripting is not all wrong, yet comparative tally sheets will never adequately weigh harm. The resulting reduction of Congo's history in public memory (and much African history teaching and texts) suggests a single trajectory with two hinges: first "red rubber," then Lumumba's assassination (now often extended by a third point: terrible rape and war in Congo's east since 1996). Such a storyline of continuity and repetition has history moving from violence to violence, malfeasance to malfeasance.

A few years ago, historical geographer Nigel Thrift remarked: "To produce a sense of trajectory" is the "nearest thing to what *used to be* called history." He proposed exploding simple narrative lines into an *unresolved* set of spaces, dynamics, and lives. An *unsettled course of multiples* would impart friction across "plural events" and locations.[16] It is time to set aside epic-like narratives emplotting the Belgian king as villain and Morel as redemptive hero. Many scholars are rethinking history and event in relation to duration and immediacy, experience, memory, historicity, and futures. This book joins the ferment while taking up harm and pleasure in a shrunken colonial milieu and in postcolonial historiography too.

Combining *event* with *afterward* enables tender complexities and surprise. Circumventing the ungainly word from the trauma register, from *aftermath* and its condescending counterpart *resilience*, enables something fresh.[17] Historical excess, wrote Nietzsche, is "detrimental to life," to human *plasticity*.[18] An openness to plasticity is important for a part of the world that knew such terrible harm and injury. Narration with a traumatic structure will not do. Maurice Blanchot's *The Writing of the Disaster* challenges such simplicity while writing, poetically so, of *undecidability* in and also in the wake of, catastrophe: "disaster ruins everything, all the while leaving everything intact."[19] *A Nervous State* tracks perceptions, sounds, and the everyday, and it uncovers brutal rape, nervous laughter, and flight. It embraces toil, reverie, even joy, albeit largely *after* the Free State's end in 1908. A dizzying range of topics and persons appear: nervousness, therapeutic insurgency, a penal colony, modern dance music, sexual economies, wonder, and song.

Southern Equateur positions analysis where spectacular violence erupted, terribly so. Reproductive trouble followed, alarming the nervous and the natalists. We cannot disregard such facts and artifacts, yet we *can* dispense with catastrophe as our scaffolding. Blanchot's method for interjecting incertitude lay in writing by fragments. This history, not a *writing of disaster*, blasts apart *event–aftermath* as narrative. It seeks to unsettle the scholarly fixation with social suffering, an anthropological subfield that with trauma studies has shaped the humanities and interpretive social sciences since the 1990s.[20] I value the best of such work,[21] yet seek to flag persistent *figurations*. A good reason to hesitate before portraying Congolese as forlorn and bereft, set within an aftermath of "social suffering" or "zone of . . . abandonment,"[22] lies in the predictability of the *segmented, straight line*—before–after, shock–aftermath, disaster–ruin. The hinged shape positions subjects as under impact, and disregarded is the therapeutic, steeped in risk and surprise.

A traumatic structure *with hinge* breaks into a brittle two: causality | effects. Reducing the force of event to *aftermath* limits angles, flattens perceptibility, intellects, and moods. Not unlike a continuous linearity, a doubled *event–aftermath* form misses layers, accidents, the uncertain, in a word, the *aleatory*—a concept that takes historical writing beyond necessity, in and through encounters, traces, and surprise. Althusser called for history to be "open to a future that is uncertain, unforeseeable, not yet accomplished," while distinguishing the "lasting" from the "ephemeral." Aware of "the openness of the world towards the event, the as-yet-unimaginable," method turns to "cases, situations, things that befall . . . without warning."[23]

Congolese in their shrunken Equateur milieu were open to futures. Avoiding the *event–aftermath* straitjacket does not mean dodging rape, childlessness, or lasting harm. Yet the eschewal does mean asking about past futures,[24] about how to make our histories capacious and unsettled, with diverse kinds of *crossing*.[25] Knowing that *catastrophic logic* was common among colonial experts from Equateur's interwar years is an excellent way to begin. Using "techniques of nearness"[26] and staying open to what Nietzsche called "plastic powers of life,"[27] such formulations work to counter stark causality and open attention to the unforeseeable and the senses. A *spectral frame*, reveling in haunting, would restir "excess of history."[28] Instead, *A Nervous State* demonstrates that Equateur's diverse subjects drew on lithe powers of the imagination, sensing—and making use of—the wondrous and the monstrous.

Nervousness

We have not thought enough either about colonies as nervous places, productive of *nervousness*, a kind of energy, taut and excitable. This word, with a modernist historicity, traveled from colonies and back to them again. Nervousness should not be confused with anxiety. *Nervosité* has been applied to corporeal systems, historical epochs, nations, bodies, dispositions, and moods. It suggests being on edge. Its semantics are unsettled, combining vigor, force, and determination with excitation, weakness, timidity. Nervousness yields disorderly, jittery states, as in a *nervous wreck*, *nervous exhaustion*, a *nervous breakdown*, or, as history has shown, a nervous national mood.

As emic, contemporary terms describing those who colonized, their conditions and states, nervous and nervousness fade into analytic concepts with multiple registers. The diverse agents and subjects of the Congo Free State and the Belgian Congo moved among violence, refusal, paranoia, and insurgency. Congolese also developed maladies with uneasy, restless, convoluted dimensions that unsettled, while their seemingly frantic treatments often *calmed* (quieting troubled, unwell women, as we will see).

Conrad wrote of the breaking of "civilized nerves" in Leopold's Congo. He joined repulsion and lost bearings with going native, with European selves lost in magical ritual and racialized violence. In his short story "An Outpost of Progress," two Europeans found themselves alone in savage forests, minus "the high organization of civilized crowds," nervous, unable to sustain a "belief in the safety of their surroundings." Their "contact with pure unmitigated savagery" yielded more nervousness, "sudden and profound trouble into the heart," while the "suggestion of things vague, uncontrollable, and repulsive, whose discomposing intrusion excites the imagination" was trying "civilized nerves of the foolish and the wise."[29] Conrad's diagnostics endured in fact and fantasy, with images of lone, nervous white men who lost it, through alcohol, sadistic violence, and suicide. Such facts and dreamwork are a part of *A Nervous State*. His interpretation offers a glimpse of the same colonial, Leopoldian world where Conrad spent time, and as one where Europeans acted fretfully, especially toward "natives" deemed dreadful.

Conrad's reading opens up a wide semantic range for *a nervous state*, an idiom kept at play in this work. The word *nervous* was part of European vocabularies in metropolitan and colonial life, in medical, psychiatric, military, aesthetic, and domestic domains. The Free State came into being just about the time neurasthenia became fashionable, from Vienna to the United States. When Max Weber sought care in 1890s nerve clinics, he liked to "play the nerve specialist" in private, while also interpreting comparative religious phenomena as "a nerve specialist of religion." Weber's intellectual reckoning with the "spectrum of . . . nerve semantics" coincided with nervousness reaching epidemic proportions, with "nerves" as code for mental disturbance: "nerve trouble." The ubiquity of nervous states "characterized the age,"[30] well beyond Europe and its intellectuals. Weber was busy diagnosing bureaucracy as the state's "true nerve centre." At the same time, in Germany, rumor warned of "neurasthenics" weakening "the nerves of the whole nation."[31] In European and American medical discourse, nervousness became a "disease of civilization,"[32] with neurasthenia paired with willfulness as its antidote. This doubling remained significant. While "tropical neurasthenia" characterized European colonial maladies, this diagnosis does not seem to have entered Belgian Africa under this label.[33] Nerve specialists and nerve clinics hardly found their way to Belgium's colony either,[34] though neurasthenic idioms were legion. The vocabulary suggests a range of behaviors and practices, including European suicide and vernacular forms of disturbance and treatment.

Above all, an emphasis on nervousness signals that moods *matter* in historical interpretation. Tension, edginess, and volatility were pervasive in colonial

Equateur, where rubber bonuses once fed terrible, nervous excess. Nervousness endured in everyday modes of presence and kinds of dissent in this once-shattered world, left shrunken but most alive. Uneasy alternations of fright and force, dread and vigor, recurred over and over again within this willful, nervous state, while uprisings fed its tenacious, overwrought, fearful edge.[35]

Modes of Presence

Frantz Fanon wrote about medicine as one of the colonial "*modes of presence.*" He showed how doctoring combined in late colonial Algeria with another mode of presence, policing.[36] When and how medicalization and security crossed, acted in concert, or diverged—as state modalities and as terrains of colonial experience—is a fundamental question here. It goes with the challenges of writing a new kind of medical history and of rethinking states: how to *sense* such modes while rendering them in relation to *matters therapeutic* writ large.

Compelling work in imperial medical and sexual history has produced an emphasis on "the biopolitical state." Historians of race, empire, eugenics, and epidemics have thought with *biopower*,[37] a concept elaborated by Foucault in relation to governing life, population, and territory.[38] Biopolitics, he theorized, embraces security, the aleatory, and risk.[39] Yet historians of colonial medicine have tended to labor in relation to the sanitary and epidemiological, sometimes the sexual, the reproductive, and health promotion.[40] For colonial situations, where policing, violence, nervousness, and medicine persisted and crossed, the concept of a *state of exception* also inspires.[41]

Colonial states governed through technologies of numeracy, screening, diagnosis, and security. Yet medical historians have tended not to move not far beyond the clinical and demographic and the state-derived. Historians of Africa have been exceptional in mobilizing expansive notions of healing and embracing the vernacular, sometimes shunning Foucault in the process.[42] This book began as a contribution to the recent spate of literature on biopolitical states, imagining it would be fruitful to marry South Asianist (Foucauldian, state-focused) and Africanist (vernacular, subaltern) approaches to medicine and empire. But the project morphed into something quite different as not only security and the carceral but also *nervousness* came to the fore. In Equateur, *therapeutic insurgency* incited colonial policing and *nervous states* on all sides. *Dread* seeped into worries about the birth rate and saturated the high incidence of clashes over insurrectionary healing. Dread and multitudes went in pair, forcing this reconsideration of colonial practices and dispositions far beyond the narrow brief of conventional medical history.

Medical anthropologists have, since 9/11 and Guantanamo, been quick to show the biopolitical and the securitizing coming together in early twenty-first-century biosecurity.[43] Yet few historians have investigated similar intersections in a colonial situation. I have found it useful to think of the Belgian colonial state as having two guises, tracks, or *modes of presence*: with a biopolitical face and a nervous one. This foundational *heuristic* here yields neither a dichotomy nor parallel domains but a constellation of mobile, shifting elements, composed more of "figures of the third" than pairs.[44] While akin to bureaucracies, the guises became like moods—one more guilty and humanitarian, the other energized by dread. The biopolitical worked to promote life and health, whereas the nervous policed and securitized as it sought to contain menacing forms of therapeutic rebellion. Each track faced roughly the same "natives," yet colonial perceptions divided by guise—into ailing, grotesque, needy bodies on the one hand, and unruly healers, prophets, rebels on the other. Sometimes separate, sometimes intertwined, the nervous also went with a fearful, jumpy mode of presence. This tonality fundamentally shapes this history of colonial power; edgy, agitated, restless, it grew more paranoid with time.

States and Persons

The biopolitical state in Equateur moved from sleeping sickness to research regarding *dénatalité*, the venereal, and sterility. The nervous state began with the tense, aggressive Free State, fierce Stanley, taut officers, wrathful, inebriated concession agents, and armed sentries. The same nervous state culminates with a penal colony named Ekafera, while the biopolitical concludes with an infertility clinic some fifty miles away. The penal colony and infertility clinic were in the same territory, sited where a notorious rubber concession produced terrible abuse in the 1900s. The brutality became spectacularized through the camera lens of Alice Harris. Several photographs became well-publicized, anti-Leopoldian propaganda (with some specifying those pictured as Nsongo, a label that persisted in colonial consciousness, we will see).[45] By the 1950s, the penal colony and clinic were spaces of experimentality. Doctors were conducting sterility and demographic research; the penal camp confined and punished *relegated* therapeutic rebels.

The two trajectories complicate this history with moods, subaltern therapeutics, and securitization. Much evidence comes from the archive of the nervous state,[46] busy policing the risk of "xenophobia." Yet the heuristic of two lines with a doubled culmination—clinic, camp—ultimately proves too neat. Medicalizing and securitizing spilled outside these spatial bounds, sometimes crossing, bleeding with effervescence or paranoia.

While the biopolitical knew uneven intensities, Congolese expectations, performances, and claims erupted, sometimes with force or rage. The idea of exposing intricacies and layers complicates the heuristic too. Present are doctors at the march, gloomy biopoliticians, prison wardens, and daydreaming subalterns. The positive *and* negative registers of vernacular therapeutics are fundamental. Healing and warlike qualities formed a rich "argument of images,"[47] with recurring idioms of protection, elimination, refusal. Congolese healing *fed* outbursts of official nervousness. Refinements in state technique resulted. In tracking *crossings* among not two but three domains—the biopolitical, the securitizing, and the vernacular—this book immeasurably widens the compass of a colonial medical history.[48]

The last three neoliberal, postcolonial decades, a time of venality and penury, have roused much debate about antecedents: about colonial states, in and outside of African history. Scholars have taken to a range of notions: commandment, arterial power, bifurcation; or gatekeeper, shadow, and fragile states; and the politics of bellies, wombs, and sorcery.[49] This book neither engages or challenges such abstraction and its use, but rather suggests how to bring the state *near*, to make it perceptible through reading sounds, images, persons, and moods. This rethinking begins with traces in the archive, investigating how persons, often individuated at that, acted, wrote, and made up the state, enacting its deeds, applying its regulations, while using words and techniques and sometimes duplicity or flight. When state agents sensed and realized, so too a mood—collective, institutional, individualized—may often be discerned. Insisting that persons composed the state and its guises engenders much about tonality and the dispositions of specific administrators, governors, or chiefs.

Sometimes the person of the state was a territorial agent, sometimes a military officer or sanitary agent. While usually Belgian, a few were Swiss, Italian, even Congolese: a chief, soldier, or court clerk. Some white men lived in an urbane mansion of sorts, others in a humble abode hours from the next post. That some slept with guns under pillows is suggested. Some journeyed by steamer or took to poetry. Some had children and helped shape Equateur's shadowy *métis* culture of Belgians and Congolese mingling, letting in some Portuguese. Europeans sometimes found each other obtuse, pompous, or manic. Some worked in the metropole—Brussels, Antwerp, Flanders, Wallonie—

such as tropical medical specialists who critiqued from afar. The tenor ranged from clichéd gloom, reminiscent of the timorous *Heart of Darkness*, to cold, willful bureaucratic talk about extinction or confinement in reserves.

Rarely was the state anonymous in Congolese eyes.[50] They long daydreamed about forcing out "Bula Matari," their sobriquet for the "rock-breaking" Henry Morton Stanley, the king's early, violent broker who had wielded dynamite. While Congolese extended this nickname of destruction to all Europeans, the state appropriated the phrase to invoke mighty state power. Bula Matari, hyperreal, spirit-like, was also concrete, present in taxes, prisons, flagpoles, and passports.[51] While individual agents toured, ordered, menaced, and reported, some took time off. Some sought out lovers or angled for hens, eggs, and game for meals. That such traces hover in the archive suggests much about subtleties worth gleaning and the value of an approach privileging "nearness."

Belgians commonly approached the colony as empiricist, masterful, relentless engineers. This observation has been made in relation to their energies in road, bridge, and clinic construction, however, rather than their development of a secret police, penal colonies, and relegation and surveillance technologies. Few would contest that Belgian Africa, from the 1920s, had the most impressive, systematic, natalist, family health programs and epidemiological routines in colonial Africa, aiming at sleeping sickness, leprosy, safe childbirth, venereal disease, infant nutrition, and kwashiorkor. These aspects earned the Belgian regime much praise, though criticisms for its "paternalist" orientation also followed.[52] The relative prosperity of the colonized during the postwar years went with rigid racial logics and deeply hated inequalities and segregation.

The degree and effects of Belgian medical relentlessness have been evaluated as part of new research on the emergence of HIV/AIDS in central Africa, leading to a sobering appreciation of the problem as one of technological fervor.[53] As Belgian Congo publicized itself as a "model colony," its glossy semiotics effaced forced labor, chains, the *chicotte* (whip), the color bar. This analysis grapples with the efficient, machine-like "smoothness" and "happy engineering"[54] of colonial Congo's middle and late years. Partly from the 1920s, forcefully from 1945, a developmentalist machine worked with sophistication to create the unique Belgian imperial model: a skilled, stabilized labor force; the highest standard of living in sub-Saharan Africa; early, extraordinarily intense welfare capitalism fueled by pronatalism; ubiquitous clinics and maternity wards; and gestures of urbanity from modernist, high-rise buildings and air conditioning in big Kinshasa to copious bicycles almost everywhere.[55] Did the reasons for this eager momentum lie in unspoken, unconscious guilt about early colonial violence and scandal? *A Nervous State* broaches this delicate question. If in Equateur the weighty facts of population—fright before widespread childlessness—played a part in driving this developmentalist push, so did nervousness and dread.

Therapeutic Insurgency

Congolese often met new medical technologies with vivid rumors about autopsies, doctors, and blood collecting.[56] Some have explored the biomedical in Africa as forms of policing and subject formation aimed at managing subaltern bodies and producing healthy, docile, semi-modern persons.[57] In Congo, religious movements seemed foreboding, ever menacing to turn violent. This is the first study to consider *relegation* and the carceral technologies developed to arrest, control, segregate, and remake Congolese *therapeutic rebels*. Two analytic moves are combined: one toward "the carceral,"[58] the other returning to Eric Hobsbawm's prescient, useful, if still jarring 1959 expression, "primitive rebels."[59] How primitivism bred state readings of rebels, sporting scant garb and wielding ritual devices, deserves more attention, as does the ever-canny, subaltern rousing of primitivist nervousness within a colonial state.[60]

African medical histories are deformed by language likening biomedicine to vernacular therapeutics, as if corresponding *systems* within a pluralistic domain. The pluralization of medicine, a theme first introduced—and beautifully so—by John Janzen, no longer may suffice as framing.[61] Too often, scholars have intimated that African healing was—is—parallel to biomedicine. The distortion deserves correction, and not only because it risks romanticization. Although interrogation of therapeutic multiplicity has been lively, with entangled strands, mixtures, and conflations,[62] a binary framework undercuts the negative dimensions of African healing by seeking equivalence in visibility and patterns of resort. Murray Last challenged the 1970s inclination to romanticize "traditional medicine" as a potential counterpart health system.[63] His notion of "knowing about not knowing" is helpful for what it says about latent knowledge, secrecy, and skepticism, as for the refusal to construe varieties of therapeutics—African, colonial, postcolonial—as "systems." Last pointed to asymmetries among the biomedical and vernacular, and the dearth of systematized knowledge in many medical cultures. In turning to thriving vernacular therapeutics in Africa, he pointed to their furtive, shadow-like character often as a "non-system," with secretive, unintended, and harmful aspects.

That the Belgian Congo targeted therapeutic, religious movements as "contagious" dangers needs scrutiny. In the 1950s, when Georges Balandier, Basil Davidson, and Thomas Hodgkin first tried to understand the Congolese prophet Simon Kimbangu and his imprisonment, they underlined *messianism* and *proto-nationalism*.[64] By the 1980s, Karen Field zeroed in on colonial states and the politics of antiwitchcraft movements,[65] while Steven Feierman has long shown how spirit mediums led battles against colonial conquest, stirring movements of "public healing" involving "social criticism" of harmful, "extended crisis of health, of reproduction, and of well-being."[66] Jan Vansina and colleagues instead underlined mobile, charm-based movements as reactive rituals of destruction and substitution, techniques that have erupted within central Africa over a very long *longue durée*, and well before the arrival of colonial duress.[67]

Healing and harming is a salient pair in Africa's histories, long and brief.[68] This work also owes much to Feierman's notion of public healing. Yet I pursue the secretive, negative, and harming side of African therapeutics much more than has been the case by most historians of health and healing.[69] Since 1996, the ubiquitous use of dreadful forms of sexual destruction among Maï-Maï combatants and other militia in eastern Congo has prompted important historical rethinking about how anti-kin outcasts, insurgents, and mobs of earlier epochs wielded violent charms with therapeutic aims. Often, the protective achieves force through being brutal, harmful, ruinous.[70] Armed Simba and Muleliste rebels deployed an array of technologies to make war and heal in guerilla battles of the 1960s.[71]

Likewise, the punitive, warlike edge of much collective healing in colonial Equateur was sharp. Speaking of *therapeutic insurgency* as well as war is helpful. The use and destruction of charms to expel colonial rule began at least in the 1890s and lasted until decolonization. Healing worked through spirit mediation, trance, and possession, medicinal assembly, use, and destruction. Charms would speak to hunger, misfortune, and penury, to fertility in hunting, fishing, and wombs. Yet words and deeds often signaled poisoning and revenge. This book traces such forms and techniques in relation to a nervous colonial state, ever ready to declare "states of exception," create "camps,"[72] and remove the eerie, the unfathomable, and the "xenophobic."

Infertility, Zest, Hedonism

Infertility disquiet in central Africa dates back to at least the seventeenth century, perhaps much earlier, in worlds where low population densities generally fit equatorial ecologies even after farmers arrived.[73] During colonial times, from Uganda to Cameroon, reproductive worry often turned into distorted scares. Whether in moralizing figments or fretful angst, fear ran contrary to reproductive realities.[74] So, asking whether a colonial infertility scare was veering toward fact, fiction, or fantasy—and when, how, and in whose minds—is important. Nervousness was significant and on all sides, as was whether something structural—material or economic—underlay perceptions and facts of childlessness.

Harsh, extractive colonial economies intruded from the 1880s, with profound demographic effects.[75] From the 1930s, infertility became a major scientific field for producing knowledge about peoples of southern Equateur (those, also increasingly glossed, assembled, and standardized as "the Mongo"), as well as about groups such as the Nzakara in nearby Afrique Equatoriale Française. By the 1960s, this entire wide region became pivotal to a demographic notion: the "central African belt of low fertility."[76] Statistics have effects. Using them to map Africa's equatorial zone suggested high sterility within and beyond bounded, contiguous, purified groups like "the Mongo." In the process, idioms of natural history coincided with the notion of a "primeval" region, with persons decadent, libidinous, and pathological. Reifying this "belt" *as* reproductive crisis suggested a uniformity to this tropical ecology, a world without children.[77] The result was to flatten complex, diverse histories of conquest, violence, and forced labor. Intricate detail about circulation, rape, healing, and infection ended up effaced, as did the economic and racialized structures shaping livelihoods and biologies—and surely psyches too.

Colonial *catastrophe logic* of a reproductive kind was not subtle. Nor was it singular. A stir about "race suicide" followed genocidal violence directed at the Herero in Deutsch-Südwestafrika.[78] W. H. R. Rivers, the prominent neurologist, anthropologist, and psychiatrist who played a large role in British treatment of shell shock during the Great War, also intervened in depopulation discourse in Melanesia. There, "race suicide" or "dying-out" races had long been tropes of imperial fantasy and overrule. Rivers was unusual in downplaying the role of venereal disease. He psychologized and politicized instead, while remembering the refrain of colonial subjects: "Why should we bring children into the world only to work for the white man?" He pointed to melancholy as defeatism underlying "racial suicide," expressed in conscious birth restriction and abortion. Declaring the problem had nothing to do with "original decadence" among races, as if they were necessarily headed for extinction, his vitalism accused, while pointing to the colonial reduction of "zest." Depriving colonized communities of economic intrigue had worked to eliminate "nearly all that gave interest to their lives."[79]

A similar kind of anti-catastrophic, romantic vitalism emerged in Flemish

Catholic circles. The antiliberal, anti–big finance views of Equateur's priests went with their yearning to rekindle a keenness for life through a common tongue; above all, they wished to nurture an emerging Mongo nation, soul, and language.[80] These priests could speak only so loud. From the 1930s, the idea of a "dying race" surfaced in Equateur, and state doctors joined officials in speaking a dark language entangling race, biology, and death, degeneration, shock, and extinction.

While the notions of race suicide and an infertility belt deserve skepticism, not *all* colonial infertility scares *were* distortions.[81] Alarm paralleled milieus of stark childlessness, widespread venereal infection and genital lesions. Among the Nzakara (in today's Central African Republic) as in a few Belgian Congo zones, venereal disease, barren marriages, childless adults, and a scarcity of infants and children became social facts, as well as metaphors for injury and tedium. Rich and wonderful evidence produced by the sensitive, creative French medic and ethnologist, Anne Retel-Laurentin, speaks powerfully to sterility-associated "ennui" among the Nzakara and an escalation in sorcery accusations.[82]

Some have shown how infertile Africans suffer from exclusion and shame. Others consider barrenness within narrow medical terms or as individualized suffering.[83] Significant is female knowledge about reproductive mishap in relation to bodies, diets, circumstances, aging. As Caroline Bledsoe has shown, contraceptive use may extend reproductive potential across a long life course for some, whereas the less fortunate are vulnerable, their bodies aging more quickly from overwork, fatigue, poverty.[84] Also relevant here is Retel-Laurentin's focus on sorcery allegations and metaphors shaping bodily and reproductive processes. Attention to ritual and everyday bodily practice is often as important as material, epidemiological conditions. *Fertility* is much broader than *the procreative* in Africa. Fertility may embrace getting married, building a house, attaining cloth, or enhancing the image of a strong chief. Yet the basis for all such symbolic repertoires remains the human body, a humoral zone, which in Equateur required irrigation to keep life and death flowing, to avoid the perils of blockage.

In central Africa's Lower Congo region, affliction manifested itself through fertility angst. When Atlantic slaving increased, women joined fecundity and healing associations like *kimpassi*.[85] In twentieth-century Equateur, subfertility stirred copious studies, abundant vernacular treatments, and movements of insurrection. But Congolese melancholia and mourning also proved difficult to find. No professional ethnologist—no one comparable to the talented Retel-Laurentin—ever arrived in this part of the Belgian colony. Medical doctors objectified, counted, generalized. Protestant and Catholic missionaries left behind rich archives in Edinburgh, Nashville, Bamania, and Flanders, but they and their Congolese literati never recorded life stories about childlessness. A few story slices, a couple poems, and many a song still give a strong sense here about how infertility enfolded with fright *but also* acceptance. Compensatory nimbleness surfaces again and again.[86]

Instead, hedonism and urbanity come to the fore,[87] especially as 1940s development-speak produced new desires and capacities. Security concerns fueled developmentalist logics, often spoken in humanitarian terms and aimed to end subfertility, raise standards of living, and shape aspirations. An old economy in kind, involving the gifting of women, wives, and hunted and gathered forest products, morphed, as the songs tell, into a colonial economy of money first and new kinds of eye-catching consumption and display. At the same time, more available and often strongly coerced venereal screening arrived as care, and not without the punitive edge common to most colonial medicine.

Historians of Africa have spilled much ink over whether the word *modernity* is acceptable, real or idiomatic, useful or mimetic, indispensable or hopelessly confused. This book sidesteps this debate as one of wheels spinning in vain. While not reluctant to use the words *modern* or *modernity*, I suggest the word *urbanity* may be more fruitful. We know that modern–traditional and urban–rural polarities are mobile fictions, unmappable in any firm, stable manner. It seems more fertile to note bleeding across categories and spaces, persons, and worlds. Urbanity underlines fluidity, and it shifts the idiomatic and material toward valences, manners, tempers, appearances, pursuits, and style. The urbane suggests elegance and sophistication, aspirations of refinement in a town, city, or worker's camp far up an equatorial river, but not remote either. Urbanity sits in a semantic polarity with the rustic, a semantic advance on the traditional and rural, it seems to me.

For Congo, urbanity has long been mixed up with hedonism, but we have been missing its historical textures. Hedonism did not begin with stylish *sapeurs* or Kinshasa bars in the 1950s, just as HIV histories need to move beyond mechanical logic (as in prostitutes or trains). At the very least, the Congolese search for pleasure fed emergent, complicated, sexual economies[88] in ways not always easy to decode. That is a key challenge here. All these aspects suggest urbanity as *latitude*, a word to which we will return.

A Shrunken Milieu

A Nervous State joins the insights of the major French sociologist of the colonial, Georges Balandier, with those of French philosopher and historian of
science, Georges Canguilhem. Balandier's insights into the pathological and
experimental within a "colonial situation" have simply not received the attention they deserve. This book marries them with Canguilhem's "shrunken milieu."[89] In many senses, Equateur was precisely that: a *shrunken milieu* undergoing compulsion, exhaustion, distress, but also refusal and insurgency from
the 1890s.

In this setting, we see a colonial medical science drawing on endocrinological, psychiatric, and psychosomatic ideas, all in global circulation at the time.
Equateur's doctors never spoke of *stress*, but they circled among the ideas that
produced this new 1960s buzzword, which emanated from the skill and flair of
an Austrian-Hungarian endocrinologist, Hans Selye, with a laboratory in late
1950s Montreal. In the 1930s Selye began experiments on "general adaptation
syndrome," on distress, breakdown, and shock.[90] About the same time, the
talented Jewish neurologist Kurt Goldstein was working against mechanical
ways of thinking about injury from Berlin. Goldstein's holism pictured human
organisms within *a milieu*, sometimes confronting catastrophe, though often
revealing a capacity to adjust and thrive even after devastation. Canguilhem
spoke of a "shrunken milieu" to draw attention to structural issues, even the
catastrophic, inhibiting a world and its inhabitants. In speaking of "latitude"
or plasticity, he used Goldstein's findings about human flexibility, adjustment,
and manipulation.[91]

Mechanistic logic about shock lurked in medical thinking about the birth
rate in colonial Equateur. Canguilhem's notion of latitude within a shrunken
milieu enables appreciating how men and women might fashion lives within
this colonial situation of forced labor, fatigue, and widespread sterility. *Milieu*
is a spatial and ecological concept. It suggests broad, inclusive diagnostics.[92]
Forged to counter mechanistic shock models, like those favored by doctors
in colonial Equateur, *milieu* aims its holistic approach on critical perplexities.
At the very least, if many Congolese were ailing in Equateur, countless strived
with agility and creativity, often outwitting or dodging the constaints and cap-
tivities of this colonial situation.

A colonial situation should be tackled as concrete and heterogeneous, Balandier wrote in his prescient essay of 1951, widely cited in recent years.[93] He often
wrote from Congo's neighboring French colony, from the vantage point of this

imperial borderland. Both the French and Belgians dealt with equatorial fallout from earlier times of concessionary violence and from cross-border currents still surging long after Simon Kimbangu's first emergence, arrest, and fame. An exuberant urbanity also joined Léopoldville (Kinshasa) and Brazzaville, and from this transcolonial position Balandier diagnosed colonial power as a "fragile edifice," usually in a "latent," unmistakable "state of crisis."[94] He declared most everything germane to colonial analysis: dimensions economic, moral, economic, psychological; collective representations, ruptures, symbols; colonized rejections, refusal points, and *adaptations*. A colonial situation was not one milieu but two—internal and external, of the colonized and of Europeans. He did not forget about troublesome, interstitial categories and figures either.

Balandier's method lay in tracking fault lines, crises, and "antagonisms" as the best "standpoint" for reading all the categories and forces at play. He suggested that colonial situations knew perversity, becoming sick and strange, and that sociological method in broaching the colonial had to be "in some measure clinical."[95] Few have noticed Balandier's interjection of a diagnostic, pathological register into theorizing the colonial.[96] As "a kind of social pathology," a colonial situation involved fixated, phobic aspects, and these drove late colonial emergencies. Fear and resentment transpired within what were lopsided, racialized worlds, with a tiny, "dominant minority" reigning over the large "numerical majority" ever lodged as a "sociological" minority.[97] Balandier pointed out that colonial situations were experimental, but not in the sense of living in a laboratory. Rather, writing long before experimentality became fashionable within Africa's Science and Technology Studies, he suggested brash, makeshift methods: "Colonialism appears as a trial, a kind of test imposed" on societies. It meant rather living within "a crude sociological experiment." A doubled process resulted, with the "'crises' created by colonialism" orienting more knowledge collection, while also manipulating in creating, imposing "sociocultural facts."[98]

Canguilhem never invoked the colonial, and he diagnosed plastic milieus. His language turned around health, capaciously defined, asking about tensions between "experimentally constructed conditions" and those who composed the milieu. Tackling disaster logic, the idea of being "commanded from the outside by the milieu," he saw potential in the catastrophic, in being caught up in a grim milieu: "A life that reaffirms itself against the milieu is a life already threatened." The person with a "healthy life," "confident in its existence, in its values," is able to manage "a life of flexion, suppleness." A catastrophic situation might entail broken, ruined persons, or "a certain latitude."

Canguilhem left room for "debate between the living and the milieu," whereas Balandier's colonial eye grasped debate erupting between the living and the living, appreciating how racial "opposition" became the phobic and fanatical.[99]

Both angles are useful. A contracted, shrunken milieu was surely basic to colonial situations everywhere. In Congo's Equateur, colonial demands yielded fatigue, likely withering and emaciation, yet not gaunt, childless persons alone. To suggest such a thing would follow the logics of colonial catastrophe with a narrative about suffering. The challenge, rather, is to rummage for traces of motion, plasticity, exuberance, and debate—forms of *milieu-making* all—while never losing sight of shrunkenness as fact and provocation.

This book points to healing as vernacular *experimentation* and seeks to understand constraints, breaches, and latitude within a vexed milieu. Healing often expressed itself *as* opposition, dissent, and security, *through* medicines, gestures, and the production of an event, *in* song, flight, and insurgency. Imagination was a resource. It was plasticity and it enabled debates that developed among Congolese about colonial hostility and their contracted lives. Canguilhem once wrote: "life is poor in monsters, while the fantastic is a world."[100] Colonial life in Equateur was rarely "poor in monsters," living or imagined, not in this part of the forest where children grew up hearing thrilling ogre tales and memories of battles and disfigurement. Through their stories, performances, healing, and rumors, Congolese kept the fantastic and monstrous alive as part of their concrete and imaginary worlds.

Canguilhem once sought out Bachelard to think about how the human imagination "incessantly deforms or reforms old images to form new ones," proliferating more images in the process.[101] In colonial Equateur, for Congolese and for Europeans, images thrived, trembling among the fantastic, the monstrous, the marvelous. While some images vented nervousness or terror, others fed reverie. *Nervousness* suggests visceral energy, alarm, and fear, quite unlike the appreciative wandering of the imagination as in *reverie*. In this book, spry daydreaming merges with idleness and distraction, joining horizons, wonder, and consciousness. Two concepts, nervousness and reverie, anchor this historical interpretation, enabling close readings of clashes, predicaments, the weird, and strange. The pair joins affect and moods with ideas, often uncanny,[102] while the aim is a new way of writing a subaltern history of *health* amid the shrunken and pathological.

Multitudes, Reverie, Dread

Reverie suggests the fantastic, fanciful, and impractical.[103] With the concrete embedded, as Gaston Bachelard suggested, reverie comprises the poetic, material imagination. This leading French philosopher moved between epistemological ruptures and wonder, showing reverie to be awake in its daydreaming, in its musing about hypothetical lives and futures.[104] Daydreaming may reckon with brutality, yet reverie begins not from trauma, but from wonder. Neither hallucination, delusion, or trance, reverie may be aspiration or suggest a claim. While fantasy may enter, reverie is conscious, even consciousness.[105]

In this work, reverie detects the material images motivating dance, rebellion, and vernacular healing: concrete matter like a flywhisk, flag, or tree. It also engages "tonality."[106] Equateur's Nkundo, Mongo, and Ekonda knew reverie. Yet the same concept may pry open the imaginations of Belgian, Flemish, Portuguese, and British subjects living in Equateur. Reverie becomes a technique for reading imaginations within this world of once village-sized micropolities. Equateur men and women were still traveling to sing under the magical sign of Lianja and his cast of originating figures, those who first showed how to live, marry, and reproduce amid forests and waterways, seasonally expanding and receding marshes, spirits, and medicinal trees. These persons went deep into forest for the bounty of edible, illuminative (copal) resins and vines as well as the fertility of mud- and barrier fishing. Objects, images, animals, and technologies—some reproductive, some violent—were part of their imaginations. With such bits from a rich poetic archive, this history thickens the contents of public healing.

Matters fanciful, fantastic, and impractical entered into the musing. Though secrecy was critical to healing, reverie often expressed itself in public ritual and visible performances. Such fancy and its spectacular qualities could panic Europeans, especially when images of eviction aligned with spirits and charms. The ingredients often became folded into an enduring poetic imagination, one that integrated the likes of gynecological devices and umbilical cords.

Similar processes of knowing, observing, and imagining developed in medicine, dying, and war. Drawing attention to dreamlike pictures—their material images and figurations, like visceral moods, go with an authorial capacity to complicate historical subjects in relation to event and futures. This skill widens understanding of the range of maneuver, the plasticity brought into play by individuals. It is not unlike gauging "structures of feeling," to smuggle in Raymond Williams at his finest. His notions of "residual," "emergent," and "dominant" time may be used to *sense* generations or social categories, and thus tease out historicities within a colonial situation.[107]

Yet reverie suggests rather a daydreaming *multitude*, a collective, political subjectivity that worked like a magnet for colonial nervousness, igniting perceptions of a fearsome crowd. Fear and revulsion piled up quickly in colonial Equateur. Some nervousness was protean, alighting upon object or event, inciting further energy as it moved and stirred. State rejoinders sometimes knew excess within such relays. Dread forces wondering about racialized terror, the ways it materialized alongside violence and state techniques, feeding on deep fears in the face of a throng. Paolo Virno's "grammar of the multitude" encourages this kind of thinking about collective subjectivity, the latter comprising individual subjectivity shaped into group belonging. *A Nervous State* extends dread and multitudes to fear and horror, to the kinds of police reaction that a subaltern, colonized crowd wielding charmed power objects could stir.[108]

Concrete elements also are embedded in Lomongo tales, a spirit peering, a dancer possessed. How are we to unknot insertions, congruencies? An intimate simultaneity often emerges between an imagined and material thing. Bachelard persuades that the two are fused, inseparable: thus his concept of material imagination.[109] Yet when a pairing turns monstrous as in a *physical, dead human hand, smoked, lying in a basket* (allegedly a commonplace in 1900s Equateur), and an *imagined, detached human hand* (a repetition within Nkundo ogre tales), such simultaneity needs investigation across registers of the real and legendary. We know that metropolitan spectators who watched magic lantern shows in the Northern hemisphere saw photographic images of such mutilations, and we know more than one generation of Nkundo and Mongo remembered severed hands filling baskets into the 1950s. Both were partial to the monstrous, which grisly material images stirred.

Thinking colonial reverie permits a fundamental rewriting: releasing colonial subjects from being slotted in *as* the downtrodden, as prey. African history is at an interesting juncture, peculiarly at risk of dividing strangely between those who aspire to the intellectual and those who reduce everything to the affective. A focus on material, poetic images combines and blurs these veins.

Reverie also helps rethink colonial mobility as *motion*. Walter Benjamin, like Simmel and Kracauer, wrote about urbanity, strolling, and capacities for refined observation, idleness, movement, and *distraction*.[110] Relocating *flânerie* from Paris to this colonial tropical backwater may seem an odd, unlikely move. Yet thinking about colonial spaces as more and less *urbane*, as well as the capacities required to amble or move, is productive. The method means grappling with sensibilities and also skills in wondering *and* wandering in relation to concrete places and horizons. Equateur's daydreamers were ultimately not wrong: with decolonization, the Belgians or at least their regime went away. Relentless reverie fed colonial nervousness and this exit.

Archives and Futures

Debris once served well as a method for attending to material remains, often mired within postcolonial lives or revealing nostalgia.[111] This book instead takes up a *past present* of nervousness and *past futures* of reverie. Useful is Reinhart Koselleck's asymmetrical pair of "spaces of experience" (memory) and "horizons of expectation" (hope). While seeking relationships between lived spaces of memory *and* futures,[112] my archive has pushed me toward *combining* past horizons with reverie.

Vernacular healing was often a zone of distraction and refuge for Congolese. Using Benjamin's "technique of nearness" to isolate bits, detect repetition, parse import, and sense moods,[113] I have navigated diverse kinds of document making: by the Flemish humanists of the scene, by their Congolese literati, and by persons of the state. The region's Catholic missionaries along with their Congolese protégés generated an important archive. These Flemish priests were linguists, anthropologists, and folklorists, with passions for history and conservation. Seeing themselves before worlds seemingly in the process of disappearing, they noted down, preserved, and published all they could, while encouraging Lomongo speakers to write as well. Their immense, vernacular archive is poetic, and it yields bits of song and performance, sometimes thickening or surfacing as event.

Memory often was brimming with a sedimented, magical past. Tensions abound between the way these missionaries wished to keep this zone alive and enchanted and the ways inscription reified "tradition." Their corpus comprises Lianja epic variants as song and origin stories, performed by Lonkundo and Lomongo speakers and collected from the 1930s. This archive suggests orientations toward an ancestral, residual time of mending and generation, widening therapeutics as experience and expectation.

Reproductive idioms are pervasive, as are medicine bags, trees, ancestors, leopards, a dwarf spirit, pregnancy, and battles of vengeance. A pregnant wife craving a forest fruit keeps her devoted husband absurdly busy climbing trees. A big man threatens his wives that each better be pregnant when he returns from a pending journey because he will kill the one who is not. Ogre tales likely haunted, though their missing hands and detached body parts, and surely produced a kind of laughter too. Poems contain a refrain about a man beating his wife, a wife beating her husband, with tittering suggested by the back-and-forth cadence. In a bountiful collection of women's dance songs, many salacious, women yearn for lovers, urbane casseroles, and high heels. Such material images marvelously enrich what we know about history and reverie.[114] There is much more in this bounteous archive, including some 170 vivid essays written in Lomongo for a 1954 contest in memory accounts. They record adversity, destitution, cruelties, exchange, and war during the Free State years.

Among the state-based archival streams are numbers and statistics, diverse narrations, and visceral, nervous assessments of conditions and beings. The security archive announces emergency, looking to the future with an urgency to avert disaster. A hurried, panicked modality, rushing to deflect and arrest, such nervousness reminds us *why* Balandier wrote of the *pathological*. In security transcripts, interrogators sought information about the upcoming, the anticipated. Subaltern reverie insinuated trouble, the need for more tracking, and became grounds for arrests and relegations. Reverie in the security archive also emerges *as repetition*, telling of collective dreamwork and a wholesale Belgian departure from Congo.

Present in 1915, this daydream about rescue figures, arriving almost magically and helping Congolese to end Belgian rule, recurs through the mid-1950s. In 1915, the images embraced leopards, copal, cannabis, soldiers, and Germani. By 1931, flags and flagpoles were the fixation, while the rescue figures hovered as African Americans, at a time when Marcus Garvey imagery took over imaginations in much of Africa. Flywhisks came to the fore about 1937, whereas letters, name lists, and a high-tech infertility apparatus became nodes of the networked imaginary around 1953. In all, Belgians would be driven out, replaced by other, kinder, sometimes black foreigners. Sometimes a massacre was suggested, but regardless the Belgian state would end, opening up a bright future. Such eviction reverie suggests lively energy, feisty dissent; it usually came beside therapeutic insurgency. It often appeared as a few typed lines within the security archive, even if also circulating as rumor. When interrogators questioned suspects, their spare, awkward answers, typed in French upon an official document, suggest hedging, dissembling, and fear.

The Chapters

A Nervous State considers everyday life in Equateur during Congo's two colonial states: King Leopold's Congo Free State, 1885–1908, and the Belgian Congo, 1908–60. The chapters imply a temporal sweep while avoiding historicist logic, instead offering up a sequence of dense crises, antagonisms, and emergencies, following Balandier, whose heterogeneous elements are unpacked.[115] Interrupting the sweep are bits and layers of time, story, image, inserted to *snarl* any universal calendar of progressive time. Clutching *perplexities* and suturing them in[116] is a method that goes well with a history that must grapple, more than most medical histories, with wounds and scars.

Each chapter elaborates a juncture or "critical event"[117] when colonial power, vernacular practice, and persons came to loggerheads and diverse mediations ensued. The immediacy of aggression, gendered excess, and persistence across generations matter much. This is a history of a nervous colonial state on edge, terrified by the facility of "primitive rebels"[118] to stir daydreams, ply charms, and harm colonial symbols and persons.

This history begins with searing violence. The first chapter examines the immediacy of unfolding aggression during the Free State years, drawing on the words of Congolese sharing memories much alive fifty years later. Evidence collects around the violation of women, suicide, and Ikakota charms as therapeutic war technologies. So begins a long thread about trafficking in medicines, poisons, and therapies. The interpretation parses evidence of Congolese claims and pleas, the wealth and abuses of sentries, rape, flight, and devastation. Much is gained by attending to Equateur as a war zone, by reading dynamics of combat through *acoustics* of hushed silence and sadistic laughter.

Each of the middle four chapters elaborates conjunctures when state power and subaltern wills clashed. A healer named Maria N'koi animates chapter 2. Arrested and relegated in 1915 for naming the "Germani" as ancestral allies, she caused a tax rebellion and inspired armed insurrection. Speaking out against copal labor and sleeping sickness, she became a security crisis just when most military officers and soldiers were away fighting in German Kamerun. Her movement fractured the nervous state, while the size of her crowds produced primitivist dread in state agents. The nervous state banished this woman to calm this volatile healing insurgency.

From the 1930s, state persons were acting within the two guises of state power, as the global economic depression fed nervousness. Medical touring began, while rumors about flags, loyalty, bribing, and spies circulated. Police interrogations in the riverain provincial capital focused on salvationist images, marked by pan-Africanist Marcus Garvey and his liberationist ideas. While the drama at hand spoke to colonial eviction, charms and healers did not surface in this town milieu. Yet a woman's association, *métis* subjects, and a Kimbangu-like figure in a hospital lockup did.

Later in the same decade, infertility awareness was swelling from many a side. Chapter 4 discloses Flemish priests spreading news about a low birth rate, intensifying official efforts to investigate *dénatalité*. A research tour investigating depopulation was under way, and the lead doctor downplayed gonorrhea and stressed degeneration and shock instead. A kind of healing procession called Ewewe yields insight into the purging dynamics of therapeutic practice. Likili followed more a mode of initiatory, charm-based, mobile healing, and it turned insurgent, colliding with the state. When Likili followers confronted state doctors, their dances sent up alarm about "xenophobia." A Catholic priest and Congolese protégé were not far away when police arrested many Likili. While Likili entailed eager healing journeys, dreamlike stories told of medicinal trees splitting open, ending barrenness. Likili was not welcome everywhere, leading to conflict and symbolic rape in one chiefdom, suggesting the sorcery-laced, destructive dimensions of all charms.

An infertility clinic and a penal colony are the subject of the fifth chapter. During the postwar years, the state helped fund an immense development project at Befale, embracing major medical installations and a specialized infertility clinic. These experiments went with demographic censusing, which suggested some 35 to 40 percent of women were childless. This specialized clinical space was a short distance from the penal colony at Ekafera, founded in 1939 for dangerous *relégués*—mostly Kimbanguist and Kitawala religious rebels relegated to this special carceral site from Congo's key cosmopolitan, industrial, and prophetic zones in Katanga and the Lower Congo. Both clinic and camp were located in the former Abir rubber concession, which produced nervous, violent excess in the days of Leopold's Congo.

The two were the brainchild of Pierre Ryckmans, the governor general, visionary, and micromanager who articulated the Belgian colonial motto: "dominate to serve," *dominer pour servir*. A social Catholic, intellectual, masterful technician of colonial numeracy, and man of letters, Ryckmans published captivating, moralizing colonial short stories. Governor general for two decades from 1934, he first arrived during the Great War, leaving Flanders's lethal battlefields for those of the Sangha river valley in Kamerun.[119] The detail matters, since *A Nervous State* provides a fresh glimpse of this head of the colony, among other European figures, with an eye to ideas, sensibilities, and moods. Ryckmans supervised the two prongs of the state, resulting in these technical, experimental spaces of development and security, of life and risk. While the clinic and camp culminate the heuristic of two states operating on separate tracks, their increasing junctions become pronounced in chapter 5.

The symmetry and separability is further challenged in the final chapter, which turns to motion. It asks: who could stroll or otherwise move in this situation? The question elicits vignettes speaking to some who sauntered, whether in fantasy alone or more concretely. An urbane nurse, a Kitawala healer, and the famed, modern music star, Henri Bowane, are included. Many Congolese ambled in late colonial Equateur, even if only in reverie. The last chapter also returns to social pathology, well-being, and latitude in a shrunken milieu, with troubled surfaces, invasive venereal campaigns, and subjects astir. Many were seeking pleasure and extravagance in fashion, Rumba, and dance bars. At the same time, that some chiefs were using hygiene routines to capture Kitawala offenders tells another story, less about a nervous state than nervous chiefdoms.

On two occasions in this history, when mobile, insurgent healing—Likili and Kitawala—ended up banned, nervousness in "customary" chiefdoms produced tension, nightmares, and allegations of sexual violation. In Wangata, vulnerable women sleeping alone at night would find a visiting Likili spirit's fluids between their legs come morning. Similarly, a nervous customary authority in Loma used the profound medicalization of late colonial life—relentless village routines in medical censusing—to arrest Kitawala suspects, fusing the biopolitical and nervous within his figure as colonial chief. On the eve of Congo's chaotic decolonization, therefore, deep in its rustic interior, the two colonial modes of presence—the securitizing and the medicalizing—became not only deeply knotted, but profoundly vernacularized.

| Registers of Violence

Even Mark Twain took on the Congo cause. In 1905, his *King Leopold's Soliloquy* poked fun at the plight of the Belgian king, caught out by Kodak cameras sparking international outrage. But the famous American novelist soon "retired from the Congo," pulling back from further campaigning for the Congo Reform Association in 1906. Being "tangled up in the Congo matter" menaced his independence: "What *have* I been doing?" he wrote, "Dreaming? Walking in my sleep? . . . I wake up and find myself tacitly committed to journeys, & speeches, & so on—perfectly appaling [*sic*] activities." Twain also compared himself with the masterful publicist who organized the humanitarian campaign: "I am not a bee, I am a lightning-bug. . . . If I had Morel's splendid equipment of energy, brains, diligence, concentration, persistence—but I haven't; he is a 'mobile, I am a wheelbarrow."[1]

There was good reason to liken E. D. Morel to a buzzing automobile. Entering into the immense humanitarian corpus about Leopold's Congo still takes tenacity and resilience. The stories are graphic and gruesome, the layers thick with repetition, the photographs stark, shocking, and insistent. The reasons we want to recoil are not as simple as refusing knowledge. There is an unrelenting, grisly logic to this propaganda about violence and suffering, an economy to the way it snaps images that produce horror and revulsion. Voyeurism was at play when Europeans and Americans traveled to Congo at the time. They chased to spot a mutilated person, to snap another photograph, if they could. Frederick

Starr learned that none could be found anymore near Ikoko; he was advised to continue up to Abir territory instead.[2] Anti-Leopoldian rhetoric became hackneyed, the violence often reduced into simplified stories or photographic assemblages of Congolese amputees. Pro-Leopoldian propaganda also soared, spreading images of good works and technology—bridges, engineering, schools, obedient soldiers, and efforts in civilizing, including photographs of military brass bands or schoolchildren playing as part of a *fanfare*. We will meet fanfares, music, and fond memories again.

Some images travel, others fade away. Many, like photographs of violence from Leopold's Congo, are repackaged and reframed over and over. Adam Hochschild's moving, redemptive *King Leopold's Ghost* includes some of the most recycled photographs:[3] one of a Congolese father looking at the severed hand and foot of his young daughter; another of two youths with handless black stumps on display against white cloth. Each was part of a magic lantern show that circulated in Britain and the United States during the anti-Leopoldian campaign. The photographer was Alice Harris, a missionary at Baringa, a Congo Balolo Mission station in the Abir rubber concession territory (see figure 1.1). Her pictures and the lantern shows enabled Morel's propaganda machine to gather force, moving ever larger British and North American publics. By 1907, the Congo Reform Association in London had sold ten thousand copies of *Camera and Congo Crime*, a brochure with twenty-four Harris photographs.[4] Riley Brothers Ltd. was marketing a standard show, "Lantern Lecture on the Congo Atrocities." An image of "A savage Abir" appeared quickly, then a whipping scene, followed by one of women chained: "The treatment of women hostages." Six pictured Congolese men and boys with missing hands or feet. An advertisement arranged the sixty slides into a salvationist trajectory, moving from violent rubber system to the redemptive promise of missionary work.[5]

The Congo atrocity photographs overwhelmed. They still do. As "shock-photos," they produced "public revulsion" in Europe, America, and Britain, ultimately working to "change the course of history."[6] The Free State came to a halt. These photographs reify maimed, black bodies, producing a traumatic form with an "insistent grammar of sight." Their persistence, as Cathy Caruth has suggested, yields an "effacement of the event."[7]

Effacement is one subject here. It is time for a fresh reading of Leopold's Congo that moves beyond humanitarian earnestness and does not blame, publicize, or shock. Conquest in Congo and its extractive rubber economy produced spectacular violence in Equateur. Yet we know little about the ground and senses of everyday lives. The region was an intricate milieu with

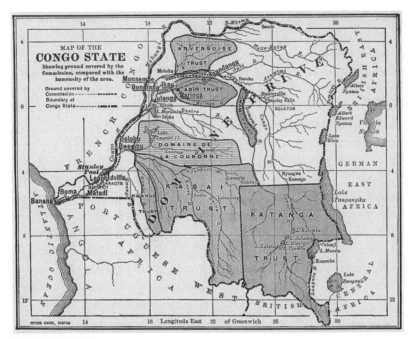

FIGURE 1.1 Note the location of the Abir Trust in this disapproving humanitarian map of the Congo Free State depicting concessions and trust domains. From Congo Reform Association, *The Indictment against the Congo Government*, 4.

a wide range of categories and individuals, many with knowable names. A rich documentary record enables thinking about witnessing, immediacy, duration, and memory. This chapter rethinks the production of violence, visceral and sensory effects, and their sexualizations.

Hochschild's conceit is that the history of violence in Leopold's Congo has been suppressed through manipulated politics of memory invested in public forgetting.[8] This is not untrue—for Belgium at least. But it is not right for Equateur, where memories were vivid through the 1930s and knew substantial rekindling during the harsh years of the Second World War. An epic story line, with an altruistic hero (Morel) battling against a greedy rogue, the imperial king dreaming tall, is not only too simple. It is too remote.[9]

Seeking the immediacies of lives, imaginations, and injuries, this interpretation moves toward the visceral and acoustic. Fresh source material, read obliquely, paves the way. Hochschild evoked a familiar evidentiary problem when explaining why within his book "nearly all of this vast river of words is by Europeans or Americans." He acknowledged: "Instead of African voices from this time there is largely silence."[10] I would be the last to propose "African voices" as the best corrective, especially given the unsettling quiet still over parts of Equateur.[11] Rather, the point is Congolese *did* speak and write during this time of wars and abuses to British Consul Roger Casement and appalled missionaries. In 1904–5, they testified before the Commission of Inquiry, sent to investigate by the King after the release of Casement's devastating report to the British Parliament. Some fifty years later, as part of a contest organized by the Catholic mission, teachers, students, clerks, and chiefs wrote down some 170 memory essays that tell of making war, maneuvering, overtaking, sowing terror, and weeping aloud.[12]

While of course all sources are mediated, ranking evidence for African histories by racial provenance is misguided.[13] European diaries, journals, and reports are invaluable, and I draw on the critical investigatory report of Casement and the private record book of a Belgian colonial hero, famous during its foundational "Arab War." In 1904, Baron Françis Dhanis became inspector for the notorious rubber concession, Abir company, just before the King's Commission arrived.[14] I use bits from these sources to unsettle simplicities about atrocity, many produced by Morel's propaganda machine.

I do not want to haunt. Nor is it possible *to know*, in a simple, unmediated way. Yet partial knowledge about matters urgent emerge from striving to *hear* senses, words, and images not only *of* Congolese, but from the texts produced by these contrary figures, Casement and Dhanis.

Visual evidence embraces photographs and images in explanations, accounts, and memories. Mutilation photographs of severed hands and became phantasmagoric among humanitarian spectators in the West.[15] Roland Barthes's notion of "shock-photos" is useful, since these photographs still shock, and fright and scandal have endured.[16] Their circulation then and since matters, while the images that *never* made their way into contemporary circuits are also important. Disaggregating the visual is useful. An image of a basket of human hands in an *immediate field of vision* is unlike the counting of hands in *memory's eye*. Both differ from a maimed youth pictured in a photograph that once circulated, as it does today, influencing memory's eye wherever it alights. Photographs may be projected onto large screens for audiences too, and magnification produced humanitarian distress in Europe and America at the time.

When the photographic becomes relentless, its disruption is important. I track the acoustic to short-circuit the tenacity of the visual, to push beyond the effects of photographic shock blotting out all else. Instead, the idea is to move *near* to structures and perceptions of violence, distress, and dismissal.

Pushing beyond *seeing* as the primary mode of perceiving the past enables being wakeful to other senses and capacities, especially *the field of hearing, producing, and muffling sound*. Working with bits and a few dream images, this chapter considers persons laboring, refusing, ailing, and abiding within one region with many armed men, probing visitors, and busy inspectors crossing through. Reading with an attentive ear yields sounds, but also smells, sights, peering, sensing, and the invisible.

Listening is a "technique of nearness," in the senses proposed by Benjamin.[17] Such moving in close conveys the everyday and the spectacular. Minor moments and slight words bring near a human scale within the immediacy or remembering of violence. It means attending to dins and echoes, the unsayable and silenced, but also wondering about nonnarrativity and agitated, disturbed sounds of madness. Laughter is a thin, instructive thread here. Nervous, twisted, anguished laughter erupted alongside violence in Congo's Equateur.

The approach highlights immediacy more than the duration of duress. Leopoldian milieus bled into post-Leopoldian ones in Equateur, through imaginations, ongoing traffic, and the reproduction of capital and extraction in this forested world. *Afterwards* are important. The history of Free State violence has hardly ever been told from the standpoint of results, endings, and aftereffects. Nor has it been told from a vantage point of *near*, with immediate sounds and images offsetting jumping too quickly into a narrative of *aftermath*. Violence in Congo's Equateur was structural, corporeal, symbolic, psychic, and sexual. These modalities intertwined.[18] Hunting persons as animals, commandeering girls, stealing wives, raping and sexually tormenting women, all went with bodily and psychic effects and forms of refusal.

How aggression became repetition, perhaps somatizing over time, is a critical, refractory problem. So are questions about assertion, dissent, and flight. Sexual economies were critical, and some injury was surely reproductive, literally and metaphorically. Somatic effects surfaced as an implicit colonial question from at least the 1910s. An emphasis on *making claims* enables discerning how bodily, mental, and aggressive processes crossed.

Sexual economies went in tandem with immediate fields of vision and remembering eyes: who could *see* whom, who liked to *watch* whom, and *who* acquired and had access to whom. In aiming at elements of a *soundtrack* that secures a new handle on Free State violence, harm, and fright, this reading examines sexual, visual, and racial economies as well as kinds of refusal and desire. A biopolitical daydream emerged in the years that followed, telling about opposition and avoidance during and after these "red rubber" years.[19]

Nearness with Casement

It is time to skirt the spectral prose of Conrad's modernist novel, *Heart of Darkness*. I instead parse another canonical source, Roger Casement's serious, rhetorical investigative report. Optics and acoustics operated with studied restraint in this circumspectly composed indictment of Leopold's Congo.[20] Casement wrote of emotion and "mental depression," of a man who broke down in tears before him. Yet his report did not brood or haunt. Once he witnessed several instances of mutilation, he saw his work as done. Material objects were present. Some rubber collectors received shirt buttons as payment.[21] Casement based his sense of extensive depopulation on what he *saw*, contrasting this sight with what he remembered *seeing* some ten years before. His idea of slavery came from a *past* trade, which the Free State managed to end. He did not comprehend that much population dispersal accompanied the breaking up of big, riverain trading "houses,"[22] managed by Congolese entrepreneurs, when the strongly armed Abir moved in (see map 1.1). Immense commercial houses like Basankusu and Wangata expanded by the early nineteenth century, absorbing large numbers of raided slaves, followers, and dependents. They were still in place when Stanley first arrived in 1877.[23] Casement did not understand the complex layering of chronotopes with a new rapacious rubber economy building networks right on top of, often with the same human material as, the Zanzibari- and Sudanic-associated economies in war and persons[24] that had been linking Equateur with the East and North since at least the early nineteenth century. Casement's access to Congolese worlds was limited. This sensitive Irishman hardly left the central river channel and its zones of partial "civilization." Even his lodging usually came through English-speaking missionaries and their riverain posts.[25]

Some sounds were words, voiced out loud. Casement heard many, including of five young girls rescued near Lake Tumba. One girl's fear meant her "voice was very small." Some sound was visceral or eruptive. A chief "broke down and wept, saying that their lives were useless to them." Some sounds were technological, emitted by new objects that moved, killed, and made troops march to time—steamboats, rifles, cap guns, bugles, and the military bands known as *fanfares*. To Bonsondo's young ears, memories of a bugle call suggested a white officer was present when soldiers attacked her village. Not all sound-making objects were new. The "noise" of brass anklets slowed Bonsondo's pace when on the run, at risk of being sighted and caught. Death produced weeping and sounds of lamentation. Yet fright also led to a loss of voice. Bikela remembered that after one massacre, those left buried the bodies amid

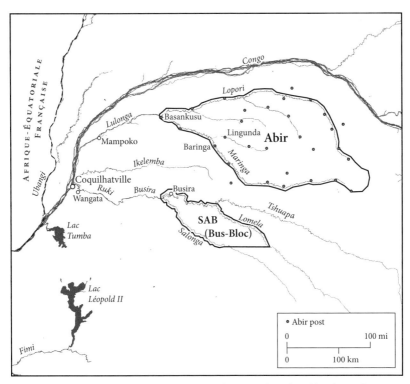

MAP 1.1 *A Nervous State*'s terrain, ca. 1900. Note the rivers, the colonial border, and two major concessionary companies, including many Abir posts. Map by Jake Coolidge.*

"very much weeping." When soldiers killed her mother with a shot: "I cried very much." Afterward, when soldiers told her sister to call for her, Bikela "was too frightened and would not answer."[26]

Casement was hyperattentive to visibility and audibility, in keeping with the charged atmosphere of imperial accusations, investigations, and denials. One of the king's commissioners told some American missionaries their "*ears are too long.*" Reverend Clark snapped back that "*their eyes were sharp. . . . We see and know.*" Casement observed, and people offered up visible evidence: "Several . . . *showed* broad weals," while "a lad of 15 or so, removing his cloth, *showed* several scars across his thighs." Images of cruelty are plentiful in Casement's report. Ncongo saw a basket of two hundred hands being counted out for a white man. Casement himself saw "fifteen women in the shed . . . tied together, either neck to neck or ankle to ankle, to secure them for the night, and in this posture *I saw them twice* during the evening." In the morning, a sentry ordered "*in my hearing* to 'keep close guard on the prisoners.'" While writing that those in the Abir zone "were not happy," Casement wrote: "it was *apparent to a callous eye* that in this they *spoke* the strict truth." The consul knew that whatever he reported on—as *seen* or *observed*—became a fact, adding that things heard "*from their lips*" might double the truth effect. Casement made his readers aware of the scopic economy at work: eyes watching and guarding, the filling of sacks "taking place *under the eyes* of . . . a State sentry." Casement used his eyes and ears—"*viewing* their unhappy surroundings" and "*hearing* their appeals"—to argue that Congolese felt "a very real fear of reporting." Though some did speak, "the broad fact remained that their previous *silence* said more than their present *speech.*"[27]

Seeing took precedence over hearing in the Casement report. These were the only senses seemingly at work as he observed. The memory accounts from 1954 are mostly from the Ruki and Tshuapa river valleys, though some wrote about former Abir territory. The stories of girls rescued in 1893 by the American mission are from Ikoko on Lake Tumba (near Irebu and Bikoro, not far from Bokatola, central to the next chapter). In all accounts, sound and hearing were at least as important as sight. Casement took pains to collect the Ikoko accounts, which show that as soon as the girls began running for their lives, they became attentive to sound as risk. A misguided or inadvertent thud or rustle could cost a life, Bikela learned, running far into the bush with her mother. Soldiers followed. When armed men came "near us they were calling my mother by name, and I was going to answer, but my mother put her hand to my mouth to stop me." Bikela knew that "if she had not . . . we would all have been killed." The noise of gunfire produced flight, while crying was dangerous: "we went into the bush to look for people, and we heard children crying, and a soldier went quickly over to the place and killed a mother and four children."[28] A similar sense of peril comes through in the memory texts of 1954, too. Antoine-Marcus Boyoto wrote one of these: "When they perceived a noise or the rattling of shots, they went further into the forest. Mothers buried alive their small children because of their crying."[29]

Dhanis, Abir, and "Bassankussu"

The journal of Baron François Dhanis gives us stark counterpoint.[30] Abir seems to have asked him to come investigate when supplies of wild rubber were nearly exhausted, amplifying abuses, atrocity, chaos, and scandal.[31] A retired Free State officer, Dhanis was towering hero of the so-called "Arab War" in Congo's eastern Zanzibari zone. He arrived in Equateur in June 1904, just before the King's Commission arrived; he was gone again by mid-September.

An ally of Abir and the king, Dhanis entered into a scene of ruination. He kept a private journal, studying conditions inside this rubber concession, where those with guns were not soldiers of the state but sentries of Abir's militia. He worked as diagnostician, and his daily entries progressively identified these sentries—their wealth, power, idleness, and guns—as the chief factor that made the Abir system terribly violent and hopelessly uneconomic. His writing suggested a second factor, however: unhinged white male agents left to work and live alone.

This colonial star, as famous as Stanley in Belgian circles, did not shy away from death and abuse. In contrast to Casement, he moved far from central riverain posts and missionary meals. While not a humanitarian witness, Dhanis was hardly backed into a defensive mode. It was probably impossible to be neutral, much less affirmative, about conditions in Abir territory at this time. His unstudied, spontaneous, often quite pained personal jottings about the visible and the heard—never intended for publication—are a precious contrast to the "studied realism"[32] of Roger Casement.

Not a worked-over text, Dhanis's record book is a diary. He visited Basankusu, spying sentries with so many women as wealth that clearly some of their wives worked not at all. Many women in this town were waiting for steamers to arrive, he noted, keen to latch onto men who disembarked. He went to rubber markets, observed Congolese collectors receiving merchandise for their rubber's weight, and listed objects exchanged: machetes, knives, salt, beads, belts, and pieces of brass rod or *mitako*. He specified kinds of cloth: Checkered was not well liked. Less common were spoons, forks, goblets, hats, and bells. Dhanis spent time tracking things, noting transactions, and bemoaning the fact there were not enough of those commodities Congolese most wanted. He praised a few well-supplied Abir agents who gave Congolese a chance to choose and shop. Dhanis was annoyed to discover others paid with vouchers instead of goods. His entries also mention all kinds of stuff, and not all for sale: Albini rifles, cap-guns, whips, ivory tusks, letters, photographs, goats, pigeons, bats, chickens, eggs, hammocks, and even, as we will see, a chief's tufts.[33]

Diverse registers combine in Dhanis's journal. Sometimes the sound of anguished laughter cut through optical powers. Visible were occasions when people came to complain, protest, or seek an intervention. Dhanis made notations about his conversations. Most were claims, appeals for help. Chiefs, "natives," one Abir agent's "boy" were among those who came forward. These interactions suggest forms of duress, whether visible, tactile, hidden, or heard. Some injuries appeared as faint traces. Dhanis jotted spare words about a chief's swollen finger. He wrote laconically about body parts, the kind that instantly became global visual debris through Alice Harris's circulating photographs. But he was present, we will see, soon after the Baringa missionary couple confronted an Abir agent about a massacre and detached body parts.[34]

Unlike Casement, Dhanis saw rubber extraction through eyes of experience. His earlier time in Congo's Zanzibari zone meant he knew quite a bit about the swelling energy of a central African raiding economy. Pillaging captured new people through rifles, battles, and theft, while assembling wealth in ivory, food, slaves, and wives fueled the devastation. Too often it is forgotten that Free State brutalities had antecedents that bled into and shaped early colonial concessionary practice.

Since at least the early nineteenth century, trading and raiding economies in wealth had been in motion. "Bassankusu" became a pivot point in commercial grids stretching downriver to Bobangi networks and north into the Ubangi and Sudanic regions (see map 1.2).[35] E. J. Glave, an Englishman working with Stanley from 1883, remarked that the Lulonga river valley was "studded with stockaded villages," and "monster war canoes were ready to launch at a moment's notice" in these "piratical regions" of warriors, "slave-raiders," hunger, and ivory markets, with many "slaves seen in the markets."[36] Located at the confluence of the Maringa and Lopori, the strategic Basankusu became headquarters for Abir from 1893.[37] It was likely a bigger center for captive trading earlier in the century and again more intensely after Tippu Tip's Zanzibari world, centered on the Lualaba (Congo) to the east, sprawled westward following Stanley's downriver path in the 1870s. Ivory became important from the late 1870s through the 1880s, when Belgians like Lemaire, Coquilhat, and Delcommune arrived.[38]

Such predatory violence arising from big-man networks or gangs, those seeking quick wealth, raiding, and pillaging, tend to be effaced by scholars seeking a villain in King Leopold. The layering of raiding economies was complex and uneven, especially once concessionary rivals arrived. Though the details of mutilation practices will never be fully known, this terror tactic was old. It stretched within a region as far east as Mirambo's worlds near Tabora, and embraced the colorful, kinless, marauding *ruga-ruga*, with their dreadlocks and hemp who surfaced into view from at least the mid-nineteenth century.[39]

Corrosive violence emerged from access to guns, while these enlarged petty power and capacities to accumulate women, spreading chaos, hunger, and devastation. More than anything in the Abir world, Dhanis deplored the sentries. They were thieves, dispossessing the unarmed of all they owned until they were left with nothing, wives included. Four from Bongulu, in charge

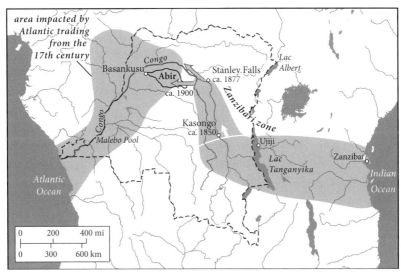

MAP 2.1 Trading and raiding networks and frontiers from the late sixteenth century. Congo Free State borders from 1885 are shown. Two trading frontiers most influenced Equateur terrain. An Atlantic one associated with the export trade in slavery extended inward from the sea and Angola. A second Zanzibari or Swahili frontier arose from the mid-nineteenth century, extending westward by caravan from Zanzibar to Ujiji and Kasongo. From 1877, it moved north along the Lualaba with Henry Morton Stanley to Stanley Falls. By 1900, it expanded westward into the Abir concession. By this time, Nile trade centered on Khartoum was also important. Thus, trade and violence did not arrive first with colonial rule. Rather, complex layers of traffic coincided and interacted, notably in the 1890s and 1900s near Basankusu. Maps by Jake Coolidge.**

of sixty-five rubber gatherers, wanted to take their women. They killed their dogs instead. "We can keep nothing" was the lament Dhanis heard. François Bombute wrote in 1954 that when there was a patch of bananas, only the sentry could cut them: "If he discovered that you ate those bananas, he killed you straight away."[40] A gun—an Albini rifle—comprised a sentry. Congolese conflated armed men with their instruments and sounds. Joseph Imome called sentries "guns" (see figure 1.2). Bombute penned: "the guns spoke."[41]

Some sentries became petty police, working for tyrannical, state-appointed, and often socially disconnected "customary" chiefs. Dhanis's notes suggest that whether Abir sentries were familiars or strangers made a difference in their brutality and how they were remembered. When Abir met dissent, it sometimes introduced sentries from another region to brutalize the unproductive. At Nsongo Mboyo in May 1904, terrifyingly harsh punishments forced the uncooperative back to work.[42] Dhanis noted that violence also developed among those who knew each other's names. Some Basankusu became *capita* (over-

FIGURE 1.2 Three Abir sentries pose with guns beside a chained Congolese, perhaps a noncompliant rubber gatherer, ca. 1905. Photograph by Alice Harris. Courtesy of Anti-Slavery International, London.

seers) over low-ranking Basankusu required to collect rubber. If a chief agreed to act for Abir, this overseer could decide who would receive a rifle. When a chief controlled sentry selection, he might choose loyal captives, slaves, or clients. Either the sentries or chief would turn lesser persons—probably slave-like dependents—into gatherers. Such patterns kept alive nineteenth-century dynamics of trading houses expanding by "composing"[43] ever larger networks of clients, dependents, and captives, as beautifully described by Robert Harms on the Bobangi stretch of the middle Congo.[44]

Abir used Congolese identity readings to name and punish. *Readings* is a helpful word, since social categories were fluid and multiple. Ngombe sentries appeared as fierce, imperious warriors (not unlike the nail-studded stools, back-rests, and execution swords labeled after them today).[45] While they had been raiders near the confluence at Basankusu for decades, Basankusu big men competed for trade through battle. The powerful towered over humble Mongo living inland along the Lopori and Maringa. Lowly dependents, subjected to looting and slavery, they were likely the first forced into gathering rubber for Abir.

Europeans saw Mongo as frail weaklings and degenerate, and this language is a critical part of the history to be disentangled here.[46] Yet the historical record also tells of bullies and gangs. Dhanis hated sentries as the "gangrene" of the Abir system, for theft and murder and abducting wives and daughters. Some chiefs also were gifting women to sentries to receive exemptions on the amount of rubber their villages were required to collect. When a sentry came to Dhanis with a complaint, the baron asked him how many wives he had. Some women, nearby at the time, later gestured toward yet other wives whom the lying sentry had omitted from his tally. On another occasion, when Dhanis untangled a complex murder, he listed out the cast, naming each sentry and his servants, working out a series of clashes between rival sentry factions and their *boy* subordinates,[47] surely operating as shadow networks and gangs.

Of some twenty-five claims made to Dhanis, chiefs introduced ten, five involved groups, and individuals made another four. Sentries pleaded twice. Six asked for caps for their muskets, insisting they needed Albini rifles instead. Only a few complaints involved a soundtrack beyond words spoken. Dhanis called some entreaties, of women making baskets in a rubber drying site, *supplications*; he passed while approaching a jail where he spied a "skeleton" of an old man. When he asked how long he had been in prison, the frail man's wry retort—"Judge for yourself. I no longer know"—stirred Dhanis to make an exceptional intercession: He sent him home and with a generous gift of cloth.[48]

Nervous Laughter

The old man's irony came in words. He did not laugh. But fright, shame, and the unsayable often produced the sound of laughter. A crowd "roared with laughter" when a sentry claimed he did not recognize a maimed youth. The throng knew he alone had hacked off the hand.[49] Laughter "out of place"[50] sometimes produced a brutal, punitive death, as Ncongo explained: "when we were coming to Bikoro, the soldiers saw a little child, and when they went to kill it the child laughed so the soldier took the butt of the gun and struck the child with it, and then cut off its head."[51] This story became a mainstay of humanitarian propaganda about Congolese cruelties. It traveled far, also becoming a joke in a caricature circulating about the king's cold denials. A cartoon at Lormoy castle showed someone telling King Leopold with the same words about the child who laughed and then was beheaded. The punch line was the king's reply: "I wish she had not laughed!"[52]

In the Abir concession, laughter knew a different tonality. Dhanis encountered chuckling, snickering, and cackles. A Boande man asked for help in getting back his wife abducted by a sentry some time ago. The husband had never complained before, and the baron asked why. "He laughs. The response is sufficient," Dhanis noted laconically. The sentry also had been laid off,[53] possibly losing his gun in the process. The husband's nervous laugh was akin to what Baudelaire called "trembling laughter."[54] Or as Bataille tells, with laughter, there is usually "unknowability" and "anguish." While "the unknown makes us laugh," anguish is "in some form necessary" for laughter to begin.[55] The husband's laughter came from a realm of the immediate and visceral, the instant and direct, but its erupting sound suggests something crucial about the duration of duress.[56] A delayed laughter resulting from a delayed claim and an uncomprehending white man's question suggests prolonged, diffuse suffering in a world of dangerously shifting stakes where men vied over women.[57]

As Casement traveled, he also heard laughter. In Nganda, a state soldier from far up the Upper Bussira spoke to him "fully of the condition" of people. When Casement asked why he had stayed with military work for so long, the soldier explained that "his own village and country were subject to much trouble in connection with the rubber tax," so much so "he could not live in his own home, and preferred, he said, laughing, 'to be with the hunters rather than with the hunted.'"[58] His laugh suggests uneasiness and also anguish about maintaining his dominance through pursuing others.

The laughter of an Abir agent entered Dhanis's jottings more than once. Van Calcken laughed in mid-May when Baringa's missionaries showed him detached body parts from a massacre at Wala. Once photographed, the images became iconic of excess, as if lantern show viewers far away were moving between pity and abjection in fast motion. Several weeks after this Wala massacre, Dhanis visited Baringa and learned of letters written and the brutalities committed by sentries sent to Wala with rifles. The missionaries showed Dhanis some Alice Harris photographs: a father looking "with a sad air at the foot of his child" taken on the verandah, and two of dismembered hands and feet. They also told him that Mr. Harris wrote Van Calcken the day after Wala, and when the agent arrived, they showed him the detached foot and hands.[59] Van Calcken had long tormented these earnest Anglo-Saxon missionaries. He had ordered sentries to forbid children from attending their school. He had accused that their goats devoured his rubber trees, and he sometimes took to killing their pigeons. This time, faced with body parts, the man broke into laughter, seeming to "make fun of everything."[60]

Dhanis saw Van Calcken's ridicule as the method of an agitated man. When the two met again days later on the Maringa, Dhanis visited Van Calcken's stores and counted his Albini rifles. When he questioned quantities and also Van Calcken's station departures, the man began to talk and talk. Dhanis jotted: "real chatterbox." There had been battles and knife wounds during his absences, Dhanis stressed, leading to complaints about sentries trying to abduct wives and steal much else besides. Dhanis quoted rubber gatherers: "'We can keep nothing.'" Van Calcken cried out again. Dhanis never labeled the excitable man as unhinged, but ordered him to answer questions. Afterward, each time the baron spoke, the frantic agent interjected: "'I'm listening.'"[61]

Hochschild uses the valuable word *frenzy* to grasp what happens when killing "becomes a kind of sport, like hunting." He also provides telling examples of European "sadists,"[62] torturing Congolese with castor oil, rubbing faces in excrement, and shooting holes through ear lobes. Relationships among laughter, domination, pleasure, and anguish are complex. In the racialized situations common in Abir territory in the 1900s, seeking power or safety were often less linked to capacities for observation and silence than to controlling and modulating sound.

Sexual and Visual Economies

Congolese mutilation photographs have directed attention away from the hidden, tactile, and out of sight, away from a key modality of violence: the sexual. The latter was often transgressive, punitive, and reproductive.[63]

Enter Boali. When she resisted the sexual advances of an Abir sentry, he shot her in the belly, took her body for dead, and then cut off her foot to run off with the brass ring fastened just above her ankle. This substantial anklet would have been reproductive, marital wealth, a sign that she was worthy, valuable, not a slave. Boali became one of Harris's photographic subjects. The image shows her almost naked, a mere apron around her waist, holding onto a long pole to stay erect (see figure 1.3). Her belly, traced with scarification marks, had been misshapen by the gunshot wound. The missing foot is a present absence at the bottom of the frame. Boali's image traveled far as part of magic lantern shows, her name deformed as Boaji in the process. Slide 34 carried the caption "Boaji, Mutilated for her constancy."[64] With these redemptive, evangelical words, she became a model, faithful wife. Since this time, her image has largely disappeared, though it appeared in a Congo Reform Association pamphlet[65] and in a *Penny Pictorial* piece denouncing Congo as "Murderland!"[66] By contrast, photographs of young men with missing hands, their black stumps in high contrast against white cloth, became cropped and reduplicated over and over again. They were brought together into an assemblage of mutilation shots, as in Twain's *King Leopold's Soliloquy*.[67] Usually, just as individuals went unnamed, their stories disappeared. Instead, the quantity

FIGURE 1.3 Photograph of Boali, taken by Alice Harris, ca. 1905. Reversed image, courtesy of Anti-Slavery International, London.

and simultaneity of photographs summarized all, less as "Murderland" than with Conrad's lingering word: horror.[68]

If we insert Boali back into the complexity of Free State violence (or in relation to war in the Democratic Republic of Congo since 1996),[69] the urgency of rewriting these atrocity narratives becomes marked. Historians have tended to get caught, obsessively so, on the malevolent, naughty King Leopold who never set foot in his colonial place or on the mute row of victims with stumps for arms.[70] Some have sought to put the king on trial posthumously.[71] These narratives tend to end not long after Casement's incriminating report to the British Parliament and Morel's energetic, effective propaganda campaign. They end with a *reprise* in 1908, when the Belgian parliament intervened and forced the king to relinquish his colony.

There are other ways to tell the story. They require not evading the fact of the King's Commission of Inquiry sent to investigate conditions in his colony. Boali's voice can be located in the Commission files, closed for decades though now open at the African Archives in Brussels.[72] There are 370 depositions, 258 by Congolese and 112 by Europeans or Americans. Of the sixteen women who testified, thirteen were Congolese, of whom five introduced evidence of a sexualized nature.[73] Boali of Ekolongo was one of these. She testified at Baringa, the Abir post and mission site where Harris and her husband worked. Boali spoke of a day when her husband went to gather rubber, and a sentry, Ikelonda, found her in her hut and asked her to give herself to him: "I rejected his proposition. Furious, Ikelonda fired a gun shot at me, which gave me the wound whose trace you can still see." When she fell, "Ikelonda thought I was dead, and to get hold of the brass bracelet that I wore at the base of my right leg, he cut off my right foot."[74] Boali's *claim* concerned her wound as "trace," her missing foot, stolen anklet, and refusal to be raped. She knew the sentry's name, while Ikelonda's fury and gun seem to have blasted through Boali with life-altering noise. While she managed to stay "quiet as death,"[75] his sharp blade separated foot and anklet from body. This human capacity for lying silent, giving no "sign of life" while a body part was "hacked off," had intrigued Casement in 1903.[76]

The British Consul found some forms of violence "unfit for repetition."[77] Likewise, the testimony of women before the King's Commission confirms something long sensed about Free State violence: rape became epidemic. Women's words push against the grain of Congo Reform Association propaganda. Whether produced by Morel or missionaries, humanitarian tracts lumped together women and children as the most vulnerable and injured. Their troubles related to the "hostage houses," where they were confined until husbands produced the requisite rubber.[78] Such representations reduce women to suffering alone, with no faculty or scope for struggle, reflection, negotiation, witnessing, anger, or mockery. Morel's generation of humanitarians rarely used a sex card or alluded to rape when speaking about the plight of Congolese women.

Casement told a story about some sentries before two sisters: "'We might keep them both, the little one is not bad-looking'; but the others said 'No, we are not going to carry her all the way; we must kill the youngest girl'. So they put a knife through the child's stomach, and left the body lying there where they had killed it."[79] Wife-stealing, like aesthetic admiration, is present in the Casement report, while "delight in slapping and ill-using them" was suggested.[80] When and how violence became sexualized is absent, whereas Commission testimony suggests modalities of sexualization. Several women told stories about voyeurism, torture, rape, and escape, with some living among a few decent white men and some cruel Congolese. While attempted rape surfaces starkly in Boali's story, the other female depositions suggest the complexity of sexual and visual economies. Together they tell of sexual capital and abuse, how some women used the first for protection, whereas many became reduced to objects of torture and sexual violence. They permit glimpsing women negotiating to their advantage, sometimes bettering their situation, and sometimes refusing sex or insisting on their autonomy.

Among the depositions by women, at one extreme was Boali's sexual refusal and severed foot. Sadistic pleasure combined with sexual torture in Mingo's testimony. She did brickmaking work at an Abir post, Mampoko, where sentries punished her: " . . . N'kusu, Lomboto, and Itokwa, made me take off my cloth and put clay in my sexual parts, which made me suffer a lot. The white man saw me with clay in my sexual parts. He limited himself to saying: 'If you speed up in my work, they can throw you in water.' The white man Longwango also saw the clay in my sexual parts, and he had the same attitude as Likwama."[81]

Something twisted, if less physically violent, went on. It is impossible to know who dreamt up the idea of filling private parts with clay, of using work materials to threaten, abuse, and humiliate, though Vigdis Broch-Due reminds us: "violence can lead to a macabre form of creativity." In Mingo's case, authority and observation combined: A white man, present and watching, did not quite approve, yet did not intervene. Twistedness is suggested in words legible but struckthrough ("~~Three women are already dead; if you [continue] this will be the fourth~~"), an excision officially approved at the close of Mingo's deposition. Voyeurism accompanied this spectacle: "the sentry made me take off my cloth," "the white man saw me." There was a division of labor. Black men "put clay in my sexual parts," while white men watched at a remove in a situation involving racial layers of authority and capacities for observation. A white man sat apart and looked, while another white man was there with eyes looking. It is as if there is an ellipsis in Mingo's deposition through which almost sounds the twisted pleasure and tittering attending this sexual torture. One white man spoke with a mixture of threat ("you may be the fourth to die") and an offer of escape ("work harder and we will release you from your pain").[82] The expunged words likely warned sentries they might soon kill another woman.

In three cases, white men sought sexual relations, and a range in coercion and sentiments appears. From the Lower Congo, Kapinga testified about spurning the approaches of a European telegraphic line overseer, who "proposed I become his concubine. I refused, and I even said that I was sick and could not have sexual relations." Undeterred, "he prowled several times around my house." Kapinga hid herself from his view: "he did not manage to see me," until "he sent one night some men who took me and led me to his place." More recently, "the white man sent a canoe, with paddlers led by a black clerk who came to take me again and lead me to Yambi. I refused, and they left again without using violence." Kapinga concluded by naming the man—perhaps Congolese—whom she preferred: "I want to stay with Moamba."[83]

Tema found protection with a white man named Nina. She testified at Basankusu about the arrest of her husband; when he fled, sentries imprisoned Tema at Bilange. For three days, the white man watched her and then "made me his mistress." She stayed with him for four months, "never object of any violence." One day, he "dismissed me because I fell sick," and Tema departed; Nina gave her three pieces of cloth as she left. But, a "sentry took me at the exit to Nina's place," and he also "appropriated the three pieces of cloth." A month later she complained to a white agent Schoort. Tema spoke of the other women at Bilange who "remained in prison after the white man noticed and took me." Something approaching sexual capital allowed her to escape captivity, while Nina's kind gift of cloth suggests an understanding of obligation and gift giving. That the sentry both stole the cloth and "took" Tema suggests a vengeful, harsh sexual servitude.[84]

Mausato testified at Bokotola, recalling being taken from her village with other women, all conducted to Mampoko. More joined them "when our village was burned." She recalled the hitting of women at work, "neither with a whip or stick, but rather a cane." One day she ran away with others, after a time of drawing water, cutting rushes, and making bricks: "When we went to draw water, white man Ipama made us take off our cloths." A benign, erotic voyeurism is suggested with this image of restraint: a white man who enjoyed looking, as female shapes moved through running water. He found pleasure, asking for repetition. While the gentleness surprises, the scopic economy underlying the sightings is plain. The contrast with Boali, a foot lost for refusing sex, is stark.[85]

Not all sexualization was aggressive or sadistic. Some was protective, suggesting some female strategies, marshaled well. Several found refuge in white men's arms or homes, becoming *ménagères*—"housekeepers" doubling as sexual partners.[86] The range suggests more than one sexual economy at work, and possibilities crossing in complex ways. One economy brought together white men and Congolese women, sometimes with affection, sometimes with force. When Ikengo ran to glimpse a steamer about 1890, a white officer sent someone to seize her. She landed, despite protesting, "locked into his room until they were underway again, when he assaulted her and compelled her to become his mistress." The young Ikengo managed to run away, though a decade later near Coquilhatville seemed a "scarlet woman" on another steamer.[87]

Relations often began through looking and sight, forms of voyeurism that ranged from white men peering to sighting that unleashed prowling. Health mattered. Illness led to dismissal, while claiming sickness could serve as a ploy in avoiding relations.

A linked, different economy connected armed Congolese men and women, while being distinct from the marital economy suggested in testimony. The relatively new sentry economy became manipulative and ruthless. When white men joined Congolese men in torturing women, solidarity and mocking laughter appeared. In Dhanis's journal, a third economy may be glimpsed: older practices of gifting women. The most visible chiefly ally of Abir was Evokolo. Dhanis spotted this powerful chief traveling through more than once. At one juncture, Evokolo passed through and danced "a dance" for the baron and others present, at a time when the arrival of the sensational traveler and author, May French Sheldon, had attracted women and then a large crowd.[88] Evokolo and Dhanis exchanged gifts, while Dhanis lectured the chief about getting people to work harder before the chief slid away. Later, Evokolo reappeared and offered Dhanis three *something*—resulting in a journal entry which Dhanis concealed, switching over to his inscrutable stenographic script. Likely, the offer proposed a gift of three women.[89]

This patrimonial economy appeared again in June at Van Calcken's post Lifundu when an investigating judge was there. An attack seemed imminent. Van Calcken claimed Chief Lopombo wanted him dead and his Abir post burned down. Dhanis noted that all the white men of Lifundu were so nervous that they were getting two sentries to accompany them "to the WC" at night.[90] Chief Lopombo had not appeared in Lifundu for a long time. "It was necessary to end this," Dhanis decided; he ordered calling for the chief and offered the help of his ten soldiers to make it happen. Lopombo finally appeared: "I came now because I learned a big white man of Bula Matari had arrived." He also spoke to avoidance and humiliation, reminding everyone that when he last came to Lifundu: "van Calcken shaved my hair, and the whites hit me and sent me onto the chain in Basankusu. A house was under construction for me: they demolished it. There was no indignity that they did not make me undergo."[91]

The judge knew more. When Van Calcken asked Lopombo for a woman, the one received turned out to be sick. Soon Chief Lopombo was prisoner, with the pretext that he had not furnished meat. They cut his "too many tufts," sent him to prison in Basankusu, though Abir authorities there sent him back again. Dhanis drew an easy colonial moral about "the prestige of native chiefs," which if reduced only served "to diminish the authority of the white man."[92]

He also confronted the Abir agent about the chief's refusal to visit, his "perfect reason after you shaved his head." Van Calcken admitted the shaving, but "turning the thing into a joke," he echoed his earlier "method" before a missionary accusation of atrocity, turning everything to ridicule.[93] Did Chief Lopombo send a woman with venereal infection as a punitive, mocking gesture? It is not impossible. The agitated agent seems to have read the soiled gift in this way. In public spectacles that followed, cutting away a chief's tufts surely went with biting laughter, debasing power.

Rape and Specters of Sterility

The sexualization of women's dealings with Abir agents, sentries, and chiefs, therefore, knew a wide semantic and practical range. With violence often sexualized, rape ever a risk, the sexual still could be as subtle as tone or gesture and part of intimate politics among men. A sick woman was at the crux of the Van Calcken–Lopombo wrangle. Chief Lopombo breached colonial expectations with a brazen agent whose nervous derangement may long have had cerebral and venereal dimensions.

Humanitarian critics, Morel in the lead, pointed to the widespread loss of life in Leopold's Congo. Others aimed criticism at the venereal, the psychiatric, and the reproductive. Dhanis found many with syphilis while wishing for regeneration.[94] Casement suggested the specter of sterility, after discussions with critical missionaries. He found people frightened and frail while traveling from Lac Léopold to the Lulonga confluence, then into the Abir concession. He noted visceral effects of terror and trauma: "suspicious looks," "evasive eyes," "flutterings." He quoted Reverend Clark of Ikoko: "a lower percentage of births" partly because of weak bodies "lessen the population," in addition "women refuse to bear children, and take means to save themselves from motherhood. They give as the reason that if 'war' should come a woman 'big with child,' or with a baby to carry, cannot well run away and hide from the soldiers." Others pointed to hunger and starvation. A missionary near Lukolela spoke of a disappearing, "dying people," suggesting "fear and punishment" were producing loss of appetite and, among women, amenorrhea.[95]

A less sensitive observer, more aligned with King Leopold too,[96] was British journalist and traveler Viscount Mountmorres. He found much to admire in the Free State, arguing that violence tended to be confined to Equateur's concession areas. Noting the violent squeeze of the Abir bonus and sentry system, he pointed out that rubber supply was almost exhausted while hunger often *became* war.[97] New pressures to collect scarce rubber produced uprisings or conflicts between rubber villages, or battles in which rubber villages fought food villages. Many simply took refuge from the Abir zone.[98]

Mountmorres imagined Mongo as "indolent, timid, and sulky, desiring only to be left alone to lead a slug-like existence." He did not acknowledge how war, grueling labor, and hunger were producing the images of frailty and brokenness appearing before his eyes. "The villages are smaller and not so well kept," he commented, "one scarcely sees a village worthy of the name." Occasionally he would glimpse "one or two huts," "occupied by a surly, silent, depressed people, who neither greet one nor flee before one, but accept one's presence with a dull indifference." Nor did he hesitate to judge: "*Physically the race is degenerate*, being extremely small of stature and meager of build." But health and harm were at the core of his judgments: "The rapidity with which these people fall ill and die is almost incredible," though he presumed an acceptance of "death with a fatalism which goes far to encourage it."[99] Mountmorres's degenerationist language returns us to matters of sexuality and reproduction.

Casement's report never used the word *rape*.[100] Nor did he use the ambiguous word of his time, *ravish*. Historians have become less reticent on the topic, though evidence is rarely explicit. "Institutionalized rape was not uncommon, and such sentries often lived *en pacha*," Síocháin and Sullivan state about rubber districts near Irebu, without indicating quite how they came to this conclusion.[101] Hochschild speaks briefly of "raped hostages," quoting from the 1895 diary of a Force Publique officer working in Uele, northeast of Equateur: "The women taken during the last raid at Engwettra are causing me no end of trouble. All the soldiers want one. The sentries who are supposed to watch them unchain the prettiest ones and rape them."[102]

Ikakota and Memories

We have a sense of how those at a remove *saw* Leopold's Congo, from viewing lantern shows and humanitarian exposés. In Congo, young Elima's visuality extended as daydreaming about the terrifying state, monstrous, a crushing figure. When she dreamed "Bula Matadi was coming to fight," her mother told Elima to stop making up stories. Soon together, they "heard the firing of guns."[103]

What Congolese saw, heard, and remembered at the time, as well as some fifty years later, comes through in memory accounts written about 1954, when Father Edmond Boelaert organized an essay contest in the pages of a Sacred Heart Fathers magazine, published in Coquilhatville. Boelaert promised compensation, with the best receiving 2500 francs. Some 170 men participated.

While few claimed to be direct witnesses, most were a younger generation of students, teachers, catechists, and mission workers who collected memories from elders and wrote them down in the mission language, Lomongo.[104]

Many began with the arrival of missionaries and traders, giving away beads and cloth. Nicknames were many, as were stories about first interactions, with someone killed or a battle erupting. At Wangata, some played with a ball of wild rubber when white men asked for two bouncing spheres to send home to Europe.[105] Soon, rubber was sinister and deadly. War and massacre combined with flight. Often a treaty followed, with the first brave enough to exit the forest becoming chief. Rubber collection constituted part of the truce; this new imposed, taught work even brought some rewards in cloth, beads, salt, and brass wire money. Rubber collection ended abruptly, inexplicably, while new corvées followed. The arrival of colonial money and taxes in coin was a signal moment in these memories, while several also complained about the horrendous return of rubber corvées during the Second World War.

Memory may smell and shudder. In 1954, several Congolese recalled the stench of rotting corpses when many wrote essays in Lomongo with fine penmanship for the mission contest (see example, figure 1.4). Their accounts are rich with sounds. The first boat arrived "like the noise of large wind that precedes rain." An old man crooned an inebriated song about war taking some and sparing others. Mocking insult met the first white men who arrived with unkempt hair. The bang of firing combined with sounds of drizzling rain. Children sobbed with hunger.[106] Images are ubiquitous too: the trees used to hang people, baskets of severed hands, and blood running like a river up to the thighs.[107]

Their texts suggest distress as well as remembering after duress. Stories of cut off hands, detached feet, and removed ears abound, as do whole baskets piled high with smoked human hands. Tswambe recalled sentries forcing people into transgressive, sexual violence against their own kin: "Soldiers made young men kill or rape their own mothers and sisters."[108] Tallying supervising agents were suggested by some. Objects included guns, machetes, and a therapeutic charm called Ikakota. The skills for making this embodied tool of war were also there.

Protective charms enabled a special visibility. Jean-Ambroise Yolo wrote of looking into an Ikakota pot, seeing rows of troops at war.[109] An Ikakota, or *bote*, was a medicine, charm, magical practice, and also a tree.[110] A human-made mixture of tree and plants, hair, nails, blood, and fragments of objects, Ikakota appeared with fondness, delight, and sometimes consternation. One mission man gave credit to God: "War in the morning, war at night. Right

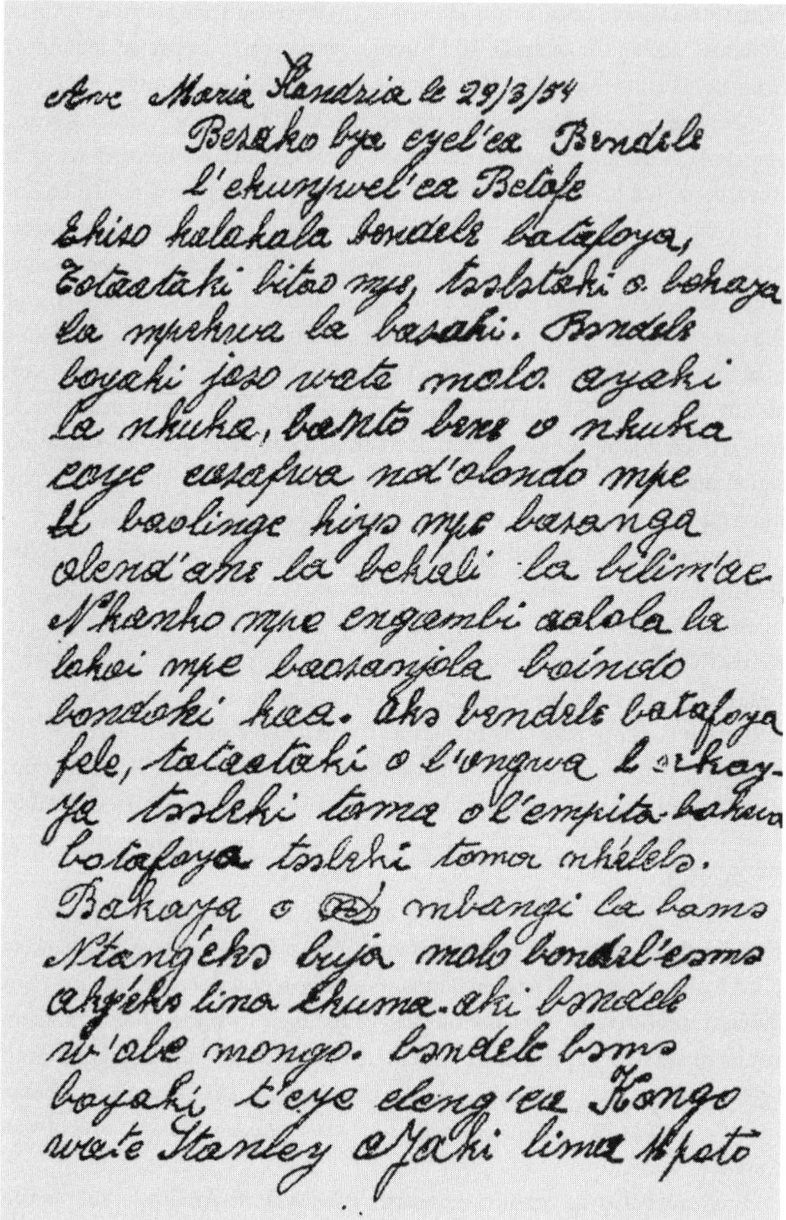

FIGURE 1.4 One of some 170 handwritten memory texts written in Lomongo. Authored by François Bompuku, a student at the HCB Flandria-Boteka school, this page was one of four he submitted for Edmond Boelaert's contest of 1953–54. Courtesy of the Archief van de Missionarissen van het H. Hart, Borgerhout, Belgium.

there, maybe God stirred up a charm called Ikakota."[111] Some spoke of wars among spirits, wounds small when entering and large when exiting bodies.[112] Ikakota produced invulnerability: "bullets no longer crossed through skin, but fell flat."[113] A common narrative began with ancestors and Ikakota; it made them impenetrable, then some soldiers died. They continued to fight powerfully, killing soldiers in stations until a white man sent in reinforcements.

Resorting to Ikakota went with the need to fight gunmen. Often they prepared the charm, placing it in an antelope horn. Many would leave for war, the first carrying the horn, a second an arrow, a third a flywhisk. With these three in lead, Bolampunga underlined, the troop would shake while chanting about a smoldering smell adrift, which might not retreat: "Small smoke of the charm in the horn, oh small fume, you left promenading, you must return to the village, oh small fume we have mixed and put in the horn, oh small smoke!" Upon arriving, dividing into combat positions, the man with the horn would dare the gunmen: "Shoot me." A time of slaughter would come, he concluded, while the ones not dead held the horn, the arrow, and the flywhisk.[114] Flywhisks, like trees, will return in this history.

Most accounts do not suggest Ikakota saved lives. They do imply the dangers, smells, bravery, and walking associated with war. Ikakota went with initiation and journeys: "our ancestors went to look for Ikakota to get the upper hand."[115] Or: "Seeing the strong man killed, Boleja of Losilika went to be initiated into Ikakota."[116] Ise'Ekafela went to Elanga with this "very powerful war charm."[117] Joseph Ilanga remembered Lokolonganya arriving with Ikakota. Though himself a sentry, Ilanga sought the charm after being imprisoned and still furious with the authorities. Lokolonganya fought against sentries of two big whites, Ntange and Wilima,[118] killing many, carrying off their guns. As others learned of his success with this charm, they went to be initiated and killed some more. Lifuma used Ikakota to fight against Ilanga and his soldiers, hurting him "with seven arrows." Ilanga concluded his paradoxical account: "I killed many people. Then they put me as sentry at Bokele."[119]

Some suggested partial victory, with the ancestors more powerful and sentries posted in the stations killed.[120] One remembered whites making battles more fierce, killing "because of Ikakota." It was a turning point, at first called peace: "Now let's make peace, and you furnish rubber."[121] Many stories of defeat revolved around prohibitions. The white man would send in reinforcements. Defeat would follow after the transgressing of Ikakota commands. Ikakota became effective through its rules, as in: "*Bote l'osise, ndeki nko bosise*," "the charm and its interdiction, the most important, it's the interdiction."[122] The semantics for *bosise* embrace message, order, as in a drum's message. A judicial palaver produces a bosise.[123] A bote's command is its message; obeying it keeps the medicine working.[124] Wartime inverts the normative, leading to special commands.[125] Contact with women was perilous in war, just as Ikakota "forbid eating anything a woman prepared and drinking any water she fetched."[126] Transgression stripped the war charm of both its murderous *and* protective powers. Reversals could be sudden: "The Whites conquered our fathers and dominated them until now, since our fathers broke the Ikakota prohibition to not sleep with women, they desired to sleep with women, and the medicine lost its force."[127] At the close of Is'e'Ekafela's successful fight against SAB forces,[128] Ikakota abetting, he was with a woman. Soon, the "state killed us," and everyone took "refuge in the forest."[129]

The Ikakota command required arresting sex, desire, and reproduction to ensure life and survival. The rule was a poetic commentary on a grave time of emergency. In enforcing an ultimately impossible *state of exception*—zero access to women—Ikakota was in contention with the fragility of male forbearance before its sexual command. Ikakota memories mix pride with sorrow. These late colonial memory accounts tell much about therapeutic insurgency, the basis of might, and its foundation in a charm.[130] But these memories also contain grim threads about failed manliness and defeat. Also vivid is sexual violence as transgressive excess.

Some wrote about sentries forcing mothers and sons, and fathers and daughters, to have sex while they watched. One mentioned sentries "amusing themselves while pounding the insides of women's vaginas with sticks."[131] This graphic image suggests acute pain, writhing bodies, arrested desire, and damaged reproductive tracts, a kind of intimate injury to women[132] in an era long before gynecologists arrived, as in the recent war zones of eastern Congo where clinicians speak of psychosocial trauma and proceed with fistula repair. The memory texts suggest gratuitous, grotesque violence, sometimes in a repetitive, fanciful mode of remembering:

> The one inflicted with the chicotte who defecated right afterwards, they forced eating this excrement. If you refuse to eat it, they kill you. . . . A woman is pregnant, they order: 'Eviscerate her so that we see how the baby is inside.' The death of the woman follows. They cut one ear from someone and left him another. They forced a woman to have sex with her son. If she refuses, they kill her. . . . They cut a breast off a woman and left her another. . . . They forced a boy to have sex with his mother, if not they kill him.[133]

Such violence was fantastic, but not implausible. The repetition suggests monstrous phantasm, almost reverie,[134] whereas other evidence suggests much violence involved excess and derangement. Years later, a Belgian observer recalled being among Abir agents, in a milieu where, as we saw, many were worked to the bare bone. He did not remember skirmishes or gauntness, but the madness of this place, where Chief Evoloko boasted some three hundred wives and where rubber agents paraded too. A Swiss agent was ever keen to hoist the Swiss flag in this colonial world of many well-dressed alcoholics.[135]

Ekuma and Suicide

Several memory texts discuss another Swiss man, Ekuma or Charles Liwenthal, a nervous, violent Swiss officer who shot himself at Bokatola in 1902. He was often remembered in the 1950s for his music-making fanfare, as we will see in chapter 6. *Ekuma* means hair plucker, suggesting torture.[136] Known for cruelty and eating native foods while on the run, he still fascinated in 1954. Fierce, severe, he killed and punished.[137] Jean Boenga wrote about him arriving with soldiers: "too many to count." At first assigned to Bokala, where those with Ikakota lived, Ekuma sent many suddenly into a battle and then lost. When the "old men attacked him and his soldiers by surprise," they used Ikakota, making Ekuma and his soldiers scatter. He fled far away until appointed to Bokatola.[138]

François Bompuku recalled this "very bad White" coming to Bokatola "at the time of rubber gathering," when people looked for latex furiously, "from the height of trees."[139] Ekuma arrived with hundreds of soldiers, two hundred workers, and a hundred women who worked fields and lived in a common hut, each with a booklet, blanket, and regular payments. He had the post paths planted with palm, establishing himself as a strong leader who knew how to obtain rubber. As this substance became a fact of life, his soldiers brought back hands cut from the dead and rebellious. Smoked in Bokatola, the hands may have moved by basket to Mbandaka, demonstrating orders well followed.[140] Some remembered instead corvées in roofing material and *chikwangue*[141] or cruel exactions for those not supplying as they should: "hands cut off," "tied to trees, then shot."[142] Ekuma commanded Lomboto, "chief of Blacks," to issue orders. Those remiss met cruelties: "cut a hand or an ear" or "killed with a bullet."[143] New construction began in Bokatola: Ekuma's impressive house with mud bricks, two stories, floor mats, ceiling cloth, fine pillars, and also a big prison with individualized cells. So memories in the early 1950s went. Prisoners received fifty to a hundred whiplashes at a time and were often freed in lamentable shape, dying soon afterward. Ekuma also owned brass instruments and offered feasts. His two Ekonda ménagères joined him as night fell.

Some thought Ekuma took his life for all the lives he had taken. Disgrace prompted him. "Covered in shame, he committed suicide with his own gun," wrote one.[144] Another penned: "his friends learned he killed many Blacks," then he was so ashamed, he killed himself.[145] Others pointed to conjuncture. His death came when state policy shifted, and he was found acting contrary to newer, less violent times. Imbamba recalled a letter from superiors, delivered by soldiers: "'You still kill people, and the bosses call you to Coq because they no longer want someone killing as you do.' Ekuma read the letter and killed himself by gun shot."[146] "Fury" was the cause, suggested others. He struggled over wealth with bosses. Commander Polo wanted punitive killings stopped.[147] Ekuma was recruiting former soldiers and ignoring boss Polopolo. Sinking into shame, some had him planning a new post at Bonginda,[148] others trying to escape downriver one day.

Known to drink, he drank more when his troubles began. One day, he wrote a letter, left it on the table, and called for his servant Efumba: "After asking his boy to give him food to eat, right away, he ordered: 'Take the gun, kill me.' Efumba refused: 'Me, I do not kill a Whiteman.'"[149] Dressed in his best clothes, sitting in a chair, the 1950s Congolese memories have Ekuma placing a gun under his chin and lifting the trigger with a foot. As soon as he did, the questions began: "Where does this gunshot come from?" Then a bugle sounded and soldiers assembled, seeing through the window the well-dressed, white man. A crowd gathered. When the corpse appeared, social memory resounds with a single cry: "Ekuma killed himself with a gunshot."[150] People mourned and wept for this man, "they loved very much." Hundreds added bits of earth to his grave during the spectacular funeral "for a big chief."[151]

Ekuma's was not the only suicide during the Free State years, though it is perhaps the best recorded in Congolese collective memory. We will never know their total number, only the prominence of a few. Two 1905 suicides—of the colony's governor general and the Nigerian merchant and photographer Herzekiah-André Shanu—suggest that nervousness became destruction. It took lives. Governor General Costermans took his life shortly after the King's Commission shared its findings with him. A biographer attributed his exit not to moral outrage but "excessive *nervosité*."[152] The educated merchant Shanu worked as clerk, postal director, and archival assistant for King Leopold II. After opening his successful Maison Shanu in the colonial capital of Boma, the elegant Shanu traveled to Belgium, giving talks within colonial circles. Yet the urbane, talented photographer and businessman became suspect when anti-Congo tensions flared. Intermediary for Casement and Morel, he wrote the latter about the destruction of official archives, his forced removal from Brussels's Cercle Africain, and the hardships of being involved in politics and "the cause of truth" as a black man. Just before taking his life in September, shortly before the release of the Commission's report, Shanu began to worry about epistolary replies missing from Morel. He sensed the mounting suspicions about him as black British spy were resulting in the boycott of his once thriving business, Maison Shanu.[153] Shanu's suicide was but one of several human exits realized during these years.

The Biopolitical Meets Bandits

Dhanis instead took refuge in his travel journal as he tried to imagine, for his king, a broader colonial exit from the destruction near Basankusu. Much of his journal was an effort to find a way for Abir to overcome its notoriety and state of disaster through a future of well-organized rubber plantations and markets. His technical reverie included working with those present and creating a middle rank of industrious, partly "civilized" Congolese. The vision embraced counting and inscribing names in registers. Dhanis was planning a future based not on those whom Mountmorres found to be feeble, huddled in meager huts, nor frail rubber collectors, but on the armed sentries. Their wives would get paid to clean posts and harvest fields.[154] Dhanis daydreamed in the midst of ruination. But these were not idle reveries. As the 1954 memory accounts recall, from about 1910 on, a new kind of state emerged. Belgian Congo agents showed up, distributing identity books and insisting on tax in coin. They also sought a new kind of forced labor, glossed as "customary" and "educative."

Colonies create diverse kinds of camps, enclosures containing persons and curtailing mobility, though with porous boundaries. A mission station was one kind of camp. A state post, school, hospital, and prison were others. Camps required work; they had to be built, defended, and maintained. A colonial camp could fall into ruins. Many Abir posts and factories seem to have done just that, as the concession dissolved and agents departed. During the Abir years, many simply fled as conditions produced countless refugees.

This chapter closes with a vivid chronotope from just beyond Abir territory, several years later in time. It is about a fruitless state attempt to get control over a group of Songo fugitives and bandits in a refuge zone near the Tshuapa during the Great War years. We jump forward to think better about camps and escape in Abir time and track Dhanis's biopolitical daydream. The number of refugees produced by rubber and war in Abir territory is unknowable. The empty villages sighted by Mountmorres told of death and withering away, but also willful departures and flight (see figure 1.5). Several times, Dhanis

FIGURE 1.5 These "old men of Mangi" survived the raids of Congolese sentries and soldiers in or near Abir territory, ca, 1905. Their eyes suggest vigor, fierceness. Perhaps they fought back against abuses or took flight for safer parts, joining other refugees in marshy zones. Coursez perhaps met men like these a decade later. Courtesy of Anti-Slavery International, London.

mentioned people on the run to the Tshuapa river basin and also whole villages not returning home.[155] Areas of flight embraced the Ikelemba and Busira, a realm of non-camps and safe havens within marshy forest, where not only the emaciated but spirited runaways and bandits gathered.

Seasonal journeys surely had long taken people to these refuge places, for camping out in *nganda*,[156] to catch the best spells for fishing and copal collection besides. Such refuge spaces were as ancient as Lianja, the magical founding figure of material life and therapeutic performances in this region, whether people identified—or were labeled—as Mongo, Nkundo, Ekonda, Wangata, Basankusu, Songo, and the like. The marshier the land, the more water levels receded and rose twice a year, creating plentiful seasons of barrier and mud-fishing in a world where nganda time was a way of life, a special "timespace"[157] marking life with seasonal rhythms and bountiful spirits of water. By the interwar years, nganda had become favorite second homes in Equateur, places where people hid out from tax collectors, census keepers, and the tedium of village schedules that officials named "customary."

In 1916–17, territorial officials moved into this rebellious Songo area with a police operation. From at least 1903, Abir refugees had fled east of the Ikelemba, between the Maringa and Tshuapa. A strong impression of the landscape emerges from official reporting, as does a sense of many different groups of Songo, with the Songo-Eose especially unruly and rough. The far-flung name also appears in documents concerning Basankusu and Songomboyo. Refugees may have carried the name with them or fled to areas with distant Songo kin.

A long, detailed report of the Force Publique officer in charge depicts the maneuvers of his task. Coursez began by making a meticulous map, scattered with streams, hideaways, and fishing havens. Lasting months, the operation involved battles, loss of life, and an intimate official knowledge of many names, persons, and *ituka* (houses) involved. Coursez was pursuing an evasive set of troublemakers, many called "runaways." He spent much time trying to hunt down ringleaders within their refuge spaces. Some confrontations were verbal. Others involved war maneuvers. Official territorial borders were confounding efforts to securitize the space. Prescribed limits stymied the reach of state agents; boundary lines split chiefdoms still working as familiar networks; and various Songo rebels were moving into elusive refuge spaces sprawling across borders and maddeningly difficult to find or pin down.[158]

After days, Coursez accepted that he was unable to capture the main ringleader, a bandit figure and popular hero. Mopindji and his gang, including troublemakers Isekoale and Isekalanga and two runaways Zako and Bongo, had assembled an intricate shadow network. Some secured protection from his mafia-like ring by providing a wife; others paid up with other forms of wealth. Those managing their reputations and security through these nganda had collected all kinds of wealth. They were able, perhaps brilliant, tacticians of war. They used sound to caution, frighten, and repel. At one point, Coursez witnessed a war dance. Otherwise, hints were few about whether Mopindji and gang were using war charms to make battle. Visible were tactical practices of making war. At one stage, they had strewn entire pathways with sharpened wooden spikes, designed to wound the bare feet of those who dared to pass. They felled huge trees across paths to signal no one should proceed any further— or else! There is no hint they had or needed guns.[159] Their methods worked terribly well, and they kept an upper hand through their intimate knowledge of terrain—each marsh and stream, mound and hollow, surely also special places where spirits collected. The felled tree was powerfully medicinal in nature, as we will see: This book is littered with trees as charms. A key definition of *bote* is tree, and Coursez's soldiers were terrified to cross these fallen ones. Others were astounded when some dared to help chop up the immense obstacle in their path.[160]

Biopolitical fantasy and work were at play in Coursez's police operation. The method was akin to Dhanis's reverie: to count, census, and also encourage singing to persuade. Coursez made conciliatory, patronizing speeches, trying to explain why he was there and why it was important to come out of hiding, be counted, and listed by name. Slowly some appeared. He kept returning from forest maneuvers to village settings to count more and assign more tasks. Often, he busied himself with persuading people to settle down, build new and better villages, and do assigned work to pay taxes.

Disease was absent from his report, though population and counting were paramount. Depopulation, frailty, degeneration, and children never emerged.[161] Whether women were part of Coursez's many counts is never clear. Not pathology but crime was central, not only of bandit ringleaders, but "runaways," with Coursez constantly trying to get some to settle down, often in a new village with fresh roads they themselves constructed. Also present was copal. Subjects would seek permission to go collect this resinous product in the forest, but Coursez would refuse, fearing a pretext for escaping or engaging the forest bandits. His account suggests that many of those hiding out were doing well from the new commercial product, which gathered in the forest and sold unprocessed was supplanting wild rubber in economic importance.[162] Traders were at the margins keen to buy this raw, resinous substance used to make industrial lacquers and paints in Europe. Many were finding furtive ways to sell their copal to Portuguese and other itinerant traders on the move between small trading posts.

Coursez was unable to get a consistent policy in place. Territorial agents wanted everyone to return from the forest and work to pay taxes, now reckoned in coin. The anticolonial, nganda-based ring seems to have let a few return to village life and census books in an unsettled truce of sorts. Yet the police operation suggests that Songo were still fiercely protecting nganda as space-time, knowing full well that the colonial insistence on sedentarization represented an attack on social reproduction and pleasure, too.

Reworking refuge spaces into sanctuaries through combining escape needs and protectionist tactics surely began earlier, during the Abir years, when flight into areas abundant in fish and game would have been a shrewd way to reconstitute livelihoods and community during a time of assault and war when mafia-like gangs produced hierarchies and felled trees.

Conclusion

The Alice Harris photographs became a global force of historical significance.[163] In setting aside these tenaciously visual marks of pity and the abject, an intimate sensory scale enabled a new reading of Leopold's Congo. Sounds opened laughter and also a jittery, agitated Abir agent picking off pigeons, terrified of nocturnal assault. Listening with nearness enabled hearing sadistic violence and laughter convulsing around forms of sexual violence basic to reproductive ruination in Congo's Equateur. Dhanis saw some Harris photographs at Baringa, but these seem never to have circulated as shocking phantasmagoria in Congo. While distress was enormous, the visual still risks reducing subjects to frail parties, just as any lens of suffering may exaggerate anguish and flatten volition. Women and men were maneuvering, making allegations, hiding out, and taking flight, with many running after Ikakota or taking refuge in nganda.

This reading probed claims. The sexual and erotic opened wide rape, bemused peering, and sexually transmitted disease. We met incest and vicious sexuality that cut off a foot at the ankle and blocked up another woman's private parts with stiffening clay. The demographic historian Voas shrewdly pointed at women confined in hostage houses and guarded by sentries, hypothesizing rape as the reason a low birth rate followed.[164] There is excellent reason to conjecture that for women hostages sexual violence was as excessive outside as inside these camp-like spaces.

Present were kinds of sexual entrepreneurship, patronage, gift giving, and hints of pleasure. Some women steered among sexual, juridical, and domestic opportunities, it seems. Others were waiting for the next arriving steamer to watch their next prospects disembark. These milieus knew suffering husbands and brilliant revenge, with a vindictive chief presenting a white agent with the sour gift of a sullied woman. The kinds of language in circulation included the humanitarian, the biopolitical, and the degenerationist. Mountmorres's idea of a degenerate Mongo race endured, repeated for decades, as Equateur became a relative backwater with sinking population, and as finance capital made industrial mining in Katanga the fulcrum of the colonial economy.

Diverse kinds of dreamwork combined in Dhanis's journal, Casement's diary, and the 1954 Congolese memory accounts about Ikakota, battles, white men, and a suicide. Casement worked to bring scandalized attention to the abuses, helping Morel close down the Leopoldian regime. Congolese had their own remedies, with flight to refuge spaces a critical maneuver. Dhanis was more special remedy man on the spot. He, like most officers and agents, could hardly master the intricate ecology of marshes, forest, and rising and falling waters. Still, these white men helped shape the knotted sexual economies of these worlds, shared with sentries and chiefs, joining intimate gestures and brutal rape with an unbridled, predatory colonial occupation.

Dissent ran deep a decade after the Free State came to a close. Memory perhaps inflated the awful transgressive sexuality of these years. Yet these remembered scenes of sexual horror stand in a blunt contrast with the tight control expected of men during times of battle, with total arrest of the sexual to win at war. Ikakota and its commands helped win some important skirmishes, but by the 1950s, memory was more about the faltering; failure in sexual forbearance had yielded sovereignty to these petty white men with relentless censusing and corvées.

The chapters to come think more about this disappointment in relation to childlessness, its fact and fictions, and its mediations by venereal infection, somatization, and new sexual economies. But other questions incited by material in this chapter are now pressing. What did happen to those charm-like devices for making war under less spectacularly violent colonial conditions? How did nervousness, laughter, and fantasy surface in the decades to follow? Tracing the many layers to Maria N'koi's story, we enter into some of these riddles now.

| Maria N'koi

A Belgian priest first heard about Maria N'koi at Ibele. It was the same Sunday in May when he heard Congolese talking about the Germani, close by and at war. This Maria was a healer with an amalgamated name, suggesting the elusive spiritual powers of Christ's mother and crafty, alarming leopards (*n'koi*). Maria N'koi spoke of Belgium's archenemies as ancestral spirits, ready to punish Bula Matari for all the troubles this colonial state had sown. These Germani would appear and help her charms drive the Belgians out of their colony. This vision, a form of *eviction reverie*, ignited colonial emergency, the subject of this chapter.

This healer named after leopards resembled and used these animals of stealth. Antoine Sonzolo Efoloko shared stories with me in 2007 about his grandmother's powers. One day when quite young, she went to work in her fields and encountered a leopard. It approached, ready to kill. When this predator tried to seize her, she fought back. Its paws scraped across her head. She fell faint. The leopard died. Her wound turned white. Until she died, hair never again grew at this place of scars. Forevermore, she was known as Leopard Maria.

In the 1960s, Sonzolo and other grandchildren would accompany her when she went to harvest cassava and medicines at her Lolifa fields. Sometimes, late in the afternoon, Sonzolo's father would follow in his vehicle, giving everyone a lift back home. One day, the elderly woman gave her grandchildren bundles of wood and corn to carry and instructed, "I am behind, following you. Walk quickly now." Sonzolo and the others started out, hoping all the way that their grandmother was following behind. Yet when they arrived, there she was, already sitting in her Mbandaka yard. "Grandmother was mysterious, truly," this middle-aged man concluded. She could bring to life those already asleep, dead from sorcery.

Her first and foundational journey deep into forest near her natal Ikanga had erupted, mysteriously, with a loud, drum-like sound like the gigantic crash of a tree. The sound announced her special powers. Soon, crowds were gathering. When she came out of the forest, Sonzolo's grandmother possessed a calabash. Working like a mirror, it sent messages long after she was arrested by colonial authorities. Her healing disturbed. Some were so unhappy they wanted her *gone*. They went to the State, who relegated her far away, along with her children.[1]

This chapter examines *figurations* of Maria N'koi and the events surrounding her public emergence as a healer in 1915. The evidence comes from memory work conducted in 2007; Maria N'koi's relegation dossier; a lush and valuable colonial short story; and its rebuttal by the territorial who arrested her. A magistrate charged with undertaking an official inquiry, Joseph-Marie Jadot, wrote the story, published in 1922. His interpretation provoked the irritated attack of Armand Collignon, in a thin tome of 1933.[2] This pair of texts, each unsettling in its way, was published not in Brussels but Paris. (The two later ensured Maria N'koi important lines in historical overviews about Congolese dissent.)[3] If Jadot's papers still exist, they seem in hiding.[4] Yet Maria N'koi's dossier, unearthed in Brussels amid a long series of relegation files, includes documents produced by agents straddling two districts. I garnered invaluable traces during field work in 2007, moving by canoe along the Ruki, through narrow streams to Bongale, then by foot and bicycle to Bokatola, Ikanga, and Besefe, before meeting Sonzolo back in Mbandaka (see map 2.1).[5]

These complex layers of memory and archive suggest that Maria Nsombe (Sombe) lost her way one day when she went to fetch water. Sounds and visions pulled her deep into the forest, where *bekali* spirits[6] told her how to prepare medicines, extract poisons able to kill, and heal the maladies of those on the verge of dying. Upon emerging from the forest, a sickly young son perhaps first named his mother *N'koi*. Regardless, the leopard nickname linked her to a key symbol of chiefly power in central Africa, while suggesting her talent for moving gingerly, with imperceptible, enigmatic slyness. A leopard is deadly and secretive. It hides and stalks, devouring prey suddenly in and out of trees. That she may have killed a leopard would have heightened awe about her powers over this lethal animal.

Her words and medicines attracted. Congolese from a wide area listened to her commands: refuse taxation, stop copal labor, and wait, since soon she would signal it was time to kill all white persons around. She pointed at Bula Matari as cause of death and misery. Her instructions stirred. People, white hens, and letters were on the move, far and wide, linking Ikanga with Bokatola, Kiri, Bikoro, and beyond to Waka, Monkoto, and Bianga. She gave out many a copal piece as a charm while insisting people stop collecting this commercial product. The multitudes and skirmishes became less a movement of public healing perhaps[7] than one of *therapeutic insurgency*, not unlike Ikakota during the time of terrible Free State wars. Her movement combined power medicines with an armed uprising, and it drew on and escalated nervousness about world war battles not far away. That Maria N'koi claimed the Germani as protective, ancestral allies was among the factors that incited the nervous state to arrest and deport—*relegate*—her in 1915.

Thinking of these elements as *figurations* of history is useful. A sure grip on Maria N'koi is out of reach. While she sometimes seems all figment, the *layers of perceptibility* are complex, grasped by diverse subjects in assorted documents, while memories about her surface, as in her grandson's remembrances of her singing and healing in the 1960s. In 1915, she enthralled and frightened, though her figure brims with problems of recoverability. Depictions are plentiful, incongruous, sometimes baffling. Above all, no direct rendering of *her* experience, motivations, or person may be had.

In another sense, Maria N'koi and her figurations give us something precious: a slim, fresh angle on the Great War years in equatorial Africa. The colonial milieu that produced her knew borderlands: Nkundo and Ekonda mixed and competed, often in dance, where Batswa and related pygmy communities stood out as averse, submissive Others, though as powerful medicinal specialists besides.[8] Maria N'koi's world straddled two colonial *territoires*, each part of a different, official *district* (see map 2.1). Hers was near a charged part of German Kamerun, a pointed slice of the Sangha River valley transferred from the French to German hands in 1911. This triangular area touched down at Belgian Congo's riverain border near Lukolela, at the edge of Equateur. The region where she stirred awe was already on edge, therefore. It stood near a critical theater of the same Great War that produced fields of death in Flanders and Germany's occupation of Belgium.

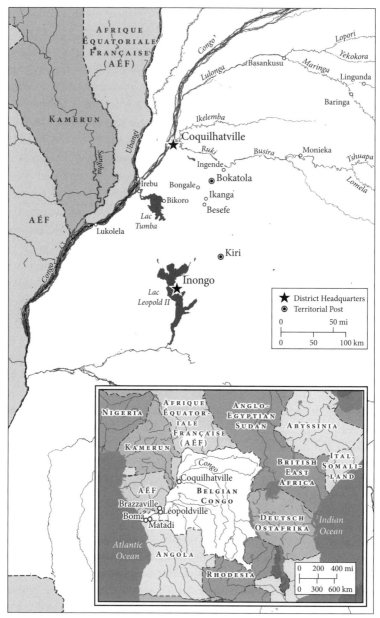

MAP 2.1 Maria N'koi's world, ca. 1915. The map suggests the proximity to a Great War theater: the one that moved up the Sangha River. When the Germans acquired this stretch of land from France in 1911, a slender border between Belgian Congo and Kamerun resulted.* The inset map, Belgian Congo and its colonial neighbors, 1911–18, shows the region during this time when Kamerun slightly bordered Belgian Congo.** Maps by Jake Coolidge.

"A Special Situation"

Armand Collignon, the territorial administrator (or *territorial*)[9] of Bokatola territory, heard nothing about Maria N'koi until the third week of June 1915. When he went to collect taxes from tardy chiefdoms, three chiefs told him about this woman with a shrine at Ikanga, making "an enormous impression" in the region. Chief Elongolo's subjects had headed there with gifts of game. Chief Engelengele expressed astonishment that the white man was unaware. His subjects had been going in crowds for weeks. He "insisted strangely" that people saw the healer woman "as their white man, as their God." Tax collecting in Lombala's chiefdom had been reduced to none at all. His subchiefs were ignoring him, and when his subjects came back from Ikanga, they refused to work in copal.[10]

God had sent Maria N'koi to preach the "true religion," one chief reported. Collignon asked about her "precepts" and learned that leopards carried her away, along with a voice insisting she heal. She told people to discard amulets and keep her charm alone. Chiefs would die if they dared arrest a soul. It was whites who caused sleeping sickness, and now death was a risk for all.[11] Collignon's chiefs seemed to disapprove of her. Lombala wanted her stopped. They knew their bonuses were at risk if taxes went unpaid, if "not another cent of tax enters State accounts." Collignon sent a messenger to Monkosso, where tax collection was stalled. Some were refusing to work for another week or much longer. The Monkosso subchiefs said Maria N'koi was banning all forest work, threatening that her leopards would devour the disobedient (see figure 2.1).[12]

After some five days listening to his chiefs, Collignon sat down and wrote his district commissioner at Coquilhatville: he was confronted with a "special situation" caused by a "purely native" woman. Collignon signaled less panic than a need for reinforcements. Having written that he would leave for "the Ikanga region" the following day, this agent instead returned to his post at Bokatola and summoned more chiefs. Chief Pia had recently been demoted to subchief during what had been a time of official tinkering with customary hierarchies and asserting new control. Surely not pleased, he said chiefs did not dare not show allegiance to Maria N'koi; the slightest sign of defiance put one at risk before her "spells."[13]

Collignon sent his Belgian tax collector to Ikanga, with orders to neither touch nor disturb. Monsieur Lhoir came back exclaiming he had seen paths seven to eight meters across, suggesting visiting caravans were many and wide. Collignon never made it to Ikanga. His 1933 account implies he planned a

FIGURE 2.1 Leopards and leopard attacks remain strong in religious imaginations. This house painting is from Bongale, near where Maria N'koi's reputation for slyness mixed with leopard powers. It suggests that spiritual powers to menace and protect still involve reminding passersby about leopards: their lethal, invisible, covert propensities and the risk of a sudden attack. Photograph by author, 2007.

nocturnal sweep but it became too risky to undertake. Instead, he listened. A state-paid messenger, Lokwa, advised simply calling her to Bokatola.[14] Maria N'koi arrived at Collignon's post, "followed by a whole cortège, enthusiastic but tortured." The word *tortured* intrigues: Perhaps the accompanying throng performed duress? The healer herself wore brand new cloth, carried a staff, and shook wooden bells; she presented a hundred francs, a sign of wealth. (The sum might have covered tax payments for about a dozen persons at the time.)[15]

When Collignon asked her to explain herself, her narrative went like this: One May day, six leopards carried her to a secret place. There, God charged her with announcing that those not hurrying to convert would be punished. She had been telling people to obey state laws and missionary regulations, make peace, use hunting weapons alone, not eat certain foods, and end polygamy. Maria N'koi's account hardly resembled the stories Collignon had heard, and the territorial asked why. Contrariness is "natural," she explained. She sought to stop lying, though her followers were going "home and telling the opposite." These persons were "bad, lazy, and liars," keen to "use me to coerce their chiefs." She defended herself: "I am the first victim of their falsehoods." Yet things had also changed, since now "no one accuses me. It is why I dare appear here." Collignon described Maria N'koi as "sincere," "audacious." His focus remained on the tax dodgers whose "taste for the mysterious and super-natural" drew them to her promises of driving out the white man and "an era of happiness." Yet he came close to finding Maria N'koi innocent during this bewildering day in Bokatola, when he advised her to further dismantle the "inauspicious situation" resulting from her "advent."[16] In the following days, he continued convoking chiefs, now catechists too, while confirming a dramatic shift in the contents of her words. Chief Lompoko found her blameless now. Other chiefs, once disturbed by the "cancellation" of their authority in chief-doms "in upheaval," now asserted Maria N'koi was preaching the good word, while favoring chiefs and the colony, too.[17]

As opinion turned upside down, a marching military column shattered the emerging calm. It entered Bokatola post on the morning of July 17, telling of disturbances and stealth in a wide region.

Column on the March

News of Maria N'koi had reached Kiri territory to the south in early July (see figure 2.2). There, administrator De Laveleye learned of troubles emanating from Ikanga, situated on the Kiri-Bokatola route. He moved into action to lay hands on this woman, who was threatening that those who did not bring her tribute would be eaten by leopards. Promising "to free blacks from white rule," if allowed to carry on she would "become a big worry." Some had stopped a letter from crossing a chiefdom; they shot arrows at the Congolese policeman whose assignment was carrying mail. While wondering if the Bokatola ter-ritorial was yet aware, De Laveleye set out to seize the woman on July 8. His commissioner sent Lieutenant Durbecq and a troop of soldiers to join him. (The same Lac Léopold district commissioner at Inongo advised his counter-part at Coquilhatville that the armed column would soon cross district lines.)[18]

As the column marched, Lieutenant Durbecq worried about war: He knew his men were needed in Kamerun.[19] The opposition in Kiri had been so fierce it seemed long prepared, while military needs for the Kamerun theater of war had reduced the size of his column to twenty-five soldiers with a thousand car-tridges. He would need reinforcements if this "movement" spread, especially since his soldiers were mere wartime "volunteers." Most had never fired a shot; they came from garrisons supervised by retired soldiers. Calling home the

Kiri. — Hutte indigène.

FIGURE 2.2 Customary homestead with a grass roof in Kiri, the territory where Maria N'koi's influence became armed insurrection and through which the armed column marched. The original caption was banal: "Kiri—Hutte indigène." The soft, romanticized image appeared in a lavish, colonial coffee table book, however, and Jadot wrote the Equateur chapter, Pierre Daye et al., *Le Miroir du Congo Belge*, vol. 1, 77.

more experienced soldiers, the ones sent into battles "up the Sangha," might become necessary.[20] (Most probably came from or were conscripted into the Ruki, Irebu, and Lac Léopold II platoons, all situated close to where the Maria N'koi disturbances erupted.)[21] Durbecq's commissioner anticipated fighting. As soon as they crushed the rebellion, he reported, his armed "volunteers" would depart for "the front," by which time they would be seasoned soldiers. The commissioner at Inongo requisitioned nine thousand more cartridges, while seeking to upgrade the column from a police to military operation.[22]

A "sure source" told of eight Kiri chiefdoms already departed or still readying "tribute" for the healer woman. Two chiefs could no longer collect taxes or supply their required foodstuffs. Whole villages were disappearing toward Maria N'koi, "surrounded by six leopards!!!" One snippet had her declaring: "I don't have guns. I have my leopards and my natives. The white man may come arrest me if he likes." A Father De Winter spotted few chiefs: "villages are no longer tidied, nothing is done." Maria N'koi was speaking about an expulsion to come: "Return home. The hour has not yet arrived. Soon you will receive my final word. Then all must come to my place and we will oust the whites." She also was heard saying: "If a white man . . . wants to arrest someone, kill him, along with his soldiers and the chief."[23]

Events confirmed the urgency of the military expedition. Durbecq and his men came under attack at Weti, where three villages combined forces, hitting private Elonga's shoulder and mangling M'poi's hand. Soldiers were to shoot only when fired upon. At Weti, they killed four and wounded a few more. Afterward, a chief warned of four more villages attacking up ahead, while three more would prevent their moving forward. The column met deserted villages. In one where they passed the night, a chief arrived with food and porters as requested. They saw no one passing through others. At Bondongo, they met three men and asked about everyone else. A blind elder uttered, "go look in the forest." A chief's candidate said the men were hunting and the women had gone "to check on their *chikwangue*[24] soaking in water." The third, a catechist, leaked: "They are all in the forest or at Maria N'koi's place."[25]

At Bolo, they saw cannabis all around. The Kiri administrator and the column had joined forces by July 16, and it was De Laveleye who began the uprooting. As soon as he did, bowmen in hiding began shooting arrows at the rear guard. Small, finely pointed, bamboo slivers were strewn everywhere, many hidden under dry leaves. Specially cut, these jagged darts were designed to pierce and impair bare feet; when stepped on, they broke into pieces, aggravating initial punctures into wounds.[26] When lieutenant and soldiers began lighting on fire the uprooted plants, they found themselves in a blaze of arrows.[27]

On they marched. Near Lokongo, a group hiding in banana groves attacked. When the column moved toward a clearing, they glimpsed several taking cover in a hamlet beyond. All the while, arrows were flying. When three fell at the feet of Durbecq and his bugler, the soldiers fired two more shots: "one native killed, another wounded, the others flee while carrying away the two bodies." They returned to the main route, and at the long village of Lokongo, both the advance and rear guards came under attack. The column fired twice more, with the fate of those shot unclear, "wounded say some, killed say others." They would bivouac and hear the sound of arrows at night, until soldiers fired blindly into the night and calm returned. The flying arrows did not frighten unduly, while military logic moved between firing an exemplary shot and "judging it not useful to respond."[28]

Fields of hemp, planted on all sides in some hamlets, suggested industry, a thriving trade.[29] Durbecq and De Laveleye spotted pipes. Smashing many with delight, they grabbed a few as souvenirs. Cannabis signaled defiance, and it produced uprooting and more battles, up to the Bokatola border. A couple years later, the cultivation of hemp near Bokatola periodically erupted like an "explosion," inspiring police operations. Chief Ikenga at Boteke reported on Kiri subjects traveling up to the Ruki with "the unique aim of selling hemp." At Bokoro, Chief Niamanene could not find a single subchief who would suppress this "nefarious custom." Chief Ieli-Ininga at Bosanga advised that many "did not want to collect copal because hemp" was "lucrative."[30] The men from Kiri were punitive when uprooting in 1915.[31] That officials were working so hard to eliminate cannabis suggests that its cultivation, as well as its commercial, medicinal, ritual, and recreational uses, were diverting attention away from colonial duties. The plant was like a currency with commercial sway, while its many powers made it a symbol and fact of dissent.[32]

When the column crossed into Bokatola territory, they spotted a chief and three *capitas* with bows and arrows. An obedient Kiri chief soon turned up, a reminder of turbulent conditions in Kiri territory. He had followed orders to carry food to them until he came under attack for supplying the enemy. Fighting in retreat, he then cut through forest and across the border to find them. Besefe was five more hours of marching away. Its residents returned, after a day working in the forest, to find their village occupied. They threatened to attack at night, but Durbecq warned that a single arrow shot would mean their village would be destroyed by morning. With the column nearing Maria N'koi, such a verbal threat proved effective in a way infeasible in the more remote and volatile Kiri.[33]

Relegation Time

Collignon strangely skirted the men who arrived with a military column from the neighboring district. At first he refused to meet with them until the next day. When their first meeting ended, nothing was settled. When De Laveleye lay down for his siesta, he was incredulous, writing: "I go to bed without him having made a decision." When he awoke, he wrote his Bokatola counterpart, "begging him to give me his decision." If Collignon dithered, he also listened to the men from Kiri and admitted a "resemblance" in "rumors spread" and "results observed" across the two territories. De Laveleye still fumed because Collignon again delayed a decision; he "promises it to me the next day." While the standoff continued, the two wrote each other letters across the minor space of a territorial post.

By morning, Collignon admitted Maria N'koi must be detained. His reinforcements had arrived along with orders from his commissioner to make the arrest. But Collignon still waited. He claimed that an absence of instructions for joining forces across two districts was the reason. On July 19, he told the men from Kiri to wait two more days. He wanted to summon Maria N'koi to Bokatola again, rather than going to Ikanga. De Laveleye was incensed. Still, Maria N'koi arrived on July 21, and Collignon called the Kiri administrator to come see. Collignon's act of arrest, in De Laveleye's eyes, resembled a conversation about "complaints," "grievances," and "her advent." Collignon told her that the rumors and "dangerous crowds" had become untenable. Each time Collignon posed a question, it seemed Maria N'koi asked another. By the time De Laveleye's turn came, he was bursting with anger. With the march from Kiri freshly bitter in his mind, he asked her why so many "attacked us in your name." He remembered their cries: "'You will not have Maria N'koi; we will kill all of you.'" Maria N'koi claimed that she had not wanted people to abandon their villages for Ikanga. Furious, the man from Kiri blurted out: "how come you did *not* send mine home then, after they had been at your place for a month?" He also accused: "Why did you tell my Weli and Bolongo, who did not want to go to your place, that if they did not come you would send your leopards after them?" Maria N'koi hollered back: "Because your natives are bad . . . !" De Laveleye was fed up. He picked up and left, along with his soldiers. A search warrant seemed pointless now.[34]

When Collignon wrote his district commissioner again on July 25, he argued that even the "simple presence" of Maria N'koi had become impossible. Unable to say whether she was "voluntary or involuntary instigator" of serious revolts, she had become an "object of a cult," which she could "no longer lead . . . in a good direction or stop." Over a large region, crowds who were refusing "our simple penetration" saw in her an "ancient ideal." They also "translated" her promise into words they believed came from her: "'We no longer want to pay our taxes or sell our products or provisions to the Whites. We want to live and be at rest like long ago.'"[35]

Some days after the arrest, a boat took Maria N'koi from a riverside stop at Ingende to Coquilhatville. By August 9, an interrogator in Coquilhatville began his work with these words: "Rumor pursues you." Again, she declared people were fabricating lies "brazenly," whereas her orders came from spirits who told how to heal. Defined as a security risk, relegation became the obvious next official step. When the interrogation ended, a relegation order was readied for approval by the governor general.[36] Relegation was long a political, administrative expedient, initiated by territorials to remove the disorderly away from a site of disturbance or calm unrest. In 1903, a Free State circular instructed how to keep *relégué* registers, and a 1906 decree specified relegation use in relation to infringements and the movement of kin.[37] Maria N'koi's destination became Buta in Uele, over one thousand miles away. Her children accompanied her, and her husband followed.

While a basic version of Maria N'koi, as story and event, has now been told, intriguing elements remain. The remainder of the chapter turns to several of these: white hens, sleeping sickness, copal, and Germani at wartime. Certain *tellings* become more distinct in the process: Jadot's short story, Colligon's rebuttal, and Congolese recountings in memory and practice. Complex, conflicting layers of perceptibility come into view—among colonizers, among colonized, and across various divides. Different readings were at play in relation to "red rubber" violence and micropolitics surrounding Maria N'koi.

Importantly, the concept of *the nervous state* undergoes a critical transformation in this process: *away* from the Leopoldian and early Belgian Congo *states* with agents busy at task, away from the Kiri military column or the tentative Collignon, and *rather toward* Maria N'koi's powers, patients, followers, and *spirits*. These narratives suggest that vernacular nervousness was integral to a widespread template of harming and healing in this region, expressed in and through trembling and trees.

Copal Charms and Sales

Maria N'koi's commands produced alarm. She called everyone to come forward and, upon arriving, each received an *"n'Kissi"* charm and words: "This will protect you from all ills."[38] Loniamela of Dongo received his copal bit in 1915, after offering gifts. She told him it would protect from leopard attacks and police arrest, and keep guns from firing.[39] While copal could be protective, its labor produced ambivalence, affliction even. This kind of coerced work was to be rejected.

In Ikanga in 2007, some described Maria N'koi as one who took leaves and bark, boiled them into drinks and internal washings, and roamed to heal. She would invite people forward, lighting some copal on her hand. As the flame healed, copal became a miracle. While letting it burn, her skin remained unharmed. Copal, though medicinal, remained ordinary. It made light. The flammable product could prevent theft; fixing some near a woman's soaking cassava roots kept thieves away.[40]

About 1900 and not far away, Holman Bentley saw a patch of shore, sand, and pebbles as a "wonderful collection of the gum." The light resin dropped from trees and "floated at flood time," with winds pushing bits together. Copal seemed plentiful, there for the taking. Potters rubbed "hot ware with copal."[41] George Grenfell spoke of "copal varnish" smearing clay dishes with a "handsome brown, red, purple glaze,"[42] while many burned it for "illumination at night."[43] Copal's value shifted in the twentieth century, when it became a commercial product and tax medium. Exports fluctuated from 21 to 845 tons in the Free State years, soaring to 17,088 tons in 1929.[44] Stanley pointed to its in-

GUM COPAL FOR SALE, UPPER CONGO.

FIGURE 2.3 "Gum Copal for Sale, Upper Congo," ca. 1911. Copal collection coexisted with rubber collection, even replacing it in importance. Both knew violent coercion. Four Congolese gatherers in assorted attire display baskets of their collected copal. Photographer was likely Alice Harris or John Harris. From John Harris, *Dawn in Darkest Africa*. Courtesy (for physical rights) New York Public Library.

dustrial value in 1885. There were two kinds "useful for varnishes": white gum copal in "large cakes over 18 inches in diameter," and the white and red fossil type used for lacquers. This fact of modern industry was "too well known to need remark," Stanley wrote, belittling Congolese who "contrive to make torches of it," but who seemed to know nothing of its other uses.[45]

Often secreted by legume trees in marshes, copal became a major collectable product (see figure 2.3).[46] When Roger Casement journeyed and investigated in 1903, copal seemed almost as sinister as rubber, and also served as taxation in kind. He observed people "engrossed," "chipping and preparing the gum-copal for shipment" or filling "basket-sacks" with the stuff. Copal became onerous work.[47] In 1911, those collecting copal drops exuding from tree fissures poked special sticks at the foot of trees and into banks of sand. In 1910–12, most of Equateur underwent conversion from the large concessionary tracts of Leopoldian times. Independent, private exploitation became possible. Although the new autonomy did not last, for the first time, Congolese were able to collect forest products for sale on their own account.

When Jadot wrote his story, he suggested that the months before Maria N'koi's movement had been relatively "good times." He included a scene with her husband heading off to Ingende to sell his copal, coupled with another where he purchased a glamorous piece of cloth for his new lover or wife.[48] The independent sale of copal offered some autonomy from chiefly control, at least for some. Then collectors were securing new wealth, as their copal yielded manufactured things, such as cloth, machetes, kerosene, and matches.[49] Others were removing impurities, like insects, before selling their copal to factories, a process that involved more cleaning by the basketful at these factories before export to Europe.

Maria N'koi suggested copal labor was abusive. Her call to halt collection *and* disobey chiefs suggests exhaustion and exasperation amid coercion. Perhaps there was some scuttling aside of best copal bits for independent sale outside chief-controlled tax routines as well.[50] One thing is sure: the Maria N'koi emergency dramatically disrupted sales to the Ingende factory of the powerful company, SAB. The Ingende manager knew something was not right. He had been away. When he returned in early July, he told Chief Baosse his factory on the Ruki was open again for copal purchases. He expected the chief to spread the news. Instead, Baosse told him it was "useless to wait" for sellers with copal. Maria N'koi "had stopped all work" and declared an "imminent return of all whites to Europe." SAB-Ingende exports came to a near halt.[51]

Chiefs were surely trying to benefit from the new, post-rubber commercial economy; copal was key.[52] With wartime likely came new pressures to produce even more copal, at a time when prices were falling.[53] Tensions existed between larger trading companies and itinerant Portuguese who had long wandered pathways, dazzling with "bric-a-brac"—old cloth, soap, casseroles—while purchasing copal. Arriving where people lived, they often secured better deals from copal sellers than a company like SAB.[54] For Belgians, the Portuguese were a threshold category that disturbed sensibilities of propriety, nation, and class. Efforts to eliminate these darker, métis persons were under way, surely from the 1920s, perhaps earlier.[55] Jadot's pejorative inclusion of such a trader suggests competition even repulsion, though also connivance. A drink of whiskey shared between one trader and the Bokatola commandant (Collignon's fictional counterpart) invokes transgressive complicity; it was also one of the insinuating details in the Jadot story that had Collignon most irate.[56]

How exactly chiefs fit into such tensions and venality is difficult to read. Struggles over the new Congolese economic autonomy likely intensified during the war, when copal labor became mixed up with taxes in money. With chiefly power mediated through taxation and ensured through paid-up accounts at the village level, there was still room to require collective, forced labor,[57] reckoned as taxes in kind, even if in 1911 Bokatola people were officially paying in coin.[58] Surely chiefs determined conversion rates between product produced (copal) and coin equivalents within this shadow economy at wartime, when lower prices made labor feel more coerced. Some chiefs carried special medals and received larger bonuses.[59] Such rewards likely represented another way to channel more copal to larger, favored factories that were buying, bundling, and cleaning volumes of the stuff.

White Hens

Some heard Maria N'koi say: "When you kill an animal, give only a little bit to the white man; the largest part should come to me." Chiefs complained she was summoning food supplies to feed her followers, thereby usurping a colonial prerogative: the prompt delivery of food. People had given her so many white hens as well as smoked antelope and game that she had several huts full. Some chiefs said she had received six ivory tusks. Other gifts poured in—beads, brass rings, and arrows. Some said she insisted on quantities and kinds, while for those bearing the stuff, it was often like tribute.[60]

Loniamela of Dongo said his village gave him two white hens to take to the "fairly young woman" at Ikanga.[61] Maria N'koi once explained: "Bekali spirits forbid me to accept other hens."[62] Her stockpile astonished, including after her arrest: "Hundreds and hundreds of white fowl were found in sheds near her house."[63] When the Coquilhatville interrogator asked about her white hens, she said they were gifts. Yet she also gestured to ongoing colonial life, where many created amity through gifts and food: "I give them to those who I want to do well and to the white man as well." Her interrogator obsessed about their whiteness: "Do you make a comparison between Whites and white hens?" Her reply was perhaps sly. The Bekali spirits had not told her why, though personally she did not link white hens with white men.[64]

Inquiries followed her arrest. Near Kiri, a man who claimed to be her brother was stirring revolt. The men from Kiri were convinced that without their column's arrival, Collignon would never have made the arrest. After all, he had only done so "after four days of reflection," and in a way "disapproved by us" since no authorities ever went to Ikanga and no search occurred. Thus her gifts were never seen or seized, while "it would have been interesting for everyone to see the camp of this woman," wrote De Laveleye.[65] Why did Collignon avoid her charged ritual space? Was he trying to avoid death, prevent a massacre, or shelter his wife? Or, was he simply nervous, dawdling, inept?

While his watchword remained more verification, the clues suggest compla-
cency. He was never punitive toward Maria N'koi. His avoidance of confrontation suggests some sympathy for this unusual woman, as well as a colonial
modality of waiting in an era before automobiles. Letters and reinforcements
moved slowly. So could he. Tax payments were tardy and thin, but nothing
was terribly new or alarming about such a rhythm of refusal. That she was
attracting crowds for ritualized, festive dealings may have seemed like more
of the same, too.

Events interrupted his modality of waiting. Afterward, he came under a
cloud of suspicion. Collignon's own letter suggests some jockeying to make
himself look resolute during these days.[66] That his wife joined him in welcoming Maria N'koi suggests a clue. When the healer went to meet Collignon the
first time, she brought along food provisions. Collignon duly noted paying
for the gift (which may or may not have included white hens). From Inongo,
the commissioner called Maria N'koi a "cunning" woman who tricked and
manipulated the territorial through providing food. This accusation originated with Congolese who claimed she furnished the Collignon household
with fresh hens, implying that the rebellion brought much choice food to this
agent's door.[67]

The sense of conspiracy may have been overdrawn. Yet this agent's everyday embraced domesticity and a wife, perhaps a taste for fine meals. Congolese rumor went in this direction. The commissioner at Inongo used the word
"indecision" to characterize Collignon, whereas De Laveleye and Durbecq
suggested his plodding permitted the "insurrectional movement" to spread.
Collignon's personnel evaluations had been mixed. In 1914, his marriage in-
terfered with excellent work. A March 1915 review found him quarrelsome,
distracted, with "a tendency to criticize more than organize." He had increased
his movements, however, while surveillance was curbing his *caractère discu-
teur*. In September, he seemed devoted and serious, though in 1918, he was
feuding with traders at his new post of Lusangania.[68] The same disputacious
man took to pen in 1933, criticizing Jadot's story and its characterization of the
agent in charge—implicitly Collignon himself.[69]

History, Clichés, Tellings

Jadot's fiction suggested that memories of the Free State years were still fresh,
and others sensed the same. When Durbecq set out with his column, his
thoughts wandered to previous dishonor in the region. Memories of defeat
ran deep, and he thought nervously about northern Kiri around 1898, when

FIGURE 2.4 "Clackety-clack." This 1902 gravesite of Charles Liwenthal, nicknamed Ekuma, is set back from the main path near the Bokatola state post, where it still forms a little cemetery all its own over a hundred years later. Photograph by author, 2007.

Free State forces faced guerilla warfare. A Scandinavian officer saved himself after some eighty soldiers lay dead or wounded. Another officer met "a similar defeat."[70] Durbecq was marching toward Bokatola, a post that had known scandal before.

Collignon surely had heard stories of Ekuma and his unusual death in Bokatola.[71] A compact, singular gravestone is still set back from the main path near the post buildings. The tomb commemorates the death of this wayward Free State officer who (as we saw in chapter 1) shot himself through the head in 1902 (see figure 2.4). When I visited in 2007, some Bokatola residents let slip that passing near this burial place late at night goes with hearing "clackety-clack," the sounds of the cruel commandant busy at his typewriter. Collignon's post had been dramatically marked by aleatory events: rubber violence, Ekuma's suicide, Maria N'koi's crowds and her arrest. The suicide and its author remained vividly alive within Congolese memories of the 1950s, we will see, alongside Ekuma's music-making *fanfare*.

If frantic confrontations in 1915 made Collignon hesitant to act, by 1933 he was also, in a sense, typing away.[72] Why did he critique Jadot's story, twelve years after its publication? Irritated, keen to set the record straight, he pointed at many inaccuracies.[73] He stressed the dangerous, persistent rebelliousness of this countryside at the time. Yet Collignon was obtuse when he turned Maria N'koi into a quintessentially wily woman, reducing her commands into a ruse aimed at solving her conjugal problems.[74]

Jadot's embellishments were irksome, as were his plotlines diverting from fact, notably having the commandant in charge of the healer woman's arrest also overseeing terrible punitive violence. Such a portrayal of a territorial as brutal military officer, ready to mow down, diminished the rectitude of the colony's young territorial regime. Collignon attacked on patriotic grounds: Jadot disgraced Belgium by repeating E. D. Morel clichés.

Collignon's righteousness suggested a stark before and after. Jadot's story suggested bleeding between periods, reminding that the unrest that came with Maria N'koi was not the first time the area knew agitation and protest. Around 1907, "Ekwakota" had spread from Inongo up to Bokatola (as Ikakota, we saw), producing disturbances into the final Free State years.[75] This pair of Belgian accounts, therefore, suggests a stormy drama of class frictions, tensions that also surfaced in mocking colonial songs.[76] Here, they played out over the spectacular healer woman, the fragile regime that deported her, and the different sensibilities of a magistrate and territorial. The rebuttal came from a less privileged, married administrator with pretensions of respectability. Collignon's irate retort also tells how much the magistrate's stories and interracial mores could *disturb*.[77]

Jadot, a bourgeois doctor's son,[78] mixed the erotic and abject with the clinical in his stories. When he left the colony in 1931, having fathered children in Congo, he was rare in taking his children home to Belgium and declaring himself their legal father.[79] He was also unusual in speaking out about race (see figure 2.5), founding a Belgian association dedicated to protecting the rights of métis.[80] Like others among middle-class, Walloon, social Catholics, he adored primitivism in *l'art negre*.[81] His short stories, many written when young in Equateur, were overwrought, yet perceptive. The first, published in French Brazzaville, addressed the Great War in central Africa.[82] In the 1920s, he helped produce *Revue Sincère*, a Belgian literary magazine with some colonial stories and featuring the first Georges Simenon story to appear in print. That Jadot became active in the Association des Ecrivains et Artistes Coloniaux Belges, founded in 1926, is in keeping with this profile.[83]

A lone white man in a nervous state of mad violence, whether due to climate, overexcitement, or venereal mishap, has gone with imperial figurations since Conrad's *Heart of Darkness*.[84] In a bleak scene in Jadot's 1920s story, "Le Campement," a colonial doctor wrestled with Congolese detainees ailing

FIGURE 2.5 Evidently the only photograph in print of this unconventional man of colonial letters, Joseph-Marie Jadot. Shot from an unusual angle, it suggests a radiant, avant-garde man with lively eyes, pleased expression, balding part, and drooping curl, ca. 1949. From J. Leyder, "Jadot (Joseph-Marie)," in *Le Graphisme et l'expression graphique au Congo belge*, 47. Courtesy of Société Royale Belge de Géographie.

in a gruesome *bagne*[85] of a prison, venereal lesions exposed. This imaginary topos mixed the sexual and the nervous. An overwrought administrator was mismanaging the bagne because his Congolese lover had vanished into other colonial arms just when his departure approached.[86]

Jadot's story about Maria N'koi was crosscut by loathing, too.[87] It told of colonial hierarchies, while lurking were thresholds of repulsion.[88] The central one concerned nation, class, and miscegenation. As it rippled through Jadot's story, it suggested antagonisms between "proper" commercial firms and Portuguese traders. Friction between Collignon and Jadot was also about class, politics, and distinction, and difference in their marital, sexual, and intellectual lives. A humble territorial with respectable wife remained rare at the time. The magistrate's lofty, literary airs wended into how he traveled, wrote, observed, and surely with whom he slept; later, from Belgium, the Congolese mother of his children was invisible, though he was protecting métis children's rights.[89]

A rare biographer once flagged Jadot's "interest in sexual problems," suggesting he handled the fixation "with the muffled discretion" of his generation.[90] If Jadot stifled, he left much *un*concealed. A 1914 poem eroticized black

FIGURE 2.6 Suggestive drawing, showing three Congolese policemen entangled with dignified fez hats and draped cloth. It suggests calm, rest, and poise, while the tallest reads in a sensuous, recumbent pose. Parodic, it illustrated the satirical colonial song "Policeman." Artist: P. R. De Meyer. From P. Hubin, Alexandre Leclercq, and Léon Pirsoul, *Chansons congolaises par trois moustiquaires*, 14.

male bodies with the words (compare, figure 2.6): "My blacks, naked torso . . . And their fervent march is the joy that moves."[91] Valor and transgression combined in a homoerotic, patriotic war story about a stunning Zande man, Mambamu. This husband, father, and Force Publique officer, repeatedly marched off to military prison for having sex with his soldiers, died a brave hero during a dangerous, victorious assault. He and his soldiers saved Belgian lives as they broke through a German battle line in Kamerun.[92]

Wartime Reverie

When the military column started out for Ikanga, its lieutenant was the only ranked officer left in Lac Léopold II district, enfeebled by wartime. After the Weti attacks, it seemed troubles might erupt far and wide. Durbecq wondered whether the Maria N'koi rebellion had been long in the making through German machinations. Regardless, the conscription of Congolese into the joint Belgian-French military maneuvers pushing Germany out of the Sangha River valley complicated Congo's colonial situation with ambivalence, dissent and death.

Shortly after crossing into Bokatola territory, De Laveleye spotted special

FIGURE 2.7 "Mongo Wives Mourning for Deceased Husband at Mompono," ca. 1910. Fourteen wives in a former Abir post. With bodies and foreheads caked with white clay, these spirit wives were in ritual mourning. From: Postcard, A. W. Banfield Collection, ROM, 950.257.81. With permission of the Royal Ontario Museum © ROM. See also *Customs of the World*, vol. 1, ed. Walter Hutchinson, i.

shelters for drinking and mingling, noting: "in this region here, it is every-where a big party." At Banza, they saw three sculpted figures "not too badly done"—elephant, naked man, naked woman—whose "disproportionate sexual parts" disconcerted.[93] Mourning and festivity often go together, while the reproductive spirits suggested a funeral gathering combining death and life with reproduction (compare figure 2.7).

Other layers of figuration come from Jadot. This man of colonial letters relished Equateur, and his many stories resonated with his colonial generation and class, as we will see.[94] As magistrate, Jadot would have read the Kiri military report, and he later included drinking shelters and sculpted figures in his story, beside a funeral for the first local man killed at the front. The shelters welcomed those mourning, while animated political conversations came just days before Maria N'koi's "hallucinations" in the forest.[95] We will never know how imaginary Jadot's interpretation was. Yet the implications remain interesting. Loss and bitterness arrived with the Great War. It took the lives of some Congolese during battles being fought in a war between European nations far away.

When the commissioner at Inongo requested an urgent military action against Maria N'koi in 1915, he nervously wrapped her in leopards, with the

"Germani" as her imagined protectors.[96] Some Congolese were skeptical about fighting for their Belgian "whitemen" in Great War campaigns,[97] and pro-German sentiments seeped into Maria N'koi's eviction reverie. Thomas Lubaka heard the Germani would be present at the moment Maria N'koi announced killing should begin. After her arrest, an investigator asked Biko if the healer woman spoke of the Germans. Chief Boma's wife reported her depicting them as Congolese "allies," who would help in "fighting the whites of Bula Matari."[98]

At the very least, the Germani and Maria N'koi arrived in Congolese consciousness within the Bokatola and Kiri territories about the same time. Germani reverie featured in the official decision to relegate, the verdict of a nervous state before a colonial emergency. In these equatorial territories, not long after terrible rubber wars and just after wartime conscription, nervousness met agitation. It also met the future horizon offered by Maria N'koi. The word *Germani* alone suggested an expansion in scale during this time when both imaginations and lives stretched beyond Congolese territories and up the Sangha.

Sleeping Sickness and Extinction

Maria N'koi pointed at the body, at sleeping sickness. Europeans caused and spread the disease. Collignon heard her linking the risk of black extinction with the necessity to expel whites. The interrogator pursued the subject, asking if she had spoken of "the black race" at risk of disappearing. Maria N'koi dodged his question: "why would I make war with the whites?"[99]

Although demographic efforts to enumerate seem to have been slight in this area, trypanosomiasis campaigns had been intense and coercive in other parts of the Free State. Doctors had arrived with soldiers, insisting on lumbar punctures, "dosing . . . with arsenic," making some "mad with it." Many ran away. Some places watched the sick overwhelmed with "mania" and "fits," then restrained with "chain and locks," "legs in stocks," or feet in fetters, before the "somnolent stage" preceding death.[100] Treatment produced terror, in other words, with sleeping sickness often appearing skeletal, as a terrible colonial plot (see figure 2.8).

Maria N'koi gave birth to four children and was expecting Sonzolo's father when the first crowds arrived. Some said she told followers that a pregnancy kept her from traveling more to heal.[101] Although she may have alluded to extinction, this healer woman was a mother. Not all women were. Biko jour-

Photo by]   DYING OF SLEEPING SICKNESS.   [*Mr. Black.*

FIGURE 2.8 "Dying of Sleeping Sickness." The bleak emaciation of a moribund patient near Baringa, as printed by the Congo Balolo Mission. High mortality from sleeping sickness coincided with and followed "red rubber" violence. Photograph by a Mr. Black, in "Congo Scenes," *Regions Beyond* (June 1908): facing 118.

neyed to Ikanga because she was "feeling sick" and had no children.[102] But the celebrated healer sent this wife of Chief Boma "back to my village." Biko sensed politics; she "refused me medicines, surely because I am wife of an invested chief, a man of the white man."[103] Being married to state power aligned Biko and her infertility with those who taxed and arrested. This memory of a refusal to care suggests taut micropolitics and swirling rivalries over fame and wealth. The tissue of conflict is opaque, though chiefs, messengers, white men, and gifts were likely involved, as Jadot's short story suggested.[104]

Pathology and a Magistrate's Story

Perhaps it is Jadot's florid, "outmoded" prose that has deterred postcolonial critics from delving into his fascinating, enigmatic oeuvre.[105] His Maria N'koi story is a diagnosis of this equatorial corner turned riotous through wartime conscription and its humble woman in distress. Catapulted into the limelight

FIGURE 2.9
Sensuous, romanti-
cized photograph of
a firm, knowing
Nkundo woman.
With her bare shoul-
ders, scarification,
and necklace (of
European shirt
buttons?), the im-
age was a form of
colonial erotica, ca.
1930. Original cap-
tion: "Nkundu, Frau
mit Tätowierung."
Photograph by Paul
Schebesta; and in his
*Vollblutneger und
Halbzwerge*, pl. 42,
no. 88. Courtesy of
Anthropos Institute,
Sankt Augustin,
Germany.

as phenomenal healer and public spokeswoman, Maria N'koi became *the
hinge* in this insurgency and tax revolt. Jadot had her preaching an end to
polygamy, too.

He admitted embellishing the story to study the "black soul."[106] While at-
tuned to trees, dancing, and war-related healing, an ethnographic register was
not his only refrain. His story begins with a long, affectionate portrayal of
forest as an idealized, eroticized Eden (see figure 2.9),[107] lush and rotting, sensuous and abject, with dazzling nature, magic, and suggestive female dancing.
He mixed in Conradian gloom with damp, decaying, tangled vines and rank
persons, too, while marveling at Maria N'koi. But physical beauty he made her
not. The sexual in the story touched on the nervous and venereal, while he
moved causality to a historical plane. He pressed the significance of Equateur's
violent past, not letting his readers forget rubber, atrocity, rape, or female labor.[108] Placing her birth about 1890, Jadot had this Nkundo girl growing up
during harrowing times. Her first sexual experiences came after long days
spent carrying heavy loads to the nearest state post, Bokatola (a notorious
place, as we saw, under Ekuma and others). When she and her mother needed

somewhere to sleep at night, soldiers were welcoming. With this suggestion of rape, Jadot heightened the somatic effects, and Maria N'koi became a touch grotesque under his pen. He called her "degenerate," marred by stigmata, though he maintained an affection, showing her as a busy healer tending to yaws and other sores. Burdened by syphilitic chancroids and children who inherited the disease, spectacular healing developed in keeping with his central cliché: alternately luxuriant and putrid forest in a sodden, seductive world.

The magistrate pathologized. The powerful language of his day, degeneration, took him to the venereal and violent. His diagnostics also turned psychiatric. He sought to prove that Maria N'koi had had hallucinations not visual but acoustic, a point about degeneration and instability clinched via a footnote to a 1911 psychiatric text. Auditory hallucinations spilled forth as commands, which when mediated by chiefly struggles produced the Maria N'koi rebellion of 1915. Drawing on dermatology, gynecology, and venereology, all sciences of degeneration in his time, he declared the somatic imprints of her mental infirmity. He spoke not of neurasthenia but rather of the *nervosité* of this woman whose malady began as a spurned, unhappy wife.[109]

Maria N'koi became a special woman of spirits, one who could collapse everyday coordinates of space and time and invoke invisible powers. She was as if in *a nervous state* when she first lost her way as a young woman and spirits pulled her into forest. Her early story also suggests a template for psychic disturbance among women: first taut, tangled in trees, or suspended leopard-like from boughs, before therapeutic dances to coil and uncoil their bodies begin, quieting cares all the while.[110] We now turn to this reading of her, enmeshed with trees, as a spirit named Njondo. It takes us to Maria N'koi's post-arrest lives, her countering of enmity, and her soothing of nervous conditions. Trees recur, packed with medicines and meaning.

Afterlives, Njondo, Trees

When the men with soldiers from Kiri passed through Besefe in 1915, they found Maria N'koi's village already aware of its significance. Residents claimed her marital home as the place from which she "vanished upwards toward Heaven, to come down again near Ikanga, after receiving instructions from God." They had made the house a *lieu de mémoire*. A tear in the roof suggested her sudden upward flight. When the two white colonials went inside, the rip seemed slipshod, contrived: "the hole is cut out with a knife."[111] Yet this invitation to tour and see suggested the commotion Maria N'koi was stirring in little Besefe, with hundreds passing through daily. It is unclear if these travelers were also invited to enter the little museum with torn roof, yet the pride and impulse toward claiming heritage suggests a consciousness of the historical significance of their heroine with extraordinary powers.

When interrogated in Coquilhatville, Maria N'koi explained, "I went to fetch water one day, and all of a sudden spirits surrounded me." Soon, "the voice of a man, a being who I did not see, called me, and I went forward." When she saw three dogs walking, she followed. Then, a being from behind pushed her into the forest's midst, she recalled, and "I was taken and placed on a tree branch." Trees and branches lingered and in all kinds of ways, including after her arrest, when "tongues unfastened." In Kiri and Bokatola, many remembered aloud as part of official investigations. Maria N'koi, they recalled, began enmeshed with trees. Old man Bokolo testified about her wedged amid woods and vines, while spirits hesitated about where to have her dwell. He explained that her journey began while drawing water at a forest's edge; her husband searched long and hard, finding her deep in woods. Soon, some heard her commands: "give the chief two francs for the white man, instead of eight." Maria N'koi said to no longer fear the white man: "As soon as he sets out en route, shoot arrows at him." She threatened those who dared defy her: "I will put *likokoloko* on them, and my leopards will devour them." Biko recalled the large crowd at Ikanga, where she listened for a long time. Everyone wanted a charm, while waiting for the time when "all whites, including missionaries, would be killed." Maria N'koi had promised that "bullets would not wound, touching without hurting."[112]

In 2007, many were keen to speak.[113] In Besefe and Ikanga, no one knew about tax refusal, copal, or the Great War. One called all these aspects "a lie." Yet they spoke about her healing and small bell, how her drums ignited, producing crowds. Some talked about her taking leaves and bark, boiling them into internal washings and drinks, and announcing prohibitions. Articulate and eager was Sonzolo. He grew up in her house in Mbandaka and his story perhaps resembled his father's version of events. She was the child of parents who fished and trapped. Their world knew few Catholic colonial chapels, priests, or catechists, though they named her Maria: Maria Nsombe. When she spoke of her initial visions, he said, she pictured herself dressed, wearing shoes, and holding a bottle of palm oil.

While the idea that she was arrested because of her large crowds remained present in social memory, salient were stories of betrayal. Bad persons keen to harm plotted against her, Sonzolo insisted. They saw that she could reverse the murder of those put to sleep, their souls hidden. She would put a dead body in a house for days, until this person walked again, alive and resuscitated. When people saw these powers, they turned against grandmother with anger, he suggested. These persons were not of a single village. The whole countryside divided into those for and those against her. Sonzolo invoked a parallel with Jesus:[114] "his country did not love him, and then people killed him. It was the same for our grandmother; in her village, she was not loved." She was not loved because she worked against those who used medicines to harm, he insisted.

In Ikanga, such narratives met another specificity, resonating with Jadot's interpretation. In 2007, men competed by asserting their ties to Maria N'koi. They detoured into who had been a lover, and whether Nkundo or Ekonda had most right to declare her as theirs. Camille claimed he became her servant at Mbandaka: "she took me as her Batswa" when "the money of Mobutu" was in use and she had plenty because she divined so well. Mboto Y'Ofoya claimed his Ekonda blacksmith grandfather had been a love partner. As he did, another man blurted out that Maria N'koi's possession had begun when her husband took a pygmy as lover.[115] This disgrace perhaps turned Maria N'koi weak, nervous, and unwell.[116] A painful transgression, it degraded. This world was one of loathing before tiny Others: those servile toward Nkundo and Ekonda masters.[117] Yet these pygmy-like Batswa were paradoxically powerful too. Most potent medical practices, including—so say many—Njondo, come from these same diminutive, uncanny Batswa, known as masterful magicians.

Sonzolo, ever proud of his grandmother, was saddened by the story of her relegation and imprisonment in Buta. The prison warden's wife had doted on this inmate who took to caring for fellow prisoners. One day the white woman fell sick and Maria N'koi cured her. Soon, she found herself released from prison and given a house with an annex for healing.

Especially after her husband Lomputu died, Maria N'koi began to long to return home.[118] Buta officials sought to lift her relegation order in 1926, quoting the magistrate who conducted the 1915–16 inquiry and knew this *relégué* "very well." Jadot (based in Buta at the time) vouched for "exemplary conduct," that this woman once of "hallucinatory crises" was now "utterly calmed down." Governor Duchesne denied the request; territorial agents and chiefs alike feared memories, still "quite alive" among those once moved by "her subversive words." In October 1929, the governor general finally removed her relegation order. But her home was fixed in Coquilhatville, a town with "climate, hearth, and food" of "evolved natives," and of her "same tribe."[119]

Maria N'koi sometimes showed off her liberation documents, her grandson remembered, though her first decades when Mbandaka was still colonial Coquilhatville are shadowy. When Father Hulstaert met her in the 1930s, she avoided speaking of her "youthful trifles," gesturing disdain for this past.[120] Her children grew up learning about this time when villages "did not want me." Many did not want to live near her, grandson Sonzolo noted, while being amazed by her powers. When troubles surged, they accused that she was the cause, that it was best for her to depart, to live under the state's care. Some conspired against her because she exposed their work in sorcery, telling themselves in Sonzolo's words: "'better to chase her out.'" They betrayed her. The result was her arrest. She did not flee, though she hid her special calabash in a hole and leaves grew there. Many came for these leaves, Sonzolo said, while the calabash's power endured within her.

In 2007, many in the remote forests near Ikanga and Besefe knew where Maria N'koi's house stood in Mbandaka (in Ilongowasa quarter, on the road leading to Bamanya). She died there in the 1970s. She stayed with a brother, eventually bought land and farmed, purchasing an urban plot where she lived with a man from Bokatola under a safou tree in a house with seven rooms. Papa Joseph Bomgombe first arrived as a patient; he was present for her grandson's baptism. Bomgombe had no family near, so Maria N'koi had given him a room. For years, the two searched for medicines together or Bomgombe went off alone, following her instructions. She became known as an excellent healer of maladies of the mind, though also healing women not menstruating or wanting to give birth. Sonzolo displayed her remaining papers, including a postcolonial identity card (see figure 2.10) and letter from the early 1970s state of Mobutu. The letter advised her that she had been chosen to work for the "revolution" and the public health department.[121] During Maria N'koi's final years, therefore, she practiced as a recognized *guérisseur*, at a time when Mobutu—soon Zaire's leopard skin–capped ruler—was busy launching his *authenticité* program.

In Mbandaka, at least from the 1960s, she walked and walked in a wide space, tiring not. Many came, from Besefe, Boyeka, Pombo, Bikoro, Bandundu, and Ingende. Some arrived in a group of up to ten. Sometimes, they slept over. She provided medicines or instructions, welcoming, chasing away none. Sonzolo recalled her singing while she healed, sometimes with a tempo of hasty patient arrivals. Her songs were about motion and not knowing, just as healing went with journeys, urgency, and uncertainty. Someone far away would come to visit, not knowing what she would find, and his grandmother would sing that this "one longs to stay: she is coming, truly very quickly." Another song was about marvelous charms of magic and healing, received without human intervention: trees, leopards, winds, and bells. A third was about danger and harm, with an antelope, mud, and bad people who left something "over there" and arrived, menacingly.

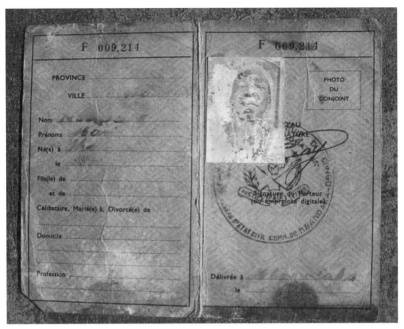

FIGURE 2.10 Maria N'koi's postcolonial identity card, ca. 1963. In the possession of her grandson, Antoine Sonzolo Efoloko, 2007. Photograph by author.

At Ikanga, Bosango sang me a song about Maria N'koi as author of Njondo, creator of all, the spirit who spread divination through the world. In Besefe and Ikanga, she emerged as important less because she caused a rebellion or underwent arrest, but for founding Njondo. (A few Njondo healers still live nearby, I learned, jotting down their names.)[122] Some recalled that when Maria N'koi was first seized by a spirit, she began to weep. At first, no one could get her to leave the forest, and then for two days after she did, she spoke not a word. Sonzolo said that she left the forest carrying the name of a dancing spirit, and that this was the first time Njondo appeared.

Njondo means spirit, though also anvil.[123] Throughout central Africa, iron smelting draws on medicinal, sexual, and procreative metaphors to do its miraculous, technological, reproductive work. Ekonda were known as leading ironworkers,[124] and also extraordinary dancers in spirited, warlike theatrical productions.[125] Iron-working and reproduction go together. Ekonda blacksmiths go in pairs with honored women in special dress, whether mothers emerging from seclusion after giving birth, or *elima* spirit women wearing bells, amulets, and calabashes with copper nails.[126]

In Maria N'koi's world, njondo brought together smelting, fertility, and women seized by spirits. Njondo often calms disorder, soothing trembling and seized-up states of being. Lonkama and Kanimba even speak of it as a "mental illness," common near Ingende, with Batswa origins. Njondo healers long created red paste from bark and palm oil, applying this *ngola* salve to corpses during wartime. They still use it to calm maladies of the mind or skin. Smearing a body with ngola restores equilibrium by pleasing the spirits. An njondo illness may attack with headaches, fevers, rambling thoughts, or aggressivity. A woman suffering from njondo begins to recover when her healer receives an assortment of gifts, whether a goat, machete, earthen pot, gas lamp, or cloth. Ingesting potions and taking vapor baths may cleanse. The process depends on payments made by kin, while the patient may stay at the healer's for months, even a few years. When baths are readied, the healer and assistant dance and sing. Plunging a leaf in boiling water, she splashes the patient and those gathered for protection from njondo.[127]

She would sing about *wengengo* or wavering with insecurity. Wengengo is like a teetering drunk or the shaking of a still-standing, yet cut tree, vacillating in the wind before tumbling down. The Njondo healer applies this trembling tree metaphor to family troubles, promising children all the while. She might sing: "I dig up charms, Wait for me, I am standing, I stop, The things of spirits, Uncertainty." Another song suggests a strong mother or tree trunk pitted against a troubled family: "The family of Papa, a bad family, The family of Mama, a bad family, Ask me for my money, The reproach for a fault is a lesson, The heart is a trunk, Let's judge the palaver . . . Stay Mama Bompoto, With many children."[128]

Maria N'koi's own agitated, possessed states are clues about illness and calming in the larger region. Her methods resembled therapeutic forms still found nearby today in this central African region—Jebola, Yebola, Cibola.[129] Her own malady knew trees, met trees, and used trees. For days, spirits gave her medicines, though when she was finally found, she was in the roots of a *musenge* tree. In Ikanga and Besefe, people also spoke of her "mysterious vision" as a "miracle." She took a huge piece of wood and hit it against a tree, producing a loud sound heard far and wide: "From that moment, the world moved. Then, people came from everywhere."

Sonzolo no longer heard much about Njondo in 2007. Yet he knew that some living far away suffered from the spirit and used to come to town to see his grandmother who would give medicine, sometimes with songs. She sang to heal, not for applause. She danced with her patients, healing and treating those ailing from Njondo, but not as part of a public spectacle of distraction.[130] She was known for healing those "on the edge of death." Sonzolo had her working through metaphor, cleaning out bellies full of *bad stories*, snails, or frogs. She purged, discarding the refuse, just as *stories may shift and empty*. When she would take away the animal bone possessing someone, madness would vanish.

Her serious cases stayed at her place as inpatients; she often spoke of them as those who arrived quickly, in much pain, yet departed slowly. Some stayed for a month, a year; others lasted a week and were gone. Before treating someone, she sang Njondo songs. She sang and called forth spirits. Afterward, with the patient better, this was not a time for drumming, but traveling back home. Patients arrived with urgency; healing ended with a calm journey homewards. The cool composure achieved is significant. Njondo possessed women knotted up in branches, like a tree cut asunder, trembling in the wind, a distraught state.

Sonzolo spoke of her powers over trees turned malignant. More than once, she ordered people to cut down a fat tree, laden with toxic medicines, perhaps the hair and clothing of children and wives. Such a tree *killed* good fortune. Someone who placed perfectly good hunting traps could not feed his family; a farmer came out of the forest with empty hands. Placed by those wishing to harm, such tree charms might prevent pregnancies, her grandson recalled. In chopping down the tree, dividing it in pieces, its *bad stories* would depart. When Maria N'koi emerged as a healer, she found more than one tree with bad stories. When she ordered one such tree chopped down, her command stirred struggle, mayhem. Many refused to allow the tree to be felled. This woman named for leopards could collapse everyday space-time when calling upon the special powers of spirits or producing an instant gust or fierce storm. And so, in this case, she did. Her enemies remained. Yet "she sent in a violent wind" and the tree fell down while its bad stories tumbled and dispersed.[131]

Trees return us one more time to Jadot, fond of poetry and *l'art nègre*. In 1914, he published a poem about a healer, a woman famous for her dancing at Inongo years before. She promised peace through a tree of medicines, and she danced and sang in relation to mourning, mass graves, and ruins of war. Invoking "wasted huts," "debris that eluded the looting," and "rage in the blood," through her, Jadot insisted that extinction was at stake: "the race might die." Yet when the special tree would split open, the dancer's song told, medicines would spill forth and end the awful massacres. This "old dying woman" with her "fierce dance" was also like a tree.[132]

His pungent, erotic, primitivist stories were reminiscent of Rabelais and Bruegel at least for one Belgian critic of *l'art nègre*.[133] His negrophilia was unlike varieties of primitivism found in Europe's interwar francophone metropoles—Paris and Brussels.[134] His passion repeatedly turned to the extraordinary, erotic dancing found in his Equateur. Jadot's keen ethnographic eye for song, trees, healing, and insurgency meant he also understood something about violence during and since the Congo Free State years.

Conclusion

A Ugandan nurse confronted a Congolese soldier in 1915, just when Belgian troops entered into battle in Deutsch-Ostafrika: "Why do you fight for *your* whiteman?" he asked. He proceeded to explain recent history and events to this Belgian colonial subject: "The Germans took all his villages in Europe. It is because he has lost everything there, that he comes to make war here."[135] The African nurse understood that the Belgians wanted to use their colony and their involvement in African military campaigns to reassert national honor. In a sense, the nurse was telling the soldier what the Belgians wanted to keep secret in the colonies: the fact of German occupation. After the war, Belgian general Tombeur claimed that Congolese subjects had never faltered, their "loyalty to the flag" and to "European chiefs" having been "without limits." Belgian Congo had only known "proud calm," never once "revolt or native mutiny." Pro-German sentiments also had never reached Congolese subjects. This chapter has exposed these conceits[136] as patriotic, national and colonial fictions. A striking therapeutic insurgency deeply shook this Kiri and Bokatola border zone just after conscription began. The unrest was profound, complex and unexpected, emboldened by memories of earlier experiences of colonial coercion and bloodshed.[137]

The result was *colonial emergency*, starring Maria N'koi and a subtle range of nervous states—territorial, intimate, and vernacular. Her only quoted words are ones she enunciated in 1915 ordeals of duress, underlining how much security interrogations *form* a nervous register to the colonial state. That they often yielded relegations underlines the "factor of distance" within colonial punitive spectacle.[138] Distinguishing between *everyday* and *emergency healing* may be useful, but the separation should not be carried too far. The two fused in Maria N'koi. Still, urgent healing may fell trees and make war. In 1915, when healing became *aleatory*, an *outburst-like historicity*[139] developed around the healer's leopards and name. Maria N'koi's realm was tenuous and shadowy, separate from formal spheres of political authority. She and her crowds wracked the nerves of chiefs and Belgian men of state. Recent Leopoldian violence was vivid in memory. Forced copal labor pressed upon lives, as did conscription into Kamerun and other Great War theaters, from which not all returned alive. These processes spilled into households, imaginations, shadow economies, chiefdoms, and a fractured state. As Bula Matari moved the armed column toward Bokatola, the state's nervous face tightened, fracturing, until in declaring a state of exception, it calmed the volatile through relegating this woman of leopards.

The biopolitical hardly appeared in figurations of Maria N'koi's uprising, though extinction fantasies did. Jadot's stories featured titillating elements: doctors and degeneration, interracial sexuality, venereal sores, concubines, and homoerotic desire. While these topoi suggest the equatorial, the coming chapters take up *repetitions*. Maria N'koi became a degenerationist specimen, while Jadot's fixations suggest that such logic surfaced readily in colonial conversation. (Degenerationist discourse will return as a theme in the chapters to come.)[140] Jadot, self-appointed diagnostician, combined *nervosité* with the abject, painting Maria N'koi with a dash of the grotesque. His somatic logic *historicized*, suggesting event *marked* bodies and skin. His extinction fantasies anticipated the biopolitical state to come. Soon, many were investigating Equateur women as barren, albeit less nervous than diseased.

Another register for a *nervous state* came through in Jadot's story, when he used the word *hallucination*. In a vernacular register, visions, visceral shaking, and tears suggest trembling bodies, minds, and beings. That Maria N'koi vanished until found on a forest branch, this foundational strand suggests restlessness and spirit possession. Wavering unmoored before she came anchored to a tree, the figuration suggests somatized worries and a path to healing. Soon she was medium for multitudes,[141] while her crowds sowed dread up to high colonial levels.

This chapter explored the elements that formed her pattern of healing in the Kiri, Bokatola, and Mbandaka region. This template became history, event, and song, even a colonial short story. That much involved trees, loathing, and expulsion matters. In the 1930s, near Flandria and Bokatola, it was not uncommon to see healing initiates hanging from trees.[142] Getting lost then found on a tree branch is a sign of leopards and spirit illness, even today. Maria N'koi lingered as memory, in words and images, in Njondo spirits and healing practices. The figurations tell of her shaken state as she left home and entered a forest of trees, visions, sounds, and stark uncertainties. Once she began spelling out commands, her orders transformed her, producing eager crowds. Her words ignited, touching on "conditions of survival."[143] They enabled less "states of fantasy"[144] than daydreamed futures without colonial masters. Such reverie fed wonder (to follow Bachelard),[145] intoxicating some. A spectacular future was on offer when she suggested a massacre yet to come. Insurgency shaped time into storied intensity and a conflict-laden *event*. A keenness to daydream went with her leopards, trees, and copal charms.

The theme of eviction reverie returns again and again in this long history. Undergirding collective healing and colonial emergency were visceral metaphors of separation, riddance, and expulsion. Jadot's historical candor—in print—was unusual. His figurations suggested Free State rubber violence, rape, even amputees. That he linked Maria N'koi with the Leopoldian regime and its sexual risks for girls secures a critical point. Memories of Leopoldian violence shaped Belgian imaginations and deeds into the Belgian Congo years, including experiences in reading and writing the colonial.

This chapter read the *fray* over this healer woman's aura and import. It also sensed a long duration of motifs, from an Inongo woman dancer with tree in Free State years through Zebola in Mobutu's urban Zaire. It teased out a regional template for healing such nervous trembling, infertility too. Attention to history as *figuration* enabled. Concepts proved critical: not only the nervous and biopolitical, not only the therapeutic turned insurgent and aleatory, but also *event-aftermath* logic within degenerationist thought and the *futures* of eviction reverie. In extending a fresh reading of the Great War in one corner of Africa, the chapter also suggests that historians need to rethink conscription: in relation to anger and mourning, and as prone to barbed interventions from healers, publics, spirits with their human, animal, and arboreal media.

CHAPTER 3

Emergency Time

Nkundo men seemed feisty, angry, and demanding in Paul Schebesta's eyes, "negative towards Europeans traveling through."[1] They always asked for fifty francs, no matter the item sought. This priest-anthropologist took to mockery in 1930, hastening to ask if something cost fifty francs before the seller named a price. Noting struggles over newly appointed chiefs, with a "usurper" often eliminated "through magic," Schebesta never had so much trouble in provisioning a caravan. He concluded that the difficult Nkundo acted "out of spite." The game of trying to "fleece whites whenever possible" seemed to be their way to compensate for a harsh history, as if they wanted to be "paid back for the wrongs done to them."[2]

While the Nkundo seemed "prosperous, not poor," Schebesta rarely saw children. Estimating 300,000 persons in all, he spoke of crisis. These refractory, resentful people were in reproductive trouble. Their once "vigorous tribe" was "rapidly going downhill." The "catastrophic fall in the birthrate" translated into one child for every two and a half married women. Everyone was aware of the problem. Women tended to spoil the few children around. Nkundo were adapting in other ways: When a first wife bore no children, she usually became "mother" to her co-wife's first child, with both women sharing the care of this infant. Abortion preparations of leaves and bark seemed a factor, though men blamed licentiousness in women. Regardless, the many small or childless Nkundo families stood in contrast to teeming Batswa households, where husbands lived with one wife alone. Nkundo women were less "bound" to spouses. Forms of "friendship marriage" were on the rise.[3] At the same time, Schebesta spared no praise for the marvelous Nkundo bards who enlivened dance performances with story and song.

Schebesta assembled a cluster of issues at the core of this chapter: wealth and material conditions, anger and suspicion, barrenness and sexuality, and *festive zones*. His brief stay, in one Nkundo corner inland from Flandria in 1930, came just before economic depression made its mark. This chapter considers this conjuncture and nervous eddies in 1930–31, while the diverse spatialization of this colonial milieu is suggested. The low birth rate was under investigation when crisis hit, and doctors were touring and speaking of reproductive mishap. A mixture of the festive and the therapeutic enable thinking about sexual economies and reproductive disappointment. Nervousness had diverse hues, from securitization and reverie at the depression's height to women's therapies. Set largely in the early 1930s, the chapter's first section considers parallel confrontations in the early 1920s.

Pan-Nègre Traces, White Trash, Rebels by Fire

Pierre Daye evoked Congo's mood after traveling from one end of the colony to the other in the early 1920s. The Belgian journalist took in a *dancing* (French for dancing house) at Boma as well as installations of HCB, the British palm enterprise Huileries du Congo Belge.[4] The *dancing* was under surveillance, not for fox-trots but for "pan-nègre" politics. Congolese cosmopolitans in Bas Congo appeared "one quarter civilized" and dangerous in the postwar world where "races" were global "rivals."[5] With glances at England, America, Ethiopia, Brussels, and Accra, Daye painted his picture of the pan-Africanist movement. Included were Marcus Garvey's alarming New York City speeches about reclaiming Africa for blacks, ordering all whites to depart. He found copies of Garvey's *Negro World* in Kinshasa and concluded that Bolshevik plans for colonial revolution lay behind the newspaper and movement.[6]

Daye moved on to Equateur, where a perilous bungling of white-black relations had occurred. The revolt emerged from competitive enmities among men who oppressed: imposed chiefs; unscrupulous Portuguese traders ("forbans, à la peau plus or moins clairs"); and deceitful *capitas* who forced product-gathering in far-off places. The rebellion, which began in 1920 Sankuru, arrived near Bokote and SAB's Bus-Bloc concession (see map 1.1) on the Upper Busira, where independent traders competed. The discontent erupted with violent destruction and led to work stoppages, commercial crisis, and much money lost. The events demonstrated that colonial catastrophe would result "if we do not improve our relations with the natives."[7]

A healer named Boambokai inspired dissent with his *ikaie*. Made from ashes, camwood powder, coins, and chiefly medals, the charm claimed to disable bullets. The first officer to arrive had his soldiers fire with blanks. Ikaie's fame swelled instantly. As the troubles spread so did reverie: whites would run for their lives. The rebels attacked with fire. As their insurrection moved along the Busira and beyond, factories, state posts, residences, trading stations, and a Catholic chapel went up in flames. Military operations, which began in March 1921, lasted over five months. At least 115 rebels and 7 soldiers lost their lives. Everywhere, the results were "ruin of the country, devastation of plantations, desertion of work."[8]

This Busira rebellion remained on colonial minds, though some worried more about Communist infiltration and Simon Kimbangu's 1921 arrest. This Bas Congo prophet healed and drew large crowds with words about a *God near Africans*. The clamor suggested *xenophobia*, a word entering the colonial lexicon.[9] Fear and aversion also ignited the Busira revolt. Congolese detested the exaggerated corvées in food, rubber, or copal, imposed by greedy white men pursuing gain. Their clumsy gestures inflamed. Fury exploded over a ban on ritual dancing. Declared a matter of moral uplift, clearly such festive, therapeutic time disrupted copal labors. Other white men claimed to civilize while profiting from the sale of tawdry used clothes and hats in factories.[10]

Who were these white men who produced indignant fury? A hint comes from Monieka in 1917. The Protestant American doctor Louis Jaggard wrote of this unsavory world: "Usually 30 (traders) or so are at Bussira only 4 miles distant." With no other "doctor or hospital for 400 or 500 miles up river," they came to his mission hospital for treatment. Jaggard scorned these petty merchants, noting that he would prefer "100 times over" to treat an "ordinary Christian native" than this "low down white trash we have to put up with" here.[11]

The Bus-Bloc or Busira revolt became the subject of colonial critiques and lessons learned. One journalist wrote about the area's "rare and fragile population," a process of collective "suicide" through the "refusal to have children." Bare force, part of blunt moneymaking, he also suggested, was a key cause.[12] *Force* in colonial Congo was euphemistic, condensing violence and harm, chains, prisons, and floggings. Schebesta also effaced violence when perceiving spite and childlessness in 1930. When the depression began to mark lives with hardship and disquiet, the birth rate was already under investigation, though with little attention paid to constraint and aggression as actors.

Touring Doctors and Gonorrhea Logics

"I crossed from Bokote to Basankusu, a region of the Mongo race. The villages are big, but give an impression of emptiness. One hardly sees children." So wrote Dr. Mouchet in 1931 about his trip through Equateur and Lulonga. Dr. Mottoulle arrived before him, traveling for the colonial labor commission, for five months in 1930. He visited state posts, worker sites, and towns (Coquilhatville, Basankusu, Bokote, and Flandria) and studied the effects of recruitment. Mottoulle came up from Katanga's industrial belt, where since the 1920s, he had been architect of Union Minière's programs of stabilizing skilled labor for this copper mining company, engine of the colonial economy at the time. He was shocked at forested Equateur. With little mechanization, strenuous, forced labor was plain. He saw men and women building roads and airplane landing strips, breaking up earth with hoes, and carrying large loads on their backs and heads.[13] Mottoulle counted, and he listened to agents, missionaries, and chiefs. Village girls married old polygamists and became pregnant too young. Miscarriages resulted. Wives took refuge from marital conflict at mission stations. Shame from barrenness figured in many of their departures.[14]

Mottoulle's report in 1931 unleashed alarm. Instructions followed about undertaking demographic investigation.[15] Many noted the stronger fertility of Batswa (Bacwa "pygmies"). When territorials complained about evasive answers from dim Congolese, Mottoulle sneered. Belgian technicians were the incapable ones, whereas the chief gave Mottoulle precise numbers and pointed to out-migration and barren women as causes of the declining birth rate.[16] The chief colonial doctor Mouchet questioned the validity of demographic data. He preferred having a chiefdom clerk register births and deaths by inscribing individual names rather than another method: placing sticks in death or birth baskets.[17]

In the early 1930s, most of Equateur's few doctors and sanitary agents worked from towns. Coquilhatville had seven physicians, whereas there were none in the Bokala or Ekonda chiefdoms.[18] After two state dispensaries opened in Basankusu, Dr. Schwers began studying whether they improved the birth rate. Those near Boende were reducing stillbirths.[19] The birth rate was 2.12 per one hundred women in the *cité* and 3.78 in Force Publique camps (whereas in Katanga, Union Minière raised the birth rate over four years from 6.9 to 15.25 percent).[20]

Cités and single women suggested immorality. In 1930, Coq had 3,400 men and 2,178 women, with 294 single women or *filles publiques*.[21] Prostitutes were aborting with bark pieces or a fish bone, it was said. Mouchet heard that women unhappy in marriage would abort in order to be repudiated by their husbands. Venereal disease was an important cause of sterility, doctors assumed. Miscarriages also played a role.[22] Neosalvarsan injections available for syphilis and yaws, as in much of interwar Africa, were not always for free. They produced excellent results when patients stayed for two rounds of seven injections. At Bokote's dispensary in brick, supervised by a nun, injections were fashionable and, Mouchet thought, too easily lavished upon patients. Those from far away disappeared after an injection or two, which "whitewashed" lesions and left patients contagious.[23]

Equateur's doctors knew gonorrhea could sterilize,[24] whereas syphilis caused miscarriage and congenital disorders. Effective gonorrhea treatment was not easily achieved anywhere in the world in the 1930s, even in specialized hospitals in Europe and North America.[25] Dr. Dratz, one of several district doctors, argued treatment was "illusory" because of "constant reinfection."[26] Incidence was high. Bonura examined 11,000 near Bokote and found 32 percent diseased, with gonorrhea prevalent at 14 percent. In Lilangi, 75 of 249 women of childbearing age were childless.[27] Chiefdoms on the Busira's right bank had few children. The situation worsened when the impact of the depression hit in 1932. In Bokote and Bakala, where SAB presence was strong, births were few; stillbirths and infant deaths were frequent. Syphilis was at 8 percent, with secondary lesions like hair loss and nervous cases among untreated elderly.[28] Wangata-Tumba was healthier than upriver; only 2 percent of adults had gonorrhea, though the rate doubled among soldiers and state workers.[29] Only near Bokote, the SAB labor hub with Catholic dispensary, was infant mortality low; clinical work was also reducing yaws and syphilis.

Thirty percent of young Basankusu women were unable to conceive or carry a pregnancy to term. At Lingoma, 38 percent of 2,169 had gonorrhea. Dratz attributed sterility to uterine adherences; he did not specify gonorrhea, but many did. Gonorrhea was a clinical challenge. Men seemed indifferent to this infection causing little discomfort, not fathoming that it sterilized wives.[30] Nicolas Favre caused pain and required the longest treatments, sometimes thirty emetic injections.[31] Several women who had had a miscarriage carried another pregnancy safely to term after receiving arsenobenzene injections. Dispensaries should identify them for treatment, Dratz argued, because miscarriage outnumbered birth in the region. Perhaps his suggestion became practice where he held sway.

This avid researcher was keen to hypothesize while working to shape an experimental vogue.[32] Dratz was not shy to criticize. In 1934, he disapproved of Wangata-Tumba's new post at Ingende. Soldiers were sleeping too close to

HCB's plantation and countless mosquitoes at night. Lacking a home for the doctor, he had to sleep in the sergeant's house. Still, with more than a hundred Europeans living nearby, many passed through to see the visiting district doctor on tour.[33]

Diagnosing who had "the clap" was work for district doctors. Often the patients were European planters, traders, and workers. Physicians rarely indicated *how* they diagnosed gonorrhea, though some mentioned examining Congolese men alone. Men were the unmarked category in this situation where doctors had little access to women. Doctors found themselves "practically disarmed" from examining women, Mouchet noted. But a few did pelvic exams; Mouchet and Strada examined 144 in Bokala's Boleke. Five had syphilis and twenty "abundant white discharges."[34] Dratz examined seven women at Ingende, finding five with gonorrhea. He did gynecological exams at Bokote dispensary; the stillbirth rate was high. Many had inflammation of the cervix and uterus, one an inflamed fallopian tube and ovary with appendages. Such conditions produce miscarriage, he cautioned.

Treatment options were few. Bonura used the expensive *gono-vaccin*, usually reserved for Europeans, to treat a Bokala man with gonorrheic rheumatism. Dratz used leprosy treatment—methylene blue—for gonorrhea complications, with better results than the costly, recent gonacrine and gono-vaccin.[35] Gonorrhea regulation was never simple, hence the venereal archive abounds.

As early as 1928, Dr. Barthélémi asked about sexual secrets and venereal disease among European men. Cerebral syphilis was producing agitated mental states, while patient privacy routines prevented aggressive treatment.[36] Long an interracial zone, Equateur retained more of a mixed, métis atmosphere than other provinces. A recent emphasis on respectability, with state agents arriving with wives from the 1920s, entered this humid zone less strongly. Still, interracial sexuality, like matters venereal, remained a realm of nervousness (as we also saw with Jadot-Collignon tensions in chapter 2).

Jaggard had watched venereal incidence grow very slowly over his twenty years.[37] Syphilis remained rare, and he was only beginning to see gonorrhea at his hospital on the upper Busira in the early 1930s, some fifteen years after Monieka was clinic of resort for "low white trash" traders along this labor and trading zone.

The situation was different downriver at Flandria-Boteka where the HCB palm enterprise had a clinic. The HCB doctor seems to have been the only clinician regularly examining women for venereal disease. For every ten examined, eight had gonorrhea or syphilis. The territorial service criminalized "defaulters," those who did not return for care.[38] Treatment went undetailed but included repeated, deep washings with permanganate (as was common in much of the world at the time if uneven in efficacy, notably as Janet's *grand lavage* treatments). As in Belgium and much of Europe at the time, Belgian Congo hygienic policy focused on regulating the sexual and the venereal. No one imagined criminalizing prostitution or disease transmission.

Policing was part of health care in the palm zone south of Boteka and Ingende, however. The size of its labor force required HCB to follow Congo's hygiene laws on medical staffing and disease surveillance. The company doctors zeroed in on its workers and *femmes libres*, an ambiguous term straddling autonomy and prostitution, as we will see. That the most systematic gonorrhea treatment in the region occurred at this riverain site with HCB worker camps, near Flandria's Catholic seminary, tells us about state-company collaboration in disease containment. Such alliances became more fraught in the context of economic troubles and a HCB squeeze, when worker indiscipline became a revealing predicament.

The Slump

Everyone in Equateur had been hard hit since 1930. HCB was no exception. The chiefs in its palm zone ignited with fury in 1932, months after colonial commerce came to a virtual standstill in late 1931.

The Unilever affiliate had implemented a new bonus system, using "good for purchase" coupons convertible only at HCB stores. The chief of Bongili demanded an immediate return to the old system, pointing to his payment card specifying his right to money bonuses. Indignant chiefs stopped persuading their subjects to work well. The unyielding, patronizing HCB encountered much vengeance during these lean years. When transport costs spiked and the company stopped removing palm fruit near Bokatola, it asked cutters to go work along the Ruki, fifty kilometers away. As many refused as went. When production dropped at Monkogo, the two best cutters seemed like plotters. Long valued for speed and skill in cutting down large oil palm bunches, Djusu and Bogendankeka became known for sowing laziness among all cutters in the area. Convicted twice, the pair continued replying to the poor conditions with sluggishness.[39]

Many European traders and planters also were having troubles making ends meet. Richard Vereecken began an Equateur concession in 1930 after receiving state subsidies for colonists. Soon his capital was tied up in livestock and fifteen hectares of coffee; he had sixteen workers to pay, nothing left for improvements, and no way to get another loan. Not able to pay taxes or rent,

FIGURE 3.1 Colonial advertisement for an imported, everyday amenity: pure, high-quality, pasteurized butter, specially prepared for the colony. Consuming butter from Liège furthered patriotism and strengthened Belgian commerce. From *Annuaire des importateurs, exportateurs, entreprises commerciales, industrielles, minières et agricoles opérant au Congo belge 1934*, n.p.

he desperately sought to pass his land back to the state. He stressed his veteran status, his fifteen years as colonial postal secretary, and begged for reappointment to the post office. Pleading was hopeless: no one who resigned would be rehired.[40] Thus, Vereecken's attempt to get rich as a *colon* ended in disaster.[41]

Those still employed by the state were not faring much better. Inspectors confronted soaring costs. New rules magnified the expense of traveling on the province's eighteen navigable rivers, and family reimbursements were no more.[42] When Governor Duchesne insisted "sacrifices" were necessary for one and all, Coq's judges tried to go over his head. They wrote to the colonial minister in Brussels about skyrocketing costs for fresh European vegetables.[43] Production costs had gone up for steamer fuel and thus all imports. While the judges worried about how to afford fresh Belgian butter (see figure 3.1), Congolese food sellers were under duress, lowering their fees for eggs, ducks, and hens.[44]

Not only Congolese were under surveillance. Territorial administrators were subject to petty scrutiny about where they slept, for how long, how they used funds, and speed in inspections. The idea of cutting back their number surfaced. Some suggested having one cadre for long careers, another for short, technical stints; critics pointed to resignations resulting from the province's steamy conditions and recalcitrant natives.[45] Questions of authority met complicity in this zone, since territorials often took orders from the big HCB. Agents were escorting porters with fruit balanced on their heads, even though such policing had officially ended. One territorial quietly paid workers to build a road that would decrease company costs.[46] Another alternated between doing police hearings for the state and HCB production supervision, between disciplining the refractory and steering work. Brumagne understood he was to track production drops and pursue lazy cutters, while HCB supervisors told him who counted as lazy. Slowdowns did not reflect on his authority, Brumagne rationalized, while he kept telling chiefs how to motivate good work.[47]

Asked to assess whether revolt might sweep through, Brumagne projected calm. It was a time of disturbances in Belgian Congo, with turbulence erupting from Pendeland to Léopoldville and fears of Communist plotting stirring nervousness everywhere.[48] In Equateur, the governor's desk was piled high with telegrams about a rebellion shaking Dengese, a region to the south that had never been forced into tax-paying or missionization and now erupting with murders of white men and threats of war.[49] Brumagne posed as if undisturbed. A minor "movement of insubordination" had not spread, and such tensions seemed confined, distinct from any "systematic disaffection" against the state. Still, regional unrest might erupt, Brumagne did admit.[50]

Brumagne wrote, "I don't feel physically or morally depressed." Sometimes he had trouble facing all his duties but, "I don't hesitate to devote myself to these tasks during all my holidays and most of my evenings."[51] Why the obsequiousness? Was the man afraid of losing his job? Or was he seeking more merit points in personnel reviews? Working on holidays sounds obsessive in a life filled with minutiae. Yet such devotion during a time of staff reductions was apparently wise. This territorial knew HCB only had two men in the region. He had long wondered why this firm did not commit more personnel to purchasing and surveillance. He learned more state support was on the way, with another agent soon to join him during this period of tight budgets and difficult workers.[52] Territorials dedicated to company profits, such were colonial politics during these years of shoring up the economy and avoiding unrest.

While seeing no reason to fear a "movement of revolt," Brumagne admitted many Congolese worried about upcoming taxes. Reinforcing soldiers at Bokatola seemed wise since the many defaulting 1932 taxpayers would soon be imprisoned, like the year before. Morale seemed worse. But troubles in supplying white visitors with hens were nothing new.[53] Indeed, such transactions produced altercations, as Schebesta discovered at Bolima (see figure 3.2). When

FIGURE 3.2 Father Paul
Schebesta shown at
an awkward moment,
reprimanding his uneasy
but remarkably well-dressed
"boy," likely Bernard
Bongonga of Boulama. From
Schebesta's brief stay in
Bokuma, 1930. Photographer
was possibly Father Gust
Wauters. Courtesy of Archief
van de Missionarissen van
het H. Hart, Borgerhout,
Belgium.

he asked for two for "my cooking," the chief had none. Others refused to sell theirs. When a man came forward with two tiny as doves, asking fifty francs each, Schebesta erupted in anger at the "insolent" price. Seizing the "sparrows," he paid his going rate of ten francs each. The man seemed aggressive, prompting the visiting researcher to advise the nearest territorial. Soon, two policemen with medals and "red caps" turned up (see figure 3.3), followed by obedient food bearers from all directions. The man who agreed to sell the tiny hens ended up in chains and locked in a hut.[54] Tiny events could trigger larger altercations, beside resentments, rumors and dissent.

Flags and Garveyite Reverie

The depression disturbed livelihoods and ignited anger, with foreboding stealing in everywhere. The unfolding in Coquilhatville and nearby often reads like parody, a byproduct of broaching security interrogations with "nearness."[55] The point here lies not in satire, but in disclosing nervousness, hedging, and

FIGURE 3.3 Missionary-crafted block print, likely created by Flemish missionary Petrus Vertenten. An idealized caricature of a policeman with fez cap, jacket, and shorts, it suggests pride more than mockery. Published in the Lomongo-language Catholic magazine, *Le Coq chante* #4 (October 1, 1939): 5. Courtesy of Archief van de Missionarissen van het H. Hart, Borgerhout, Belgium. (Compare with figure 2.6.)

guile. Amid fissures, the documents tell of imposition and duress, of inscrutable procedures of transcription, translation, contraction and ellipsis.

As 1930 came to a close, rumors were flying. Officials were busy with undercover investigations, tracking talk about a scheme to end Belgian power. An American takeover would begin with African Americans arriving by airplane. Along the Ruki and Busira, people were entering *boseka*[56] pacts and speaking of a holiday upset. Authorities spoke of aggressive threats, "plotted" by "malcontents" and "laid off workers." The governor ordered the doubling of surveillance.[57] By December 2, rumors had spread into a nearby chiefdom and Congolese headquarters of SAB. Wangata announced a New Year's revolt.[58] At the same time, the cost of imported goods was rising and prices for local products were falling. Many lost their jobs. Plantations were going bankrupt. Europeans began packing up, heading home. Many sensed calamity.

Reports from South Africa had conversations overheard about African Americans arriving to the rescue.[59] On December 18, Coq's police commissioner began interrogating suspects (see figure 3.4). Louis Bontala admitted

DU CALME MONSIEUR LE
COMMISSAIRE DE DISTRICT

FIGURE 3.4 Caricature of two colonial agents, one startled, one agitated. It accompanied a satirical colonial song, teasing a nervous district commissioner and telling him to calm down: "Du calme, Monsieur le Commissaire de District." Drawing by P. R. De Meyer. In P. Hubin, Alexandre Leclercq, and Léon Pirsoul, *Chansons congolaises par trois moustiquaires*, 97.

overhearing a conversation about black Americans. Three sawyers had been speaking in Ilolo's yard, saying an administrator offered Chief Bongese five thousand francs to hoist *not* the American but the Belgian flag on New Year's. If he raised the American flag, he would end up dead. Bontala overheard talk about an American plane flying over the colony to collect intelligence.[60]

Bontala was secretary to Monsieur C. Marée, cité administrator. Congolese imaged Bontala as their "chief." The sawyers, Lomela, Ilolo, and Ekulu, had worked at Belli and Costa. Lomela claimed not to remember when Bontala appeared. "I had just taken my bath," Lomela hedged, suggesting Ilolo had been in the yard. Ilolo ducked too: "There was a young kid, Léon Bombomba, he came along and said a plane was going to arrive with Americans inside." Bombomba overheard Europeans speaking similarly, but Ilolo "told him to shut up and stop telling stupid stories." That was the end. "We didn't talk of anything else."[61]

The interrogator wanted specifics about Bongese receiving five thousand francs. Ilolo was precise: "No one spoke of that." Ekuku claimed he was absent when others discussed Marée buying off the chief. He pointed to Bontala's spying methods. When Young Bombomba was discussing the bribe, Bontala overheard from a neighboring yard. "I can name a witness," Ekuku said. When

Timothée Bongongo passed by with his lady companion, he asked who would be killed. Standing in the yard, they had learned about a possible murder. Bongongo was the first to suggest Chief Bongese's life was at risk.[62]

Bongongo entered the interrogator's office as Ekuku left it. The commissioner overheard Ekuku say, "Pay attention to what you say." Soon Bongongo was so nervous he was unable to take his oath. After several minutes, he insisted on being asked only about matters he knew. He admitted meeting the spy-like Bontala while walking along the fence at Lomela's. Bontala had asked what people were discussing. Bongongo said they were saying Bongese would soon be dead. Bontala interrupted: Who said such things? Bontala wanted names. Bongongo only gave a location: Lomela's yard.[63]

And so the interrogations went on. Bombambo said no one at Lomela's spoke of Bongese. They were only talking about their chances of finding work and an arriving airplane. Bombambo recalled, "I told the mason Ilolo that Monsieur De Dobbeleir said there would probably be work from Sunday through Friday, on the occasion of the arrival of the Secretary General of the Colony who would most likely appear by airplane." The commissioner returned to Lomela and the gathering in his yard, Who said someone would kill Bongese? Lomela, angry, bypassed the question, bursting out against Bontala as "a liar." Instead, he turned to the day Bontala's son stole a wallet from Belli and Costi. Ever since, Bontala had been angry with him: "As for this story about Americans, I don't know anything at all."[64]

The next day, the commissioner interrogated a Belgian in the colonial service since 1928 who supervised public works in Coq. Joseph-Oscar Delrue overheard a conversation about arriving Americans between a public works capita and the *boy* (servant) of Monsieur Scheys. Delrue asked his foreman, Jean Kemba, for help following their Lonkundo words. Kemba explained that in Coq's cité, Belge, "they speak like that," whereas "we others, we don't want to hear talk like this." The capita Lokwa admitted hearing about arriving Americans from Samuel Momptesi and Isanguma. Momptesi spoke of risk. If the Wangata chief sides with the Belgians, they will kill him. Lokwa mocked the pair. "Before, you were 'Basendji' [uncivilized], and now you are speaking like that against the Government? Who made you clever, wasn't it the State?" Momptesi and Isanguma snapped back: "You are paid to speak like that." Lokwa threatened to tell the boss Delrue. The commissioner asked about the rumor that Ekofo would soon be named police commissioner. Lokwa claimed ignorance. Kemba denied speaking about arriving Americans, even hearing such a thing. Lokwa only knew about boss Delrue's request, "If I heard something, I should alert him."[65]

The questioning continued. Another mason claimed to know nothing about the impending killing. Efoko overheard Lokwa speaking with Monsieur Scheys's wife the day he went to ask this Madami if she didn't have clothes to sell. Efoko complained about tightfisted white people, raising that same irksome problem of hens and prices. "When you people wish to buy a hen, you want it for a mere ten francs. You whites want to sell everything too dear." The interrogator turned back to the first black police commissioner. Efoko remembered Madami asking about the number of commissioners. He explained how things worked. "When palavers arise between blacks, Bontala the head of Belge cuts these. If the parties cannot agree, the case goes to the Comississaire de la Police." Madame began mocking, "Is that it then? I thought you were a commissioner too."[66]

Finally, the time came to interrogate Bongese. Commissioner De Bisschop asked the Wangata chief about the revolt that might erupt on New Year's. Bongese learned of the rumor from two Belli and Costa capita at Ifeo Monene who had learned it from sawyers. "Americans are going to arrive and present two flags, one Belgian and the other American." If Bongese chose the Belgian, he would end up dead. Most were sure he would choose the Belgian flag because "the Administrator gave him a lot of money and promised him an automobile car." The sawyers suggested the state gave the chief guns to ensure he took their side, to guarantee death. "We will kill Bongese right there in front of all the Whites of Government."[67]

After two days of questioning, the authorities arrested nine, charging them with penal code infractions.[68] Monsieur Marée continued inquiries in the cité and some villages.[69] On December 22, he ordered searches of seven, including the homes of Belli and Costa sawyers. Many were clerks. One was unemployed. One worked for Unatra, another for SECLI at Wendji, and a fourth was notable Tchoambe of Ipeko. Asikani, clerk for Chantier Naval et Industriel du Congo, was under suspicion, as were clerks for the Secretariat, and for Maître Weeste, Maitre Pecqueur, and Bakimbiri fils.[70] Also to be searched were the "recognized mulatto" Garzoul and Maria Mabille, both without professions and living in Coq. The objects found included a notebook with oilcloth cover, two films extolling France (*La vie politique au Palais Bourbon* and *Le Père Normand*), a French-German dictionary, and a bill with receipts, letters, and papers. At Bakimbiri's, papers in Lingala seemed promising. At Garsoul's, a photograph of soccer players perhaps suggested métis prestige and an attraction to this sport. Nothing useful seemed to emerge at Maria Mabille's,[71] but her name should make us pause. Mabille, a common Belgian surname, carried a hint of the Belgian "Loi Mabille," a law obliging fathers to recognize children born out of wedlock. Her name may have signaled the ambiguous rank of a mixed-blood woman, and her in-between standing within a racialized Congolese town.[72]

The commissioner asked about the several times in 1928 when he went to see a Russian engineer, asking him to defend blacks. Asikani replied, "I don't know M. Estchenko and never was in touch with him." The commissioner pressed: "You never asked for employment?" Declarations came from Estchenko,[73] and De Bisschop had himself seen Asikani leaving the Russian's several times. He assumed Asikani sought work, yet Estchenko had said Congolese came "to ask me to stick up for blacks mistreated by Whites." His words—"I wonder why they come to me"—rang as naïve.[74]

By Christmas Eve, a security commission had been established. Its remit expanded beyond "Communist plotting" and calming minds, as it instituted careful scrutiny over suspects and things arriving and departing by boat.[75] When December 31 arrived, it increased undercover observations in the cité, among some in the European *ville*, and over boat passengers stopping in the town.[76] Nothing unusual happened. There was calm all night. By January 8, the situation had been declared normal. It even seemed plausible Congolese were no longer spreading "tendentious rumors."[77]

Yet, on January 19, rumors were bursting out in Coq and the interior, and the governor opened a new investigation. Some spoke of the dwindling power of the Belgians, of Americans about to buy Congo, of black Americans taking over, of armed conflict erupting. Congolese soldiers would be disloyal, "Africa" would disembark and take charge, and all tax monies would be reimbursed. Even voicing such was a security infraction. Everyone was supposed to pursue the implicated.[78] The focus turned toward stopping strangers from entering the province. That ship workers launched rumors when stopping at riverain docks became a reigning theory. Congolese "undesirables" from big Bas Congo towns—Boma, Matadi, Léopoldville—were often Compagnie Maritime Belge shipmen who should be prevented from entering Coquilhatville. Three arrived recently. Exposed to Communism in Antwerp, their ideas threatened to distort Equateur minds. In the future, they should be kept from disembarking in the first place.[79]

The nervous strands were several. One entangled rumors about a chief, bribes, flags, and a takeover by mostly black "Africa," the latest rescue figures in Equateur reverie. Marked by the arrival of Marcus Garvey within global black consciousness, these ideas began entering central and southern Africa in the 1920s. The Belgian impulse to see Communist plotting embraced Congolese exposure to labor militancy, Antwerp, literacy, and foreign ideas.[80]

Kimbangu's continued salience fed nervousness, too. At the height of the depression in Coquilhatville, a Kimbangu strand met a man undergoing clinical incarceration. Esukula had been found praising "Kibango," the prophet arrested in Bas Congo in 1921. Kimbangu's person and spirit morphed into several banned, Kimbangu-like figures over the years, including Simon Mpadi and associated movements (as we will see in chapters 5 and 6). Esukula was one of dozens who imagined himself as "Kibango" during these years. He was enough of a worry that during the other interrogations, he was placed in Coquilhatville's hospital for medical observations. In the end, though not at all blamed for the surge in rumors, he was kept under surveillance. On January 31, Esukula was "freed," repatriated to his village. The case was closed,[81] though his medical certificate was attached to the security report.[82]

Such conjunctures recurred. In this case, medicine and security crossed over a risky individual. With the hospital as site of carceral enclosure and the patient as suspect and possible madman, his imagination and state of possession were colonial hazards to be managed. Esukula's story fascinates. Yet it became a banality in this colony where the pursuit of religious rebels became an everyday part of security. A keenness to produce and hide colonial knowledge was not unlike using rumor to terrorize. These intersected in this context where modalities, fears, insults, and reverie fueled imaginations and interrogation sessions alike.

Roads, the Overworked, Pueperal Infection

Another kind of nervousness was more everyday. It knew guilt before the frequent sight of files of women carrying heavy loads as part of required corvée duties. This welter of humanitarian feeling knew several dimensions. One was mobility, exits, and disappearance. Single women left villages and, it was often claimed, became prostitutes in towns. Bachelors, leaving for Coquilhatville or Léopoldville, would surely never return. Territorials monitored those exiting for public works jobs in Bas Congo, learning that Lac Léopold men were the least resistant to disease. Those who remained behind were hunting, fishing, and collecting copal. Yet most men had worked in a commercial center at some point, often in nearby enterprises, returning home often. That the back and forth—between workplaces and villages—spread debilitating, sterilizing venereal disease was global epidemiological logic at the time. In Congo, it first became salient beside industrial hygiene in Katanga. Even in Equateur, work contracts, "detribalized" labor, and family health care entered discussion in the 1930s as remedies for the future.

Mottoulle combined porterage work and demoralizing towns as causes of the low birth rate. State posts and commercial centers meant growing numbers of *rationnaires* (food recipients): soldiers, patients, and prisoners. Feeding them involved the carrying of food, a duty imposed on those nearby. In 1930, when Lisala had one thousand rationnaires, women and children carried seven hundred tons of food to this northern post. The administration fixed the day, and porters arrived in long processions with cassava, corn, and bananas. The porters were almost always women, who had less time for planting and harvesting fields. Food scarcity resulted. Echoing Jadot's interpretation of Maria N'koi's harsh girlhood, Mottoulle emphasized that arriving with loads, then looking for a place to sleep, meant many ended up in a military camp or popular cité: "How many return to the village contaminated and in any case corrupted!," he exclaimed. He returned to roads as the best remedy. If only the state would construct these thoroughfares, women could stay in their fields, suggesting that state agents would drive to villages for their food instead.[83]

District doctors knew that women were doing the brunt of forced labor, their loads putting them at risk. To avoid crushing them with corvées in porterage and paddling, roads seemed the optimal answer. Doctors pleaded for more motorways. Other provinces had fine transportation networks, and Equateur needed to catch up and improve working conditions for doctors in this way. The province had never been penetrated, went the complaint, and its rivers were inadequate. A "tangible presence of civilization," roads would spur "evolution": dispensaries, courts, and schools would arrive. In 1934, the governor blamed not only the birth rate but also "corporeal misery" on the lack of roads.[84]

When asked to prepare census reports, state doctors received a chance to speak. Some seized it with relish and flair. Notable was a fifteen-page digression by Dr. Armani, which consumed a large share of his twenty-two-page report on a chiefdom near Boende. He was impatient with those worrying about the negative effects of colonial rule: "We have exaggerated the destructive role of our presence." Armani's favorite word was shock (*choc*), suggesting distress as an inevitable result of two civilizations meeting. Not all would survive. Selection of those best able to adapt was unavoidable. Too many were linking *shock* to state force and pressures (quietly alluding to corvées, flogging, and incarceration without specifying them). To create a new "native" society, compulsion was needed. Fond of Darwinian language, Armani painted Europeans as a stronger race, while native demographic regression seemed inescapable.[85] Yet he also challenged the idea of Equateur as technologically backward and of roads as the obvious remedy.

Armani pointed to a sight so common it had become iconic: a long line of women walking single file, carrying loads. While the image stirred pity and regret, Armani spurned such sentimentality about women walking "slowly in Indian file with their baskets." He insisted that they were "not persecuted by civilization." Rather, "They work, they earn, they live." He challenged, while commenting on everyday speech, "Why do we say . . . each time we see a few dozen women loaded with small baskets of cassava, that we should substitute this carrying work with trucks, the modest native path with a road for automobiles?" Mechanization would be brutal. Using such female energy without destroying this human resource was difficult, he admitted. Yet: "Do you want to help them? With trucks, with roads?" He warned that they "would then be obliged *to be on the big road*, first making it and then repairing it during the entire year?"[86] Armani's words may have been anti-humanitarian, though they were prescient, as we will see.

Most saw the dangers of carrying loads, none more so than Dr. Jaggard, the ornery missionary straight shooter who wrote of Busira's "lowdown white trash" in 1917. Present since 1911, this keen elephant hunter from Texas and other parts in the American south ran a small mission hospital near the Bokote labor zone.[87] From his intimate and constant perch, he saw the situation differently. Commercial centers were draining the healthy from villages, with the young, old, and infirm staying behind. Yet since the economic crisis, many commercial centers had shrunk and hunger had increased.

Chiefs left their subjects little freedom to pursue livelihoods. Forced to keep up with every chiefly call, men had trouble providing meat for their households. Diets were imbalanced. The many long trips made raising poultry and livestock difficult. One chief sent his men hunting on his behalf when he did not have other tasks for them. Debility and malnutrition resulted from poor diets. Ritual prohibition of high-protein foods affected pregnant women. Many were living on cassava, plantains, cassava leaves, and palm oil, yet had to neglect their gardens during long trips to collect copal or maintain bridges. Not a single new domestic garden had been planted during six months in 1935 in a region with a long bridge requiring regular upkeep, where women were ever busy carrying food.[88]

Jaggard also invoked women moving in single files. They carried forty-five kilos of food in baskets toward markets, factories, or territorial residences. Often a village was utterly emptied of food after a caravan departed or a state officer, who could "ask for whatever" he wanted, had passed. Carrying heavy loads harmed fertility. On this point Jaggard was explicit, while district doctors, though haunted by the long lines of women porters, were not. Conditions varied for women from riverain and forest villages. The first rarely carried big loads or spent long periods amid marshes; their husbands combined copal collecting with fishing. Among the riverain Eleku, for example, men stayed close to home; their women kept up gardens, poultry, and goat raising and avoided carrying heavy baskets. Women of the interior carried forty-five kilos of bananas and cassava for three days, even during the rainy season and then without decent cover. This porterage put young women at risk of dislocated wombs, Jaggard asserted. The trips weakened. Robbed of vitality, many suffered from miscarriage or premature births. Others lacked the strength to give birth to a child at term. Many stillborns resulted from long delays or panicked maneuvers by midwives. When a woman was too weak to give birth to an infant of normal presentation, Jaggard tried to save lives through surgical interventions. Many who came to his hospital already sensed death was near.[89]

This rural missionary doctor placed the blame for the low birth rate on malnutrition and postnatal infection. The early age of intercourse and marriage was putting girls at risk. Precocious sexuality meant some were expecting a child before being large enough to carry a pregnancy safely to term; some were even misrecognizing a miscarriage as a first menstrual period. Unsanitary conditions exposed many in childbirth to infection. Many mothers complained of never becoming pregnant again after a first birth. Puerperal infection due to poor sanitation was common. Midwives understood that delivering a viable infant from a small mother was often impossible, with the girl dying, so they provoked abortion with infection and sterility often resulting. More risk came from the use of internal irrigation (douching) during menstruation as part of "their desire for personal hygiene."[90]

Flight, Copal, Nganda

Few detailed the intimacies of causality like Jaggard. District doctors saw overworked, exhausted people. Images of empty, childless villages surfaced. At Bokote, Dr. Bonura spotted lethargic people with shabby huts of dried mud and diets of banana and cassava, antelope and warthog. They still hunted as villages, producing copal and palm oil.[91] While coerced female movements were debilitating, Congolese sought mobility and fled. Men moved with wives for hunting, fishing, and copal collection. When Bonura showed up in Bokote in 1931, he discovered everyone "in the bush" along streams, searching for copal. It took him five months to census two chiefdoms. He succeeded only through establishing makeshift dispensaries offering free injections, suggesting the rarity and value of clinical care: it brought people near and home.[92]

FIGURE 3.5 This domestic structure built above flowing streams suggests a temporary encampment or *nganda*. Near Bongale, 2007. Photograph by author.

Near Bokote, Mouchet observed that the group with the largest population deficit was the one producing the most copal. The paradox challenged the validity of village-based censusing. Whether these people evaded being counted or were occupied elsewhere, some labor was less coerced than gainful. Eagerness and copal often went together. By the 1930s, Congo was one of the world's largest producers of this resin from marshy countryside used to make industrial varnishes and paints.[93] Since becoming an important commercial product especially since the 1920s, the intensity of its extraction had meant that many copal trees had fallen or died. Gatherers were now using sharply bladed iron lances to find it, standing in knee-high water while driving these *bosuki* into mud and current. After striking some, a gatherer would thrust his arms into stream and sludge to pry out the copal. A good day might produce two or three kilos. Conditions meant some came down with coughs, fevers, and rheumatism.[94]

That many collectors were living in provisional forest camps, called *nganda*, became a colonial health problem. Work rhythms followed the rise and fall of waters, a seasonality that defined this ecological zone.[95] In two seasons of about three months each, people left their villages with their foodstuffs and possessions. They created delicate, palm leaf–made hamlets on firm strips of

FIGURE 3.6 While learning about nganda and fishing and also arriving into Maria N'Koi's former realm on a shallow stream by canoe, I met this old man standing with his traps near Bongale, 2007. Photograph by author.

land, from which they could access currents (see figure 3.5). This mode of living enabled barrier-fishing, copal gathering, hiding, and escape. Often empty, villages became mere official homes. Residents showed up when summoned. Living in their nganda refuge places, "the true permanent residence of the black man,"[96] enabled tax evasion.[97]

In medical and territorial eyes, nganda were seedy, "unhealthy," mosquito-ridden, and aimed at neglect of villages and fields. Copal, depopulation, and abnormality became a discursive bundle, while tensions over the contrary meanings of copal—abuse or flight—remained. In 1919, the native welfare commission discussed excessive copal work in Equateur beside "abnormal" neglect of fields.[98] Soldiers and capita were forcing children into copal production in some areas. Tensions remained taut and mutable. Copal sales at "official markets" coincided with tax payments, whereas selling copal at a factory counter often meant sly, ugly transactions.[99] Yet others were enjoying copal wealth and seeking refuge in nganda time (see figure 3.6).

Disapproval grew before the intensifying appeal of these zones of flight and respite.[100] The regime and the firms it supported were losing many to nganda. Some of the demographic crisis stemmed from this doubling of space, with people moving in and out of this shadowy realm at the edge of "customary" villages. During these same years, Equateur's colonial economy was moving from copal to palm, from gathered products to formal plantations. But the shift was more on paper than realized, with many Congolese seemingly hardly working or only in copal.[101] Calling copal *unhealthy* concealed economic motives in a biopolitical language. Fixing Congolese in space and establishing modern plantations became the goals.[102] The enemy became copal as steering toward wage labor began.

Customary cultivation corvées of sixty days a year pushed many toward plantation work.[103] New buying monopolies excluding Portuguese traders emerged. In this world of marshes, where people had long subsisted from hunting, collecting, fishing, and trade, the state favored big capital and large companies like SAB and Unilever's HCB.[104] A plantation economy of workers with passbooks and contracts developed, as did living in worker camps. New regulations limited copal collection to four months a year and prohibited women and children from participating.[105] Little suggests the new rules were effective. If a few were aspiring to colorful urbanity, nganda continued to thrive as alternate spaces within shadows; their gentle rhythms enabled more daydreaming and wonder than the grinding routines of a tawdry "customary" village with corvées. Congolese kept nganda alive into the 1950s, while illicit departures out of the region remained a demographic worry.[106] In the early 1930s, doctors were not sure nganda would ever be eliminated since people "love this life," noted Mouchet. Copal also "enriched," at a time when many were keen to dress "in European style."[107]

Congolese also had their own therapies. Some mixed care with distraction in a ritualized, almost anti-European style. Yebola combined madness with healing through rest and dance.

Yebola and "Neurasthenia"

The depression years were also a time when women fell ill, and when some had men who showed off their wealth by paying for daughters and wives to undergo long, expensive Yebola treatments. Boelaert, charmed by Yebola, got in close to observe. He noted that travelers on the Congo, Lulonga, and Ruki had a good chance to glimpse a performance. The healing dance originated southeast of Coq, and Elinga river-dwellers recently "picked it up again," plying it with "great success." The patient often disappeared into forest, not unlike Maria N'koi.

Yebola was a "very old custom" and serious disease, which revealed itself slowly with aches and pains, and the patient became "incapable of heavy work." After trying medicines and watching her lose weight, a case appeared "definitely disturbing" when, with a deep cough and drowsiness, she began to talk "gibberish" and disappeared until she could not be found. Upheaval followed. The woman became Yebola—one possessed—living with spirits while learning dances and secret languages. She would play tricks, climb thick trees, come down head first, or dig herself deep into the ground. The way to bring her back to the world of the living began with a dancing drum, calling her name, making her dance. Husband, kin, and Yebola healer would go looking for her, "singing and hitting and banging the drums under her tree" until she came down. The healer would give medicine, "the drums playing twice as hard." Still unable to "speak sensibly," slowly she became stronger and would sing "her first spirit song and drag her body along in an uncertain dance rhythm." The return from forest was theater: one "played her part brilliantly," with "many spectators . . . truly captivated."[108]

The woman might flee several times, walking into water for hours, immersed to her chin. The husband would entrust her to a "sickness-mother," who went through Yebola herself. A small hut covered with palm leaves protected her from the "eyes of passersby." She stayed for months, coming out wrapped in a mat. Relatives might greet her with a small coin. She replied on a hand drum. The healer, busy with herbs and salves, trained her in songs and dances of the spirits. She could not work or eat chicken. If her husband touched another, his wife would die. No one could sit on her chair, whistle before her, walk over ropes wrapping her up, or else spirits would sweep her back into the forest.[109]

The treatment ended with a feast. The Yebola came smeared in reddish *ngola*, body wrapped in leaves, wearing a wreath of hen feathers. Everything used in treating her was set ablaze. Her husband arrived with a hen, and the healer sprinkled the patient with its blood. Later healer and patient ate together to "banish spirits from her forever." The healer led her star pupil before a waiting public for their spirit dance. Her husband paid a "royal sum" of three to five hundred francs, perhaps a thousand. The patient remained Yebola, going out periodically with hand drum and two bells. On festive occasions she performed her spirit dance, keeping the audience in suspense with strange singing and movements. The "fantastic coilings of her whole body" showed her tussling with spirits. Boelaert watched once while one "illustrated the struggle to get spirits out of her body." The crowd watched, "fearfully and breathlessly," taking "part in her pains." Finally, her dance conquered the spirits, and she threw herself triumphantly, headlong onto the ground, while the crowd "jumped aside to make way for the fleeing spirits."[110]

That Yebola resembles Maria N'koi's possession fascinates. Similar conditions of distress perhaps motivated the parallel idioms: Njondo and Yebola. As we saw in chapter 2, Maria N'koi's trajectory suggested a regional template of healing in and through trees. This pattern embraced her and Njondo, as well as the more spectacle-based Yebola, and the postcolonial Kinois counterpart, Zebola.

What were the motives of illness and healing? Marital conflict, colonial corvées, economic uncertainty, or reproductive mishap? Or all of the above? We know marriage troubles pushed Maria N'koi into the forest, though she later named excessive corvées as bad. Many factors may have weighed on Yebola patients in the early 1930s, a time of nerves for one and all. It was also a time of humiliation for those unable to achieve a pregnancy or a surviving child. Only women became Yebola: "men with Yebola are extremely rare, and then they die immediately." Women were never quite cured, holding on to their Yebola identities. Most were adults. "Married women like it a lot," and "may live with the disease as long as a long tongue."[111]

Yebola began flourishing as the depression hit and also as doctors began touring. Colonial experts were pointing to venereal disease and sexual license as causes of households without offspring. Was Yebola competing with biomedicine? Doctors were dimly aware of it. It is unlikely husbands would have taken a wife with garbled speech (or any illness) to see a state doctor. The sickness was a nervous condition not unrelated to reproductive disappointment and ridicule—this understanding hovered on Yebola's surface. The wealth required to sponsor a patient in a journey that ended with ostentatious spectacle surely carried old meanings linked to the way lineages and husbands used to select and promote a nkonde wife as specially named, decorated, and celebrated as a reproductive treasure. Nkonde wives were rare well before the 1930s.[112] Independent women were those who left marriages or never entered them. Were they able to gain in prosperity or fame through becoming Yebola?

Boelaert took an interest in etiology, translating between European and Nkundo illness categories. He once called Yebola "even a contagious disease," while translating it into a still prominent, if fading, diagnostic term of his day. "It even resembles a beginning neurasthenia."[113] That he associated this malady with the high-strung is interesting. When neurasthenia emerged diagnostically as a "disease of civilization," associated with the cultured and well-to-do, it was manifest in dizziness, fainting, exhaustion, and mental collapse. Boelaert noted that Yebola knew "rest cures," a neurasthenic treatment in Europe and America. Why apply this diagnostic for "nerve sensitiveness" to the tropics and its seemingly overwrought, "primitive" women? The simple response is that *neurasthenia* had become a household word.

A more complicated answer involves thinking about the pressures Equateur women were under, how strain became expressed in a somatic, performative language. Neurasthenia tended to emerge as somatic, associated with shot nerves rather than madness or a fragile subjectivity. A sign of prestige among the "civilized," cultured, and wealthy, the American neurologist George Miller Beard, who coined the term in 1881, spoke of "nervous energy" and "nerve sensitiveness." It might worsen in an "evolution of nervousness" toward insanity. In North America and Europe, the cause was frenetic, fast-paced city lives and high-strung dispositions. Cures lay in withdrawal, rest, and simpler living.[114]

In Congo, another "evolution of nervousness" was at work with nervousness culminating with a "patient" tangled in trees. Perhaps some Yebola were overworked porter women or self-paying femmes libres. Regardless, this healing form flourished when women's bodies were undergoing medical and gynecological investigation for the first time. The word *neurasthenia* suggests their suffering involved weakness, dizziness, fainting, and exhaustion.[115] Neurasthenia as diagnostic category mixed the psychiatric and the venereal in early twentieth-century American and European clinical practice. Beard defined it in 1869, as produced by "civilization."

Independent women, those who bought cloth and perhaps sold their bodies, were spirited. Striving to evade state impositions, perhaps pregnancies too, they were accumulating social capital in cloth and style. A similar liveliness produced Yebola, though it was likely partially related to reproductive disappointment. What did women claim through Yebola healing and dancing? Joy, for one, in spectacles mixing pleasure and awe. Yebola as sickness allowed for time out, rest from toil, removing some women from labor while producing time for dance exercise in relative seclusion. Its labors focused on singing, moving and tending to the body. Boelaert once spotted a Yebola in town. "I have seen one walk straight across Coq, aloof but self-assured. The bells rang as in a procession. And all blacks looked at her with respect and awe."[116] He knew the long, enclosed therapies mended uneasy beings, while in concluding ceremonies, they displayed health in startling, intricate dances. If this Yebola figure suggests a bleeding of the rural and urban, it also tells that some proudly introduced healing dress into urbane space, where tastes for modern cloth and bar-associated leisure were thriving (see figure 3.7). Still, that Yebola flour-

Danse de femmes Bokala à Bumbuli.

FIGURE 3.7 Women knew violence in colonial Equateur. They also danced. Many European men encouraged the festive and liked to watch and photograph their dancing. This image accompanied Jadot's impressions of Equateur in Pierre Daye et al., *Le Miroir du Congo Belge*, vol. 1, 63.

ished when the depression hit suggests material worries furthered its edge when the global economic slump shook lives and imaginations. Though we will never know how reproductive mishap fed a Yebola malady, it is clear that sterility was a laughable condition, one that could produce illness as shame. We turn to this evidence now.

Reproductive Disappointment, Lianja, and Baby Theft

It is time to more deeply think about reproductive disappointment, its sorrows and compensations. Being childless often went with diminishment, being reduced to a laughingstock. No children or few offspring usually meant pain, shame, and sorrow, a sense of being cursed through words or theft.

Mottoulle, the doctor from a more cosmopolitan Congo, noticed exaggerated "vanity" in and near Coq. Bicycles, sewing machines, fancy fabric, cigarettes, and beer were common desires, if not purchases in the tough early 1930s. Mottoulle noted European beds, mosquito nets, and iron trunks. In more "primitive communities," a common European sign was a folding deck chair. Clay pots were in decline. Blacksmiths were still active, though many bought European axes, machetes, and hoes at factories.[117]

Mottoulle contrasted "miserable" Batswa huts with "often pretty" Nkundo homes. Chiefs had solid, impressive houses. At Pensele, Father Boelaert noticed one with "a big pendulum clock . . . framed pictures . . . a colorful almanac," another in brick at Boyela with varnished doors and windows. Mottoulle observed mimetic, sturdy copies of "white civilization" at the edges of Equateur's big town.[118] He commented on a futile urbanity: houses with too many

FIGURE 3.8 A romanticized image of a Nkundo bard, ca. 1930. He would have sung Lianja episodes, perhaps Ewewe songs, too. With stringed instrument, headdress, and bare feet, and piles of wood to the rear. Original caption: "Nkundu, Bardensänger singt zur harfe." Photograph by Paul Schebesta, and in his *Vollblutneger und Halbzwerge*, pl. 45, no. 94. Courtesy of Anthropos Institute, Sankt Augustin, Germany.

rooms, Europeanized doors, large glass windows, and straw roofs. Expensive to build, these oversized homes readily fell apart, their high mud walls collapsing. These lofty, "fragile monuments" concealed a paradox, perhaps about grief and compensation. Their ostentatious owners tended to be "barren," with the head of household having "only one or not even a single child."[119]

Barrenness, considered within the poetic archive assembled by this region's remarkable priests, opens toward festive dance, song, and theater. Ekonda performance was famous for its warring idioms and extensive preparations organized by competitive teams. Lianja theater produced moral dilemmas.[120] In 1930, the Nkundo impressed as well-fed, with plentiful forest, rivers, plantings, and oil palms. Meat and vegetables were available. The average man seemed a polygamist with a "tranquil, idle life," with most work done by women or Batswa. Settlements possessed goat pens, chicken coops, and slit drums. Talking drums sent news. Fur-covered ones enabled dancing. Bards wandered with guitar-like instruments and head wreaths, singing long stories about their legendary heroes (see figure 3.8). People would avidly watch, sometimes all day long. One show used a large doll for an old woman's corpse. Many were hesitant to mourn, until actresses depicted spirits taking revenge.

A few fell down dead, until one came forward with a medicine that instantly brought the corpses back to life. The show captivated, the audience sang, and Schebesta judged this genre of entertainment dances "highly developed and harmonious."[121]

He likely witnessed an episode from Lianja, the "epic" that Boelaert observed and assembled in an era before tape recorders. Arguably Congo's first oral historian (the Flemish Vansina followed), he thought Lianja was at risk when deciding to "write it down, while time is still there." Boelaert learned that the "most colorful parts," with "hundreds of echoes in . . . thoughts and emotional lives," disappeared upon inscription. Lianja's malleability was striking: "Everybody tells it . . . after the standpoint of his surroundings." Boelaert's standpoints were the Flemish figure Reynaard the Fox and the Bible. His "first small tryout" drew from three "wells"—creation, the forbidden fruit, and resurrection. Seeking "unity," "purest headlines," and biblical "connection points," Boelaert made this "living, oral tradition"; some fifty-six textual versions are available today.[122]

Boelaert saw parts performed many a time by elders, as familiar, fantastic figures came to life. Crowds "in almost a trance" interpreted refrains, with youth in awe, children "trembling." Boelaert suggested Lianja's vitalist powers: "From where it has come, and to where people have taken it in their movements, I don't know. But it is still alive, ever young and powerful within the lives of its creators." Plastic, Lianja "can still change." No one claimed to know the whole story.[123] Lianja had no beginning, no end. With each performance unique, the hero was ever on the move, protecting lives or causing calamities.[124] Among "important distinguishing marks of the Nkundo-Mongo" and their "oldest monument," Lianja narrated creation: first humans, ghosts, ancestors, miracle people, then material elements, *bote*, *lokole* drum, bows, and arrows. An immense migration, with fighting against those who did not want to move, seemed the core plot, with episodes about Lianja's mother's pregnancy, conquests, crossing a river, and Lianja's rise into the sky. Hunting, food, fertility, tensions over wealth, and reproducing women were themes.[125]

Lianja trafficked in healing: wealth, distress, fatherhood, and pregnancy. When Boelaert published his first version in Flemish (Dutch) in 1934, it began with a stern husband departing on a journey. He warned his three wives that the one not pregnant when he returned, "I will kill you."[126] Boelaert edited out the episode in 1949 along with its suggestion of permitted sexual friendships (or "friendship marriages").[127] Pregnancy remained as teasing, repetitive, and droll. An expecting wife repeatedly hungers for *safou* fruit. Each time she is hungry, her husband climbs another forest tree to obtain more safou for his ravenous, pregnant wife.[128] The *barrenness as risk* and *pregnancy as ludic* went together.

Many more bits in the gigantic, Lomongo-language archive speak about pregnancy, bodies, the transgressive. Lullabies and body part songs tease with faces rubbed in, or feet squashed into, excrement.[129] The terror of plentiful ogre tales suggest nightmares old and repetitive but perhaps new in relation to memories of the monstrous, colonial, and grotesque. Some colonial nick-naming may have begun with ogres, like the hair-plucking Ekuma. The paths of an ogre are imaged as strewn with horns and excrement. An ogre may pluck out eyes or be lured by honey until its head ends stuck up a beehive, absurdly so. A "grotesque echo" of negative human conduct, as Brunhilde Biebuyck has beautifully shown, ogres appear as severed body parts: nails, heads, hair, eyes, mouths, necks, arms, stomachs, buttocks, eyelashes, knees, or jaws. An ogre as body part may eat a woman alive. Given Equateur's history of spectacular violence, it seems unlikely ogres never had a "counterpart in reality."[130] Some appeared as a troublesome child, a sapless tree not bearing leaves, a sterile wife turned black anthill.[131] These echoes suggest how ogres spoke to violation, aridity, shrunkenness.[132]

Within the same archive, a therapeutic zone widens along with the ludic.[133] Schebesta observed matters of marriage, love, and sexual friendship. He ad-mired Nkundo beauty and boldness in style: "Tall, wiry, and supple. . . . Fea-tures express courage and decisiveness, a twinkle in their eye. Bright-colored clothes and flashy ornaments." Body marking went with esteem and pleasure, while "enhancing beauty" aided in "arousing sensuality."[134]

The festive intermingled with the medicinal, suggesting fertility. Beside their creator god, *elima* power permeated all, especially places of water and the insides of trees. Elima had to be purchased or procured: going to an elima place, saying words, putting earth, leaves, or bark into a horn was one way to get some. Worn in amulets, a mother would hang elima sticks around her child's neck to ensure walking. A person would wind wire into an elima arm-band. When Schebesta naively tried to purchase an armlet off a man's body, the fellow barked, "Are you trying to kill me?"

All lineage members lived under one elima.[135] Elima power was vital for re-production. A man would put an elima object under his bed when seeking to father a child.[136] Elima came in *nseka* or scare amulets, small "vigilant things"[137] that frightened away thieves and shielded property, while working through metaphor. An nseka might protect an unharvested fruit. An nseka assemblage placed at a field's edge would prevent theft. An nseka's menacing verb was *nsesekya*, to terrorize. Placing one as interdiction required powerful words.

The poetics worked by analogy and suggested ancestral spirits interceding with harm: a fluttering piece of paper yielded an upset belly, a knotted cord gave stomach pains, a stem with thorns caused limping. The one who stole became a fool, the butt of joking, like a woman not finding a husband. Defying nseka commands produced sterility.[138]

The one who could heal an nseka violation was she who placed and empowered the charm with words. Payments to undo an nseka were analogical. A powerful nseka required complex correlative medicines in treatments lasting months. Two months after Jeanne Boso of Bongale stole pepper from a neighbor, she was terribly sick. Her elders diagnosed bewitchment via *embossment*, suggesting embossed colonial documents with raised seals. Her treatment lasted a year until her own embossment—a hump on her back—disappeared. Her payment doubles included an *ingonda* plus umbrella. A short sword with raised blade and rounded top, an ingonda may decapitate or enable (as bridewealth) a wedding. The counterpart, a coveted commodity of similar length, was an umbrella. Its design pivots around reaching into the sky, mixing urbanity, chiefly regalia, and refuge from the sun. This intricate payment pair, which joined colonial embossing, manly reproduction, and prestigious dress, tells about the complexity of diagnosis and treatment within poetic imaginations.[139]

In tales, mothers and fathers who deserted their children in the forest were scoundrels. The deprived appeared as celibate men, orphans, the poor, and hungry, and those marked by sores or missing body parts.[140] Some nseka curses menaced similarly, with reproductive and sexual maladies. "He who gathers my fruits shall die without children. All shall laugh at him for his infirmities and poverty." Laugher as risk, sterility as shame: the one without children was ridiculous, pitiful. In this world of nseka and conflict, sterility and theft were ever lurking as humiliating risk.[141] Sometimes they burst forth as minor, terrifying aleatory event.

At other times, questions about reproductive and sexual change produced terrible memories. Sorrow before an only child sometimes went with more collective forms of sensing causation. When Hulstaert prepared—with an exacting, prurient eye—his study of Nkundo marriage, men told him they blamed their decline in numbers on "first occupation," the terrible time when violence, sleeping sickness, and venereal disease combined. The moralizing priest was trying to account for the prevalence of sexual informality and concurrency, of transactional sex before and during marriage. Sexual competition and friendship outside marriage were widespread and not only urban. Husbands often benefited from the gifts wives received. When Hulstaert asked Nkundo elders to explain change over time in sex and sexual propriety, they turned to the terrors of past sexual transgressions. They pointed to collective incest forced upon women and children during Free State years of war and violence. In their memories, strangers initiated these outrages: Congolese soldiers and sentries, not European men. Their breaches tore asunder an earlier climate of moderation and restraint.

Sometimes childlessness appeared as individualized, almost slapstick vignette. In 1939, a *Le Coq chante* journalist shared a personal story with his Catholic readers. A woman passing through by river barge with her mother learned that a Coquilhatville friend had recently given birth. The traveling daughter paid a visit to the new mother, mentioning that she too would give birth soon. She also persuaded her friend to go buy cigarettes, leaving the baby alone in bed. When the mother returned, the baby was gone. So was the friend. Instantly emergency time, everyone sprung into action. The journalist and his wife contacted the authorities past curfew, seeking help. The baby snatcher returned to the barge where her mother waited. The parents sought help from diverse ranks of police who located first barge, then the thief, and at last the newborn. Some had heard the counterfeit mother feigning sounds of childbirth that evening. Others learned that her mother had cut her daughter's body to produce blood suggesting a birth had happened. Baby at hand, it became the doctor's turn to examine the two women and adjudicate rightful maternity. He looked out over his spectacles, declared one a fake and thief and the other the true mother after all.[142]

Much fascinates in this account about a woman in a nervous state, bereft of child, willing to steal, feign, and be cut upon to end not only her but also her mother's shame in childlessness. Set in Coquilhatville, it tells of the tight regulation of space and time in this colonial town. The emergency suddenly collapsed the rules until an ultimate theft was resolved, the stolen treasure returned. With its bereft mother-daughter, moving by river, it also perhaps suggests a femme libre or two focused on maternal distinction.

Amicale and Distraction

In 1931, during the same security roundup focused on Kimbangu's supposed double (Esukula), as well as Communists, Chief Bongese, and rumors about flags, another focus was a women's association. Amicale, active in Coquilhatville's cité, came under suspicion along with a métis woman, Marie Mabille, searched and arrested for a time. The organization had a second name, Etoile dorée. *Amicale* suggested pleasure and sociability. *Etoile dorée*—golden star—intimated regal majesty and Congo's flag. Eight days after closing it down

FIGURE 3.9 Congolese *fanfares*, part of civilizing missions in the 1900s, bled into colonial minstrelsy humor, as seen in this belittling, humorous caricature: a Tetela brass band in a muddle in Congo's Lusambo. The caricature accompanied a mocking song: "La fanfare de Lusambo." Artist: P. R. De Meyer. From Hubin, Leclercq, and Pirsoul, *Chansons congolaises*, 71.

over the holiday, the authorities decided Amicale was *not* seditious. Rather, it was innocent, a social group whose members met for modern dancing.[143]

That forms of distraction were active in Equateur's major port town is hardly a surprise. *Dancing* bars, we saw, were the rage a decade before in Boma, Congo's first capital in Bas Congo. Dancing turned modernist throughout Congolese towns and work sites from at least the 1920s, about the same time that mimetic, music-making fanfares became basic to town life (see figure 3.9). Associations of women, whether independent or married, intersected with fashion and cloth, with meeting in bars for drinking and dance. These were sites of idleness, sensuality, conviviality, and music too.

Independent women in Equateur were wealthy enough to buy stacks of cloth. Whether they exchanged their bodies for gifts or payments is not so clear, though doctors sometimes used the word *prostitute* in speaking about them. While some evidence about femme libres comes from the biopolitical archive, other clues may come from the poetic archive assembled by this

VIENS PRÈS DE MOI
MA P'TITE YAYA!

FIGURE 3.10 This sexual parody suggests everyday colonial practice, ca. 1920. A distinguished official, etched with detail, peers down slyly at a Congolese "Yaya." His words and her emptiness reinforce the colonial agent's capacity to seduce and coerce: "Come close to me, my tiny Yaya." Her caricatured, rudimentary shape suggests blankness: bosom wrapped in a sunny cloth, elementary curls, gaping mouth, and vacant eyes. Artist: P. R. De Meyer. From Hubin, Leclercq, and Pirsoul, *Chansons congolaises*, 87.

region's missionary humanists collecting epics and song. Equateur women, we saw, seemed overburdened in European eyes, their heavy loads carried in single file. A woman's association as counterpoint suggests pleasure—even independence in dancing and attending to the body surface.

This early women's association at Coq seems to have bordered on mixed-race sociality while enabling a sexual economy of distraction. How are we to characterize Equateur's social complexity? When Boelaert journeyed in 1931, he encountered manifold lives coexisting within this milieu: a wife harmed by a spouse's angry spear; a Catholic seminarian turned Protestant catechist; a Nkundo student stammering his way through a letter written in Lingala; and a Belgian Catholic with a Congolese woman partner.[144] This spectrum—Congolese households, missions in competition, linguistic discord—was also a sexual contact zone. Its métis tinge was pronounced. At Bolingo, by the 1940s, a Belgian planter's *ménagère* would welcome Congolese women and their Belgian partners for parties, while others danced, seemingly available for the taking (see figure 3.10).[145] Thus, that Amicale was not shut down in 1931 is significant. To have banned it would have hindered modes of pleasure and release for Congo's white men, in a context where Belgian policy toward commercialized sexuality lay more in disease regulation than in criminalization.[146]

Many *makango* or femmes libres were plying the Congo and its tributaries as they sought lives in forms of trade. Some were based at Coq, Ingende, the Boteka plantations, or in riverain villages. Doctors sensed these women intervened "to not have children," knowing "*bocks* for this purpose" were available for sale. Such clyster devices came equipped with a hose, ending with a small tube to insert into a body cavity. These items were the focus of population debates and contraceptive politics in Europe during these same years.[147] Independent Congolese women had considerable purchasing power, observed merchants passing through Ingende. Some women bought hundreds of francs' worth of cloth at a time. Nkundo had new needs, habits, and tastes. Clothes, dancing, card games, and gambling were among them. Women sometimes sold their bodies, many thought, while husbands and fathers benefitted from their revenues.[148]

Among traders near Ingende were independent women.[149] Some femmes libres settled in work sites, bought and sold cloth, became wealthy, and asserted themselves as entrepreneurs of leisure, fashion, and dance. Probably, they also sang. Images of them appear in dance songs suggesting extramarital lovers were an everyday source of amusement, pride, and competition, neither shameful nor hidden from view. They also tell of their appeal, by evoking rural women longing for material items of urbane living, like high heels and manufactured cooking pots.[150]

Song and Sexual Economies

Song lyrics are valuable for sensing the wide range in reproductive sorrow and sexual exuberance. Bishop E. Van Goethem, present in Equateur from 1924, extended oral tradition collecting to women's dance songs. They tell about pleasure, distraction, sexual friendships, sorrow, and shame.[151] Women danced, they suggest, often allusively, luridly, and about love, sex, and the obscene. Song performances produced frenetic excitement, and the mission fought to stop their associated dancing and purify the songs through education and control. Yet the bishop continued to collect the lyrics, and in 1982 Hulstaert published many, though sanitizing some as he went.

Balinga, which imitated a "European" dance found in 1920s Kinshasa, spoke about dirty clothing, refusing to marry by custom, and a mother giving a *lave-*

ment (enema) behind the house. Those with names like Airplane, Bird, Moon, and Jew came and went. The remarkable Thérèse Bokaa performed Beskya, an old women's dance, singing lines like: "She does not want lovers who do not complete a year," and "He married a woman with many blemishes." Many songs spoke of wanting, competing for, or ridicule in love. One featured a man "wanting to marry only a special woman," noble or "civilized." Another had a woman seeking an educated man: "I will not take up with someone who is not intelligent, Me Marie, I promise to take as husband, a teacher. When he will die I will remain with his leaves of paper." Lingala signified the modern and cosmopolitan. Some wanted just that: "I want a lover who speaks Lingala." Stranger lovers brought trouble, "like those who came to trade, misled mothers, infants." Some specified age and generation: "I am going to look for a young lover, born in the time of francs." This "time of francs" created distance from old men. Youth were "playing cards with money in their pockets," unlike "elders of former times, who gathered rubber, who saw war."[152]

Some songs suggested extramarital sexuality was everyday, mixed with the erotic and competitive: "your wife is traveling, don't desire her, you desire her, but she sleeps with another." Pleasure and the sensual went together, as in "beautiful tattoo markings and their delicate touch." Or "Don't be too slow, the duration is not exaggerated, I feel my heart open." Some clarified competition: "My lover and I, we were like the sun and the rain, the lover with his lies, the wife with her ruses." Some quantified: "Six lovers: show a forehead of bronze; eight, that is enough." The nickname for the woman with many lovers was "a hundred of mothers of lovers."[153]

The risk of getting caught out and owing indemnities cautioned restraint for men: "One unwinds leaves . . . but does not unwind the cloth wrapper for fear of an affair." Another sang of a European with contagious skin problems and accused of jealousy: "but I do not fear him." Some commented on adultery resulting in compensation payments and the dirty, diseased women involved: "The wives for whom they kill us with indemnities, are those who wear underskirts with lice as clothes." Sarcasm entered: "I took a dirty lover who does not wash well," "a new concubine who does not know how to cook." Culinary metaphors surfaced too: "I return to my old lover, tinned, reheated spinach."[154]

A basic message was about perplexity: "Love is like a stumbling block." Illness and sorrow spilled forth. One sang "her lover did not warn her, and he was sick." Another featured Iobana who lost reason like a madman. Violence lurked, especially in "taking a maltreated woman whose body was marked by blows." Many broached disappointment. Households with single children were ubiquitous in these songs, a matter of deep shame, suggesting the social fact of household "enclosures with a single child." One sang about the only toddler: "Unique child, don't die, your mother cries, only for a child."[155]

Conclusion

Distraction, though critical to many a colonial milieu, is a dimension often missing in African histories, or reduced to "leisure" alone. By the early 1930s, Equateur was a highly cosmopolitan world of doctors, officials, planters, merchants, and workers. The Belgians were diverse, and also in contact with American Protestants, Portuguese traders, and at least one Russian, a Communist suspect some of the time. Jaggard spoke of "lowdown white trash" in 1917. Barthélémi wrote of venereal secrets turning white agents madly violent. Yet a climate of interracial sexuality and festivity had developed by the 1930s, and it was not slender. When a *mulâtre* came under suspicion, missionaries discussed the case, while a growing number of planters had parties with card playing, betting, drinking, and dance.[156]

Economies of distraction extended beyond Amicale and mixed-race revelries. A splendid dance was long a chiefly offering contrived for visiting Europeans, tourists by night; when Boelaert traveled with a trader, territorial, and prosecutor in 1933, the four took in a special dance prepared for them.[157] Lianja performances and dances underline this varied festive zone. Sometimes a public dance fused with the therapeutic or mingled with theater, while the mythological came to life. The ludic also permeated the sardonic dance songs of women, competing over lovers and gifts, though singing about one-child households. Theirs suggests a complicated picture: of sorrow alternating with laughter in a vibrant world of rival, *revisable sexualities*. Many were dancing, seeking pleasure while finding lovers, high fashion, and amusement. If some were distraught about losing a pregnancy or being mother of a unique child, others avoided motherhood or ended pregnancies using the irrigation devices for sale.[158] The femme libre figure of the medical archive likely knew wealth, cloth, and clyster devices. She blurred with other women across the region who had a modicum of ease—some married, some mothers, many not, all often sarcastic while humming for joy. They included Yebola.

Mottoulle spoke about how the monumentality of fragile homes suggested compensation for being one of the region's many single-child families. A nursing nun at Bokote evoked of sorrow through the example of Bambo. This old polygamist lost many babies as stillborns or shortly after birth. He had six wives: Buya lost seven babies, Likunda eight of ten, Djoku all of her three, Esombo two of five, and Bomba had none. Lokuku, his most recent young wife, seemed "sterile."[159] To comprehend Bambo's situation, we need to think not only of syphilis and gonorrhea, not only about infection circulating within and beyond marriages with many wives, but also about the colonial milieu of which they were a part.

Bledsoe signals the importance of knowledge about reproductive potential across a life course. African women know about their greater susceptibility to mishap if aged from overwork and fatigue. The Equateur doctor who thought most about milieu (as social ecology) was Jaggard. From Monieka, he raised questions about Equateur as, to return to Canguilhem's words, a "shrunken milieu." State doctors spoke with hyperbole while diagnosing gonorrhea. Jaggard pointed rather to the intensities of forced labor, malnutrition, and natal and postnatal infection. He signaled the high incidence of secondary fertility. He was aware women were using internal irrigation (douching or lavements) for personal hygiene.[160] His complex, intimate reasoning was based on decades of observations at his small hospital on the Busira. He clarified porterage as forced labor. His insights about pregnancy and vulnerability were fresh. Childless women were not his focus. No, this rasping doctor drew attention to the many unable to have a second child. This affliction stemmed, he insisted, less from gonorrhea than from infection arising during childbirth or the postnatal period of the first child.

Equateur's few human stories about reproductive disappointment rarely reverberate through households, marriages, and lives. This milieu of much barrenness never knew a Retel-Laurentin, the talented ethnographic doctor who listened, probed, and came to understand *ennui*, pain, and sorcery accusations, all stemming from widespread infertility in neighboring French Equatorial Africa.[161] With stories so few, songs are even more precious. They confirm that having only one child was common and an experience of grief and disgrace. They also suggest compensation: mockery, courtship, sexual camaraderie, and pleasure in distraction.

This chapter contained a set of extended snapshots within the conjuncture of the depression. The interconnections amount to perceptions: ways of seeing and describing a population, especially its women who were not reproducing. Causal readings aimed at venereal disease, overwork, abortifacients, but also at bawdy sexuality—as in keen, competitive, and unbound, known for few rules with many lovers before, during, and after marriage.

Some observers spoke of links between a harsh history and spite, suggesting vengefulness was producing this collective "suicide." Most doctors focused on promiscuity and venereal disease, while being haunted by the sight of single files of porter women. That North American and European doctors read gonorrhea and syphilis as nervous conditions linked to neurasthenia from the 1910s through the 1930s encourages reflection.[162] Boelaert—like Jadot in 1922—suggested connections among Yebola, the venereal, and neurasthenia. This Flemish priest's diagnostic word of translation came well after Maria N'koi. It came when state doctors were first touring these parts, diagnosing gonorrhea and enumerating miscarriage and stillbirth. His word "neurasthenia" means reckoning with Yebola.

It is important to recognize that Yebola never became public healing in an insurgent, threatening mode (the next chapter will wonder why). Nor was there a singular dancer, healer, or prophetess who animated Yebola, unlike Njondo and Maria N'koi. The evidence suggests many Yebola women suffered from nervous conditions, their subjectivities and concrete situations destabilizing speech and their dwelling places. They tangled themselves with elima medicines and also trees. Yebola drew on ancient reproductive methods of removing women from labor, feeding them copious meals, and requiring dance.

Perhaps the slump incited the new rounds of Yebola, plied by those profiting from its fees. At least the weary were able to stop working during its long healing. Yebola began as nervous illness and exhaustion, before dancing out of spirits yielded calmer, strengthened selves. All the while, doctors were extending images of drained, overworked, pitiable women. Some beleaguered porter women may have entered this template of healing, though situation and rank likely separated the depleted from those able to access pampering in and through Yebola.

Regardless, the early 1930s saw a certain liberty in expression: The state did *not* crack down on Yebola. Still, it flourished just as doctors began examining women's bodies in new, invasive ways, a simultaneity that suggests another reason for mounting nervousness in Equateur. Such simultaneities are worth weighing. In the early 1930s, everyone—doctors, missionaries, and Congolese men and women—was confronting reproductive mishap, childlessness, and single-child marriages. Biopolitical inspection and Yebola may even have been competing modalities. Each mediated nervous energy. Medicalization was increasingly mixed up with rules and coercion. At the same time, reproductive disappointment joined the therapeutic, the festive and wondrous, notably in Yebola, where being knotted with trees, spirits, and possession came, ritually, before rest and dance cures at a healer's homestead.

In 1922 Boma, pan-Africanist ideas ignited alarm, not long after Kimbangu's arrest. Soon, in Equateur's commercial zone with a shrinking population, revolt erupted, suggesting revenge and social suicide. In the early 1930s, the conjunctures became dizzying with doctors in motion, an economic slump that set in motion speculation about a chief's allegiance and Belgian and American flags, and a surge in healing. The nervous state went into action against spies, cosmopolitans, and the unemployed. The rumors told about a possible takeover by black American "Africa," the latest figures promising to liberate. Marked by an emergent global black consciousness and Marcus Garvey, the rumors complicated Belgian nervousness about Kimbangu and Communists. Soon, a man who dared identify himself as Kimbangu found himself in lockdown in the Coq hospital. Amid the turmoil, the authorities declared a woman's association in Coquilhatville innocent.[163] Town life had opened horizons for many, up the Ruki and Busira and downriver to Léopoldville and Bas Congo, including European traders and colonists. It perhaps seemed wisest to simply let such a cathartic place of dancing and drinking be.

These junctions—traversing medicine, security, nervousness, paranoia, and reverie—recurred, as the following chapter explores. Unlike Yebola, the next therapeutic edition to our regional template—Likili became embroiled in a sharp, police crackdown. Doctors were still nearby while medicine and security crossed more explicitly—over risk.

| Shock Talk and Flywhisks

Ewewe, kiii
Ewewe, kiii
We show out Ewewe
Ewewe,
We escort you away
Ki, ki, ki
Give us food,
Give us fish
Ewewe kiii
We usher out Ewewe,
Nsongo and Lianja, kiii
Sweep away sickness,
Carry away coughs
Ewewe, kiii
Ewewe, kiii
Give us food

Ewewe embraced song about this mythological ancestral figure. His grandson and granddaughter, Lianja and Nsongo, often came to life in village performances. Yet Ewewe was more than his figure or this refrain about ushering him out while removing illness and harm. The lyrics tell of a festive drama periodically performed to remove affliction, receive abundant food, and weave together a cluster of villages. An Ewewe procession was also about purging and mending, ridding and relinking. Negative, harmful matter underwent elimination, entwining anew. At its center was Ewewe's wrapped-up corpse, a package of energetic matter carried up high until the container holding death reached the big river, where porters placed the bundle in a stream. Ewewe floated away.[1]

In southern Equateur, those identifying as Nkundo, Elinga, and Ekonda performed Ewewe likely from the 1920s, though perhaps through much of the nineteenth century too. Boelaert once described Ewewe as "an epidemic removal procession."[2] Illness, death, or calamity necessitated a performance. The music of the patterned dance sometimes became the whistles and pounding footsteps of porter men alone. They carried the imagined grandfather of the key figure in mythological imaginations: the hunter, trapper, and magician Lianja (who we met in chapter 3). A procession produced nervousness, with special transitional work as a group of carriers shifted care for Ewewe's hidden dead body to a next set of porters. Ewewe also worked through fear, joy, and wonder in removing the rotting waste symbolized by this corpse figure.

Lianja has been a favorite hero of Africanist folklorists since the 1930s, though these specialists of oral tradition have tended to treat Lianja as epic, text, or performance, not as integral to therapeutics.[3] Ewewe linked villages in a web akin to a reproductive body, taking in and eliminating food, a lattice of flow and blockage, childbirth and wastage. As Ewewe became an energizing force within time and process, the funereal qualities would have worked through motion, physical and of the imagination.

This chapter turns to a parallel kind of therapeutic practice. Likili also worked through logics of motion and purging, while it more clearly met confrontation and discord. An initiatory, mobile charm and healing association, it became event during the brisk year of 1937. Likili crisscrossed the Nkundo and Mongo zones along the Ruki, Busira, Maringa, and Lopori rivers. (A 1935 colonial reorganization joined these zones into Tshuapa district, headquartered at Boende and embracing Coquilhatville, Basankusu, and the former Abir zone.)[4]

In 1937, much was circulating—doctors, police, letters, charms, and fear. Quarrels arose. So did arrests, journeys, trials, and dance. The crux of the commotion lay with paucity in pregnancies and live births. At the height of this mania over the birth rate, provincial doctor Georges Schwers received orders to undertake a medical survey analyzing the causes of infertility. At the same time, Congolese were taking to pen, as a public sphere of publishing and reading in Lomongo emerged, with writing becoming part of practice in churches, schools, customary courts, and the new therapeutic network gripped by one *bote*, Likili.

Likili's power came, in part, from the motion it inspired, including among persons of the state or members of the emergent Congolese Catholic intelligentsia. Colonial worries about fertility failure were multiplying. The fixation crossed with vernacular modes of treatment. The nervous and biopolitical also became more pointed as uneasiness about childlessness thickened from all sides. Three new departures converged: Likili itself, an alarmist missionary pamphlet, and a colonial medical mission. Each altered perceptions and entailed diagnostic categories. The nervous state began assessing risk arising from charm-based, vernacular movements with its new word: *xenophobia*. The diagnostics for fear and hatred remained a work in progress in this colonial situation where the key strangers to loathe were colonizing whites. Nor were territorials the only interpreters of Likili.

Congolese were more aware than ever before of sterility as social fact, one producing colonial investigation. Present in marriages, households, and communities, reproductive disappointment came in diverse kinds.[5] The new climate of colonial investigation altered the milieu. Curious facts emerged from research and observation: 254 of 359 Christian households at Baringa Mission were childless, for example. Other details came from evolving practice: Old notables were asking priests to bless their young wives with a pregnancy.[6] Knowledge became printed matter in Lomongo.

Losilo Pamphlet

By the 1930s, Fathers Boelaert and Hulstaert stood out as substantial figures within the Tshuapa scene. They founded the distinguished, bilingual journal *Aequatoria* in 1937. Published in Dutch (Flemish) and French, it challenged the transposition of Belgium's linguistic hierarchy (with Flemish beneath French) to the colony.[7] *Aequatoria* pushed a provocative, "indigenist" line. Sometimes called *négrophiles*, these priests were in constant contact with literate Nkundo and Mongo, categories they increasingly merged within their romantic vision of a single Mongo nation. Reluctant to condemn the magical as "superstition," a stand that sometimes stirred the wrath of the Church, their *Flamingant* sensibilities had them keenly preserving Lomongo, standardizing its use and extending an appreciation of this language.[8] With interests embracing linguistics, ethnology, performance, marriage, and jurisprudence, these prolific scholars spoke out about depopulation in the Ruki region. In 1937, they shook up public opinion with a fifteen-page, didactic pamphlet written in Lomongo: "A region that dies."[9] Making thousands available at the mission press, they urged territorials, doctors, magistrates, and *colons* to disseminate it to all Congolese. Just ten francs bought one hundred.[10]

The pamphlet spoke bleakly of frail bodies, a region without inhabitants, dying clans, fathers bereft of progeny, and sterile women. It combined imagery with stark numbers, pointing out that one sector (Elanga de Losanganya) had 22,000 persons in 1930, only 16,000 in 1937, while a decline to 12,000 by 1940 was likely. Along the Ikelemba, "we see only one child for every four women." The visible and enumerable received attention. "Don't you see with your eyes that this region lacks inhabitants?" the booklet asked. "Have you an idea of the figures?" A sexualized body was lurking, and these vitalist priests stressed vice: "Debauchery rages; it has afflicted people with shameful sicknesses. Bodies are weakening and no longer have the strength to procreate." They skirted the venereal, posing an uncanny question instead: "Do you feel able to laugh about it?"[11]

A Lomongo-language pamphlet designed for Congolese was novel. It emanated from the use of vernacular poetics in mission bases at Coquilhatville, Bamanya, Bokuma, and Flandria. The Sacred Heart mission published two magazines, *Losilo* and *Le Coq chante*. For about two years, the latter featured letters by Congolese men about depopulation.[12] Some angry letter-writers pushed back with cheek, annoyed at the drawn-out fuss of the booklet. They placed the blame for depopulation on white men who hid their concubines and claimed girls for sex as they liked, offering only a few coins. In a sense, hostility mounted as sexuality and reproduction received so much attention. A major medical mission also increased indignation.

A Research Mission

In February 1937, Governor General Pierre Ryckmans charged Dr. Georges Schwers with a six-month mission of "medical reconnaissance" to determine the causes of depopulation in Tshuapa.[13] The colony's chief doctor, Lucien Van Hoof,[14] instructed Schwers to study state and mission medical zones, leper segregation, and the effects of copal production, while determining the areas most endangered by the deficient birth rate. Sampling population groups and classifying the findings by age were also part of his charge, in order to determine the duration of the problem and whether it stemmed from labor recruitment or differences among "races."

Ryckmans had been keeping an eye on matters reproductive in Tshuapa.

In Befale territory, previously free of syphilis, some seven hundred of five thousand now had the disease. That venereal incidence rose as recruitment increased seemed obvious.[15] There were more and more plantations (with more than five thousand workers in Djolu territory). The doctor should study company medical services, evaluate managerial "good will," and insist on compliance with Congo's industrial hygiene legislation. The latter required employers with more than five hundred workers to hire a sanitary agent, while those with more than a thousand required a doctor. Most paid a mission or state doctor to do the work,[16] and the governor general was envisioning family protection programs in future worker camps.

In and outside of such camps, Schwers should study infant mortality, stillbirth, miscarriage, and lack of pregnancy, and propose a better organization with dispensaries, roads, and personnel.[17] All causes deserved attention: the sexuality of prepubescent girls, mutilating forms of venereal disease, and congenital infection. He was to ensure yaws was not being misdiagnosed as syphilis, collect data on syphilitic heredity and parasyphilitic disorders, and assess gonorrhea's role.[18] Male sterility should not be forgotten, though "the examination of a good number of women" would answer many questions. This assumption, we will see, did not hold.[19]

The mission required travel, letter-writing and food procurement across several territories: Boende, Befale, Basankusu, Bokungu, Bongandanga, Ikela, and Djolu. Schwers had an excellent budget, access to a state steamer, and—a rarity for the time—a Congolese nurse-intern, Eale. State agents and plantation managers received orders to ready rest houses and walking paths and prepare for assembling populations. The journey began March 10. Convocations went with woodcutting. Each riverain stopping point had to supply steamer fuel. Schwers checked his microscopes and surgical equipment, dispensed some pharmaceuticals, considered relocating some villages to reduce sleeping sickness, and identified workers needing surgery at Boende. His main focus lay in examining village residents and company workers for endemic and venereal disease, while taking body measurements.[20]

The trip proceeded mostly by river, though his possession of a 1933 table of walking times between rest houses suggests some day-long journeys by foot.[21] The tour resembled Congolese medical census work of the 1930s: mobile hygiene on the march, with many receiving injections or medical passports, and soldiers quarantining the contagious and ensuring the disobedient went to jail.[22] En route, the doctor received letters. One territorial wrote of empty villages: people were out gathering copal. Some convocations seemed redundant to plantation managers, given regular hygiene coverage. On May 7, a Belgian sanitary agent wrote to express the great honor it would be to meet the provincial doctor. He was still four hours away but hurrying, since he had not seen a European in four months and during his eighteen months in the region had never once been checked or supervised.[23] Sometimes a sanitary agent finished a hygiene convocation after Schwers moved on.[24] One manager questioned the need to reexamine three hundred in a day, since Schwers had just undertaken a "serious control." Others wrote excuses for being absent or having incomplete buildings. One owner explained: "I did everything possible to have my camps in order: the new constructions are unfinished, but it is not my fault."[25]

In the end, only about seven thousand workers were examined as well as some thirty thousand customary subjects. Over a thousand residents and a few hundred schoolchildren of Basankusu also were part of the study. Schwers concluded that the worst demographic "deficits" were along the Maringa. Flowing from Boende to Basankusu through Befale territory, in the 1900s this river formed the southern border of the Abir rubber concession.[26]

Schwers traveled at a time when colonial doctors were not parachuted in for quick errands and consultancies, unlike global health specialists today. His time in Equateur became a long entanglement lasting years. Humanitarian impulses were nearly absent at the time of his tour. Yet for his clinical care and nursing instruction in Coq, the emerging middle class was fond of Schwers. Surely the same doctor who peered over his spectacles in 1939 when determining who was the rightful mother of a stolen babe, he spent time consumed by anxieties about advancement, about where he would next be posted as colonial doctor.[27]

Schwers arrived not as a distant, observing, literary gentleman (like the magistrate Joseph-Marie Jadot), but as a technician at the height of 1930s hysteria. He became "doctor in charge," ordered to conduct a major survey and analyze the determinants of childlessness across a wide region. If he was aware it had been subjected to a brutal rubber economy of raiding, plunder, and death in the late nineteenth and early twentieth centuries, he did not mention it. There seem to be no surviving photographs of him, nor did Schwers warrant an entry in the long series of Belgian colonial biographies. We may sense his attitudes through graphic language. His mixed degenerationist and Darwinian registers, and he carried out his mission with lurid fantasies in mind. His dread sometimes became shrill.

His mission sought to clinch the extinction question long implicit in conversations and marginalia (as in Dr. Armani's tangent, we learned in chapter 3). Were Mongo destined to die out? The biopolitical in Congo went with a Darwinian logic of sizing up groups as "races" and assessing health. Congo's chief director during these years, Pierre Ryckmans, had developed a demographic calculus to protect rural reproduction and prevent too much labor from being recruited out of customary zones. In Tshuapa, these formulae faced a low birth rate and "backward" population, at a time when the plantation economy sought a big push forward in infrastructure: in roads.[28] Ryckmans thought the fertility of Congo-Ubangi's Bwaka might make up for the economic problems of this "depopulated" region: its inadequate recruitment potential. Organizing in-migration of "new blood" might "repopulate, by means of prolific and definitely healthy people."[29] Van Hoof supposed an "obscure cause" might be "sought in the race itself." Introducing new blood to "regenerate" the race, he suggested, could be an effective remedy. The Maori of the Pacific seemed the obvious comparison with eugenic parallels; "exaggerated selection" happened within a century, without disease ever being found responsible.[30]

This kind of language, thick in the air, predisposed Schwers to also think in terms of "race suicide." Yet his conclusions came out muddled and clichéd. Many elements received the term *primitive*—chromosomes, races, shocks endured, and causal levels. The low birth rate stemmed from chromosomal alterations of a "primitive" nature, he wrote. The "disappearance of native populations" seemed sudden, with these primitives of the tropics poised to "melt like snow in the sun." His journeying into the bush—also "primitive"—had transformed his thinking: "Like my predecessors, I went into the bush with a preconceived idea that I would find at the basis of the process, the gonococcus and spirochete. It was only little by little, through minute research, that I modified my manner of seeing."[31] The shift amounted to distinguishing causal levels and his reading in endocrinology. While colonial science had logics and practices, so a form of healing called Likili relied on stories and diagnosed with metaphors.

Likili

While Boelaert and Hulstaert were distributing their pamphlet, and while Schwers was speaking with his Darwinian tongue, many in Ingende territory began seeking a new mobile bote called Likili. *Bote*, as we have seen, means tree, medicine, and charm, though the idea often extended to an association or form of therapeutic belonging.[32] Colonial agents, quick to observe gatherings and hierarchy, called Likili a religious "sect," a reduction that missed how it promised to heal reproductive and economic troubles.

In 1936, a few villages began trafficking in Likili. Soon it swept through several chiefdoms. Those in Lingoi were the first to cross territorial lines into

Basankusu for initiation. Such travel allowed bringing the medicine home.[33] The one who returned with Likili became a leader who encouraged the charm's adoption in his village among men and women members.

A schoolteacher named Ekonyo studied Likili. In Lomongo, he wrote about its nature, associates, "their thinking," and commands. He ranked himself among "sensible and good people," those who had moved beyond a simple Christianity and could write. His text resembled an official ethnographic description of a "secret society," with sections on etymology, origin, purpose, rites, emblems, prohibitions, hierarchy, and tribute payments. Yet subtle detail made Ekonyo's text distinct. Likili practitioners were removing and destroying previous magical practices to protect foodstuffs and procreation. Their aim was to help women and men have children. Likili's tight focus—"so all persons would bear children"—was unprecedented. Clearing, ousting, and eliminating charms was the work of Likili. In the morning, followers painted their bodies with camwood paste, making red bodily stripes from foreheads to ears on men and from left temples to lower bellies on women. Likili persons beat drums from morning to night, while followers danced a bote song: "The owl never travels." Bekali spirits send warnings through the cries of an owl, while a moored, ready owl suggests steadfast spiritual protection.[34]

Likili knew record-keeping. Throwing away a magical remedy meant depositing it with a leader. First, this *ntombi* placed the charms on a pyre. When someone came forward with a bote, the question was: "whether or not he killed someone for it." Then the scribe did his part: "their registrar writes it down." "Implements,"[35] including imported mosquito nets and blankets, were among the many charms burned on Likili fires.[36]

Special remedies to remove previous bote were nothing new. Usually, as most knew from common *bofomela* practices,[37] people discarded medicines in *baembo*, land depressions where water collected and *bilima* spirits dwell. With Likili, fear concerned whether charms had been killing the old, the young, and women. Ekonyo disclosed that some had been taking umbilical cord bits and putting them into their charms for good fortune in hunting and fishing. The results were poisonous: it "prevents the birth of children."[38]

In official ethnographic texts, Likili emerged as periodic: something similar had occurred some eight years earlier. The charm had begun near Basankusu under the name Mondjali. Old man Bolima, a famous *nkanga*, or healer, fashioned the charm with his son Isenge. The Mondjali were worried about precarity in hunting and fishing, too few pregnancies, and too many deaths. At a meeting at Bolima's, important nkanga longed for former times while remembering the marvelous charm of Djafo. This healer had fathered more than seventy surviving children, and all his yearnings came to be. Before dying, he left his bote with Bolima, who was now ready to pass on its secrets to bring back fortune and health. Recovery would be difficult because hostile people with harmful medicines still sought to ruin others' trade. The healers also spoke about how to ensure more women began giving birth. Producing fear in those women who misbehaved was one idea. Another was an elaborate, new, superior charm whose force would destroy lesser medicines, while turning their powers back upon their owners.[39]

Those gathered at Bolima's ordered everyone working with magic to put all their medicines in one place. They began ceremonies lasting weeks. Women who had not given birth in several years danced under the care of older women who had given birth many times. Washings followed the festive dancing until—noted the territorial agent, in clinical, ethnographic mode—the medicine became "absorbed." Then each woman returned to her husband. Sleeping with anyone else would bring trouble to her and her lover. As Bolima's followers passed on the charm,[40] Likili spread.[41] So did promises of fertility, of bounty in hunting, fishing, and trade.

Likili persons often went by the name *bensaswa*, after the flywhisks they carried (see figure 4.1). When someone presented an old bote for destruction, they would beat on the charm with the ends of their flywhisks, saying the medicine had lost its power. Then they added the item to the pyre. A flywhisk, sometimes an instrument of healing, was also a symbol of chiefly authority and an everyday domestic device for sweeping and swatting. Using a flywhisk meant contact with filth, vermin and the transgressive, extending the semantic range to excrement and mocking laughter.[42]

Nervous Diagnostics

By mid-March, a couple of agents were typing up their Likili impressions, wondering whether they had enough evidence of xenophobia to intervene.[43] In May 1936, the Basankusu territorial discussed Likili as a "talisman" with "adepts," which "disconcerts by its originality." He knew his information might be incorrect because of secrecy. Still, he had seen an "impressive enough heap of material," substances to be burned in Ngombe villages. Since its rapid expansion was obvious, Likili needed to be followed closely, even if it was not possible to "foresee its results." Only after some time would the best course of official conduct be obvious.[44]

De Brier soon reported from Ingende to commissioner Vanderhallen that Likili had been performed for days. The sect had been "infiltrating" into three

FIGURE 4.1 *Bensaswa* in action. Two Nkundo posing with flywhisks and other arms and ritual devices in a region near Likili encounters, ca. 1930. Original caption: "Nkundu im Kriegsschmuck." Photograph by Paul Schebesta, *Vollblutneger und Halbzwerge*, pl. 48, no. 99, facing 257. Courtesy of Anthropos Institute, Sankt Augustin, Germany.

Ingende chiefdoms: Bunianga, Lingoy, and Bokala. He spoke the new lexicon: Likili deserved attention for "demonstrations" that might "qualify as hostile towards Europeans." While agents pleaded for caution before making arrests, "manifestations of hostility" mounted, confirming the diagnosis: "the movement had turned xenophobic."[45]

The proof arrived in bits. At Boleke, some threw rocks at a river steamer owned by the Portuguese firm Botelho & Co. At Kingunda, a Likili group sang before a European merchant, evidently Portuguese, a Monsieur Fernandes. The refrain—*que les Blancs auraient le dessous*—sang of wishing all whites to "go down," to disappear.[46] While such dissent arose from work and trading conditions, the biopolitical state began to have an unkind human face, too.

Word arrived that Likili followed the district doctor in his movements through Bokala. Dr. Charlier ended up in a face-off with some dancers. Wearing "primitive" dress, their gestures had De Brier wondering first whether Likili would "lead natives back to the carefree and lazy life of their ancestors." They performed their dances of ousting Dr. Charlier when he left a village and this more than once. Whatever clinical examinations the doctor may have conducted, this was a time of intensifying medicalization. Using their "symbol of a broom," their dances suggested more "sweeping out of whites rather than sweeping out old 'medicines.'"[47] Present was the idea, "European medicines should no longer be taken."[48] Waving their broom-like whisks in aggressive, perhaps mocking gestures, their movements enacted elimination, expulsion, sweeping away. These Likili danced as if to say the medic and his work were dirt, needing to be eliminated.

Vanderhallen joined De Brier on site to evaluate "the importance of the movement," determine "necessary measures in the event of a xenophobic tendency," and approve arrests. The major day of arrests came soon after the hostile dances. While the central clash was between Likili and the nervous state, doctors *as* the state's biopolitical face were deeply implicated. De Brier put in preventive detention several who introduced Likili,[49] and sent in supplementary soldiers. During a single day's roundup, 156 persons from 31 villages in 3 chiefdoms went to jail.[50]

While the nervous state arrested, Father Hulstaert took an interest in Ekonyo's ethnographic text in Lomongo. He published it in 1939, translating it into Dutch, perhaps to remind readers about the vigor of Flemish and Lomongo alike or to slip under the radar of the Church, completely unsympathetic toward perceived nativism or magic.

Ekonyo's language was direct. Likili produced a "clash with medical research." He added: "They were brought before the court because they would not take off their clothes before the doctor." In a footnote Hulstaert agreed, noting the state overreacted to their "resistance against undressing for medical examinations." Likili's "strict prohibition against seeing female nudity" contributed to the moment when "the white man of the state came with soldiers and took them prisoner." They first seized seven ntombi, then two more, and then their followers, sending them all to prison. The white man demanded their objects and medicines. Using the hollows found in uneven countryside, he took all their flywhisks and charms and threw them into these ancient disposal places for magical refuse. He set them all on fire.[51]

The Likili dances and police arrests coincided with the first weeks of Dr. Schwers's medical tour. Exactly how he used district doctors in his research mission is unclear, though Schwers and Charlier, in contact, had planned a March 16 meeting at Bokote. Although the study tour was a distance away when Charlier confronted Likili dancers, this region was laced with footpaths along which rumors could move at lightning speed.[52]

Degeneration

By early May, hypotheses began forming in Schwers's mind, and he wrote for additional reading material in endocrinology. Soon, letters were arriving from colleagues in Coq and Léopoldville about texts to consult. By mid-June, Schwers was declaring he had found several cases of "racial degeneration" among a group of well-fed Bakutu men. They seemed untouched by venereal disease and alcoholism, showed no evidence of being overworked, yet exhibited signs of sterility and "masculine infantilism." Van Hoof took an immediate interest in the idea of a racial problem three generations old, though suggested that "glandular deficiencies and developmental troubles" were usually "more symptom than cause."[53]

By late August, Schwers was winding down his journey. On September 20, he sent a report to Léopoldville. He apologized for his pessimistic conclusions though recommended sophisticated scientific research: "no new progress can be made without biological research of a very special nature." Impossible "in the bush," it requires "a complex and costly installation."[54] The doctor mentioned the sterilizing power of gonorrhea and found evidence for its presence (3 to 22 percent), as well as syphilis (0 to 28 percent). But, neither seemed the cause of the birth rate. He found some testicular inflammation (orchitis), though no sure relationships with leprosy, syphilis, or trypanosomiasis. Unlike yaws and sleeping sickness, he argued, organizing a campaign against gonorrhea would be impossible because getting patients to return for all treatments was too difficult. He proposed a labor-intensive medical service, not unlike the celebrated Bas Congo parastatal Foreami, but expressed doubt about conventional hygiene censusing in Belgian colonial medicine: "The ideal of working until the last patient is no longer contagious is long, thankless, misleading, and beyond the normal duty of a doctor."[55]

Schwers also sought to wash his hands of further involvement, including in the scientific enterprise proposed: "I am not competent in the matter, I think my role is finished." He distanced himself from venereal disease as a banality with futile treatments, declaring it "dangerous to propagate the idea that antigonorrheal treatment should be the chief remedy against sterility."[56]

His big discovery had come when examining patients in Basankusu's Gombe *chefferie*, where he noticed several cases of testicular hypoplasia (incompletely developed testes) and cryptorchidism (undescended testes). These men's genitals seemed reduced by more than half. He had tried to establish a method for measuring testicles, but without reference points was unable to classify size, as was done for spleens. He was curious about their functional value but regretted that sperm exams were impossible "under these conditions." He noted that men did not present with "the somatic constitution or psyches of eunuchs," but they were "less male," having undergone "a form of physiological castration." They were two times less likely to be married as well, he asserted. He then estimated that some 4 to 13 percent of men in the region had hypoplasia, with 13 percent among Basankusu's Mongo "race." The low birth rate and the genital lesions in men seemed to run on parallel curves. Thus, endocrinological deficiencies were the principal cause of the low birth rate. Schwers also developed the idea of a "primitive" low birth rate, which joined childhood cryptorchidism with adult hypoplasia. He attributed the problem to functional issues in the endocrine glands, especially secretion activity of the anterior lobe of the pituitary gland. Parathyroid troubles were likely involved, but only a specialized laboratory would enable better understanding their role.[57]

As Daniel Pick has shown for European contexts, degeneration works through a "pathologising language" with "no one stable referent," relating to "a fantastic kaleidoscope of concerns and objects." Joining ideas about a social body—a nation, a race—with fears about skin color, respectability, and birth rate, degenerationist language tends to combine "a technical diagnosis and a racial prophecy."[58] Schwers was drawn to endocrinological thinking in a post–shell shock era, when the fashion for neurasthenia had largely faded and before the endocrinologist Hans Selye coined the word *stress*.[59] Using organic metaphors, Schwers spoke of primary and secondary causes of the birth rate, combining nineteenth-century degenerationism with a strand of endocrinology emphasizing physical shock.[60] He alternated between underlining sterility as inherent in the "race" and as resulting from "primitive," "primordial" shock. He suggested that early colonial occupation led to the profound disturbance that weakened familial spirit and maternal instinct.[61] Yet Schwers spoke more in an abstract, dehistoricized language, not in structural terms about harm. His thinking had him keenly writing up his evidence about shrunken testicles and their late descent,[62] as signs explaining reproductive trouble and foretelling extinction.[63]

Rebeka Botungu and Trees

Likili did not speak of extinction. It told of origins and circulation, the movements of charms, and genealogies of destruction and creativity, often in auspicious ways suggesting reproduction, continuity, new connections and belonging.

Focusing on pregnancy, fertility, and wealth, on eliminating bad fortune and charms, Likili stories suggest that genealogical narration accompanied its spread through space, transmitting a charm to a next place with associates and kin. The insides of trees and a woman named Rebeka Botungu were vital as Likili moved and a network formed. In one version,[64] a Likili specialist produced a magical mixture. The third healer to receive Likili, Nkelengo from Bonsombe, brought the charm home. Soon after women in Bonsombe village became pregnant!

Another version began with Rebeka Botungu near home along the Botomba. She hailed from Mongo rivals, the amazing magicians, the Ngombe. One day, Rebeka worked magic with eight *lilenge* fruit near a *boilondo* tree. She took the results to the eminent Bolima, her husband. Wife and husband combined their magical substances, before Bolima passed the mixture to Nkelengo. Nkelengo joined Bolima's son, Isenge, and they passed the magic to others, ensuring Likili's arrival in Ingende territory. It spread through four Ingende chiefdoms, while its transmission resembled a line of descent.[65]

A third origin story began with a Ngombe man entering a forest and finding a Moanga tree. This huge bote was speaking as if a voice of God, ordering everyone to destroy bad charms and replace them with Likili. Abundance in fishing, hunting, and pregnancies would result. When he went home, this man told one and all about the tree's singing words. Soon they went to listen. A healer named Bokoka went up close. While praying to the tree, the Moanga split open. As the tree insides became visible, Bokoka removed ingredients: medicines for fertility, fishing, hunting. After discussing what to do next, everyone returned home, gathered together everyone else, and told them to collect all bad charms thwarting bounty in fish, game, pregnancy, and newborns. Bokoka ordered eliminating them as refuse and waste. Combining more ingredients with Moanga medicines, he put the mixture in a big antelope horn. Then he gave some away to protect houses and villages.[66] Likili forbade eating lilenge fruit[67] and women from consuming *bombende*. A woman could prepare antelope, but if she ate some, her child would be born a cripple (a *bombende*). Likili forbade foods causing sickness and taught how to mix remedies for the ill. To make these effective, a sick person had to offer a chicken, plus five or ten francs.[68]

Likili also commanded avoiding sexual relations during daylight and all "seeing of female sexual organs." After burning bote, Likili led women wishing children to a special hut of palm fronds. A man could only go inside with his wife, a woman only with her husband. Realigning marriage and sexuality was a Likili goal, the Christian interpreter Ekonyo specified: "Every woman has to go with her own husband." Likili had remedies to "conceive immediately," too. Likili's founding mother was a part of all medicines, as spirit, power, and special wife. The very act of accepting a Likili bote entailed symbolically marrying Rebeka Bontungu. A woman who had stopped menstruating—a common problem in the region—would begin having periods again. After two or three months, she would be pregnant and then bear a child. Likili suggested life "populated with children again."[69]

Brussels Scolds

The reproductive sciences in the colony fantasized about many babies too. The dream grew when recast, as Equateur's priests were wont to do, *against* the dark vision of a dying, damaged race. Hulstaert and Boelaert instead imagined a robust linguistic nation in the making, durable with zest, language, and Lianja performances.[70]

Colonial field science sometimes startled. When Schwers's report moved north to the aloof, patrician metropole, for example, it left behind the humid, "primitive" zone where dread seeped in as an everyday mood. In November 1937, it arrived at the Ministry of Colonies in Brussels, with a recommendation from Governor General Ryckmans for more research. The cover letter complemented Schwers for shedding "new light" on Tshuapa's demographic problems and working under "often difficult conditions." It warned: "saving the decadent Tshuapa population will require a huge financial sacrifice."[71] The doctor's hypotheses seemed "seductive," embracing "banal and brutal causes" of "devitalization." Three factors were salient: partial inhibition of reproductive function, alteration of the endocrine complex, and hereditary transmission of organic deficiencies.[72] Specialized research in endocrinological pathology and anthropology would require extra funds because infrastructure and specialist staffing were limited. Funds might be sought from the Rockefeller Foundation or Belgian colonial institutes. Ultimately, Ryckmans cast doubt over the "pessimistic impressions," since other causes could be battled "through means we do have," that is, intensifying medical occupation, fighting venereal disease, and promoting moral, economic, nutritional, and hygienic development.[73]

One of Congo's foremost doctors, Rodhain, convened the council of tropical medicine specialists, Drs. Malengreau, Mouchet, Duren, and Trolli, all distinguished clinicians in Belgian colonial medicine. Critique was sharp. Duren began unfavorably with Schwers's examination figures (330 schoolchildren and 1,117 adults in Basankusu town; 7,287 workers in agricultural enterprises; 30,219 customary subjects): the doctor reported on only two of the three groups. Some facts were wrong: the presence of polyandry, for one. His mortality rates at the beginning contradicted those at the end. The diet and copal sections lacked detail. A medical occupation with nineteen centers over a small area, each serving twelve thousand, was unjustified given the limited sleeping sickness. The focus should not be the three territories with the lowest birth rates but rather trypanosomiasis, leprosy, and venereal disease.[74]

The disintegration of morals, endocrinological deficiencies, and hypoplasia were the doctor's conclusion. Yet the endocrinological data were insufficient. Cryptorchidism could be caused by diet alone, and no necessary relationship between cryptorchidism in a child and testicular problems in an adult existed. Whether azoospermia (absence of sperm) accompanied the hypoplasia had been neglected. Most of all, "before launching himself into investigations with a grand style," Schwers should have tried to "sweep the terrain from a demographic and clinical point of view." All his "imprecision" arose from the "rapid medical prospection." Rodhain criticized the attention to endocrinological troubles without elucidating matters of diet and venereal disease. A specialist in endocrinology and anthropology seemed unnecessary, and such a dense medical occupation was too expensive until research suggested it was warranted. Trolli noticed "obscurities" and contradictions. A new study should focus on the once robust, well-nourished Bakutu identified in plain regression with hypoplasia and cryptorchidism.[75] Above all, these tropical specialists insisted that "in-depth medical prospecting" must include detailed consideration of gonorrhea in men and women. Like most doctors of their day, they knew this sexually transmitted disease to be highly sterilizing, so its relative absence from the report was glaring.

Fear of Massacre

Schwers acknowledged "astonishment" in Brussels, yet he remained proud of his conceptual distinction between a "primary" and a "secondary low birth rate." Knowing he had broken with "tradition" by not according gonorrhea a "primordial role," Schwers claimed he did not deny the gonococcus but sought to put it in its proper place. He knew rates were rising as a result of increases in worker camps. He knew of recent studies showing chronic genital infection caused some 65 percent of primary sterility (no live births) and 91 percent of secondary sterility (female infertility with at least one birth). Yet "no one should any longer believe in the simplistic idea: gonorrhea = low birth rate." His report had "left well worn paths," but "not by a love of paradox." Rather, he refused to reduce everything to a single cause.[76]

Ever on the defensive, however, he declared, "I was not negligent," and "I only said my report was a preface for subsequent work." He "personally" proceeded "in the search for gonorrheics, whom I generally entrusted to a native assistant. It's even in this fashion that I fell on the testicular hypoplasia." He wondered whether greater analytic "confrontation between still prolific groups and those hit by sterility" might be in order. He pondered whether he should have limited the study to a small region near a hospital and laboratory facilities. "Pained to have my qualities as a clinician questioned," he reminded that all natives had been "questioned, auscultated, percussed and examined on all sides." That a doctor could assemble good documentation without sophisticated materials had long justified colonial itinerant medicine. But because pure scientific research was in order in this case, well-equipped medical centers were also necessary.[77]

In late March, when the provincial head forwarded Schwers's justifications to Léopoldville, he also noted that Tshuapa had too few doctors for a new survey.[78] The governor general's office replied that "banal and known causes" should not be forgotten.[79] Schwers complained about the quality of provincial health care: district doctors were overworked, drugs arrived in small quantities, the reallocation of medics to better cover Basankusu and Befale was impractical, the road network was incomplete, crop development remained slow, territorials were not controlling native travel, money for new medical posts was absent, and more medical work inside worker camps was impossible given present staffing.[80] In March 1938, Ryckmans suggested a more careful prospection was in order, though money was not forthcoming. The often irritable doctor Schwers insisted that he was tired of banal causes and ordinary solutions. Everyday district health care was dreary, stymied, and broke. Fed up, he no longer wanted to hear anything more about "saving Tshuapa populations." Without new funding, he did not want a study commission either.[81] By late January 1938, bored and restless, he wrote to his boss: Would the chief medical doctor please reexamine his situation since he had practically nothing to do?[82]

In the end, the Brussels interpretation of wrongdoing, of Schwers's preference for "a grand style," was not untrue. Yet, his superiors, Van Hoof and Ryckmans, had conceptualized an unrealistic scale for this doctor's investigations. Still, why had Schwers not examined sperm? He wrote that "circumstances of the bush" limited his capacity to act. His words point less to infrastructure than patient attitude. "One mustn't think of it," he wrote of sperm collecting, adding, "If I had tried to take samples, I would have been immediately massacred."[83]

It is time to return to the hostile Likili dances, the gestures of sweeping away doctors with flywhisks. The ferment of Likili, its capacity to enable giving birth again like "before the whites," paralleled debates over medical causes. The simultaneities intertwined diagnostics and therapeutic practice with bitter, fearful emotions. Involved were the alarmist mission pamphlet, Likili's dissent before medical exams, and Schwers's intrusive tour. Nervous colonial medical practices *seeped* into Likili, its hierarchies and record-keeping. The kind of hostility that emerged stopped at least this one colonial doctor in his tracks, while influencing the way medical investigation turned from women's bodies toward the easier visibility of men's.

Anachrony and Sight

Jadot forms an interesting analytic pair with the often clumsy, expedient, self-justifying Schwers. The magistrate who investigated Maria N'koi anticipated a venereal epidemic in his degenerationist short story with notions of survival and extinction swirling around his characters. Schwers never wrote a short story. Yet he took stigmata to a new level with shock, a lexicon drawn in part from these post–Great War years and the new field of endocrinology. His words ultimately blamed colonial subjects for being unable to rally in the face of the "shock" of "civilization."

It is also worthwhile comparing Schwers with Protestant missionary doctors of Equateur. State doctors rarely left behind personal, literary and photographic documentation, but these American doctors did. A few years ago, during ten days in Nashville working in the archives of the Disciples of Christ Congo mission, I found the private papers of three doctors. Dr. Royal J. Dye grew up posing for photographs with his regal first name and fancy bicycle in Ionia, Michigan. When he came back from Congo about 1902, he orchestrated photographs showing off as an imperial, tropical star with exotic loot to display. Though in Congo at the height of the rubber boom and bust, only his wife left behind traces about the violence of this time, including remarkable biographies of women, one telling of rape.[84] The irascible hunter from Texas, Jaggard, was easily irked before the pomposity of colleagues working in the large mission hospital on the Congo River, at Bolenge and near Coq. With his frontier mentality, Jaggard relished working in a remote bush hospital, from where he would go elephant hunting when fed up with the tedium of surgery and patient care. Research was the last thing on his mind, but he left behind perceptive prose, analyzing infertility, childbirth, and infection. Dr. Barger was interwar clinician and researcher of the three. He compiled striking photographs about leprosy and treponemal yaws in children.[85]

I spent much of one Nashville day moving patiently from one Barger photograph to the next. Some showed patients receiving injections or waiting out-doors on long benches. Others were staff photos, with Barger posing with his trained nurses and assistants and one close-up of an assistant whose job was to work the bandage-pressing machine (see figures 4.2–4.5). I gasped when first seeing this photograph from about 1924. Most rubber violence ended about 1906. Iconic historical event and a slice of this man's autobiography suddenly, simultaneously parachuted themselves into consciousness. Congolese with stumps for arms? Many know images depicting them so, standing upright and posed about 1905, wrapped in white cloth, their missing hands long gone, their black stumps displayed in high, white-black contrast. These photographs were ammunition in propaganda wars over conditions in Leopold's Congo. They have been in circulation again, especially since 1996 as journalists and humanitarian organizations have grappled with Congo's violent past and pres-ent, while seeking to stir emotions and donations through publishing such shock-photos once again.

The Barger photograph seems to be the only visual evidence about a man who survived the "Rubber Wars," as the verso explains. The adult suggests a child orphan, adopted into this mission. The photograph speaks to the way a past endured and could erupt as *anachrony*,[86] disrupting the everyday with its out-of-sequence character, disordering temporality too. Suddenly, a past may turn up in plain daylight and jar. Freud wrote that a "severed hand" has an "uncanny effect."[87] Such a sight—whether of a living man or of his photograph years later—disturbs. We would do well to wonder about *shock*, Schwers's re-petitive, compulsive word. This photograph, never part of a lantern show, sug-gests that visual reminders of horrific violence and disabling injury remained part of daily life in interwar Equateur. One came in the late 1930s, when some missionaries at Lotumbe adopted and saved the life of a skeletal infant. While the mother was an obedient Christian, "The father has no hands. They were cut off at the time of the rubber war in Congo."[88] A first instant of recognition could stun with fright.

It was a world in which Equateur's chief doctor saw or fantasized about shrunken testicles. Dr. Schwers's fixations and this photograph, though chrono-logically separate, belong together thematically, analytically. As a counterpoint, it alludes to a disturbing register of the everyday, flickering with history and memory, recognition and misrecognition, terror, guilt, and dread. Biopolitics and pity reside in the hospital worker's story and photographs too. His injury occurred during a time of war, when removing hands from corpses and some-times live bodies combined weapon, ritual, and bureaucratic routine. It was a time of intense nervousness, a colonial state fraught and alarmed, while the

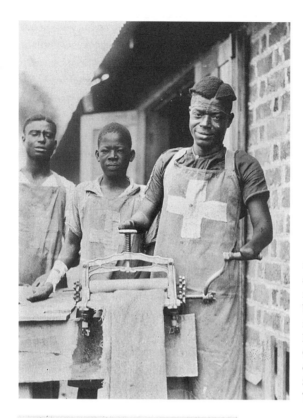

FIGURE 4.2 Hospital assistant working a mission hospital's bandage-pressing machine. Bolenge hospital, ca. 1924. Courtesy of Disciples of Christ Historical Society, Nashville, Tennessee (DCHS).

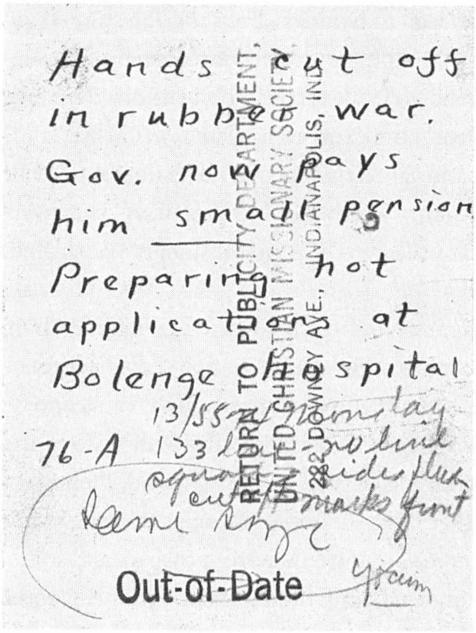

Hands cut off
in rubber war.
Gov. now pays
him small pension
Preparing hot
applications at
Bolenge Hospital
RETURN TO PUBLICITY DEPARTMENT,
UNITED CHRISTIAN MISSIONARY SOCIETY
222 DOWNEY AVE., INDIANAPOLIS, IND.
76-A
Out-of-Date

FIGURE 4.3 Verso of Bolenge hospital assistant photograph, ca. 1924. Courtesy of DCHS.

FIGURE 4.4 Uncropped group photograph of the Bolenge hospital staff, 1924. Courtesy of DCHS.

FIGURE 4.5 Cropped close-up of present and absent hands from Bolenge hospital staff photograph, 1924. Courtesy of DCHS. This cropped version draws attention to a terrible injury and perhaps too, by implication, the everyday flickering of such mutilation: between visibility and invisibility. Not only do the stumps for arms become more sharply perceptible through this magnification, but through the same infringement (tightly framing the injury), the man's incorporation within a social group—the mission hospital community of the original (figure 4.4)—is mislaid.

Bolenge mission of Dye huddled, quietly working to rescue a few perhaps, but surely too fearful of losing their evangelical perch in Congo to raise a fuss.

No one seems to have noticed that Schwers's mission covered a swath of the same region where a rubber economy in raiding, plunder, and death produced terrible violence in the 1900s. The correlation remained unsaid. Did Ryckmans, Van Hoof, and Schwers understand they were talking about groups who had been at the vortex of rubber wars in the Abir concession and further afield? Ryckmans, a refined intellectual and literary gentleman, first arrived in Congo in 1915 and became its leading governor and exacting technician in 1934. He could not have *not* known about this sinister period in Free State and Belgian history (while knowing about not knowing is relevant here). For a doctor like Schwers, who arrived a decade or more later, a deep, primordial temporality grounded in Darwinian questions seemed to have almost wiped clean any slate of historical violence, now thirty to forty years old. That was part of the seductive power of social Darwinian logic. Causality became one with "race." When it alternated with a dehistoricized language of shock, it suggested less war or violence than frailty, perhaps congenital in nature.

Schwers once suggested that shock occurred three generations back. Yet unlike Jadot or Schebesta, neither Schwers nor Van Hoof took much interest in dating or history, or mentioned violence during the Free State years. But the repulsion and fright betrays a colonial mood, at the same time that the Barger photograph confirms that likely no one in Equateur, Schwers included, could ignore a past of mutilation.

Schwers used *event–aftermath* language, not at the level of history but for hormones and secretions. He spoke of traumatism and feebleness in relation to an unspecified precursor time of shock. His language was somatic, implying a shock in a deep past with destructive, bodily effects. As the space of relevant experience narrowed to a medicalized human body, in this doctor's eyes de-historicized tremors—the shock of two colliding civilizations—marked the individual body and the collective, ethnic race. Schwers spoke of the primary as deep-seated, an obscure cause of a very long duration. When he summarized this primary level as *shock*, the word had him grabbing for endocrinology texts, whose contents he combined with a tainted, damaged race. In this formulation, the primary level preceded secondary, more recent causes. Only the latter worked at the banal level of venereal infection.

Such degenerationist shock talk ran counter to the way the Flemish missionaries on the scene viewed childlessness and suffering. They sensed the violence of such language and its implications at the level of policing and the state.

State Critic

Hulstaert also adopted event-aftermath language but in a vitalist, protective register. He romanticized Likili as hope while pointing to the dangers of disrupting healing with a stark police raid.

As Likili flared, this priest had been admiring its prohibitions against sexual relations during daylight and outside marriage.[89] The Church, he proposed, might make Likili a point of departure for teachings about divine nature aligned with ancient family and social order, in order to "reawaken their vitality." In 1957, Hulstaert's definition of Likili remained optimistic: "kind of magical practice for returning conjugal fidelity and fertility, only briefly in vogue due to the intervention of the administration."[90]

Hulstaert opposed the state for moving in rapidly, harshly suppressing Likili as a dangerous "secret society." In his eyes, Likili was a fertility "cult" that proved the Mongo will to reproduce. Hulstaert surely knew about the racial theorizing of those such as Ryckmans, Van Hoof, Armani, and Schwers. His vitalist orientation had him seeking contrary evidence about Mongo zest. He defended Likili's "magical practices" as "the right thing to do at this time," since the "aim was to have many children," making it a "success among this population suffering from a terrible falling birth rate," "trying to alleviate a dire social need."[91]

The state's "interference" seemed to increase "discouragement in a population that . . . has a greater need for encouragement." By criminalizing an effort that "natives view as a purposeful defense against dying out," the message conveyed was in his stark words: "the state wants their tribe to disappear." Congolese, bewildered by "severe action," witnessed the banning of a "practice of magic" for the first time. The practices were not "essentially different," though Likili sought to "remedy a real social distress." The use of camwood paste confirmed unruliness in dim official eyes, which suspected financial exploitation too. The state imagined it as a "rebellious movement," partly expressed in "resistance to undressing for medical examinations" as well as an "uncommonly rigid attitude of women against seduction."[92] Ekonyo spoke about nudity before doctors. Only the hostile letter writers who objected to the Losilo pamphlet's tone suggested growing Congolese anger with Europeans seducing women and girls through coin. Evidently, during Likili, access to women closed down for white agents of all kinds.

Sexual access is an important issue, as we will see as we turn now to Likili within a different milieu and archive.

A Nervous Chiefdom

When Ekonyo concluded his Likili essay, he commented on the dangers of delicate magical acts—picking apart palm nut fibers, touching a meal's crumbs—and also his research method: "I have often questioned people about it, and they have always given me these reasons for it."[93]

Yet since the arrests, getting anyone to talk became impossible: "Nowadays they will no longer reveal these things clearly because the government has stepped in. If you question them, they no longer tell it in the same way."[94]

Ekonyo was not a Likili follower, and he turned up dead, apparently eliminated through "magical practices" directed against he who divulged secrets.[95]

Ekonyo's death suggests Likili's darker side. While it often had men gathering bark and leaves with women preparing medicines, Likili also knew sharper hierarchies among men. It sometimes evoked a world of governance parallel to the colonial regime, with Likili positions translated into French bureaucratic forms: district commissioner, head administrator, assistant administrator, police commissioner, and policeman. (A *kwoko* woman leader came at the bottom.)[96] The nervous state knew layers too, of course, with a *big state* stretching from territorials and governors in Congo up to the minister in Brussels, while standing beside chiefdoms with chiefs, elders, and clerks. Wangata was like a small nervous chiefdom afraid of Likili, we will see.

Conflicts churned around Likili as doctors toured. Some refused medical exams or the doctor's presence. Police arrested Likili bearing hostile flywhisks. But nervousness about infertility extended among many in this milieu. Likili could cause ruin, the odor from a burning Moanga tree killing those who had sex by day. Basankusu's territorial cautioned that like all practices of removing medicine, Likili would prove inconstant, swinging in a perilous direction.[97] A year after the arrests, Likili was again on the move, this time in Coquilhatville territory. It assumed different forms as new personalities took it up. In Wangata, Likili never produced "xenophobia," yet it meant trouble. That the Wangata archive is quite different from the Ingende one matters: A Congolese chief and court clerk produced the documents, not territoral agents beside a priest and literate teacher.[98]

By 1938, Likili was sowing discord. Not all accepted its premises or leaders. In Wangata-Tomba (or Wangata), Likili produced a fray as well as an imaginary about violation. Court clerk Tshoambe documented it as aggressive and terrifying. Xenophobia was not his problem, and whites were almost absent. Rather, the trouble involved witches, murder, spirit figures in the night, and the duplicity of Likili officers. Tshoambe pointed at the Bekoko rank of "District Officers" who "only do commerce, stealing the money of others." Likili was changing thought so people "fall into idolatry again," misleading by promising fecundity, "whereas among the Bekoko, not a one has a child."[99] If the entrepreneurial, swindling aspect was striking, so was this accusation that the male leaders were barren.

Tshoambe's report followed the format of a territorial ethnographic report. Under "Causes," he indicated Likili "only ruins villages." He listed commands: "Don't sleep with a woman during the day. On the pain of death, don't have relations with her after 5 o'clock in the morning." Others touched on funerals, reproduction, and food, matters of not seeing corpses, returning safely from distant funerals, and properly nourishing pregnant and nursing women. Sex, hunting, fertility, pregnancy, and death converged into a linked, reproductive domain. If hunting produced food and fertility, giving away antelope would squander fertility.[100]

Tears and Rape in Wangata Hearing

On April 5, the court clerk Tshoambe summoned a territorial to a hearing,[101] asking him to preside over a complaint made by Eale of Bokala against Paul Ifenge of Boangi. Two Wangata-Tomba villages had welcomed Likili: Boangi and Lifumba. Ifenge was leader at the first, Joseph Iluwo at the second. Tshoambe asked them to provide the names of their followers, yet each refused. The invested chief was E. Bongese. After six weeks of assembling evidence, the judgment declared Likili contrary to "public order and Custom." The customary court condemned Iluwo, Ifenge, and Thomas Bokwala; each received a month of penal servitude plus fines. Judged on May 27, 1938, the court announced that if Likili reemerged, any "author" would be relegated.[102]

Iluwo introduced Likili into Tomba after receiving it at Bongese's place. Ifenge went to Basankusu for "the Sect" and then spread it. Bokwala rose to the highest Likili rank. Many in Ifenge and Iluwo became followers. Yet Boangi elders told Tshoambe that Likili caused "ruins and ravages" and should be stopped. They rejected Likili because it was spreading a charm without consent. The clerk opposed Likili because it killed: "Wherever this Sect is accepted, the village that becomes a follower . . . repeatedly dies."[103]

The case pitted Eale against Ifenge. The latter rose to Bokoka rank after receiving the "talisman (sect)" from its Ngombe master.[104] Eale accused Ifenge of being "a true sorcerer" who "troubles our Chiefdom." Rather than using Likili to eliminate curses, Ifenge poisoned with it. When old man Bongolo arrived home one night, he heard Ifenge urging everyone to assemble medicines, but menacingly so: Anyone who did not give up charms would die on the spot. Ifenge also stirred fear by demanding charms that were secrets or objects of wealth.[105]

Eale also accused Ifenge with a story about one who "did not want to cede his animals," and then "you would see tears there." The jump from wealth (animals) to tears suggests violation and escalating distress. The consequences were plain to Eale: "only a few days later, I observed five deaths in my village." Before long Ifenge introduced Likili, a charm with medicines stored in an antelope horn. Ifenge spoke to his horn each morning as "the charm of God" that wanted "all men to remove bad charms," for only Likili to remain. Eale wanted Ifenge known as the one who took five lives, who troubled with Likili, which "may poison a good share."[106]

Ifenge's testimony began with memories of being accused of sorcery after his uncle Chief Bokwala died. The accusations led him beyond the territory for old man Bongolo's charm. Bongolo came to Boangi to remove bad charms and heal. In the process, Ifenge became a Molima healer and cured twenty. Before long, Iluwo arrived with Likili, famous for being stronger than Molima yet not wanting "other talismans." Ifenge assembled everyone, removed Molima, and went to Basankusu in a healing journey "with me three strong men and two youth." Upon returning, he explained Likili's promise: "everyone agreed . . . and gave me all bad talismans." Ifenge insisted no coercion had been involved. He returned to the register of sorrow and crying: "I did not . . . *produce tears*," insisting Likili did not harm but worked to "protect villages and give fertility to women."[107]

Yet he accused Eale of possessing "bad talismans" and using fear. Ifenge painted himself as innocent and still: "I don't walk in all villages. I stay at my place. How could I trouble the Chiefdom?" Chief Eugène Nsaka was responsible because he let Likili enter Coquilhatville territory when he allowed some Ngombe to introduce it into his chiefdom. The Ingende territorial was taking measures against Likili at the time. Soon, Chief Nsaka went into hiding at the home of an old chief Bombute.[108]

Severe measures were needed to calm these villages, Tshoambe insisted. He had relegation in mind. Likili ran counter to Christianity. "Useless to allow it for natives," this clerk pronounced about this charm or sect aimed at theft, taking "as much as possible from followers," while promising women would "have enough children." Likili "only steals money" and "scandalizes," while people abandon "the true religion" and fall into "idolatry."[109]

Most alarming in the eyes of elders who critiqued Likili were its two Belanga phantoms, Boale and Lotengu, who were producing visions, dreams, and orders. "These two Belanga travel in the night, and during waking time they order people to throw away other charms."[110] The two roaming spirits were fiendish. The male spirit Boale troubled women alone in their beds. The allusion to rape was strong. Boale had sex with women, and some were in poor health afterward. More women, it was feared, would become sick and die. Murder produced less alarm among elders, it seems, than these spirit rapes. A woman haunted while sleeping would know upon awaking that Baole visited, seeing between her legs fluids shed during his stay. The liquid made her ill—unless she joined Likili.

The coercive dimension is interesting, as are the psychic, historical resonances of these violations. This evidence of Likili in Wangata speaks to experiences and nightmares of bodily violation and links them to infertility. It also suggests that the fear of rape or these nocturnal spirit visitations may have motivated female participation in Likili. Rape was once widespread among the ancestors, the grandmothers of this generation. The dream content suggests powerful "screen memories,"[111] that is, interjections of composite imprints, some historical, about intimate bodily raids, reproductive destruction, rape, and ruin, even if with mixture and distortion.

When Iluwo first went to receive Likili, another man named Pierre Bongese told Iluwo about substances excellent for women's *lavements*. The attention to women's medicine is not startling, given Likili's emphasis on fertility as well as the ubiquity of lavements in everyday therapeutic practice. That women became the focus of Likili healing and conflicts is unsurprising. Iluwo depicted Likili as a necessity, the solution to the main causes of fertility trouble: envy and conflict. In sending away bad charms, Likili was a way of removing "enmities among us." Its power was "to reconcile us, so women would have fertility."[112]

Iluwo's words point to a critical dimension of mobile charms (also discussed by Ekonyo): they often begin as a wish to heal by eliminating medicines that others used to harm. These bote navigated rivalry and envy, even an injurious sexuality like spirit rape. Likili offered, at least for a while, reconciliation—a temporary, if fictional, clean slate within a space of resentment, suspicion, and competitive charms. In eliminating invidious charms, in sending away bad medicines and welcoming the new, a collectivity tentatively formed, until hierarchy, hate, and nightmares resurfaced, calling again for riddance with purging.

Science in the Bush and Somatization

The nervous and biopolitical states clashed—with each other, with missionaries, *and* with Congolese involved in practices of elimination. Ewewe movements and gestures, we saw, involved sweeping out with song and dance in public space, but also inside women's bodies. Likili flywhisk use became an expulsive parallel, gesturing fury and distaste. Revulsion also surfaced in Dr. Schwers's language about a primitive shock, about the colonized frail and degenerate, unable to rally in the face of colonizing processes.

Colonial medicine sometimes resembled rape. During this time, when biomedicine focused on research more than care, there were confrontations over gynecological exams. Schwers insisted his demographics came "from a long and detailed questioning of each woman, and all those who know natives know the patience this required." When he examined a few in depth at clinics at Boende and Basankusu, he discussed each case with a doctor colleague and achieved "a beautiful clinical documentation." He and his Congolese assistant did not press to examine women after some first efforts. Medical exams had "fatal limits, imposed by the very circumstances of the bush." Yet after trying "several times to do gynecological exams in *gites d'etapes* [colonial rest houses]," he learned it "only resulted in dispersal." Though he examined over 35,000 during his "five hard months" of "starting at dawn and ending late to the light of lamps," he only did 196 gynecological exams. He concluded: "Gynecological exams are impossible in the bush: they would have immediately compromised the success of the mission."[113] If examining women was difficult for infrastructural reasons, even attempting the invasive practice seems to have stirred anger, refusal, and sabotage, as the Likili confrontations with Charlier suggest.

As Schwers did his work, therefore, women's bodies became more unavailable, though it seems he also never forced the issue. During his few gynecological exams,[114] he found some chronic uterine inflammation and appendages.[115] He examined seventy-nine Bakutu women in Boende territory, seventeen Bosaka at the Wema Catholic mission, and one hundred Mongo in Basankusu. The "more *évolué*" women of towns appeared for exams "after abundant irrigations that made a study of trichomonas on the basis of secretions impossible." In customary areas without "an appropriate installation," he and his assistant "had to limit ourselves to asking women about their miscarriages and stillbirths." He mistrusted their answers: "No faithful information could be obtained. It is necessary to stay a long time in the region to get women to make confidences on this point." Comprehension was a problem: "In the bush, it is useless to question women on the abundance and regularity of their periods: they wouldn't understand the question."[116]

During this time of investigation, Congolese women were engrossed in other kinds of bodily practice that mixed healing with dissent. That some Likili villages were places where men and women worried about the safety of women sleeping alone at night should make us pause. Much suggests distress not as idiomatic (as in the idioms of distress of cultural psychiatry), but distress as somatic *and* as psychic, as symbolic *and* lived. Amenorrhea (the absence of menstruation unrelated to pregnancy) was not mentioned in reports by Equateur doctors. But Ekonyo's observations suggest that it was pervasive among Likili women. Many were likely overworked and undernourished. Schwers, drawn to the endocrinological, named the harm at stake in relation to hypothalamus malfunction, hormonal imbalance and pituitary tumors. Some evidence also suggests low body weight due to high energy expenditure and overtaxation. Knowing exactly what Schwers saw, imagined, or exaggerated is impossible, though his scientific vocabulary and penchant for the endocrinological suggests he may have witnessed profound malnutrition.

Could some have had AIDS? It is plausible, given current age estimates of the "most recent common ancestor" of HIV-1 group M in central Africa, the viruses responsible for pandemic AIDS.[117] More certain is the kinds of gynecological practice at play. A doctor Prum reported Portuguese merchants selling *bocks à lavement* around 1937.[118] These enema and douching devices, widely used in Europe and condemned there as Malthusian contraceptives, were available in interwar Equateur.[119] Van Hoof assumed that such manufactured devices were recent, yet internal irrigation seems as ancient in central Africa as calabash syringes. New, commercial clyster devices may have encouraged more douching as menstrual regulation[120] or pregnancy avoidance.[121] Schebesta observed that enema clysters were ordinary, often a mere utensil in Nkundo kitchens. Enemas in the wider region have long been about food and digestion, flow and blockage.[122] But cleaning the belly was also important in preparing for and accomplishing childbirth. Women used diverse enema recipes during prenatal, childbearing, and postnatal periods, as did mothers in irrigating children, wives husbands, and within other intimate relations. Cleansing and bodily flow are a pair.[123]

Noteworthy was the accent placed on reproductive bits: umbilical cords as medicines capable of disturbing or harming. Such ingredients suggest a reproductive poetics to menstrual absence, pregnancy loss, and one-child maternity, not unlike the correlative *nseka* or scare-medicines (discussed in chapter 3). Including pounded umbilical cord in a Likili charm or an irrigation mixture may have felt auspicious, capable of restoring menstruation or creating a pregnancy—until a stillbirth or maternal death resulted. The woman who woke with a phantom's fluids between her legs may have sought out internal cleansing. Rape, however figurative, made the meanings of medicinal ingredients harmful. In symbolic logic, as in everyday experience, infertility signifies and is sensed as dryness, drought, or aridity,[124] while often being experienced as event, as a miscarriage or other marked reproductive disappointment.

Conclusion

Likili used flywhisks to sweep out intrusive doctors, at a time when biomedicine meant *more research*, more dread-filled, hypothetical thinking, *not* pharmaceuticals or care. Likili had its own experimentality. It burst into visibility with the hostile wielding of flywhisks, an excellent reminder of Fanon's words about biomedicine producing anger and ambivalence in colonial (and post-colonial) contexts.[125]

That gynecological ritual also intensified in this region complicates the medical history of this zone, where one woman in three was childless in the 1930s. Scholars have long pointed to the psychic and religious dimensions of central African healing.[126] From an epidemiological perspective, purging bodily insides that already knew infection may well have driven sterilizing venereal disease deeper into wombs. This kind of somatization has *not* received the attention it deserves. Wondering about the way bodily and psychic wounds, including the spell of rape in the 1900s, endured is worthwhile. These injuries remained not only within bodies, irrigation practices, or nightmares. Rather, the evidence suggests that harm persisted across generations, as the somatic mingled with screen-memories, history, and repetition. The past would suddenly rear itself in Equateur, with a song's refrain, a funereal dance, a nightmare about a sexual violation, or something like the sight of a man with stumps for arms, hands removed decades before.

Schwers's reporting suggests some sloppiness amid strident, florid views. Ryckman's expectations had been unrealistic. Schwers never took Van Hoof's advice to slow down, digest and organize his findings. The ambitious project was carried out when it was unlikely that many women would accept pelvic exams. How Schwers imposed himself once fear of "massacre" entered consciousness is unclear, though surely he had access to soldiers.[127] The unfriendly atmosphere had him assume it was best to stick with men's bodies. At the same time, his extinction fantasies reduced Equateur's profoundly violent past to a single, vague word: *shock*.

As the regime became strongly biopolitical, confronting widespread childlessness, its key doctor was effacing a deeply violent past. Reproductive maladies likely became rife first during and after conquest, a time when violent sexualities would have contributed to spreading sexually transmitted disease. In the 1930s, as the word *sterility* became explicit, literate Catholic men were annoyed about white men seducing their sisters and daughters. The Belgian Congo had long grappled with the forest peoples of Equateur. Once profoundly violated, they remained fretful about fertility and social reproduction, and for good reason. Memories of dreadful wars and devastation may have been conscious and motivating, as were conditions in the present.

Those of 1937 were using dance, song, and medicines to purge the toxic, mend, and reproduce worlds. While healing and harming remains an important conceptual double in African history,[128] in much of equatorial Africa, the salient pair spoke to purging and reweaving, eliminating and mending.[129] This twosome shaped event and countered event. This repetition suggests how violence and a spirited latitude endured across generations, through bodies and imaginations, intellects, and dreams.

The history covered a duration in somatic events and processes. When mediated through surprise and disbelief—the rude *jolt* of biomedical researchers inserting instruments into women's most intimate insides—vernacular healing ignited into battle. The nervous state was soon targeting Likili, and the persons of this state hovered less in watch and wait mode. Rather, they were distilling a critical, new clinical category—xenophobia. Its diagnostics aimed not at medical signs or symptoms, but at triage in relation to security, risk, and rage.

Unease about barrenness surfaced across a wide spectrum and involved all kinds of fixations and trafficking in ideas and techniques. The Schwers mission stressed infertility, and his clinical surveys noted people frail and sickly, populations "dying out" from "malaise" and "race suicide." Yet the same persons were often swift, volatile, aggressive, and resentful, especially as they pursued their own therapies and dancing. Conflict erupted over gynecological exams. When it did, Likili therapies became even more important to the Congolese women and men who acted to evict.

It is time to return to Ewewe, a periodic performance about death, memory, and reproduction. Its logics were about bodily and generational flow. Congolese therapeutics burst forth into visibility, again and again. Therapeutic ritual embraced enema logics too, moving medicines in and refuse out of the body. All these layers of healing amounted to more than vernacular *color*. Ewewe and Likili were available as critical, energizing might within social process and sometimes as *event*, with expulsive gestures sometimes fusing with insurgent healing.

Still, in this colonial milieu, not all therapeutics burst forth as event, as "aleatory encounters" of startling hostility.[130] There is no evidence that Ewewe produced a clash or skirmish, unlike Likili. Most therapies were invisible to the colonial eye, practiced at a physical or perceptive distance from territorials and their posts, police, and soldiers. Ewewe and Likili were quite unlike Maria N'koi, Njondo, and Yebola. The latter trio formed a female template that healed through an autobiographical story of transformation: from ailing and trembling in forest, soon perched amid trees, before a long seclusion of care and dance began. There was no *event* with Yebola, not one that the archive offers up as public conflict (just Boelaert's appreciation in an article). Maria N'koi, iconic in the template, burst forth into visibility before many pairs of eyes. Yielding fierceness, the storms soon militarized. Her fame, however, in many ways grew from her furtive capacity to disable, to disrupt the powers of all who harmed: sorcerers, domestic and colonial alike. Such sinister, desirous forces of envious vying and harming were part of everyday village life. The Likili evidence in this chapter vividly clarified this less visible realm of healing and harming in "customary" spaces and lives.

Colonial labor exigencies drove Schwers's research mission. The idea was to map out healthy and contaminated zones. Standard pronatalist solutions, first used in Congo's mining zones in the 1920s, lurked in Ryckmans's expectations for the future. He imagined birth bonuses and maternity clinics, even a special Equateur "fertility clinic" as an "experiment worth doing" one day. He wondered about putting prophylactic venereal cabins in worker camps, since results at the Irebu military camps were promising. The governor general scripted the Bwaka as prolific warriors, worth recruiting into Tshuapa's plantations and protecting through stringent venereal surveillance. In contrast, Songo workers received sharp and paradoxical words, as indocile, refractory, but also frail.[131] Such contradictory oppositions run throughout this history of colonial perceptions: Nervousness flickered between sensing defiance and infirmity. The next chapter turns to these dimensions, while also exploring Ryckman's daydreams and projects. At the center of them were Songo as persons and as a chiefdom, turned into a curious development project.

CHAPTER 5

A Penal Colony, an Infertility Clinic

Dr. Schwers and his grim, degenerationist theories lingered in Equateur. While his mission report was poorly received in Brussels, provincial doctor he remained, and medical and venereal matters continued under him into the early postwar years. Times were changing: the tempo of the state's biopolitical face quickened, expanding its experiments and reach up until decolonization. By the 1950s, a specialized infertility clinic was operating in Befale. The nervous state, on the move since at least the early 1930s, was organizing security sweeps and a penal colony during these same postwar years.

This chapter, more than the others, peers down from above, perceiving mostly through state archives. It juxtaposes the clinical and the carceral as contrapuntal, partially intersecting, streams of experiment, each with a focal, institutional site: with work in development, population, and health at Songo and Befale, and counterinsurgency campaigns from Befale and in the penal camp at Ekafera. This doubled seam produced a fractious, contradictory tonality in Befale territory. Medical schemes aimed high at vanity and triumph everywhere in postwar Belgian Congo, billing itself more than ever as a "model colony," while expanding its international allure.

Internally, its biopolitical largess aimed at securing allegiance, cooperation, and smiling mothers, babies, and families. With great insight, Dominic Pistor has suggested that the Belgian solution to its mounting troubles with Kitawala insurgents lay in development.[1] My interpretation

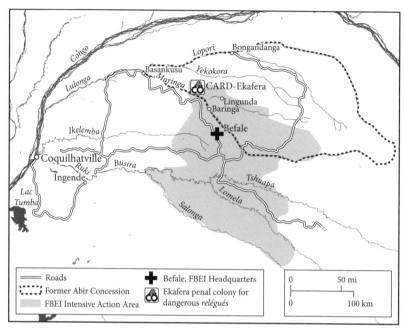

MAP 5.1 Ekafera, Befale, FBEI, and roads in the 1950s. The 1950s saw roads completed and the arrival of the FBEI development project; the map shows the proximity of the Ekafera penal colony and FBEI-Befale. Map by Jake Coolidge.*

is instead located in a region with punishing labor requirements, a charged, scandalous past, and from the 1930s, a nearly unbroken fixation with disappearance, elimination, and extinction. How the state's two faces met, interrelated, and clashed remains a key question. Each mode of presence, as we have seen, long aimed at remedies to the reproductive (the disappearing and the sterile) and to the insurgent, defiant, and evasive. Each culminated in an enclosed space: the Befale infertility clinic and the penal colony for dangerous, relegated, religious rebels at Ekafera, some fifty miles away (see map 5.1). Each space came with buildings, beds, and personnel, goals, epidemiological words, and mechanisms for triage. Both generated power, control, and discipline—investigating and treating bodies and maladies in the first, and confining and lashing persons in the second.

The two thrusts disclose a modernist, paranoid colonial state on the brink of decolonization. When Basil Davidson traveled through Congo about 1952, it was with prescience that he contemplated Belgium's colonial achievements (efficiencies in enabling skilled industrial labor and providing health and welfare) and their twisted effects. A relentless, belittling paternalism hindered post-primary schooling and fed profound disquiet. Indeed, since the armed

Bushiri rebellion, nervousness had been mounting, expressing itself in a swelling, costly security apparatus and mounting numbers of political prisoners.[2] At the same time, seduction had become a goal of development, with well-funded projects promising and engineering well-being. Enticing Congolese away from dissident religious movements was central to the agenda. Sometimes the moods of particular spaces surface: a Coquilhatville meeting room, the Ekafera penal colony, the Befale clinic. While examining state measures of diverse kinds, the chapter also reads for the vernacular—within Kitawala and Mpadisme, or through hints about verve, resentment, flight, and *motion*. Just as subaltern dreamwork and eviction reverie *motivated* state modalities, archival minutiae enable sensing experience—intended, managed, mismanaged, and lived.

Kimbangu, Kitawala, a Remedy

Ekafera began as remedy. The penal colony was devised to solve growing difficulties with religious rebels whose *movements* had been shaping security operations from at least the 1920s. This chapter necessarily widens its scale to the entire colony (see map 5.2). It alludes to the worlds out of which Ekafera detainees came, as well as the fears that landed them in this remote camp, allegedly in a region of "dying people." Nearly all men, most Ekafera "dangerous *relégués*" hailed from two *xenophobic* movements or currents, Kitawala and strands of Kimbanguism like Mpadism.

Most Kitawala arrived from industrial areas where a proletariat was emergent: the copper mining region of Katanga. The Kimbanguists were from diverse Bas Congo offshoots that splintered after Simon Kimbangu's arrest in 1921. The two strands—the colony's largest, most menacing religious movements—met in and near Ekafera.[3]

Belgian Congo had become rife with *religious movements*, as they were called by colonial officials (and have been by scholars since). The Belgian king had commuted the death sentence of Kimbangu, a prophet who healed and agitated until arrested in 1921. He ended up jailed far away in Katanga, where he died in prison in 1951. When Margery Perham visited in 1931, this distinguished British scholar of matters colonial marveled at Katanga's spotless hospitals and asked to visit this industrial world's prisons. She met Simon Kimbangu in a prison kitchen, and he showed her his Bible, hidden away in a kettle.[4] Decades later, still active Kimbanguist branches included Mpadisme and Mission des Noirs; both were associated with Simon Mpadi, relegated to Tshuapa before the district's penal colony opened its doors.

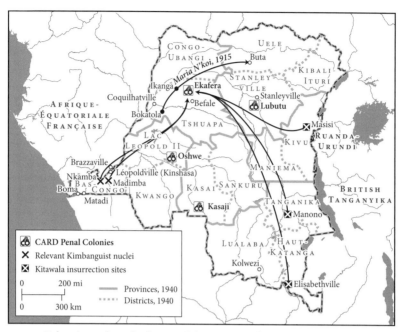

MAP 5.2 Relegation and penal colonies in Belgian Congo. This map represents Maria N'koi's relegation in 1915; the 1930s relegations of Kimbanguists from Bas Congo to Tshuapa, with many later transferred into Ekafera; and the relegations of Kitawala into this penal colony for "dangerous relégués" from the 1940s. (District names and locations were in use from 1935.) Also shown are all penal colonies (CARD institutions) in Congo, major Kimbanguist nuclei, and Kitawala sites of insurrection. Map by Jake Coolidge.**

Kitawala ended up far flung and insurrectionist. While it has received less attention from historians of Africa than Kimbanguism, Congolese historians remain keen to debate the events of Bushiri's rebellion and execution, as I learned while teaching in their midst in 2007 Kinshasa. Kitawala first surfaced in 1920s Katanga, when the Watch Tower preacher Mwana Lesa crossed the border from Northern Rhodesia. His antiwitchcraft cleansing work produced murder, then his hanging. Kitawala became an important modality of prayer and dissent in much of eastern Congo, mediating labor unrest in Katanga's copper mines, a 1941 strike at Monono, and Bushiri's dramatic revolt in 1944–45 against war effort labor near Kivu's Masisi.[5] Basil Davidson made Bushiri the turning point in his argument about Congolese resentment, insurrection, and the expanding security apparatus.[6] Kitawala knew angry rebels, workers, and peasants. They worked through underground mail networks, anticolonial reverie, and homicide. This book provides but a partial history of this complex movement with many regional variants. An Equateur focus shows how Kitawala confronted the regime more than once, as the state worked to relocate and contain them at Ekafera, while their practices spilled into chiefdoms and hygiene routines.

Belgian Congo strived for, but never achieved, the totalitarian. Technicians—territorial administrators—engineered many security matters. Other state branches aimed to win over through maternity care and forms of distraction. Such allures became part of a *glossy* register suggesting, to Belgians at least, hygiene, modernity, and comfort. Still, showdowns between sly, therapeutic rebels and the often frantic regime suggest that nervousness escalated as decolonization neared. The edginess was already there in 1937, when Pierre Ryckmans turned his attention to Equateur again. "Secret societies" and "prophetic activities" were surging dangerously throughout the colony, while a new repressive decree of 1936 aimed at stopping the spread of Kitawala and other movements deemed hierarchical and seditious.[7] Katanga's prisons were overcrowded. Its Kitawala problems pushed the governor general to establish a new kind of institution, indicated with an acronym (CARD), an "agricultural colony, where dangerous *relégués* would be concentrated."[8]

If anyone noticed that Ekafera was in former Abir territory, exactly where a rubber agent laughed at grisly crimes in 1904, they did not note this down. But all the relevant bureaucrats must have known that Ekafera would fall in the same Befale territory receiving worried attention for its low birth rate. The primary idea turned around a colony-wide problem: how to control, contain, and *concentrate* malcontents by placing a CARD penal colony in this remote Equateur setting. First in line were those attracting followers with religious languages of dissent. Ryckmans wrote Equateur's governor, seeking five hundred to a thousand isolated hectares. Provincial authorities soon offered up a marshy "no man's land" between the Maringa and Yekokora rivers, where some Boyela used to live. By 1939, an architectural plan had been readied, but soon others worries intervened.

Doctors and Wartime Duress

Ekafera's construction slowed when the Second World War intruded abruptly into everyday lives.[9] While political tensions erupted among Belgians in Coq,[10] Dr. Jaggard bought a hundred-dollar radio and accepted he would be in Monieka "'for the duration.'" Visits to fretful Belgian neighbors reminded this American of his good fortune: Congo seemed safe and free "from war molestations."[11] For Congolese, however, duress soared during the war. By radio, Ryckmans doubled work requirements and sent everyone back into forced rubber labor,[12] stirring painful memories of Free State deaths and cruelties.[13] When an official boarded a missionary vessel in 1941, a canoe followed behind, packed with guarded prisoners being relocated. Congo's war effort put countless Congolese in chains, with many forcibly "called home . . . to clear an acre of forest and plant it in up-land rice."[14]

Exhaustion, poor diets, and force became common and everyday. Many left their villages to seek work on plantations. New companies popped up all over Tshuapa, while gruelling wartime labor in rubber and road making boosted profits. Industrial hygiene laws ensured some monitoring of worker camps, and nursing schools turned out assistants for companies needing to comply with legislation.[15] In 1944, Dr. Schwers pressed firms to favor family life, increase salaries, and chase away the morally dubious.[16] Pleased that the war had interrupted the plans for an antivenereal "experiment," he remained sure that "classic methods"—"massive doses of chemotherapy"—would only produce "blind, absurd, brutal" results, in a word, "disaster."[17]

Schwers remained embattled.[18] Yet Dr. Dratz was working with his hypotheses about "deep causes" to venereal infection. In 1940, Dratz visited South Africa, where a Dr. Fox suggested studying cassava toxicity and sperm production in prisoners.[19] On his return, he researched "extinction" among "unhappy primitives," including the effects of poisonous cassava on the anterior pituitary gland. He found 60 percent of men with inadequate sperm counts, and claimed that 45–60 percent of Mongo women were sterile or prone to miscarry.[20] Dratz was still assembling basic supplies: gloves, a speculum, and a pelvimeter. From Léopoldville, Van Hoof expressed doubt about this zealous doctor's azoospermia diagnostic technique. Still, Dratz did not rest, and the number of his subfertility studies grew.[21]

A missionary doctor Bellfontaine, who wrote about the birth rate along the Lopori in 1943, took a different tack. Disease once *caused* depopulation, he observed. When the demand for rubber intensified in 1903, he noted, many died from sleeping sickness before the birth rate dropped. Now the low birth rate stemmed rather from wartime migration: men were departing with their families in search of work. Independent women were leaving too. Likely, none of them would ever return. Nor could medical efforts redress such depopulation. The proportion of departures was too large to sustain customary populations, at a time when Equateur plantations companies were benefitting from the war, ducking recruitment regulations, and rapidly expanding their work forces. Spontaneous, informal, clandestine hiring was now the rule.[22] A plantation at Bikoro, for instance, had jumped in 1940 from two hundred to twelve hundred workers in less than a year.[23]

When asked to inspect a road worksite in 1945, Schwers observed laborers arriving as families and working six months at a stretch. The work seemed "primitive," with near slaves "moving earth in small baskets." The scene reminded him of the Egyptian pyramids, yet the "Pharaohs at least had the excuse of drawing from an immense human reservoir." In Equateur, "We don't have that excuse: we knew that this road had to pass by peoples who for decades have been in the process of disappearing." Still, the doctor's recommendation did not challenge the infrastructural needs of the province's bigger companies. If the work were long term, he rationalized, it would endanger health. Instead, there was "only one thing to do: finish as quickly as possible."[24]

A worker who dared run away from a plantation job would find himself forced to build roads, suggesting the complicity between territorials and plantations. Both wage labor and "customary" rubber and road work were onerous. Congolese resented their "semi-captivity," Bellfontaine observed. Life was becoming *camp*-like, with masters, rules, and hardships in villages, work camps, and road construction sites.[25] Greater force and tedium fell on customary villages, however, where labor was punishing and often compelled by whipping and imprisonment. When the war came to an end, Hulstaert was indignant on behalf of those who "worked and toiled for four, five years," with not "a moment of respite." The Flemish missionary knew "this country of rubber and constructing roads" had become untenable, bitterly so. Congolese had learned that "there is only one God: the State." With everything oriented toward "the economy of the Whites, all for the war, all for the State," the result was "total indifference."[26]

Letters, Mpadi Escapes, and the Nervous Van Campenhout

While apathy and ennui developed during these years of semicaptivity, state agents were confronting an energetic circulation of antistate resentments, as new religious languages entered the region and security efforts grew. While Ekafera did not open until 1944, relegations to Tshuapa from Bas Congo had begun in the late 1920s. In 1934, there were 1,794 relégués in Congo's six provinces, with 559 of these in the province headquartered at Coquilhatville. Léopoldville authorities, keen to relegate Kimbanguists, learned that those who did not proselytize in their new localities were rare.[27] Relégués seemed to require greater supervision during the war, and Tshuapa became the home for those feared to be political operatives spreading pro-German propaganda. Notable was Simon Mpadi.[28] He was rumored to be fond of Hitler's name and keen to sport swastikas. Educated in Bas Congo at an American Baptist mission, catechist by 1925, Salvation Army evangelist by the mid-1930s, Mpadi took inspiration from Kimbangu and founded the Mission des Noirs movement. On September 7, 1939, he wrote a letter to Bas Congo authorities telling them their days were numbered. This act of sedition produced his relegation as a dangerous man to Tshuapa, from where he was allowed to roam at first, in keeping with the colony's treatment of most relégués.[29]

By 1941, the lead administrator at Befale, Van Campenhout, was busy scaling up security operations. Secret networks were moving forbidden letters without postage stamps through underground channels, though often using regular mail routes and personnel. Alarmed by the intensity of this postal duplicity, Van Campenhout began tracking the mail of militant Kimbanguists like Phillipe Bumba, held in awe by Mpadi because Bumba knew Kimbangu and his habits. Bumba received so many letters that listing his correspondents was a lengthy security task.[30]

Van Campenhout made it his business to have relégués searched and then sent the seized documents in Swahili and Kikongo to the governor's office for translation. He reminded his colleagues that clandestine couriers were lurking everywhere—in messengers, company servants, manual laborers, state workers, and river traffic employees. Even letters between soldiers and wives should be inspected, he exhorted, having seized grievous family correspondence from one dangerous relégué. Another goal was to arrest communications between relégués and ordinary Tshuapa residents. Zilani, a dissident from Lac Léopold, spelled disorder after penning some terrifying letters. Van Campenhout and his men intercepted and analyzed yet more mail, while their captured lists of disciples grew.[31]

Administrator Grandry interrogated a chauffeur named David Lokongo about delivering unstamped mail to Befale's political prisoners in August 1941. Lokongo claimed Biatale told him to do so, while he, Lokongo, "didn't open sheets of paper." He "did not pay attention" to the rules forbidding all unstamped letters either. Van Campenhout, busy reviewing interrogation instructions, demanded to know why Grandry had failed to ask Lokongo about Biatale. Nor had Grandry detained the chauffeur who worked for Monsieur Thirifays of Basankusu, as doing so would have meant stranding this Belgian master's automobile in Befale. By letting the driver return home, where "surely he resides among the personnel of M. Thirifays," a white man's vehicle had trumped further investigating the illicit, suspect mail.[32]

This naive skewing of priorities was not lost on the nervous Van Campenhout. Just a few months before, in May 1941, Van Campenhout had searched all relégués in Befale, placing three in solitary confinement inside the post's prison. Mpadi was among them. In October, everyone in the prison with Mission des Noirs connections ended up in solitary confinement, including Mpadi and Zilani. Van Campenhout remained diligent and energetic, issuing orders to tighten surveillance and regularly searching the huts of relégués allowed to roam. Greater severity and more body searches seemed in order. All favors should end. Why was Mpadi's wife allowed to do her own cooking in prison? This luxury must go, he declared, as he demoted this woman away from her superior diet to the same regime as all women prisoners.[33]

A year later, Mpadi was gone. The man escaped as part of an inside job, organized around a breach in guard protocol late one night. The event came as a surprise. Using tiny sticks, the famous prisoner disabled his handcuffs, pried out his hands, and wielded a knife to cut through a prison wall. Setting aside normal procedure, not a single guard had shown up for duty at the lockup's main door. While four were found at fault, the handcuffs, chains, and iron collar became a police display, along with the wooden bits that blocked the bolts open. Memorable was the voice of the first Congolese guard to notice the famous captive was gone: "*Mpadi s'est sauvé.*" "Mpadi saved himself."[34]

About the same time, Van Campenhout arrested two Bolifa overseers and learned about two hundred Mission des Noirs residing in the village. He wondered how triage should proceed. Who should be incarcerated, put in solitary, proposed for internment? Interning one and all was impossible, he assumed. Yet "it would be bad policy to not trouble them" at all. With Mpadi's movement spreading, the presence of so many Bas Congo soldiers in Befale territory was also a worry: "I no longer trust them." He busied himself with Kitawala, too. He incarcerated 275 disciples during one roundup, while searching for another sixteen. While security authorities advised that the best information came from spontaneous searches that also produced disciple lists, Mission des Noirs seemed to be bleeding into Kitawala. Those who grew up near Befale seemed unable to distinguish the two. Often dumbfounded when arrested as Kitawala, Tshuapa residents seemed surprised when being told they had done something wrong. They had joined practices that in their eyes, or so they claimed, resembled Inongo—long-standing age-grade associations not unlike those formed around mobile charms.[35] Given the circumstances, refuge zones remained the best way to hide. In 1946, several Kitawala took refuge in a *nganda* near Befale, prompting a call to clean out these places of respite. This form of hiding, we have seen, began years before.[36]

By February 1943, Befale territory seemed utterly *atteint*—"contaminated."[37] The word suggests infection, and the epidemiological idiom is telling. Likewise, the word for managing "subversive movements" was *dépistage*, detection, as in screening for disease. This scrutinizing required not sanitary agents, however, but informants and spies. Paying the latter had grown urgent, Van Campenhout suggested: "We only find them if, as soon as information is handed over and checked, we can give a bonus without delay." And "without an immediate recompense," no new information would arrive. Van Campenhout sought to pay his spies, despite official formalities thick and slow. Still, as early as 1942, a special fund was rewarding thirteen.[38]

As security intensified and breaches multiplied, keeping up seemed nigh impossible. After detaining hundreds, Van Campenhout began to invent his own system of concentration, with the idea of instituting six-month periods of prerelegation at Befale. He began rounding up all the Kitawala he could find, keeping them under his strict and wary eye at his headquarters. Before long, provincial authorities objected to such a mass containment of people not far from their homes because it ran counter to a fundamental principle of relegation: removal. The Protestant doctor at Baringa, Wide, complained in a barbed, insightful letter, accusing the state of aggravating a situation stemming from ideas first carried in by Bas Congo relégués and since profilerating amid vexation and mobilizing unrest. When security agents captured those moved by such languages of religious dissent, they enhanced their allure and stirred greater antagonism.[39]

Those already scheduled in 1942 for transfer to Ekafera as soon as it opened included twenty incarcerated in nearby prisons. The governor assumed that the new penal colony's prison in brick should be readied for them. He requested fifty more cells for "sect" members. Pierre Ryckmans objected from afar by letter: six to ten cells were plenty, since Ekafera was not supposed to imprison state charges already under lock and key; indeed, many locked up in Congo's prisons were only there because an appropriate place for them was lacking. Ekafera aimed to fill this "lacuna" for dangerous relégués. Moreover, closed cells were unwise: "no native would survive permanent detention in a prison cell." The governor general's mild and moralizing views were at best naive in relation to developments in Equateur. The 1942 Ekafera plans projected a detention house for seventy to ninety, with thirty solitary confinement cells.[40]

Van Campenhout sought to send Kitawala leaders to Ekafera's prison. Ordinary relegation within penal colony borders should have been adequate, he noted, but many leaders were *not* from far away.[41] Relegation had long meant removal across a large distance, as was the case with Maria N'koi in 1915.[42] Ekafera's locked prison became the solution for those who might escape or try to stay in touch with neighbors and kin. In March 1944, as Ekafera finally

opened, eleven "propagandists" from Befale territory became prison intern-
ees. Two were from Boyo and Loma. All came from roughly the same area
where officer Coursez sought in Belgian Congo's early years to count and fix
people in villages amid concerted flight and rebellion. Seven of these propagandists were from villages in Songo chiefdom,[43] a domain once known as
"Nsongo district." In the 1900s, Nsongo was home of several maimed youth,
photographed with their absent hands in shocking, humanitarian images circulating in magic lantern shows.[44]

   In the immediate postwar years, Songo became the site of a curious colonial trial and form of humanitarianism. We turn to this experiment with
biopolitical dimensions now.

The Songo Experiment and "Joy"

Amid the spiraling security situation, enmeshed with wartime policing and
harassment, the provincial governor pleaded with governor general Ryckmans
in 1944: "If we want to save the Kundu and Mongo populations, it's necessary
to go after 'drastic' remedies."[45] The governor insisted that "all force" in labor
must end. Instead, crop development, stock raising, village reconstruction,
and a newly designed medical service were needed. Yet he understood that
commitments to the Allies and to Tshuapa enterprises were still ongoing, so
for the time being, perhaps a commission to study the low birth rate would
suffice.[46]

   Tshuapa had long been "on the decline" and now faced new forms of depopulation resulting from labor intensification and war abuses, Ryckmans
replied. He recalled hearing about "the slow extinction of the Mongo" thirty
years earlier. Why, he wondered, were war abuses not having the same effect
in northern Equateur? Why were Nkundo and Mongo abandoning "all national pride," while the Bwaka "preserved theirs and remain ready for revolt?"
The governor general decided to institute an experiment to nourish and care
for village residents "without subjecting them to the deleterious influence of
camps or *cités*." Labor would be restricted for "the time necessary to realize
the experiment," limited in space to "the most affected part of Befale territory." The remedies would include: ending forced labor, repatriating recruits
from worksites, providing free rations, and establishing a dispensary. If the
experiment raised the birth rate, then extending it to all Tshuapa might be
considered.[47]

   Ryckmans sought to test whether Mongo were "definitively lost for the
race," whether their birth rate amounted to "racial degeneration." He wanted

to know for economic reasons, being concerned about Tshuapa's growing concessionary economy finding enough workers. It was possible that "authorizing recruitment without any limits" might even become viable, since "disadvantages for the future" need not apply if the Mongo were headed for extinction.[48] This social Catholic intellectual helped invent colonial recruitment ratios to protect rural reproduction in the early 1930s, early in his colonial career. Now the leading colonial officer was suggesting that Mongo might justifiably be worked or relocated at will, setting aside the usual colonial calculus for determining the proportion of men who could be safely recruited out of customary space. Ryckmans also wrote of perhaps creating "sufficiently large reserves" for Mongo, turning over the rest of Tshuapa for his idealized, warrior-like favorites, the "fertile race" of Bwaka (Ngwaka), whom he envisioned coming to work in Tshuapa with their emigration realized "peacefully and under European control" (see figure 5.1).[49]

We have entered a realm of colonial fantasy here, one with material effects. While Dr. Schwers's ideas had met scorn in Brussels, Pierre Ryckmans never stopped thinking in terms of degeneration, race, vitality, and extinction. He conceded that wartime labor demands produced "excess," but doubted that plantation labor yielded inordinate, harmful distress. Rather, Ryckmans coolly reiterated that customary subjects, required to work 240 days a year in village tasks and 120 more in corvées like road building, benefited from a full five days off a year.[50]

The location for the experiment in "drastic remedies" became Befale's Songo chiefdom, and a special commission met five times to discuss its progress. It convened at a remove, in Coquilhatville, while receiving reports from technicians implementing what in many ways became a development project. They discussed a wide range of subjects, with clashes among the administrative, medical, missionary, and private enterprise representatives. The provincial directors of agriculture, medicine, and native affairs took turns speaking and sparring. The first meeting in late July 1945 began with guilt, regret, and pity amid an obsession with joy. They remembered Ryckmans's recent words: "the native is tired." Mixing vitalism with fantasies of development, they bemoaned the toil of the war effort. If joy would return, so would a "will to live." When one expressed, "Let's combat disorders reigning in family life," another protested: "It's necessary to give the native more tranquility, to not pester him constantly." Prosecutor Dewaersegger spoke up for a gentle "paternalism," not wanting Songo to see the experiment as "the imposition of a new corvée."[51]

There were reservations about the instructions. How could an experiment

QUAND J'S'RAI
GOUVERNEUR GÉNÉRAL

FIGURE 5.1 A colonial caricature of a proud, stout, urbane
governor general in 1920s Congo, accompanied by a sardonic
song about power and vanity: "Quand j's'rai Gouverneur
Général." Note the tuxedo, cigar, chauffeur, and the limousine
ready in the distance, working to mock the panache and hubris
of the colony's chief officer. The image is contrapuntal to the
moralizing Pierre Ryckmans who during his tenure (1934–46)
micromanaged many pronatalist, penal, and development
experiments. Artist: P. R. De Meyer. From P. Hubin, Alexandre
Leclercq, and Léon Pirsoul, *Chansons congolaises par trois
moustiquaires*, 66.

be conclusive and provisional? How would laborers be returned home? Moral
issues embraced prostitution, the easy vacillation of Mongo hearts, old men
with young wives, education, and boarding schools. The provincial head, Van
Hoeck, suggested four causal layers to subfertility: pathological, dietary, social,
and moral. Since disease spread with increased communications, the solution
lay with drugs and upgrading medical services. The way to improve diets lay
in food crops and stock-raising in this zone long specialized in hunting and
gathering. Social causes opened matters of moods and zest, housing and refinement: "Healthy and well nourished people don't require more than a little
joy to develop a taste for life."[52]

Van Hoeck reminded that the landscape alternated between villages in ruins and worker camps. Crumbling customary areas encouraged the able-bodied to depart. Camps, artificial and new, were poorly organized, producing licentiousness. Over both villages and camps hovered an "immense sadness" inhibiting "a will to live." The remedies lay in "smiling villages," decent houses, enclosed lots, fruit trees, and "small material satisfactions"—big hunts, "folkloric" dances, and, in artificial zones, "healthy attractions." A customary and artificial polarity continued to shape thought and practice into the 1950s, with demographic surveys assuming people belonged to either a customary, artificial, or mixed zone. Van Hoeck's final causal layer aimed at joy. "Natives" were replacing "the lost joy" of custom with "debauchery," spreading corruption "in all forms." Material happiness needed a moral foundation, he announced, while thanking the missionaries present in the room. Despite all the appeals for joy, few argued for rest. The most avid proponent of new exertions was agriculture director Cuperus. He saw the experiment as a chance to create a peasant farming class (a *paysannat*). His ideas, which teemed with kinds and quantities of crops and stock needed, were transformative by implication.[53]

Schwers became a pivot of debate during the discussions, once the Songo doctors presented their findings. Van Hoeck, the most verbal vitalist, wanted to rekindle zest, with each territory having an agent who oversaw vitality. He also added stastistic-keeping to Songo's measures. Van Hoeck infuriated Schwers by alluding to doctors with "gloomy" visions, more theoretical than empirical. The doctor held tight to his causal stance: primary shock caused trouble and then heightened venereal susceptibility.[54]

There was nothing peaceful about the second meeting in April 1946. Rather, developmentalist hubris grew. Criticism surfaced that concentrating so many interventions in a single chiefdom of twelve thousand (with four thousand active men) was producing an impossible situation. The president opened with sixteen issues for consideration, from how to study "racial decadence" to whether a scientific mission with a physiological laboratory was necessary to do so. His questions were many: whether new concessions should be refused, if stock raising should be required, how to determine marriage rules for clerks, and how to reverse the situation so "blacks get more vigor." A bewildering conversation about varieties of polygamy and their reproductive effects followed. The agriculture director had told of 1945 achievements: villages still decrepit, a station for new crops created, and instructions extended for farming, land use, and stock rearing. Cuperus saw no problem in exempting Songo from other kinds of labor, since his imposed farming tasks would soon be producing revenue.[55] Clearly, his exuberance had many busy working. Indeed, Ryckmans's experimental vision—the removal of forced labor—was never respected.

Dr. Rousseau reported on the first six medical months, without a clinic and missing beds. He had learned that gonorrhea was nearly universal, with 819 cases (8.72 percent) of acute gonorrhea and chronic forms rampant. Syphilis, too, was reducing the birth rate. Schwers jumped in to interpret these facts: Conditions were worse than during his brief stay in 1937, when a "clear rupture between generations" meant a group of robust, proud elders stood beside weakened, sly, depraved youth with a few puny children. While the venereal rates in Rousseau's tables resembled his 1937 evidence, Schwers pointed at Songo promiscuity as responsible for a process which would lead to almost sure extinction.[56]

Rousseau dared to argue differently. Venereal incidence was not threatening disappearance, even though about half of adult women had never given birth. General health was average, diets rich and varied. Several mothers had many children, some of their offspring had many children, while others had none at all. As Rousseau challenged, he veered away from the somatic. Not "physical degeneration" but "psychic apathy" seemed key. Many were inserting tampons of herbs, leaves, or rags into their bodies, perhaps for contraception. He could not confirm Schwers's 1937 findings: he found no testicular inflammation or hypoplasia, no enlarged ovaries. The birth rate was extremely low. The lack of familial authority plus a new "psychic factor"—*improved material conditions*—seemed the cause. During these days of postwar plenty, Congolese were avoiding work and responsibility, seeking lives of pleasure instead. His conversations with male elders about disappearing big families revolved around departures for town and the loathing of work, especially by youth. The arrival of companies and itinerant trader-clerks had increased mobility. Flight was common and intimately related to the intensification of security measures or "penal justice."[57]

The prosecutor Dewaersegger kept insisting that the commission had to do something concrete. There would be nothing experimental if the project only suppressed excess in corvées. Songo did not need relief from directed agricultural work. Making farmers out of them would provide stability, bring back joy, and work on the "psyche," a "profound cause of the low birth rate." Adopting Darwinian language, Dewaersegger spoke of the Songo as a condemned race, likely to disappear. Yet he pressed for more evidence regarding Schwers's long-standing claims. Why was the Commission not locating a dozen human "specimens" with signs of degeneration, bringing them to a special laboratory, and proving the doctor's ideas right or wrong?

Dewaersegger also jumped to his favorite themes: the hypocrisy of native affairs rhetoric, the failure to implement protective regulations, and corruption. More than anyone else, he raised questions about recruitment abuses, excessive incarceration, and the violence of forced labor. The incessant, scattered nature of corvées was the problem. Called on to construct roads, *gites d'étape*, prisons, and dispensaries, customary subjects had to respond to summonses from irritated, hurried agents and reckon with *capita*, ever keen to punish negligence. The 120 days of required labor were never completed in eight-hour chunks of time. Workers were rarely asked to labor more than four hours at a stretch. The erratic scheduling and obsessive solicitation eliminated all sense of autonomy and tranquility.[58]

Dewaersegger returned to joy via venality and immobility. Big companies like SAB were flouting recruitment regulations and surreptitiously extending the concessionary economy. Since 1944, agreements to limit road work and halt concessions had been disregarded. Six road worksites with 1,650 workers had opened along the Coq-Boende route, and ten new concessions received approval, most for SAB. Dewaersegger became sardonic: How will the new concessions find workers if Tshuapa is actually "depopulating at the rhythm we state"? He distrusted statistics, doubting the very fact of depopulation in this context with concessions gobbling up labor.[59] This colonial jurist was no advocate of greater liberty, however. Nor did he want Songo able to exit their chiefdom. Only "when everything has been done to give birth to joy again," only then should departure prohibitions be lifted. Surreptitious hiring—with the word *recruitment* never uttered—worked to scatter. Holding Songo within their chiefdom-experiment inhibited dispersal. Deeply critical of the hypocrisies of colonial capitalism, this social Catholic authoritarian thought a new, wholesome *mystique* was in order, organized under the "continual surveillance of a European." His report envisioned a future of upright, paternalist villages, supervised by vigilant Catholic priests.[60]

Such thinking confronted the medical, again and again. By the fourth meeting on April 22, 1947, Van Hoeck was challenging Schwers, while another doctor's results arrived. Dr. Rousseau had been managing two hospital wards under construction in Befale, and he wanted prisoners to build four dispensaries in mud. By July 1946, Rousseau had left, and Dr. De Bisscop reported in December. His staff had expanded with a Belgian sanitary agent, two Congolese nurses, nine nurse assistants, two interns, and a nurse-midwife. Befale remained a dispensary, offering drugs yet without a way to hospitalize anyone. A clinic for pregnant women and a white female nurse were needed. The lack of equipment made practice difficult and ruined all "medical prestige." Patients preferred Baringa's mission hospital to Befale's mud hut.[61]

At the same time, Songo's departure prohibitions simply did not hold. In one of eight chiefdom groupings, 27 percent had either refused medical examination, were temporarily absent, or had gone off to companies or missions. The Songo doctor endeavored to study two groupings more closely. Territorial cards helped De Bisscop track birthdates over twenty-five years, and the results suggested the low birth rate began in 1905–10. He assumed that men, aged between twenty and forty, made a reproductive impact with each departure. Some 46 percent of women had never given birth, he determined; 20–25 percent were sterile. De Bisscop found Rousseau's assertions about gonorrhea exaggerated. Detecting venereal disease was difficult; before examination most women douched with astringent solutions while men urinated. Many complained of miscarriage. He challenged Rousseau's diagnostic methods, with a Congolese assistant identifying gonococcus under a microscope. De Bisscop also spoke of moral depravation; still, he knew gonorrhea treatment with *vaccin* and sulfamides had begun, promising a new medical efficacy.[62]

At the final meeting in November 1947, Tshuapa's new atmosphere was a subject of conversation. New concessions were everywhere, employing a salaried workforce with worrying consquences. Wouldn't this development stimulate new sexual economies and produce moral and reproductive disaster? Dewaersegger had blamed capitalist enterprises for spawning venereal infection. Numerical data showed how destructive a single new concession could be, with venereal rates spiking soon after a plantation opened. Some spoke of social disorganization as a "catalyst." In combining "infection and sexual exchange into a compound," the disarray caused subfertility.[63]

At the last meeting, Schwers announced Dewaersegger's resignation.[64] Exactly how this prosecutor's criticisms of excessive corruption and imprisonment produced his shadowy exit is unclear. But he left when many others simply wanted to close Songo down. The experiment had begun amid misery and harsh labor, countered by vitalist calls for joy. Schwers's hypotheses received a last airing. He struggled to remain in command, irked whenever his theories did not reign or were mischaracterized.

Schwers still spoke of "shock," loss of "vigor," and the danger of medicating venereal disease. The Songo doctors excluded racial degeneration as causality. Intense medical action was their solution, alongside increased authority and pronatalist propaganda.[65] The situation was changing by the last meeting, however, in two senses. First, penicillin was arriving. As provincial doctor, Schwers would be the one to supervise standardization and distribution in a vast pharmaceutical campaign. Secondly, other etiologies arrived. While still defending his notion of primary shock, he began using a language more aligned with the psychic as traumatism.[66] Steering his ideas into a new key influenced by reading *The Lancet* and American medical journals, the new register echoed postwar findings emerging on a global scale. Hans Selye and others were pressing forward with endocrinological research on strain and stress, while many were thinking about illness in psychosomatic terms.[67]

That any colonial problem may be converted into a scientific experiment was an idea basic to Songo.[68] That labor abuses were too extreme was contentious, clearly not accepted by all who implemented Songo. The agronomic director towed the emerging postwar line on creating a peasantry as a counterpoint to the rising salariat. Ultimately, micromanagement at Songo yielded something like direct rule, producing countless struggles over duties, rules, tasks, and punishment in the process. As agricultural reporting became exhaustive, the perception of the Songo as terribly refractory soared.[69] In the process, the goal of testing the reproductive effects of eliminating corvée obligations became mislaid. While vitalist thinking had a strong hold in Coq, at the edges of the experiment, it ultimately imposed new kinds of reviled labor upon Songo subjects. Their chief became the object of frequent, intense mockery.[70]

Serious doubts about Songo peaked in 1948, when Van Campenhout complained that Ryckmans's instructions had never arrived in Befale. This territorial declared the experiment confused and unrealistic. Not a single plantation worker had been repatriated back to Songo. The chiefdom was "a living entity," hardly an artificial or "theoretical entity," where one "can study reactions in isolation." Befale's territorial headquarters were smack in the middle of Songo chiefdom. Two main roads passed through heading to Boende, Basankusu, and Coq. The nervous Van Campenhout, who busied himself aplenty during these years, now pressed a vague case of "local contingencies." Many Songo were on the move. While some furnished fruit to the nearby Macodibe firm, many others would soon be required to provide rations for the four hundred some soldiers, patients, nurses, laborers, road workers, and detainees who would reside at the new Befale. The post would soon be a massive construction site for a medical and surgical center, mission, and convent. Such "ambiance" ran counter to the hated, overstaffed project.[71]

Van Campenhout wanted Songo dismantled without delay. He welcomed the Fonds du Bien Etre Indigène (FBEI, or Native Welfare Fund), a new development venture (see map 5.1). Its requirements would be imposed. Otherwise, nothing would be accomplished. Coercion was yielding to persuasion as a colonial technique, he acknowledged, yet abandoning discipline would be premature.[72] So it was that FBEI, a major postwar parastatal, superseded Songo at its soon thriving center at Befale.[73] As we will see, the project comprised agromony, schools, clinics, doctors, dispensaries, and research, and development became a vehicle for shaping appropriate futures. Seduction became more salient, though compulsion continued by its side.[74]

Degenerationist logic faded during Songo, foundering under the weight of new hatreds, mobilities, and the vocabularies of new postwar experts.[75] Construing this chiefdom as ailing, deprived, cut off, and clearly bounded became laughable. Set in a bursting region crisscrossed with roads, firms, and movement, Songo were rarely still. Physically, economically, intellectually, technically—never mind through the wonder of imaginations—they were trafficking in horizons of the possible (to be explored in the next chapter). The project deformed from scientific experiment in corvée removal into a detested project of rural development. It tried to fix people in place, as peasants more than as patients. While their assigned tasks fed anger and refusal, their hate fed new patterns of resort, away from adversity and toward Kitawala or Mission des Noirs. These latest forms of recourse and distraction—and healing—appealed. They were stirring the region as they interconnected with Ekafera.

Ekafera

A milieu of concentrated compulsion, Ekafera first began to function during Songo's experimental years. In 1942, many mud huts were ready, while a detention room awaited hinges and screws.[76] The war had slowed the arrival of the first relégués into this Agricultural Colony for Dangerous Relégués (CARD). Relegation had long been a carceral technique that worked through removal. The legal clause for fixing a relégué's residence came from the same 1910 decree used to deport Maria N'koi in 1915. Relegation was a political expedient and administrative measure, used by territorial administrators to get rid of the disorderly and calm unrest. Relegation determined a route of travel; it was not supposed to take away property or diminish rank, but keep a subject mobile, occupied within new spatial limits, along with a wife and children.[77]

In 1936 Elisabethville, Kitawala relegated to their home villages seemed submissive, little involved in propaganda. But relegating "subversive sect adepts" did not work: they held onto their "politico-religious" activity.[78] Kitawala was disruptive: it sought to destroy colonial hierarchies. With the slogan "Africa for Africans," it proclaimed not only racial equality, but also parity in salaries and the coming of a global theocratic state. Members were to divulge nothing to whites.[79] As Kitawala became more difficult to control in 1936, the idea emerged that their "concentration" as relégués would enable "permanent surveillance."[80] By 1938, a notice invited territorial personnel to periodically examine the situation of each relégué and deny free circulation to those posing a security threat.[81]

Those relegated to Ekafera underwent keen surveillance, arresting the mobility of ordinary relégués sent to distant posts.[82] Ekafera aimed at separation, ending contact between its relégués and ordinary subjects. In 1942, when Ryckmans was eager to transfer the first men to Ekafera, he sought to dispel confusion: dangerous relégués were to be "*concentrated*" at this penal colony for "unrepentant leaders and propagandists." Ekafera was for those too "dangerous to leave in contact" with ordinary Congolese, those whose persistent "attitude or mentality" spread "subversive ideas" throughout "all the Colony."[83]

Ekafera was intended to solve colony-wide problems posed by Kimbanguism and Kitawala. Kitawala, we saw, emerged out of labor grievances in Congo's mining zones, where unrest erupted with insurrections in the 1940s. Although Belgian Congo had long been a nervous state, these uprisings that killed suggest a rationality to state wariness. Many Kitawala joined in the 1941 insurrection at Manono that took the lives of fourteen mineworkers and deeply shook authorities and white communities. Kitawala's purpose, a witness noted, was "to drive the whites from the country and replace the blue flag of Belgium with the black flag of Kitawala."[84] After Ekafera opened, several Kitawala were forcibly transferred from Manono to its prison.[85]

Many more Kitawala arrived from the industrial zone of Katanga, at a time when this province's key prison at Elisabethville was full.[86] In 1945, governor Maron counted 178 Kitawala inmates and 21 convicts in his province's prisons. One near Elisabethville was designed for Kitawala detainees alone; they made bricks. Staffing was inadequate, brick output paltry. Yet they could only proselytize each other, not non-Kitawala inmates, as they had before. They seemed to accept escape as impossible, while bribing soldier-guards to stay in touch with kin. The prisons at Jadotville and Malonga were similar, and this province would soon have three hundred inmates of "the Kitawala type." With their kin, these men would require sixty guards.[87] Katanga's governor wondered about making them do rubber threshing in Kolwezi or Malonga, but the Rhodesian border loomed.[88] He was sure Ekafera could not absorb all the Kitawala in his prisons. But ridding Elisabethville of the most "intransigent and intractable" was urgent.

So it was that a group of eighty-three Kitawala arrived as Ekafera prisoners from Congo's industrial core in 1944. Their dossiers contained fingerprints, suggesting they hailed from a *more* hardened, sophisticated world of security management since this technology was not yet in use: The differences between industrial Katanga and equatorial Tshuapa were stark, as the wives of these Kitawala sensed. They could elect *not* to accompany their husbands to Ekafera, and many did not. Their longhand letters in Swahili suggest the allure of continuing urbane lives in a temperate city rather than risking the unknowns of a grisly penal colony set down in remote, humid jungle.[89] Ekafera arrivals came from Kivu too, after the murderous Bushiri rebellion at Masisi in 1944.[90]

At Ekafera, a system of "interior order" prevailed. For those not sent to prison, the daily routine began with a 5:30 A.M. wake-up call and three more roll calls (6:15 A.M., 2 P.M., 5:45 P.M.), reduced to two on Sunday. After morning roll, an exercise workout followed. Night curfew began at 8:30 P.M. Until wake-up, circulation was forbidden. Moving near European homes or the military camp was prohibited. Working hours were fixed: 6–8 A.M.; 8:30 A.M. to noon; 2–4:30 P.M. Those without a corvée kept busy with subsistence crops or yard upkeep. Some practiced crafts. Trap-hunting within colony borders was allowed. Each worked for himself, while also joining a work team (for a week each month) doing unpaid corvées in hygiene, upkeep, and farming. The warden designated who lived where. Some twenty-eight soldiers kept guard.[91] Built structures included the warden's 1939 home with *boyerie* (servant quarters), an apparently never occupied agronomist's house built in 1943, guard and soldier homes, and 94 relégué huts built in 1939 and renovated in 1945. A carpentry workshop was part of 1942 plans.[92] In 1945, the only European was the warden, the territorial administrator Monsieur Grandry. A mason, two carpenters, an orderly, and soldiers were among Congolese employees.

In 1945, nine relégués were "invalids," while the rest were building huts, doing upkeep, and establishing fields of cassava, groundnuts, beans, and corn. Women and children, the nonrelegated, did not have to work. Six hectares of colony crops featured banana and sugar cane. An inspector arrived and proposed a vast expansion in farming. The warden objected; the relégués had plenty to do. Some had skills: a plumber, two "mediocre" woodworkers, an "excellent" tailor, two chair-caners. The inspector encouraged crafts but wanted more corn and groundnuts produced for export to Basankusu and Coq.[93] Grandry's worry was not to instrumentalize the relégués as farmers but grapple with them as "sect propagandists" who could spread ideas and send and receive mail.

No more than five relégués could gather at once.[94] They could request visits, though a privilege like newspaper access would be withdrawn to discipline. Literacy, learning, and print culture were part of this carceral crossroads in late colonial Congo. Men from Katanga and Bas Congo had long been readers and intellectuals. Even Equateur had had its readers, newspapers, and literati since the interwar years. Yet that Ekafera assembled, in one far-flung, forested place, urbane subjects from two of Belgian Congo's most sophisticated zones, is one of the staggering facts about this place of containment and punishment.[95]

There is much we do not know about everyday violence and torture at Ekafera, especially given current archival conditions, though hints are suggested here and in the following chapter. The place also knew medical routines. At one stage, a Congolese nurse was caring for 287 relégués and workers. The regularity of hygiene visits from the flourishing FBEI project centered at Befale suggest that those relegated may have been kept quite healthy,[96] in keeping with changes throughout the postwar colony.

Penicillin Arrives

Everywhere, medical routines and capacities were changing dramatically after the war. Equateur was by no means behind. In some senses, it may have led the way. The emergence of FBEI Befale went with, indeed culminated the enduring Belgian privileging of colonial pronatalism. Unlike during the Songo experiment, however, effective pharmaceuticals became available and were in use by colonial doctors. It had become possible to more seriously tackle venereal disease. Sulfa drugs, the first strongly effective compounds against gonorrhea, came into use internationally about 1937. Within a few years, gonorrhea bacteria exhibited resistance to sulfa. In 1943, penicillin became available globally.[97] The Belgian medical campaign quickly integrated these pharmaceuticals as they became accessible. Clinical practice changed, too. For a time, mixing drugs and treatments was quite experimental. Still, when penicillin entered widespread use, gonorrhea rates went down. Before long, penicillin-resistant gonorrhea set in.[98]

Schwers had long been sure it was impossible to eliminate gonorrhea. Yet from 1948, he energetically worked to reduce the incidence—from 4 to 8 percent in villages and 40 percent in commercial centers to about 2 to 3 percent everywhere, a reduction he claimed to have achieved in Coquilhatville.[99] His earlier dismissiveness was in keeping with medical opinion worldwide. Gonorrhea was difficult to arrest or control. Most colonial regimes in Africa almost ignored it, medicating syphilis instead.[100] In 1930s Congo, gonacrine joined *grands lavages* (Janet's irrigation method) as a treatment option.[101] One doctor created a Janet lavage clinic near Bondandanga. With two assistants giving two-liter washings twice daily for five weeks, Dr. Goldman claimed to have cured 87 percent of his patients in 1939. He recommended extending the inexpensive, labor-intensive method.[102] But few agreed, notably Schwers. During the war, with much in short supply, doctors were told to prioritize Europeans for medication. By 1941, all state medical activity in Befale had been suspended. The Baringa mission doctor asked what he was supposed to do with his syphilitics.[103] Schwers instructed limiting venereal control to hospitals because itinerant care was too difficult. Inspection of boat crews still took place in 1941; 30 boats with 174 men and 45 women yielded 11 gonorrhea and chancre cases.[104]

By 1944, colonial doctors were avidly confronting gonorrhea because sulfa drugs had arrived. Dr. David researched the rapid Dagenan treatment and was eager to do a clinical trial in Coquilhatville.[105] In 1944, Dr. Stavaux in Boende had four European patients with venereal disease; their treatments by injection were hindering his travel, while the woman patient with gonorrhea was receiving urethral rinses.[106] Many medics were requesting sulfonamides in 1945. One was overwhelmed in Yakoma; not visited by a health worker for three years, gonorrhea had spread "in an unbelievable manner." He treated with sulfapyridine.[107]

Patients, previously in hiding, suddenly wanted to pay for the pills offering relief in three days. Before, some had been detained at length for a possible cure through urethral washings. Now doctors envisioned vast sulfamide campaigns to eradicate gonorrhea. Léopoldville approved a research study by Dr. Simon at Banzyville in a single village alone—fearing sulfa resistance and reinfection. Schwers was sure administering at two-hour intervals would prove impossible. Sulfa, he insisted again, should be limited to hospital use, while he reminded doctors that penicillin would be available soon.[108] Soldiers were different because they could be controlled. Treatment with sulfathiazol began at the Coquilhatville military camp in 1946 and intensified when penicillin arrived.[109] By 1947, mass sulfathiazol treatment was in progress at Befale and Coquilhatville.[110] Schwers reported a failure rate of 40 percent. That a unique penicillin dose was under study seemed promising.[111]

Schwers wrote to SAB Wangata in 1948 about its worker camps. Despite decent sanitation, the lack of a plantation doctor suggested that gonorrheics would increase in number above 3 percent; moreover, their drug list should include *sulfamidés*.[112] At Bamboli Cultuur in Lisala, 7 percent of 386 workers had gonorrhea in 1949; eleven months later, rates were up 40–60 percent among men and women. Other spikes in gonorrhea incidence emerged during these years when doctors often combined sulfa with penicillin.[113] Some were using penicillin alone. A 1948 census near Ingende reported 12 percent with gonorrhea; they were being treated with penicillin, though some received grand lavage treatments too.[114] At Basankusu, 300 received treatment over four months in 1948.[115] At Coquilhatville's Congolese hospital, 1,436 cases (with 467 women) received care in 1948. Six hundred more received treatment in rural dispensaries.[116] In 1949, at Befale, Dr. De Bisscop treated 1,400 with penicillin.[117]

By 1948, standardizing penicillin dosages was under way. Most used a 200,000-unit injection for men, two 400,000 units for women. If these failed, it was back to sulfa drugs. So far, no Congolese had been resistant to both.[118] In 1949, Schwers wrote his doctors that penicillin was available in almost unlimited quantities. So began this doctor's concerted attempt to bring gonorrhea under control. Doctors were sometimes left waiting, less for penicillin itself than for sanitary agents to undertake the injections. Schwers also investigated when Léopoldville asked about the amounts of penicillin and sulfa needed.[119] Doctors, if still experimenting, were generally moving from sulfa to penicillin as all joined Equateur's major antigonorrhea campaign.[120]

Schwers requested huge quantities of penicillin in 1949 and 1950 (costing thirty to fifty milliards in Belgian francs).[121] With sulfa hard to administer, he hoped penicillin would produce better results. Unlike his intense reticence to intervene medically earlier in his career, Schwers was now positioned between drug dispensing instructions received from Léopoldville and the district, affiliated, and company doctors whom he steered. They were all doing their jobs, while the Allies' successful wartime treatment of gonorrheic soldiers with the sulfa medication, Dagenan, was in the air, a new global fact that energized.

Everyone knew that drugs alone would never suffice to bring gonorrhea under control. Schwers hoped penicillin efficacy would persuade "the refractory to seek treatment voluntarily."[122] Some diagnosis could be slapdash. One doctor reminded colleagues about the necessity of microscopic examination: eyeballing secretions, of course, would not do. Payment was another issue. At first, doctors argued that it did not matter whether colonial subjects paid for cures. With the standard of living rising dramatically, they assumed many Congolese could afford to pay. More pressing was pharmaceutical control. How should authorities keep drugs from falling into native hands, an issue related to theft and venality as well as drug resistance, it seems. Money shaped access, sales, and treatment, while Schwers worked to control costs. State-provided drugs were designed for "independent natives," large private companies, and their workers. Private planters had to procure penicillin from the private market.[123] In 1948, a Gemena plantation doctor turned over its penicillin supply to a sanitary agent who in turn oversaw a nurse-assistant providing the injections. A few doctors still suggested charging for drugs since patients, no longer poor, were unlikely to refuse to pay.[124] A shadow network trafficking in gonorrhea medication developed. One doctor worried about illicit sulfamide sales. If not stopped, resistance would develop, he suggested: "It should be relatively easy to find the guilty ex-aide-*infirmiers* who steal the product." It was more delicate to act against plantation managers who were handing out drugs to their workers, who sold them in turn. Complaints continued that mobility and reinfection made gonorrhea difficult to control.[125] Dr. De Bisscop did not think Befale's rate could be lowered without controlling movements or intensifying medicalization.[126]

Other problems intervened. The shadow economy in venereal medication likely became paired with the sheer invasiveness of this gonorrhea campaign, increasingly trying to intervene in patterns of sexual concurrency[127] and medicate all sexual partners. At one point, Schwers instructed that patients at Bokoto could only be treated if their wives were treated at the same time.[128] He railed against doctors sending gonorrheics to Coquilhatville's hospital. If these patients arrived without their women, venereal disease would spread: "Make your drug orders. *Vénériens* need to be treated right where you are and with their women, legitimate or not."[129] Dr. Van Ackere complained from FBEI Befale that the instructions for "systematic treatment of spouses" were difficult to apply. Many wives still lived in villages in Loma chiefdom or Songo-Mboyo: "I do not have the right to convoke them a distance over 15 km."[130]

By late 1949, Schwers reported on a Coquilhatville experiment in naming sexual partners. The results were "so disastrous we abandoned it." The large majority of such naming was "incorrect, probably slanderous." Even when the one named did carry the disease, it was impossible to know whether this clinical fact was a coincidence or not. Moreover, the word *denunciation* for naming inflamed nerves. "Nothing can replace screening by methodical census," Schwers concluded, expressing frustration with the latest social phase in the antivenereal campaign. Penicillin as medical technology seemed the best answer: "I wait impatiently for the promised sanitary agents."[131]

As locating, identifying, and naming sexual partners became more prevalent, newspapers spread this astonishing news. Treating both spouses at the same time, like identifying sexual partners, had become routine. Doctors discussed how to track down partners. In 1949, Schwers advised a Lolo doctor: "All the penicillin you need is at your disposal." He also promised to have the territorial service help so as to "force natives of both sexes to follow the treatment." The Lolo doctor replied about screening difficulties, plus his penicillin had not arrived. His sector included workers of Otraco and HCB as well as three hundred *femmes libres*, with some 20 percent having no papers. While he planned to tour commercial centers again soon, he anticipated absences and protests. Police had already conducted "promenades," searching out gonorrheics in flight. Yet this highly visible method was rarely productive. Repeated examinations of gonorrheics, like monthly exams of femmes libres, were difficult to achieve without much banal surveillance involving many police assistants and considerable territorial help besides.[132]

The availability of new pharmaceuticals and screening routines, therefore, spurred a novel kind of *securitization* in postwar Congo, aimed at all persons with gonorrhea and presumed sexual partners, often femmes libres. Unsterilized injections were also surely a part of this kind of medical practice. The focus on unmarried, unattached women went with assumptions about the provision of sexual services in worker camps and towns. When the emphasis turned to controlling and naming sexual partners, another kind of relentlessness emerged: how to round up and sanitize independent women, while extending the policing of the sexual and venereal to one and all.[133]

Penal Colony as "Hoax"

At Ekafera, security revolved around neither penicillin or independent women. Rather, it was more a matter of tear gas, a dike, and sometimes even song. The penal colony stretched from north to south, making surveillance difficult; the warden proposed a new east-west road running before his house. The soldiers seemed to have decent morale, even if they were not older men of proven dedication. Since one participated in the disquieting army mutiny in 1944 Luluabourg, the warden wanted him removed.[134]

Ekafera's first inspection reports suggest order and discipline. In 1945, an inspector decided weekly speeches were needed; the warden should speak about "our civilization" and explain why Kitawala and Mission des Noirs were unacceptable. Ekafera seemed unlike notorious penal colonies such as Biribi or Botany Bay. Intended for "moral correction," its propaganda should be constant, not excessive. Missionary visits from Catholics and Protestants should be encouraged. The school for Ekafera children, run by a literate soldier, received praise.[135]

In March 1946, when several locked up Kitawala were released, all Katanga relégués celebrated with song. The sound of their Kitawala hymns so outraged warden Grandry that he arrested twenty-three, using a 1906 decree on disturbing the peace to do so. He locked up most, sent ten to solitary, and threatened two wives with prison. In the end, he released them all, but questions lingered. Had his lesson taught anything? Were his disciplinary powers wide enough? Some suggested Grandry overreacted. Others noted that his arrests and house searches uncovered Bibles and documents. Soon, he was replaced.[136] In August 1947, the new warden Hennaert issued a seizure document ordering Louisa Bembo to search Jérome Zilani's sister. Bembo found Kitawala lists on the sister's body; they seemed years old, predating Zilani's arrival at Ekafera in 1944. In the process, Zilani seemed surely the "head of Kitawala in Tshuapa."[137]

Security remained a priority. Nervousness did not relent. The number of relégués grew, as did those locked up for being hostile advocates of "subversive sects." Fearing a revolt might erupt any moment, warden Grandry wanted better preparation in case rapid repression of an event became necessary. Ekafera was isolated in full forest, eight kilometers from the Maringa. Access was difficult, more so during high water seasons. To reach the river by foot or *tipoy* (a colonial sedan chair, evidently still in use in the 1940s!) required three hours. If an uprising burst forth, getting word to Befale would take fifteen hours, to Boende four days. Quick intervention measures were needed: tear gas, a messaging device, a defense plan, military instructions, security exercises, seven more prison guards, and a nine-kilometer dike for speeding troops in by truck and ferry.[138]

Another problem was the Boyela: too many lived close by. The initial idea of locating Ekafera in a *"no man's land"* was removal and containment. Officials also sensed it was unwise to send Tshuapa residents to this penal colony in their district. Yet Ekafera's population slowly moved from no Tshuapa residents to many, while a firm boundary between inside and outside never materialized. The proximity of Boyela subjects grew more problematic. When Ekafera opened, none were supposed to come near the place. The Boyela agreed in principle. Yet they declined to leave their ancestral lands on the Loma stream beyond the Lomako, near Lingunda, where they had ninety-eight hectares of palm and lands used for hunting, fishing, roof grass harvesting, and copal collecting. The first Ekafera inspection of 1941, before a single relégué arrived, observed some Boyela; they were asked to leave.[139] In 1942, several Kitawala were living in Boyela na Nse, the chiefdom next to the penal colony under construction. Zilani was active in Bauta, baptizing two of eighty-one Kitawala of this village; a third were women. Kitawala were being baptized in Boyela na Nse, therefore, before Ekafera opened. Tshuapa district, like Befale territory, received relégués able to wander, and some sowed novel religious practices well before the first Kitawala from Katanga entered the new carceral institution.

After Ekafera opened, a Saturday market inside allowed Boyela to sell cassava, palm fruit, meat, and fish. Several capita-traders sold foodstuffs to relégués and soldier-guards too. That these entrepreneurs might sell their clerk skills—writing, typing—spelled risk. A canteen seemed wiser. The markets ended, and the warden began purchasing from suppliers. Though Boyela lived where horrific violence had taken place in the 1900s, they hardly fit the long-standing portrayal of Mongo as frail, malnourished, and degenerate. With their lands little alienated, they could generate wealth for subsistence, taxes, and trade. Forcing them to leave would risk conflict, their dispersal into others' lands. Besides, they provided meat and chikwangue, critical to this closed institution's food supply. Initially a security zone with a few villages relocated became the goal.[140] The deliberations produced a thick file of minutes suggesting amicable meetings with Boyela notables. Some moved seven kilometers north to a more populous region where trade would be plentiful. This new location would diminish the isolation that developed when Boyela, like many Tshuapa chiefdoms, lost many to wage labor during the grueling war years.[141]

The Boyela remained worrisome, while from his post at Befale, Van Campenhout continued with security campaigns against Kitawala and other suspects. In May 1944, he wrote the Ekafera warden with several names of Kitawala leaders from Boyela. Three were already in Befale, and he wanted six more sent to him in a delicate operation: "if possible, prevent them from conferring among themselves." The same day, Van Campenhout observed that Kitawala had resurfaced, along with their insignia. Often called "Ositawala," these Boyela leaders had more than a hundred disciples. In July, he sent these nine to the Basankusu prison, keeping their followers under surveillance at Befale.[142] The troubles continued. By 1946, Kitawala had been declared illegal in all Equateur; an April native affairs law prohibited associating with its activities in any way.[143]

Six years after opening, when the Tshuapa commissioner came to inspect, he called Ekafera rundown and ramshackle. Poorly planned, now dilapidated, relégué huts filled with rain. The problem of porousness had worsened. Despite constant surveillance of ordinary relégués and prison inmates, both types were maintaining contacts with the outside. Brokers were carrying orders from Ekafera's Kitawala in all directions. Boyela chiefdom had become "rotten with Kitawala." At the very least, no one living nearby should be relegated into Ekafera anymore, the commissioner declared in 1950, and any Kitawala relegated in the future should be sent to another penal colony (CARD).[144]

Similar assertions resounded in 1956, when authorities conceded a more explicit causal arrow than before: Ekafera had furthered Kitawala, spreading it well beyond this penal colony's bounds. The blunder made long ago—letting Boyela stay nearby—had been magnified by ignoring an important fact: some of these Boyela were already Kitawala. The policy of sending some discontents to Tshuapa as ordinary, circulating relégués paved the way for residents to adopt their languages of dissent as their own. Once Ekafera was in place as carceral container for the subversive, it was neither remote nor inaccessible. Rather, it became a porous "hotbed" for all Tshuapa's Kitawala. As an official sighed, "the Colony's isolation is a mere hoax."[145]

"Worse Than Death Itself"

If in Belgian eyes, Ekafera became almost a sham, the place enfolded many Congolese in misery and desolation. When Patrice Lumumba scandalized with his historic independence speech, Congo's first and later assassinated prime minister spoke of the "ironies, insults, and blows" endured "morning, noon, and night because we were *nègres*." Words less well known in his famous speech are germane here: "We knew the atrocious sufferings of *relégués* for political opinions or religious beliefs; exiled in our own country, their fate was truly worse than death itself."[146] Ekafera deserves a more detailed study, as part of a history of Congo's penal colonies and prisons. The partial archive made available to me suggests "atrocious sufferings" and forms of physical and psychic torture. In 1945, officially reported punishments for a six-month period included thirty-five whipped, with four to eight blows each, and twelve sent to prison cells. Seven received punishments for insubordination; all were from Katanga. Ekafera's police court convicted three for hitting or assault; one threatened to kill some soldiers. In the next six months, there were forty-one recorded whipping punishments with one confined to a cell for eight days. No escapes or deaths occurred. Sanitary conditions were "good enough."[147]

Among those punished of course were Kitawala, a substantial proportion of Ekafera's relégués and detainees. In 1945, there were 113 relégués: 84 men, 6 women, and a child. Nine were locked up; thirteen had just arrived from Elisabethville. Family members included twenty-six women and thirty-eight children. In 1946, there was space for fifty more relégués. The total included twenty-one Mission des Noirs (nineteen from Bas Congo) and eighty-two Kitawala; of the latter, sixty-four participated in the Manono troubles of 1941, and thirteen in the Bushiri rebellion at Masisi. Bas Congo men and women were mostly elderly and calm. The Bushiri Kitawala were peaceful and did not gather, except for two stubborn ones, Asikani and Yoka Gamasi. The "bad heads" hailed from the Manono insurrection. They were powerful and self-possessed, and disciplining one usually led to conflict: "These people did not accept the whip."[148] Also present were a few recidivist thieves from Lusambo and Coquilhatville; an Equateur man who broke his relegation; and one from Congo-Ubangi charged with insubordination.

Twenty-five came to the warden's "special" sessions in the early 1950s. Some came to recuperate deposited property or money. Most wanted liberation. These would ask why they had been relegated or how to join their wives again. Both Mission des Noirs and Kitawala clarified that they had no intention of abandoning their ideas. The Katanga Kitawala nicknamed the penal colony "Simon's path," signaling the presence of many Simon Kimbangu and Simon Mpadi followers. These relégués from industrial Congo demanded to be separated from those hailing from Lower Congo, where the prophetic notions of Kimbangu and his devotees still stirred religious imaginations.

Old man Bembali no longer had to work in 1949. He was one of seven to occupy the category of "not filled with hate."[149] The warden regarded most as incorrigible, to be kept under a close watch. Yet he also aimed to make Ekafera seem less hopeless in these years. His idea was to put a compliant relégué on display; his approved exit would represent a future to which others could aspire. His example would inspire obedient cooperation. Most requests for release met rejection. Negativity and cynicism lurked in this world of "ironies, insults, and blows," to return to Lumumba's language.[150] In May 1950, the warden tried to unleash hope by lifting the relegation of Macha Simba Levy. An important Kitawala organizer in 1937 Elisabethville, transferred to Ekafera in 1944, Levy had been "fervent, active, and very fanatical." In late 1949, however, he went to the warden with a story of turning away from Kitawala, a new perspective opening before him. Levy turned over Bibles and their annotations: "Take them, I no longer believe in them." For the warden, this "conversion" was no hoax. Levy became courageous in the warden's eyes, and he called for his release. Recent internments of two Kitawala, Stephane Mutombo and Kali la Nyololo, had raised the place's temperature. Some had even had the nerve to baptize an Ekafera soldier. The warden asked Levy to serve as a spy. Soon, as "counterpropaganda" agent, Levy was prying, eavesdropping, while also lowering the penal camp's "thermometer." He worked against those trying to form a Kitawala "Republic" inside Ekafera. Their audacity meant locking up "dangerous leaders," while a sudden, surprise release of Levy would be a spectacular illustration of promise, enabling Ekafera's "Kitawala edifice" to crumble.[151]

Implicit was an argument about hope. Ekafera's Kitawala often exclaimed: "'You see! It serves nothing to amend oneself.'" The warden knew from a good source—a spy—that "hesitant ones" might abandon Kitawala and renounce proselytizing if only "rapid liberation" were sure. Many felt caught between "two fires," between whites who mistrusted all reform and their Kitawala leaders, whose reprisals were making some lives impossible. Manono youth complained that Kitawala elders were ruining lives and futures. Reform might give this younger generation a chance to return home and create households. By adding some glow to his counterpropaganda, the warden sought to weaken Kitawala. His "draconian" interior administration was producing results, he claimed, but severity plus clemency would force the "enemy" to lose ground.[152]

The contents of his harsh, rigid side remain dim. Few clues about Kitawala networks or the harm endured inside Ekafera may be further thickened here. The growing literature on the global history of prisons, penal colonies, security operations, and torture, alongside Lumumba's 1960 words, does heighten the historical imagination. In all likelihood, conditions were terribly grim.[153] At the very least, at a certain junction the Belgian Congo became deeply self-conscious about carceral management and its choice of words. In 1952, for example, commissioner Triest declared defensively that Ekafera had "nothing to do with a concentration camp." The next year, the word *dangerous* was removed from the institutional title. Like most Congolese prisons at the time, Ekafera was increasingly projected as if a reformatory; it began to boast films among social welfare and educational activities.[154] In 1954, when several relégués received releases, mental states seemed to improve. To further elevate spirits and counter Ekafera's image as "a penitentiary without hope," the warden wanted to lift yet more relegations.[155] In 1955, one of Ekafera's oldest Kimbanguists, first relegated in 1922, was transferred near his Bas Congo home, to the CARD penal colony at Oshwe. Three others received transfers to Oshwe at the same time. The warden spoke of morale improving alongside such news, which was less about liberations than exits, movements, proximity to family and home, with more visitors, too.[156]

Ekafera had become sinister and forlorn, eerie for some. The words *hope* and *hate* flickered, ominously. A psychological register little entered official use at Ekafera, though a new era had arrived when the "psychic" and "psychological" were seeping into colonial reports, speech, even gynecological research. Usually the words spoke to volition or deficiency on the part of Congolese. We turn now to another space of experience in Equateur, a gynecological clinic. Here, the word *psychic* seemed to rush ahead, bearing new research careers, official conjectures, and everyday fears about sexuality, modernity, and reproductive disruption.

The New Befale

We saw how the Songo experiment came to a fairly abrupt halt, just when Van Campenhout enabled a new development apparatus to walk in the door. While the excessive demands of the first stirred dissent and complicated security, FBEI Befale issued in a new era of professionalized development, "native welfare," and public health. The territory became the focus of an extraordinary infusion of monies under FBEI, founded in 1947 with a considerable capital outlay and lottery funds. A large share of the budget came from Belgium, paying back its colony for the wartime contributions of Congolese. The annual FBEI budget was some 300 million francs and identified four regions for "massive action." The largest was Befale territory, imaged as one of the most disinherited regions of the colony. It received some sixty million dollars for "massive action" in rural welfare.[157]

The regional economy had long relied on the collection of raw, unprocessed forest products—first wild rubber, then copal. Palm exploitation was healthier and more remunerative but had never supplanted copal. People still spent long periods in "inundated zones," their nganda, and the region had sagged terribly as a result. This was the FBEI narrative and it went on: a missionary presence had been limited to two Catholic missions, one Protestant, with medical occupation thin. Following the recommendations of FBEI advisors, Van Riel and De Wilde, attention should turn to the rural economy, rice farming, and health promotion. The chronicle of progress grew stronger as the years passed. In 1952, two doctors were directing a specialized hospital at Befale of four buildings, where staff covered census work, surgery, maternity care, and delivery of birth bonuses. Twelve dispensaries deepened the medical occupation.[158]

The developmentalist narrative and tasks resembled the Songo experiment, yet FBEI Befale was more utopic and research-based.[159] A promotional report spoke of the Mongo as a "decadent tribe" as late as 1964, declaring that low fecundity was *not* due to gonorrhea here.[160] Already in 1948, a Louvain professor and laboratory clinician had conducted a demographic study whose findings indicated that improved hygiene in Tshuapa would increase the birthrate.[161] Other social goals for rural publics flowed from these concerns: reducing inequity in living standards, improving well-being, and especially minimize the gulf between aspirations and living conditions for a mass rural public. Designed to fight malnutrition, disease, and "ignorance," the FBEI projects at Befale included new crops, stock-breeding, schools, and highly paternalist social medicine.[162]

Comprehensive, reformist, and idealistic plans, with economic, medical, social, and psychological dimensions, produced far-reaching change. The agricultural included trucks, drivers, bridge upkeep, and brick presses. A modernist aesthetic eliminated a key visual register of the "customary," systematically removing all *paillotes* (straw roofs) in the territory. Rapid social engineering, mobile dispensaries, and the massive introduction of cash produced stark change, as did the presence of so many European experts with their families, including social workers, agronomists, and doctors.

In 1948, FBEI hired a woman doctor, Cécile Van Ackere; a year later, a gynecologist, Robert Allard, came on board.[163] Two medical nuns and two sanitary agents arrived in 1951. Four Congolese nurses and thirty nurse assistants joined them. By 1949, almost half of FBEI Befale funding went to "medico-social" action: two ambulances, six health centers, a school, and public works.[164] The medical complex with surgical center and dispensaries transformed the region's medical infrastructure. The Protestant hospital at Baringa also blossomed with two doctors, a large staff, maternity, and rising number of patients. By 1951, Befale was overseeing 218,000 dispensary visits, 27,000 new patient cases, 700 hospitalizations, 1,000 baby clinic visits, and 110 maternity births. Most of 550 some gynecological visits at Befale concerned sterility.[165] As medical touring increased, so did gynecological and sterility consultations, from five hundred a year in 1950 to over three thousand at the end of the decade. An important goal was "to create a psychological climate conducive to child-bearing," by providing maternity gifts, roads, ferries, drinking water, infant clinics, primary schooling, domesticity training, mass education, and house-to-house visiting. The broad course of social, medical, and economic action seemed "the prime cause of the spectacular recovery" in Befale's birth rate, first recorded in 1952.[166]

A small, specialized clinic was part of the pronatalist thrust. The most important rural infertility service in Congo, probably all of Africa, it opened in 1950. Its chief gynecologist, Dr. Allard, tracked venereal disease, performed pelvic exams, did salpingectomy surgery, and conducted research on historical demography, surgical results, and hormonal treatments. He worked in a FBEI world where research was well funded, serious, often quite sophisticated, and undergirded by a psychological ethos. While the biological connections among syphilis and miscarriage, gonorrhea and sterility were basic clinical knowledge, an official Belgian line had emerged that associated this region's birth rate with psychic effects of colonialism. This postwar thinking drew attention not to the negative effects of a violent past or contemporary penury, but rather to the aspirations of newly modern subjects.[167]

Subtle, thorough analysis of causes of the low birth rate, with detailed localization, shaped an influential report prepared by Allard and Van Riel. They used quantitative and qualitative demography, and Allard went on to research the effects of economic development on health. He returned to old language—we saw it in Armani, then in Schwers—of a "shock of civilizations." Yet he historicized and differentiated. Allard analyzed longitudinal data in many small study populations, usually chiefdoms. Not all, he learned, had equally undergone a reduction in the birth rate around 1900–1910. This crucial historical decade quietly pressed its way into colonial demographic analysis, therefore, but as if a function of early colonial contact and occupation, without specifying the sexual, reproductive, and bodily nature of violence and harm in the Abir concession.[168]

Allard keenly diagnosed the psychosomatic factors involved in high sterility and its sudden turnaround. The Befale birth rate seemed to rise in the early 1950s. Analysis clinched the hunch as fact, as did the number of recorded births.[169] Allard reasoned that a positive "psychological shock"[170] had grown out of the new FBEI activity, out of the enthusiastic interest of its personnel beckoning for births and infants, as well as its profamily propaganda, countless sterility inquiries, and ubiquitous birth bonuses—clinic gifts of milk, sugar, and baby clothes. Perhaps all this attention, he conjectured with an implicit vitalism, had reawakened the wish for offspring. The way FBEI enabled new ways of living had fashioned new dreams as well.

While most venereal and gynecological research became sterility research at Befale, by 1956 sterility incidence seemed to be declining. Allard's 1956 thesis traced the Tshuapa and Befale situations back to 1910, showing how decreases in "vitality" varied significantly across groups. He discredited the hypothesis of male sterility as a cause (though he later found male gonorrhea implicated in female childlessness). He emphasized that few women were fertile, with 277 of 1,000 having no children, though some married several times. While some childlessness was pathological, some was voluntary, sometimes unconsciously so. When European "penetration" began, Allard suggested, interest in infants declined as clan groups began to disintegrate. In postwar Congo, individualized longing for children was emerging for the first time.[171]

The evidence seemed mixed. By 1956, the governor announced that more effort was needed to counter voluntary sterility and feed dreams. With roads now everywhere, speed and travel were feeding new fantasies of a good life. The 25 percent of men who worked in agricultural enterprises should be able to meet their aspirations in worker camps. Otherwise, the central basin would "continue to empty itself" into towns. An aversion to motherhood was a problem. Children seemed an obstacle to comfort and ease, an attitude that was slowing the birth rate.[172] The very idea of antimaternalist women stirred nervousness, in Congo and farther afield.

Dr. Allard's Infertility Device

Part of a network of colonial researchers who were publishing internationally, Allard worked from rural Befale as state-led science arrived with force. The technological and the psychic, with a dazzle of the American, came alive in his research. The boundary between the clinical and the experimental sometimes blurred, though he insisted all sterility research should stem from patients who came forward voluntarily. He took inspiration from *Fertility and Sterility*, the American journal founded in 1951 and featuring dozens of articles on the psychosomatic and technological dimensions of sterility.

Gleaning ideas about the psychogenic, psychodynamic, and personality dimensions to sterility, notions in vogue in the United States, he modified a psychological projection test known as the Congo T.A.T. A Belgian psychologist had developed it, showing his Congolese research subjects a series of images while asking them to tell a story about each.[173] Allard instead presented six images, preclassified by kinds of infertility. With such a coding system, the signifying process of projection was mechanical, meaning deduced directly from the image chosen by the research subject. Three images signified a desire for "maternity": household utensils, a mother with child, and a woman nursing an infant. Three were coded to signify an unconscious wish for "sterility": a beer-drinking woman, a man in modern dress and busy at wage work, and a bicycle. In a sense, a moral semiotics for the modern and transgressive produced his contrived visual method for dividing subjects into types, with the research design revealing his vocabulary and gender expectations.[174]

Allard combined his projection test results with the experimental capabilities of a recent technology, used globally in sterility diagnosis and research: uterotubal insufflation devices. Designed to measure fallopian occlusion, the apparatus introduced carbon dioxide under pressure into the uterus and fallopian tubes. If the tubes were either not blocked or had become deblocked, gas would enter into the peritoneal cavity. Changes in gas pressure measured the degree of occlusion, in turn recorded by a kymograph (see figure 5.2). The legibility and validity of such graphs were under scientific discussion, and the word *spasm* became significant in Allard's diagnostics. Graphed images suggesting "trembling" indicated atypical permeability or partially blocked

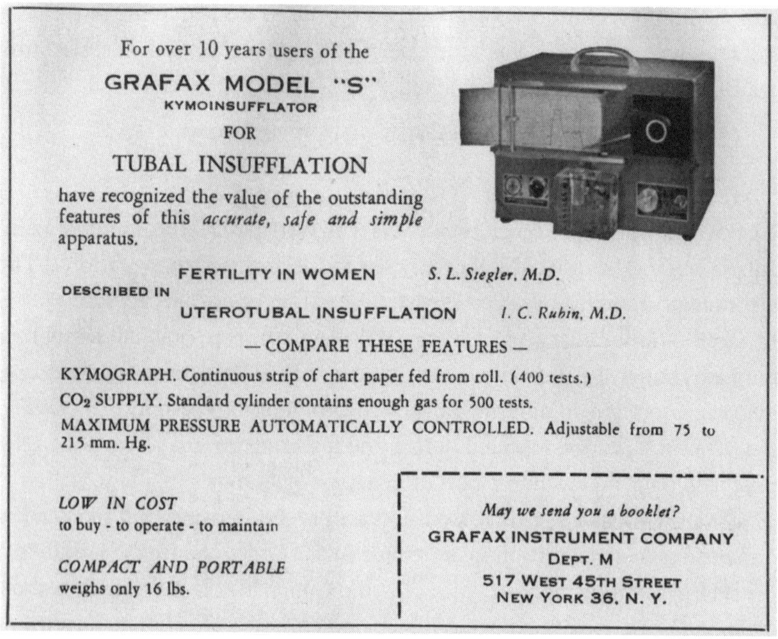

For over 10 years users of the

GRAFAX MODEL "S"

KYMOINSUFFLATOR

FOR

TUBAL INSUFFLATION

have recognized the value of the outstanding features of this *accurate, safe and simple* apparatus.

FERTILITY IN WOMEN   S. L. Siegler, M.D.

DESCRIBED IN

UTEROTUBAL INSUFFLATION   I. C. Rubin, M.D.

— COMPARE THESE FEATURES —

KYMOGRAPH. Continuous strip of chart paper fed from roll. (400 tests.)

CO_2 SUPPLY. Standard cylinder contains enough gas for 500 tests.

MAXIMUM PRESSURE AUTOMATICALLY CONTROLLED. Adjustable from 75 to 215 mm. Hg.

LOW IN COST
to buy - to operate - to maintain

COMPACT AND PORTABLE
weighs only 16 lbs.

May we send you a booklet?
GRAFAX INSTRUMENT COMPANY
DEPT. M
517 WEST 45TH STREET
NEW YORK 36, N. Y.

FIGURE 5.2 American advertisement for a portable tubal insufflation apparatus, showing its chart paper and gas cylinder. From *Fertility and Sterility* 11 (1960): n.p.

fallopian tubes. Some doctors used the device, designed for detecting tubal blockage, also in mechanically treating such an occlusion. They did so by elevating the gas pressure.[175]

Allard experimented with timing and introduced cerebral sedatives and stimulants. While some patients departed rapidly, others returned for care. Some lied about the discomfort caused, he sensed; some 10 percent achieved pregnancy, having learned that their pain discouraged the doctor from using the insufflation device. A few told him that just a single use of his trembling machine enabled a first-time pregnancy. This Congolese pattern was not out of keeping with that found by American doctors using the device to treat occlusion.[176]

Two patients who avidly sought pregnancy through their clinical visits confounded this doctor's categories. He sensed that these women earned money through sexual relations with Befale men, whether *évolués*, merchants, or others with money to spare. He also knew that in Europe the label *prostitute* would be applied. Yet these two women seemed to possess a curious mentality, since "their way of life does not keep them from wanting a child." While avoiding calling them femmes libres, their willingness to return to his clinic and provide vaginal specimens was a bonus. He learned that theirs usually came laced with sperm and carried *Trichomonas* by using the Huhner sterility test, a postcoital examination of vaginal mucous for live sperm. What were these women seeking while cooperating with the colonial gynecologist and his multiple pelvic exams? It seems that attentive care from a doctor careful not to unduly stigmatize came their way, while Allard also used his special apparatus with a reputation for igniting pregnancies.[177]

This colonial gynecologist concluded that the images produced by the insufflation apparatus, and sketched onto its graph paper, represented either tubal blockage or patency. He referred to them less as signs of physical lesion, however, than as possessing a "spastic" aspect suggesting "a nervous origin."[178] The ironies seem many. Allard, less interested in the mechanical potential of insufflation than its psychic implications, concluded that many of his patients had long had primary sterility of a spastic, nervous nature.[179] His findings adjoined nervousness, of no small resonance here. With an eye out for the psychic, this nervous lens drew him to projections, to proclivities for the modern and their effects on fertility and maternal desire. In using the latest gynecological techniques and vocabulary of the 1950s, diagnosing sterility as uneasy and convulsive, all the while he cultivated Congolese women patients seeking a pregnancy through enabling their repeated engagements with his infertility device.

Conclusion

Historians have not thought enough about the development appeals and nervous vocabularies of late colonial regimes. Fashioned to secure cooperation and quiet, we have seen that this postwar and still nervous colony worked through manipulation and technological allure. Scholars and journalists have labeled the Belgian Congo as "paternalist" since the 1950s.[180] Its populist oppositional movements have not been neglected, though they have usually been delimited—almost marginalized—as "religious movements," separated from security and development initiatives.

This chapter has considered how two strains of religious practice, Kitawala and Kimbanguism, each with therapeutic dimensions, entered southern Equateur from the 1930s. They arrived largely as a result of state practices of banning and relegation, concentration and detention. Intertwined with these attempts at containment and elimination were forms of seduction, especially once Congo's postwar development regime and its security surrogates emerged as ways to tame and calm "xenophobic," "subversive" movements.

The official decisions to target first Songo chiefdom, then Befale territory were not insignificant, in terms of history or security. Though a historical rationale seems never to have been articulated on paper, this was precisely the area that produced, via its mutilation photographs, international scandal in the 1900s. There is no evidence to suggest that these same images, surely available within libraries in a global imperial sphere, directly operated on the selection of research and development sites. Still, Songo combined feistiness with a shrunken milieu.

Late colonial fixations were twinned and knotted. They promoted medical progress, infrastructural modernity, population growth, and sterility eradication, as well as the containment and arrest of insurgent movements. The first aspect waxed proud, shining while aiming—however unconsciously—at alleviating colonial guilt about a terrible past that shocked and endured as harm and felt injury. The second was still the nervous streak, huddled, tense, convulsive, clumsy, and inept before Congolese insurgencies with amazing skill in secrecy and motion. These religious rebels, whether moderns, workers, or peasants, devised underground mail networks, rapid getaways, and languages of millennial reverie. The Belgian regime was keen to subdue and win over, not with medication and maternity care alone, but with forms of distraction. These appeals came in a shiny register, promising modern comfort, leisure time, and happiness. The confrontations between shrewd rebels and nervous colonial agents suggest that Congo's decolonization was already in process in this modernizing Equateur hinterland during the war years, if not before.

An important irony expressed itself through folly:[181] bringing together diverse categories of rebels into a single, porous penal colony, and imagining their ideas could be contained within its borders. Siting Ekafera right where the Abir rubber concession once produced atrocious rape, mutilation, and war remains an acute paradox. When choosing the site, Equateur authorities spoke of needing a "no man's land" for the governor general. They imagined isolation as achievable, not unlike the way Ryckmans and others imagined Songo chiefdom as bounded. Yet Ekafera, like the Songo experiment, proved pervious to entries, outlets, intrusions, and escapes. The penal colony neither contained nor curbed. Rather, Ekafera concentrated the fractious and ardent, many of whom as Kitawala opposed all state power while seeking deliverance from colonial rule and this carceral dispensation. The sinister penal colony became absurd—in Belgian words, a "hoax"—as it entrenched and spread Kitawala in Befale territory and beyond.[182] Befale also lay in a plantation zone where willful, feisty workers did not hesitate to ditch work when they pleased.[183] As "infection" with Kitawala increased, the nervous state spoke of pathology and contagion.[184] At the same time, high-energy, well-funded schemes for development were unfolding in this earmarked FBEI terrain.

As decolonization approached, the biopolitical state had more money, expertise, remedies, and pride than ever before. Patrice Lumumba's coarse, barbed, and heartfelt words in 1960 about the everyday humiliations of being colonized in Congo, subjected to Belgian masters, startled and disturbed. Ever since, his language and the shock of that historic speech have served as touchstones within memories and within studies of "structures of feeling"[185] in colonial Congo and its tumultuous decolonization. His words about relegation and penal colonies signal their salience in political consciousness at the time.

Though visible signs of the Abir rubber regime were likely gone by the 1940s, that many in Equateur had been forced again to do grueling rubber labor during the war was not forgotten.[186] By siting this penal colony in a former zone of monstrous death and injury from which refugees fled, the nervous state combined a curious notion of "empty" lands with scientific investigation into disturbing barrenness and abandonment. When teams of Congolese demographic workers arrived from 1955, Schwers's extinction logics had receded. The debates of the provincial commission were past. These census takers worked as part of Anatole Romaniuk's massive colony-wide census through sampling. Coquilhatville and Basankusu territories had the most women with no children. In Befale, 37 percent of women were sterile, whereas 54 percent were without child in Coquilhatville. While such exceptionally high sterility suggested a colony-wide anomaly, fact likely combined with stereotypes and deception in producing these arresting numbers. Censusing remains terrifying to Africans. Lying and flight often result, since it is felt that offspring—whether desired or achieved—may be devoured through processes of inscribing details of pregnancy, birth, and loss.[187]

Allard's infertility clinic was part of the immense FBEI installation, first established as Songo, where Schwers toured in the late 1930s. A state-of-the-art infertility machine had a novel focus: *modern* women and girls. This generation seemed to be opting out of maternity, so fresh logics of colonial nervousness went (not unlike the way abortifacients long raised alarm).[188] Its women were keen to partake in the powers of the doctor's almost magical, pregnancy-producing machine.

Those who spent colonial in colonial clinical spaces sometimes daydreamed, therefore. Dreamwork was foundational to Kitawala too. The next chapter turns more square to idleness, strolling, and musings. Ambling, moving to be seen, may suggest dance. Those who worked with letter writing or pharmaceuticals shifted and swayed, while many sauntered with reverie. Given the intensifying security in and outside Ekafera, the carceral and development schemes that inspected, channeled, and blocked, we need to ask more about kinds of motion in this colonial milieu.

| Motion

Slim threads from Befale's security archive suggest kinds and degrees of the dangerous, the hazardous, and the aleatory. Assorted persons under suspicion appeared in reports and interrogations in the 1940s and 1950s, with many *neither* detainees or *relégués* in the Ekafera penal colony. While much in this archive relates to a colonial state trying to get a grip over Kitawala persons and activities, other bits suggest oddities of the devious, shifty, or perilous, and thus in what Sureté tracked. Possible endings to colonial rule surfaced more or less dimly in official horizons of the 1950s with new futures flittering boldly alongside signs of trouble and suggesting an end to a long "time of wait."[1]

Decolonization's approach, if imperceptible or disallowed in most Belgian minds, made itself felt through new kinds of nervousness and perceptions about race. Novel kinds of trembling and discord, like registers of opposition and suppression, emerged. Throughout Tshuapa, Kitawala mixed with vernacular forms of therapeutic practice, and such bleeding combined with and emanated from maladies and dearth.

A Nervous State has tracked two modalities of colonial power and remediation. In addition to an exploding public health infrastructure, we have seen an intensifying colonial security system aimed at inspecting, blocking, and channeling movement. Not the first but the second pitted itself against vernacular trafficking in medicines, spirits, charms, and letters. Earlier chapters treated the nervous and the biopolitical largely as separate faces of the state, each imprinting itself on history while operating as its own track. Their institutionalization—within a penal camp, within a network of clinics and development—suggested a linear pair, resulting in two enclosed spaces.

We also saw junctures where the two crossed. Not only did Kitawala elements mix with Kimbanguism in Tshuapa, but the wound-up security campaign kept escalating, words of contagion abetting. At the same time, development projects produced health by lifting standards of living, extending care, and attracting via glossy, modern materialities. The medical also securitized, especially when the venereal opened up issues of multiple, concurrent sexual partners.

This chapter further undercuts this dual, analogous structuring. It looks beyond these modes, beyond bleeding among the securitizing and medicalizing. The central query concerns motion, though also the ways nervousness burst forth and remained. Who could stroll in Equateur, Tshuapa, and Befale?

Usually associated with Parisian flaneurs and urbane wandering through nineteenth-century commercial arcades, *flânerie* helps pry open a novel, capacious way of perceiving colonial motion.[2] Limitations on physical mobility were many in Belgian Africa. Receiving passports to move depended on medical inspection, while work situations shaped who could move, where and when. But not all mobility was physical. Motion suggests kinds of travel and mingling, embracing bodily movement, dance, and mail circuits, with trafficking in distraction, medicines, and reverie. All could involve work or flights of the imagination.

If we seek Benjaminian inflections as well as individualized, detached observation[3] within this zone with totalitarian aspirations and surveillance techniques, we find *strolling* in this equatorial milieu where it seems almost *not* to belong. Often unexpected, ambling pushes inquiry beyond physical mobility. Benjamin's reflections on idleness widen motion to embrace *distraction*, a key realm of Congolese motion and music.[4] Unlike Fanon's emphasis on colonized immobility or the recent scholarly focus on mobility as roads and physical travel,[5] this chapter considers *kinds of motion* and *kinds who moved*, while wondering about spectators, detectives, authors, and dancers among Congolese.

Motion returns us to reverie. When was reverie a collective daydream of a constituted or perceived crowd? When can we detect individualized flaneurs with "horizons of expectation,"[6] flamboyance, a search for fame, or readings of spaces or situations? This inquiry also asks about appropriation: How did Congolese make processes of medicalizing and securitizing their own in this time of high developmentalism? What kinds of subaltern motion and idleness were possible within this late colonial patchwork of spaces and techniques?

FIGURE 6.1 An early image of a colonial flaneur. Missionary-crafted block print of a handsome, pleased, urbane, modern Congolese with a stylish European cap, cigarette, and elegant hands. That Flemish priests were encouraging such self-fashioning, alongside reading and writing, is significant. Artist: Petrus Vertenten. Published in the Lomongo-language Catholic magazine, *Le Coq chante* 4, 1 September 1939, 14. Courtesy of Archief van de Missionarissen van het H. Hart, Borgerhout, Belgium.

Strolling seems not to have been limited to a particular social class. Congo's threshold figures included colonized men of middle rank with chances to amble along streets, roads, rivers, and texts. Among them were Congo's male nurses.[7] Yet those who wandered included independent women—cloth sellers and traders in sex, beer, style, and wares. Others were healers or dancers possessed. While some of Coquilhatville's and Befale's flaneurs of the 1940s and 1950s moved in promenade, to be seen, with daydreams of travel and upward mobility in mind, other moderns worked through medicines, letters, and music (see figure 6.1).

Many more in Equateur—plantation workers, those dwelling in villages or opting for *nganda* time—had latitude to amble, even while battling colonial strictures, work demands, and a sense of untold captivity. The question of how much space they had, where and when, is difficult to nail down. These excruciating war years demanded and inspired new forms of moving and escape. The sudden spike in standards of living in the early 1950s changed the moods and materialities of Congolese in motion. Keeping alive ecological niches deep in the forest for secrecy, hiding, and relative idleness, many so-called customary subjects still used nganda, fishing, and copal collecting to evade colonial demands. Those who spent time in these spaces seem to have relished wonder and reverie. Daydreaming was fundamental to Kitawala, while far and wide many individuals were seeking wealth and fame.

Diverse threads remind that this colonial milieu was sick and strange, producing infirmity and perversity, and sometimes seething. As light winds of decolonization began wafting through, the pathological deepened in a sense. Yet so did motion. That the Belgian colonial regime was perfecting the production of health through lifting living standards and organizing, action-packed programs in paternalist social medicine added to strangeness within this social pathology.[8]

The chapter considers two contrary spaces as well as people and ideas moving within them. Loma chiefdom was home to the former Abir post of Lingunda, where atrocious violence became sadistic in the Free State period; this chiefdom became an important home for Kitawala from beyond Ekafera and the post at Befale. The second space was the biggest town in the province, its capital Coquilhatville—or as most everyone called it, Coq. The 1959 visit of Graham Greene and newspaper sources help open this provincial capital's diverse spaces, debates, and moods. Three figures in partial motion stand out as striking within the security archive: a detainee in Ekafera's prison, a nurse at Befale's FBEI hospital, and a traveling musician who resembled an urbane flaneur (or a flamboyant *sapeur* finding fame today).[9] This trio with dreams enables probing further a range in kinds of motion. The chapter closes with the energy of colonial nervousness, with the gusts of decolonization twisting futures and disturbing sleep.

Drama in Loma

Many security operations focused on Kitawala outside the confines of Ekafera. Such was the case in nearby Loma. In official eyes, it was one of the most "infected" chiefdoms in the territory. A list seized in 1945 suggested there were 136 Kitawala, with 53 women. A year later, two of the eleven Kitawala leaders interned at Ekafera were from Loma.[10] On April 3, 1948, a sanitary agent, François Poffé, wrote to the Befale territorial from Lofiko village in a state of alarm about "a big crisis in Loma chiefdom." Loma subjects did not "want to present themselves for the medical census," and "they no longer want to pay taxes." Someone even told Chief Albert Bofola that his chiefdom was "stinking with Kitawala." Worried about such "troubles" escalating, this low-ranking medical agent cautioned of a "huge affair," which could not "be stifled without attention." Poffé pleaded with the administrator for someone to "come here on the spot."[11] His boss replied tersely: "there is no question of sending soldiers."

He also advised that another territorial, Bekaert, was already in Loma, sizing up the collective "frame of mind."[12]

Three days later, Bekaert was still in Loma conducting interrogations, asking about Kitawala insignia and baptisms.[13] Chief Bofola began with a story about learning that his assistant, Lofuko, had seized a group of Kitawala leaders. Another man, Likokoto, had denounced some men as Kitawala in Bolima-Ngere village. About the same time, the overseer Iloku reminded Bofola that gifts of salt would produce a willing crowd when the time came for an official convocation. Angry, Likokoto urged people to see this patrimonial exercise with suspicious, critical eyes, to even refuse the chief's salt. Such opposition infuriated the overseer. Iloku threatened to send Likokoto to the white man, and Likokoto menaced back. If Iloku dared to turn him in, he would betray the fact that Bolima-Ngere was full of Kitawala. "Right then and there," Iloku remembered, "Likokoto denounced the disciples of this sect to me." Soon Iloku communicated these names revealed to Chief Bofola.[14]

There was more. Likokoto was furious because his daughter had been under undue pressure to join Kitawala. Her husband was a Kitawala man, and his wife Julienne Baasa had come to her father complaining that her spouse had been beating her because she did not want to be baptized. She was the one who shared with her father all the Kitawala names, thereby equipping him to pass these on. She also told the interrogator that her husband was "always hitting" her.[15] Clearly this "stinking" chiefdom stank in more ways than one.

The chief initiated an investigation. First, he had some suspects show him their place for secret gatherings. A Kitawala leader named Jean Bakili and another accused, Makambo, accompanied Chief Bofola into full forest to see this gathering place. Sticks with flowers surrounded the clearing. The search grew violent when Pierre Bofaso, one of the accused, "destroyed the flowers." Paraphernalia found in people's huts was seized, including two small bottles filled with palm oil, five Kitawala badges or insignia, one bamboo wrapper containing three notebooks about Kitawala education with name lists, and Bakili's work booklet with writing about Kitawala.[16]

Such was the context in which the Belgian sanitary agent had been having trouble accomplishing his basic work: medical censusing to find disease and give injections at a time when gonorrhea was epidemic. Two villages, called to present themselves one Wednesday, did not show up. When they came the following morning, they arrived at 9 o'clock, three hours late.[17] Tardiness suggested reluctance and also jockeying in relation to expectations. Chief Bofola knew that some were Kitawala. He had been waiting for a medical convocation in order to locate and seize some. In many respects, this customary official had become a nervous chief, and he was using medical censusing routines—whole villages marching in at dawn for bodily inspections—to ensnare the guilty and exhibit his own innocence.

In the end, Chief Bofola had complaints against fourteen, and he directed them into the official interrogation room. The administrator used the word *tranquil* to describe Loma's "frame of mind" when the investigations began, though by the end, he sent off several Kitawala to Befale for decision-making at this higher level. Phillipe Ingonda, affiliated with Kitawala since January, had a badge. Jean Bakili had baptized him one night "in the river when we were looking for copal." Kitawala met for nocturnal gatherings on Wednesdays and Sundays. Bakili taught prayers and read Bible passages. The "lessons" embraced instructions and proscriptions. One prohibition, long part of regional healing movements from Ikakota to Likili as we have seen was there: sexual relations during the daytime were forbidden. Individualized attention to injury was novel. Flasks of palm oil enabled self-healing, and perhaps new kinds of individualized strolling required a similar protection. A slogan spoke of harm and healing: "When you have a wound, put palm oil on it."[18]

The interrogator posed questions about the "anti-State character" of Kitawala. Ingonda explained what Bakili had said: "Americans will come to chase away the state, and then Kitawala will become the state." Bakili also taught that after death, "we would be reborn whites." This reverie, first imparted as a Kitawala lesson and then expressed to the white man during interrogation, continued: "The moment the Americans come, they will give us guns to chase away other whites. And we will make medicines . . . to kill you."[19] The "you," of course, was in part the white man sitting right before them. Did Monsieur Bekaert pause? Such interrogation documents are layers, cobbled through translation and interpretation, though this one suggests the interrogator moved right along.

Marc Lokuli had been Kitawala since 1947. Bakili baptized him, too. Lokuli declared, "I possess a badge and a bottle of palm oil," while noting, "Bakili promised us that the Americans would come to liberate us in three years, and then we will be the masters. The Americans will furnish us with arms to chase away the other whites." If they died beforehand, "our god will thank us by having us reborn as whites." Calling Kitawala "the religion of the Americans," Makambo said "Americans will come liberate us, so we will be like the whites."[20]

When it was the turn of Jean Bakili himself, the leader spoke laconically. Jean Lintombe had baptized him in the Lulonga in 1945, giving him his badge, bottle of palm oil, and notebook. He still had all three. Bakili refused the idea that he was Kitawala "principal" in Bolima-Ngere but admitted baptizing Lokuli and Ingonda. He was brief when the interrogator asked, "Is it true you said Americans will come?" "No," he replied, or so the transcript suggests, with Bakili also starkly declaring his innocence.[21]

Dreaming

These interrogation snippets tell us about kinds of motion in a highly regulated colonial world. Frantz Fanon sometimes misread colonial situations as starkly productive of immobility.[22] Poetic daydreaming suggested rather hypothetical lives, collecting around images of rescuing strangers who would arrive from afar. Would this be decolonization on the quick, with one flag coming down while another shot up? Such imagery with flags was present in rumors of the early 1930s, as we saw. The idea of a quick turnaround was still at work in the late 1940s, but flags were less part of the repertoire than airplanes and guns. Such reverie has a history, predating the arrival of Marcus Garvey–influenced daydreams into central and southern Africa in the 1920s and stretching back to the times of Ikakota.[23]

"Dreaming has a share in history," Walter Benjamin once wrote. He also observed that while dreams may "have started wars" they stand as "a shortcut to banality."[24] The kind of daydreaming in and near Loma had become so ordinary, repetitive, and even rehearsed that the colonial interrogator, the stilted archive suggests, hardly paused or probed. It is as if the answers about arriving Americans had become so predictable or stale that it did not occur to him to seek elaboration. He (or the transcriptionist?) just moved on perhaps to the next question, then the next subject. But this does not mean that he was not party to this kind of reverie. He surely sensed that Kitawala as a movement was producing such horizons at a time when it also engaged in a kind of therapeutic war, even if this medical vocabulary escaped him.

Securitization was at work all the while, whether in capturing the banal or documenting the aleatory. Medicalization and the therapeutic permeated everything, including the nervous state and its processes of tracking down risk. Kitawala suspects sometimes took refuge as hospital patients, using a clinic as an alibi. On June 22, 1943, two Kitawala condemned to the Basankusu Prison were instead far away in the Boende state hospital. Authorities were waiting for the medical release of Bekungu and Beselo so the governor's carceral order could be completed.[25] Were some seeking protection and refuge in hospital settings? Or, were these Kitawala disciples and leaders sick? Likely, the answer is some of each. Kitawala recruited new members through promises of healing, offering bottles of palm oil as a novel kind of medicine that reassured.

The lowly Belgian sanitary agent was there with his village routines of convocation, censusing, and disease screening. The chief knew the drill so well that he was ready to use these early morning body inspections for his own purposes. Chief Bofola used the same exercise to catch those persons whom he needed to produce in order to clear his own name. After all, being accused of letting his chiefdom grow "stinking" with Kitawala, the chief developed an arrest and search operation, while aiming at self-protection.

Fanon also wrote about dreaming within colonial situations: "There is no native who does not dream at least once a day of setting himself up in the . . . place" of the colonizer; "the native never ceases to dream . . . not of becoming . . . but of substituting himself" for the colonizer. Fanon's dichotomous thinking had him oddly opposing "the colonial world and its barbed-wire entanglements" to "zombies" within an "occult sphere." Ultimately he sought to comprehend what suddenly could make "the lid blow off" in a decolonizing situation. Yet his primitivist reductions went with language about the "emotional sensitivity" of natives, "prey to unspeakable terrors yet happy to lose themselves in a dreamlike torment." He fathomed decolonization as a sudden reversal, while rendering the historical turning point with caricature: "After having wallowed in the most outlandish phantoms, at long last the native, gun in hand, stands face to face with . . . the forces of colonialism."[26]

Reverie, old in Equateur, long involved dreams of substitution. Yet to call it a zombified, "dreamlike torment" would miss much subtlety and individuation. Fanon's reductions distort, even if his vivid notion of decolonization as a blast of an event, like a lid blown off, remains useful as a diagnostic of temper and tempo.[27] Rage and nervousness, like other moods, sometimes permeated this milieu. We turn now to Equateur's biggest town, where the circulation of persons, fears, anger, and daydreams of substitution appear in a different light.

A Belgian Cyclist, a Lucienne Delyle Song

Nothing was beyond suspicion in postwar Tshuapa, even the sojourns of a European man on a bicycle. Monsieur Buchs, formerly an accountant in Basankusu, became the subject of a "discreet inquiry" in 1947 because he often cycled to Baringa or Befale, especially on Saturdays or holidays. His journeys emerged as an afterthought in a letter about Kitawala propaganda from the Basankusu territorial to his Befale counterpart. Buchs liked to stroll through this stretch of countryside with newly paved roads. The rarity of a white man

FIGURE 6.2 Who owned Odéon record players in Equateur? In 1934, perhaps only Belgians and Portuguese. Yet in postwar Equateur, a visiting Kinois (Bowane) wanted the phonograph owned by a rural nurse. Ad for the iconic record label Odéon, founded in Berlin but global in scope; it sold stylus-based disks, musical recordings, and portable players. Image appeared in the annual colonial guide to imported products, designed for European residents, *Annuaire des importateurs, exportateurs, entreprises commerciales, industrielles, minières et agricoles opérant au Congo belge 1934*, n.p.

on a bicycle, over such a long distance and often at night, had led to gossip among "certain people." The query aimed at finding out "the motives of these often nocturnal movements."[28]

Music, records, and books also were subjected to security surveillance (see figure 6.2). On March 5, 1948, all the colony's governors received word from the governor general that Sureté had seized a gramophone disk whose contents could "harm the Security of the State." Imported by the "Maison Patou of Léopoldville" (or "Auditorium"), this Columbia disk—no. CL 82 OIDF 3047—contained "Amalaouta," a song registered in France and sung by one of the most popular French singers of her time, Lucienne Delyle.[29] Maison Patou had imported five copies; only four had been recovered. It was possible other record companies received the same disk. Thus the instructions were these: "please search among all sellers" of this kind of article and check "if the disk is not there." If the missing disk was found, "seize it according to Ordonnance no. 62 A.P.A.J. of 14 May 1940."[30]

The song's frenetic, uneasy sounds and words suggest profound fear, reminiscent of the gloom of *Heart of Darkness*.[31] The lyrics tell of colonial nervous-

FIGURE 6.3 Lucienne Delyle, one of the most famous, glamorous, popular French cabaret singers of her day, pictured on the cover of sheet music for her primitivist song "Refrain Sauvage." Its nervous, tropical rhythms returned with intensity in her song "Amalaouta," boycotted in 1948 by Belgian Congo authorities. © Studio Harcourt Paris.

ness and alarm, with primitivist rhythms similar to those in one of Lucienne Delyle's earlier songs, "Refrain Sauvage" (see figure 6.3).

> Devant la maison du blanc
> Les noirs tournent en dansant
> Et sous le soleil brûlant
> S'élève un chant menaçant
> Amalaouta–ooh-ooh . . .
>
> . . .
>
> Prenez garde à vous—
> Ce soir c'est pour nous, fête à vaudou
> Si Dieu ce soir, pour venger pauvre noire, te choisit
> Toi perdre espoir et plus jamais revoir ton pays
>
> . . .
>
> Blanc caché là-bas—
> Et le tam-tam redoublant
> Dans l'ombre le feu jaillit

. . .

Entends-tu nos voix—ooh ooh
des Bongos
Maison du blanc devient flambé jusqu'au jour
Vaudou content, si blanc rester dedans pour toujours

. . .

Amalaouta, God of the Bongos . . .

In front of the white man's house
Blacks circle and dance
And under the burning sun
Rises a menacing chant
Amalaouta–ooh-ooh . . .

. . .

Beware—
This night is for us, feast of the voodoo
If tonight God, to avenge the poor black wretch, chooses you
You lose hope and never again see your country

. . .

White man, hiding over there—
As the tam-tam sounds faster and louder
In the shadows fire leaps

. . .

Can you hear our voices—ooh ooh
the Bongos
The white man's house burns till dawn
Voodoo pleased, if the white man stays inside forever

. . .

Amalaouta, God of the Bongos.

"Amalaouta" was hardly the only French song to invoke empire.[32] But this
one panicked nerves in Belgian Congo. It suggested "primitive," erotic, equatorial worlds in both French and Belgian Congo and terrible dangers stalking
white men there. This one might not make it home or come out alive, and
his house was on fire. Sex was part of the story of intensifying drumming
and flames. Menacing and erotic, the song embraced Africans using dance,
drumming, fire, and their gods. It speaks of avenging a poor black woman,
intimating sexual violation by the white man. The plaintive rhythms maintain
an edge of sorrow, while explosive sounds grow restless. While the drumming
suggests a primitive, savage world, the story is about a reviled, terrified co-

lonial white man. The intense pulsing music complements the panic of the words; wild frenzy is suggested by throbbing sounds, the allusion to sexual violence, and the intimate embrace of the title.[33] The idea of a "white man's house on fire," burning until dawn, was too dangerous to allow in circulation, and further alarming paradoxes might ensue if "Amalaouta" were to be played in Congo's dancing venues.

Dance music, important in town bars, was only one form of motion in the postwar years. People were moving, touring, reading, and viewing in new kinds of ways.

Urbanity and Anachronisms

In 1955, a Congolese woman went off to Lisbon to meet her husband, recruited there as athlete.[34] A few Congolese were traveling by airplane, moving about as groups of tourists in their colony.[35] A study trip made by Congolese women made news.[36] The editor of *Mbandaka*, Justin Bomboko, traveled to Belgium in 1955. As Equateur's most successful Mongo intellectual and politician, he went on to impress and steer.[37] When others from Coq came home after a trip to Brussels, it was with bitter complaints about a hotel that refused to serve them drinks.[38]

Graham Greene visited Coquilhatville and Equateur in 1959 in search of a leprosy doctor figure for his "burnt-out case."[39] The Belgian leprologist at nearby Yonda, Michel Lechat, took the famous British novelist to some of Coq's best bars. The visitor also had "duty drinks" at the governor's before he left.[40] Greene's visit began in Léopoldville: a "brand new city with miniature skyscrapers" where he "lunched fourteen floors up." There, he heard about the troubles of decolonization, many a result of "the Kibongoists [sic] who believe in the divinity of Kibongo [sic], a man who died in prison in the 40's in Elisabethville." (Simon Kimbangu, in fact, died in prison in 1951.) Soon Greene moved on to Yonda and Coq. Hygiene efficiency was striking in the equatorial town on the Congo river. "After dark an engine passes through the streets spraying DDT so thickly that . . . we were lost in our cars completely." The number of bicycles astonished: "stacked outside the dispensary as they are stacked outside a Cambridge college." Signs of things Belgian and Catholic peeked in everywhere. "Native cottons" seemed worth purchasing. So did the champagne. Greene observed a Congolese home: "a bedroom with two beds, very neat and clean under coverlets," a "sitting-room with radio, bicycle, pictures of King Baudouin, both Popes, a shop calendar (a girl advertising Singer sewing-machines), holy pictures." He also saw an "insolent-looking African" carrying "a prayer book with small holy pictures, including a film star dressed as a cowboy."[41]

A cinema had opened in Coq in 1947. Postwar media, leisure forms, and print culture entered this town, as did running water[42] and *foyer sociaux* or "social homes."[43] Novelties of the 1950s featured a radio service playing records on request, a major boon. Soon after opening, hundreds of Congolese had written letters asking for a specific disk to be played.[44] A soccer league with ten teams began in 1947, as did festive days with canoe and bicycle races.

Six libraries opened in the province, with two hundred books each for those at Coq, Basankusu, and Boende.[45] By 1948, when each territory had a library, Jules Verne was the favorite novelist.[46] *Mbandaka* began as a weekly in 1947, with one hundred subscribers and selling five hundred copies an issue. By 1949, the editors had a network of Congolese correspondents across the province, and the print run rose to seven hundred.[47] In 1950, an expansion to six pages was planned,[48] and it was an eight-page biweekly in 1953, with eleven hundred copies in circulation.[49] Missions published newspapers as well. In 1948, the Catholic monthly *Etsiko* was printing 1,475 copies, while the Protestant *Ekim'ea Nsongo* printed 2,300 copies three times a year. Newspapers produced fear; the authorities allowed them but sensed they would be used against them one day.[50]

When Graham Greene had a conversation with the governor's deputy, he learned about the Belgian intention to completely overhaul the customary and the rural, modernizing persons, towns, and villages in the process. That it was time for a new phase was evident in the way this official with twenty years' experience spoke. Expressing "admiration for the African woman," the governor's deputy emphasized the need to break down the "tribal framework" with "material incentives . . . given for that purpose." That these inducements and shattering would produce something akin to what Frantz Fanon once called "consumer" colonialism (in contrast to earlier, more exclusively extractive modalities) was suggested.[51]

In 1950, the governor had declared that acts of racial discrimination were "anachronisms" that wounded and scandalized: "We must more and more force ourselves to detach ourselves from a complex of racial superiority," even if a superior attitude was "all too natural, I know, given the psychic and cultural state of the grand mass of natives." Present in the 1950s was a sense of living through "a new era," though nervously so since: "The epoch of the total and unconditional domination of the White is over."[52] Such official cautionary words were needed, in part, because some colonial agents had been hurling Cards of Civic Merit into the faces of those *évolués* granted these special certificates of belonging to a higher colonial rank. The governor general sought to rectify such "maladroit and inopportune attitudes" toward évolués and soldiers, while scolding those agents who "like to ridicule."[53]

Humiliated or not, urbane Congolese welcomed the new, the material, and the visual. Many consumed, while some still sold copal. Advertisements in *Mbandaka* give a sense of a new economy of mixed messages. Bicycles were for sale at G. Panchal's. Aspro pills attracted customers through a paternalist, comic-based ad. Patel's advertised cloth and sardines in Lingala. Rodrigues offered his services as tailor also in Lingala. SECLI encouraged purchasing cloth and other gifts, which it would deliver rapidly by boat to interior destinations; it was keen to buy copal, too. Also on offer in Lingala were distractions: a Coq bar and restaurant.[54]

Greene asked the governor's deputy about the implications of providing modern accoutrements in a quick instant, "Doesn't this lead straight to the gadget world of the States?"[55] The reply turned to substitution and a need for "a mystique."[56] The official's words resembled those of counterparts who in 1945 fretted about depopulation in a Coq meeting. All were aware of the risks posed by movements like Likili and Kitawala with mystiques. There is room to wonder what happened to the notion of a surrogate ideal, long part of Catholic and official logics, as the dazzle of new distractions took hold.

Graham Greene did not pursue the meaning of mystique further. Instead, he found Coq's bars.

Bars and Venereal Debates

So did a Léopoldville visitor, Polycarpe. This man, whose name suggested bounty and the early Catholic martyr and saint, was embarking on no holy mission. He sent a telegram to his friend Ilanga in 1954: he would arrive by Otraco boat. On a dry, dusty Saturday, Ilanga set out to meet him at the port. The initial tour included the cathedral, the European "ville," the governor's residence, and the market. Then it was off to Cercle Excelsior to hear the Pierre Kalima orchestra. Before leaving Léopoldville, Polycarpe had gotten hold of a *Mbandaka* with an ad for the Yangard et Fils bar and was keen to go there next. At the end of the month, Yangard et Fils was swarming with automobiles, bicycles, and a large crowd. It was nearly impossible to get in the door. Once inside, Polycarpe began busily calculating how much money the owner made, while basking in a daydream of one day opening his own bar. He left without a single dance. The floor was overloaded beyond capacity, he thought, with all oblivious to "elementary rules of dance." As Polycarpe left town, he introduced doubt about pleasure and success, asking his guide Ilanga whether "Coquins" were happy with their bars.[57]

Coq's bar culture was flourishing in the 1950s alongside proliferating debates about social and medical questions, often published in *Mbandaka*. While conflicting desires for order and distraction tugged at urbane hearts in this equatorial, riverain town, questions arose about independent women and how to manage their associations, bar life, and medical routines.[58]

A cacophony of voices emerged in the bilingual newspaper as men of middle rank made it their own, writing about everything from camouflaged polygamy to racial antagonisms. Doubt and worry were everywhere, in stories still circulating about the Mongo, the "people who dies [*sic*],"[59] their low birth rate, polygamy, and their "lands without people."[60] Many articles had demographic themes, including when Governor Schmit made a major speech on the problem in 1956.[61] Firmin Molifa suggested the state reduce taxation for fathers of three and provide birth bonuses.[62] N'Djoku worried about the "grave wound of Equateur: the depopulation of the Mongo."[63] At the same time, maternity wards were being inaugurated,[64] and the papers were full with stories about nursing schools and birth announcements.[65] A new maternity ward opened in Coq in 1950, with "all comforts of modern construction": electricity, running water, showers, and water closets.[66] Thirty-four gave birth there one April week, and hundreds did so in 1950.[67] The names of the hospital director, a maternity nun, and Congolese nurses and midwives were all newsworthy, as were their photographs.[68] In 1951, a woman doctor Mlle Van Den Eeden arrived to care for women and children[69] and run a blood transfusion service.[70] Justin Bomboko suggested venereal disease reforms, while recalling cries of alarm about the Mongo birth rate and experiments tried.[71] Glimpses of hospital culture surfaced, as when Mobe observed that patients liked to wander home on Saturday evenings.[72]

Greene caught a dose of the reigning language, emanating partly from medical circles and partly from the banter of women seeking sex work. Both permeated the entire European milieu. In many ways, it became a male language of pursuit and risk before sexual traffic in women, though with violence and madness lurking at many a turn. In Léopoldville, a business man filled Greene in on essentials in the capital, where the "'method'" was "to drive around the native town until a likely girl is seen and then to send the chauffeur with an offer of money." In Coq, a Greek shopkeeper found his Congolese wife in bed with his clerk. He bought an old car and drove it over the clerk's body, crushing legs and pelvis, before the shopkeeper "shot himself through the head." Michel Lechat, talented epidemiologist in the making, made sure Greene knew basic facts, contradicting what the novelist learned in Leo: "Venereal disease among women almost universal: only syphilis rare. Many cases now no longer react to penicillin." Equateur tropes surfaced in Greene's many conversations: "Birth control here not the problem. The African a dying race owing to the sterility of the woman due to gonorrhea." One doctor "recently had a girl of eight with gonorrhea." He puzzled about the "bustles" of women glimpsed in Coq's bars: "caused by a kind of rope of plastic rings they wear round their hips next to the skin," while the larger the size, the more wealth and esteem. He knew many were "public women." He mused about two who, when they "solicited," announced to him: "'There is lots of gonorrhea and syphilis. We are safe.'"[73]

Greene moved between Coq's European hotels and "native bars." One hotel with a "terrible bar with steel chairs and man-in-the-moon lampshades" was capable of a "not so bad" dinner. He recalled "Camemberts flown from Europe" and "an excellent Portuguese *rosé*." The bar inside "the smaller of the two hotels" at Coq had "discreet nineteen-twentyish pin-ups, a tiny dartboard" and an "impertinent" waiter who did not comprehend Lechat's effort "to wait and signal the waiter" rather than just call out "'boy!'"[74] One evening, the famed novelist went to see "some native dances arranged in a native bar for a *colon*" departing for Léopoldville. He observed that the district officer watched with a "smiling proprietorial pride," not "the stupidity of the *colon*." Another evening, Greene, Lechat, and a police officer went "round the African bars till two in the morning." Greene piled up more images, such as "Polar beer advertisements," and an "old madman with his torn shirt and woman's handbag." Outside the last bar, Greene witnessed a large dispute: "a woman had drunk the beer in a man's glass." In another bar, a "young debater" with "the thin fine hands of Africans" mixed "an element of trust" with "fear and confusion," questioning "the good faith of Europeans" and then "confused when I introduced Ghana."[75] Another day, he attended a mass where everybody was "turning their chairs and themselves as in a dance." Sometimes he observed "Most unattractive colonial types." Occasionally he elaborated: "The public women—lipsticks that take a mauve tint on an African mouth, and skin under make-up looks grey as though plastered with mourning clay."[76]

The Congolese journalist Wassa worried about female liberty and prostitution.[77] Some in Coq, like the colony over,[78] complained about marriages in crisis from concubinage,[79] camouflaged polygamy,[80] and pseudo-évolués.[81] A major issue under Congolese debate was female sociality. We saw that a bar-like society organized by a métis woman as Amicale attracted security attention in 1931 Coq, when rumors about flag-raising stirred interrogations. Many women's associations focusing on dance, fashion, and beauty flourished after the war. Even in 1941, a "sect" whose traces vanished from Monkoto territory once carried the name of "Belge" or "Cabaret," suggesting that bar culture was far-flung and bled with the religious at least in some eyes.[82]

The question of probity received press attention up to 1958.[83] Also discussed was the question of a special tax for single women, a common urban colonial measure, under discussion for Coq.[84] Before the city council, some argued that a distinction should be made between long-term single women residents who had not found a husband in the city and recent women migrants. The cost of living was sometimes pressing for these women.[85] The discussion about women and their associations was a debate about *milieu*, about the social effects of "native bars" in Coq's neighborhoods.[86] Town women went to bars on Sundays. They wore "uniforms" that stirred admiration. Often there by nine in the morning, they usually did not leave until ten at night—drunk, so it was said. Men were jealous of their wealth: "Even those of us who work, we cannot pay for the number of bottles of beer" the female association members were buying. Some parents were letting their daughters join these associations in Coq's first Congolese quarter, Belge.[87]

Readers were asking moral questions. Were these associations good or bad? Donatien Bosenjdu thought women joined to signal "evolution," just as they sought to express their "civilization" through dress, abandoning "native" styles and adopting those for "modern life." Their "modernism" and independence went together, "even in language." Their nicknames evoked the mentality of an association: a de-fattened girl, a famous girl, a choice girl of value. All projected fame in beauty, surfaces, and appearances. Most condemned women's associations as antieducational, opposed to thrift, and destabilizing of marriage. The women sought the superficial, critics charged. Their leaders encouraged vanity, a desire to shine and create a sensation. Organization was lacking, with no cash drawers fed by regular contributions and no recognition by a colonial authority. Meetings focused on dress, makeup, and outings, producing an exaggerated desire for beauty. Some called for a complete transfomation of the associations. The editors agreed.[88] But when Christmas arrived in 1954, the newspaper placed a photograph of a Léopoldville woman's association on the front page, remarking that in big cities and interior posts such associations stirred passionate évolué debate.[89]

An "astonished" reader wrote about Coq évolués who supported women's associations, pretending their purpose lay in mutual assistance and progress for women. Others accused that association directors, their *Tata Mokonji*, or "Father Chiefs," had their own interests, sought to remain in charge and urged members to purchase impressive amounts of beer for meetings. These associations were also known to provoke rivalry between *femme libre* and married women members. The former had separate associations as well and were fond of mocking the married women for not dressing too as they did. Bomboko chimed in. He was not convinced separate associations existed for married and single women. Moreover, these associations were a "danger," but the women leading such "idle" lives had a "need to group together." He urged blaming not the women but the men running their associations, while changing "the spirit" and ethics of these groups.[90]

Another sore point stirring debate was marriages hurt by official antivenereal campaigns, which by 1949 attained a "new vigor."[91] Nurse Joseph Lomboto explained in a 1954 talk at Cercle Léopold II how the venereal disease campaign was organized through census work. Anyone wishing to obtain a travel permit had to secure a medical passport first, and doctors could call in anyone suspected of disease for a medical exam. At the exam, patients had to name their sexual partners so they could be called in too; *dénoncer* (name or accuse) was the ambiguous French word used, producing friction. Lomboto's audience argued that these measures were keeping many from going in for treatment. Bomboko insisted the requirement of naming partners should be dropped, while routine exams as part of census work should include women as well as men.[92]

Correspondent Testis commented on the controversial lecture. If the "evolving class" was to encourage everyone to spontaneously show up for medical and venereal exams, it needed to know discretion would prevail. Why was it necessary for a patient to name his partner? Such "denunciations" then circulated viciously in Belge, damaging marriages. Another problem was the undressing of a man with venereal disease in the clinic in such a way that everyone there instantly knew this patient carried a sexual disease. Gaining confidence was impossible in the face of these indiscretions and humiliations. A special antivenereal clinic, like the one in Léopoldville, was needed.[93]

When Dr. Schwers left Coq in 1949, gratitude and deference ran strong and thick during a ceremony honoring his fifteen years served. Three évolués asked him and his wife to never forget "their children of Equateur." They praised his organization of medical education, leprosy care, and the venereal disease campaign. In his era, so it seemed, Schwers usually treated more venereal patients himself, ensuring more discretion and individualized attention than the new screening that followed.[94] The call to make venereal screening a routine part of medical censusing for women surfaced again. At the time, usually women were examined for sleeping sickness alone. Everyone assumed it was inappropriate to have male nurses examine women, though many wondered why European women nurses could not do census examinations. Léopoldville's dispensary for examining "women theoretically living alone" seemed exemplary; a similar clinic for Coq's eight hundred single women was needed.[95]

Venereal diagnostics, examinations, censusing, and partner identifications were part of a new medical culture that was linked to Equateur's sexual economies and hedonistic forms of distraction: women's associations and bar life. Shame and secrecy were also part of this milieu, shrunken by colonial hierarchies and aggressions, where many women did not become mothers and many could not count on having children. Into this welter, the regime intervened with an often clumsy medical efficiency that magnified social awkwardness and disgrace. It is unlikely we will ever know precisely how this intensive venereal campaign stemmed from or reshaped Equateur's sexual and medical economies, or if it figured in the emergence and spread of the HIV pandemic (of HIV-1 type M) in the region. Pointed causal arrows are too brittle for the capacious, milieu-based approach extended here. Still, the wider kinds of evidence presented in this chapter are sought by HIV researchers asking historical questions, whether working with more or less supple notions of causation.[96]

In looking at two late colonial Equateur spaces—Loma chiefdom and urban Coquilhatville—the pervasiveness of medical censusing in conversations, debates, practice, and strategy is conspicuous. In each setting, censusing had *become* securitization. It met bottles of palm oil and hide-and-seek Kitawala dynamics in Loma, and it encountered ambling for fame beside bar life, venereal readings, and women's fashion associations in Coq. Matters of strolling and motion continue as we turn to three men whose lives and figurations also take us back to Ekafera and Befale.

Three Figures: Mata, Munga, Bowane

The Equateur security archive is also rich in unfinished, allusive, thin threads. We turn now to strands about three figures who drew the attention of the late colonial nervous state. It is their contrasts that illuminate. Like much in this chapter, they suggest that motion varied by spaces, but also by much more. Snatches about a suspect peter out, leaving questions unanswered, even when some storylines are suggested.

David Mata, Maurice Munga, and Henri Maliani suggest a range to state attention. Mata was categorized as a dangerous relégué, interned in Ekafera in 1948. Munga was a Befale nurse who visited Ekafera as part of his work. Maliani, now famous in the history of modern Congolese music as Bowane, was a traveling music performer, collector, and promoter, also visible in 1949. Each somehow strolled, when we stretch this word from a narrow metropolitan register (flânerie) to ambling and careening, some of it imaginary, through colonial worlds.

Mata was from Bas Congo. A sergeant in the army, he had been exposed to diverse strains of Kimbanguism in circulation after the arrest of Kimbangu in 1921. In 1946, he was imprisoned for illicit activity and by 1948, like several other Kimbanguists, found himself relegated to Ekafera. When the governor ordered the warden to keep "special track" of this man with "subversive theories," Mata's every move was covered in detail. Assigned to weekly corvée duties, he refused to do his share. The warden ordered eight whiplashes on February 1. After soldiers had to "forcibly apprehend" him, Mata stood up and began to "howl" imprecations, "his arms stretched out to his sides, his face turned up toward heaven." In this daydream performed, Mata cast himself as the Messiah. Eight days of solitary resulted. When he entered prison, he sang a kind of march: "My God, since you had me born in Palestine, you have had me tortured, had me die on the cross. . . . I was everywhere, and everywhere the Whites . . . these demons have made me suffer." While entering his prison cell, the warden searched him and "seized from him sheets marked 1–4 . . . which are, as one sees, highly edifying."[97] On February 6, he received eight more whiplashes for disturbing the peace. By February 9, having "finished his solitary confinement," the warden observed that Mata "was put by me back into his corvée team." When he refused to work, it was back into solitary confinement for another eight days. On February 23, the warden seemed to surprise Mata at a time when the Ekafera detainee was wearing a forbidden Salvation Army–like uniform—a shirt with a white cross on a red background on each side.

Mata wore spectacles with delicate rims. His figure suggested a "religious minister," as did his movements: "He shakes many hands, as if someone with many disciples." The warden sent him back to solitary confinement again for another eight days for bearing these forbidden emblems: "I have him searched and find rolled up on his chest, between a white undershirt and his shirt, a large strip of red flag." The warden concluded that Mata was waiting "for a suitable moment to break out without my knowing into some corner of the camp in Kimbanguist dress and preach his doctrine to some audience." Instead, the warden burned up his insignia in his presence. The same day, he found a sheet of paper on Mata that he labelled exhibit no. 5. When Mata was locked up that day, he accused the warden of wanting him dead. With prophetic language, Mata invoked his resurrection as Jehovah: "I will come back on earth like YAVE."[98]

A Befale doctor was asked to examine Mata from a "mental point of view." The warden feared that leniency or a means of escape might result from this clinical diagnosis, while asserting: "Mata is not mad, he is dangerously intelligent."[99] The man was strolling into a future with a robust reverie, and his singing and paraphernalia—papers, clothes, flag—helped his dreamwork move along. As daydreaming intensified for this prisoner hundreds of miles away from home, however, he was being shuttled in and out of solitary at this penal camp concentrating Congo's religious rebels. If Mata conjured up a fond past while undergoing the torment of solitary, whiplashes, and scrutiny, an imagined future of rebirth and escape from fiendish white men seems to have carried the energetic, unruly man along.

A second figure investigated by the nervous state was Maurice Munga, a nurse who was part of the medical team that regularly moved from the sparkling new medical installations constructed from FBEI funds at Befale to the Ekafera colony some fifty miles away. The security commissioner Warnant wrote to Befale's territorial in 1950 identifying Maurice Munga of Banzyville as a "dangerous element" to be kept in view: "Since this native medical auxiliary was in your territory up until recently . . . please investigate." He knew that Mlle Dr. Van Ackere, the FBEI doctor, might know something since she traveled with him as part of the visits to Ekafera. Most Europeans regarded Munga as a "strongly arrogant individual," while his haughtiness had "provoked a change in his situation within the medical service." Was Munga fired or transferred? Or did something else happen to him? The record is not clear. Yet something like a loss in rank was one of "the essential reasons for the observed modification in his behavior." Likewise, his earlier arrogance had gone with his being held in high regard, elevated in rank among the nurses in the Befale medical service. Munga had exercised sway and liked to brag about his privileged access to white doctors. At some point, vanity morphed into claims about working with the occult, and Munga began boasting about walking at night through the cemeteries at Befale and Coquilhatville. While strolling in these places of spirits and the dead, he claimed he had met two reverend mothers, the category of white person who arrived with Befale's new convent and likely served as clinical superiors over Congolese—male—nurses. Munga had claimed that these nun-apparitions extended him a "serious helping hand." The story about Nurse Munga wandering through graveyards was astir in Befale's European quarters when the security service discovered that Munga had "abused the credulity" of Congolese peers in other ways as well. One Befale nurse showed the security investigator a letter addressed to a Monsieur Diabolicus in Paris and seeking amulets to help Befale's nursing students pass their exams. Nurse Munga had written the letter on behalf of "his colleagues."[100]

Munga produced no "really dangerous deed." His audacious peddling in letters and exam scores, if not lucrative, still suggested a kind of "exploitation." His "hardly deferential" attitude toward Europeans somehow related to testing his colleagues' credulity through his contacts with "the world beyond, the hereafter." Such cheek stood in contrast, however, with Nurse Munga's visits to Ekafera. The lady doctor Van Ackere, with whom he made these tours,[101] had nothing more to report, but she had "observed a radical change in his behavior." She advised Coquilhatville's medical authorities of the stark shift after making several journeys with him to Ekafera. The commissioner formed the impression that Munga had not been especially "struck by what he saw" at Ekafera. Rather, from inquiries made, "the only things that seemed to have attracted his attention was the surveillance of which he was made object." The warden ordered that Munga "be guarded night and day by a soldier." Reduced to an object of constant scrutiny, he perhaps became like any Ekafera detainee. Some details are missing, but their effect is not. The experience in a gloomy, carceral world of isolation and punishment altered Munga. He had peddled in sorcery and diplomas to heighten his fame and power, yet he suffered indignities at this strange, remote place where the warden had him guarded nonstop. The treatment "hurt" the nurse's pride.[102] The shift to a psychic register intrigues. Security speech was often epidemiological, speaking of risk of infection or contagion. In this instance, the risk was Munga's wound, and the emotional harbored an aftermath.[103] The evidence may be thin, the sequence confusing. But this nurse's trajectory had an event–aftermath aspect to its traumatic figuration. Mistreatment at Ekafera unsettled the haughty medical worker. Perhaps the Ekafera wounds even magnified his impulse to peddle in reverie.

The third figure suggests counterpoint again. In October 1949, some Equateur security agents spotted Henri Maliani moving through his home province. The first report suggested the man was "in flight" from Ingende territory, though he had been searched. Two letters found in his baggage led to further investigations. Orders followed to seek more information from a soldier, Ambroise Bokanga, the husband of Maliani's aunt, about "who this Maliani was, where he lived, and what he had been doing at Befale; he should explain his comings and goings." A phonograph belonging to another Befale nurse Ngola had gone missing. When asked for Maliani's address, Ngola had said: "It's difficult to say because he is continually traveling."[104]

He had been living for five years in Coquilhatville, where his father worked as a chauffeur and mechanic. Maliani had a second home in Léopoldville and regularly came to the Befale region. Once when passing through, he went north to Bondanganga before returning to Coquilhatville. Nurse Ngola recalled his visit to Befale in September 1948: Maliani stayed with the agricultural assistant and returned one day from Boende, clutching a record album. Then, Nurse Ngola accused, Maliani "entered into my place during my absence and took my phonograph." When Maliani left Befale again, he took the music-playing machine away with him. The matter came before the territorial court. The fine was one thousand francs, while there were more questions about Maliani's mobility, travel permissions, and lodgings while "in the interior."[105]

Maliani also went by the name of Bowane. He seemed not to be a criminal or the type who would "engage in any subversive propaganda." He had come to Befale for work, and his vocation involved traveling with phonograph and records, while providing shows featuring new music produced in Congo's big city, Léopoldville. Sometimes he would assemble a group of girls and have each pay a ten-franc fee for dance lessons with this music star in the making. He worked for a Léopoldville music-producing company known as "Auditorium" (Maison Patou), where he helped produce the latest albums. He also had worked as a chauffeur in the capital, while singing every day at one of the first radio stations to air live dance music, Radio Congolia. He kept on the move with travels to "the interior" for another reason: "to collect native songs," so the soldier relative told. These he sent to the Greek nicknamed "Mundele ya Taris" and well known in Léopoldville for producing music.[106]

The territorial imagined Maliani as sheer idleness, alleging that he did "not devote himself to any serious work, unless it is to organize dance meetings for which he asks payment besides." While incessant mobility dedicated to new forms of distraction provoked suspicion, it also produced awe. Maliani has become iconic in the history of modern Congolese music as the famous Bowane. Security agents, too, became aware of this nickname—meaning "cat" in Lomongo—during their investigations of this elegant, sly man who seemed to be "everywhere in Equateur with his records, a phonograph." One referred to him as *le grand*, "big man" or "top guy."[107] Bowane's capacity to slink, move, and stroll made this star-in-the-making a sensation for officials wanting the truth and for young women seeking fame and fun alike.

Of the three figures, Bowane, an early Congolese dandy or sapeur, most resembles Benjamin's classic flaneur, though the feline touch is reminiscent of the leopard-like stealth we have seen before. One administrator noted: "There is certainly a question here of a fable bound to dazzle the natives of the interior."[108] The music and dance surely brought wonder, even joy. This son of

FIGURE 6.4 A photograph of a Loningisa record label for a Bowane song, combined with a Loningisa 78 rpm record sleeve. Note the photograph of Henri Bowane in the lower left. Two Greek cousins, Athanase and Basile Papadimitriou, founded the Loningisa label in Léopoldville in 1950. Bowane was critical to its success and coined the label's name: an invitation to dance. In Lingala, *ningisa* means to shake and move. This photographic montage, "Secouez-vous!," created by and courtesy of Vincent Kenis, formidable historian, collector, and curator of Congolese music.

a chauffeur wended his way to Léopoldville and went on to become a major impresario of Congolese Rumba (see figure 6.4). He strolled, perhaps once pinched a phonograph, and went on to co-write the most famous love song in modern Congolese music: "Marie-Louisa."[109]

Medicalization emerges with each of the nurse figures, bearing strong clues about the prominence of this social category in these postwar worlds of development and distraction. Agricultural assistants and soldiers were counterparts to nurses. That a nurse was wealthy enough to own a phonograph is of interest. Clearly, providing modern health care in rural Equateur went with playing recorded Rumba songs; it also made one vulnerable to theft.

With each man, we glimpse reverie. Circulation, recognition, and fame went together. The one who combined these with singing, radio, phonographs, record albums, a big city dazzled most. The Bowane fable allowed others to daydream. Nurse Munga tried to boost his prestige but ended up caught under the nervous state's thumb when on medical tour in one of Congo's terrible lockdown spaces. The warden and soldiers watched over and made him small, perhaps manhandling him in the process. That Ekafera hit him like a brutal shock of degradation tells us about security and discipline inside this penal colony. In Ekafera, Munga's capacity for physical and mental strolling came to an abrupt halt. Only Mata was a security risk linked to one of Congo's major religious movements. Only he directly faced punishment at Ekafera. Yet in and through rich reverie, this prisoner's imagination stayed in motion.

There are other stories, too, other threads in and outside of the security archive suggesting what was being tracked and how Congolese moved and daydreamed in the postwar years. Music, a form of distraction, is a strand that needs thickening to make sense not only of the state decision to ban Delyle's song "Amalaouta," but Bowane and his dancing girls, along with women's fashion associations and bar life, a modern stream dating in Equateur back to at least 1930.

Ekuma's *Fanfare*

Bowane's appeal went with other suggestions of pleasure within these forms of distraction, from the bars and orchestras visited by Polycarpe and Graham Greene to a new economy of pleasure, dress, dance, gaiety, and sexuality that swirled around women's associations and nightlife in Coq. At the heart of all of these were a kind of motion found in dance and music.

The allure enables understanding the fascination that impelled several Congolese who wrote memory texts in the 1950s to focus on Ekuma, the Free State officer who took his life in 1902 Bokatola. These writers were among the some 170 who took up Father Boelaert's challenge to write memories in Lomongo about early colonial rule, as we saw in chapter 1.[110] The fascination with Charles Liwenthal is striking. Their texts contained a sense of catastrophe associated with terrible war, rubber violence, and baskets full of detached hands, including Ekuma's roles in making war, demanding rubber, and building a prison. Yet the historical legend surrounding this paradoxical white man who committed suicide also contained bits of distraction and reverie. Around memories of this Swiss officer clustered dance, idleness, parties, and the brass instruments of Ekuma's fanfare.

Liwenthal killed, punished, and oversaw whipping. Yet these Congolese writers also highlighted his possession and use of music, a fanfare resembling a military band but used to produce festivities that sometimes merged with sexual pleasure. Some remembered Ekuma committing suicide because of shame about his role in violence, but others attributed it to "fury" resulting from a power struggle over his fanfare. It suggested to authorities an independent political realm with its own marching band.[111] Ekuma's commissioner at Coquilhatville objected that the fanfare "passed by here without us being aware. Bring this fanfare here."[112] That the technologies under debate were not guns, but the symbolic instruments of an army able to make music intrigues.

That Ekuma's parents became part of memory's cast captivates as does the military and festive detail. The fanfare's arrival seems to have converged with a recently ordered pacification, a decision to end battles and turn toward economic extraction in rubber. Ekuma had said, "'Now that war has come to an end, may all soldiers come here.'"[113] He used music almost like a prize, a gift, not unlike salt or cloth. He lured his sentries from the villages where they had been assigned to his post at Bokatola "to parade to the rhythm of the fanfare." These brass instruments came from afar, as a family gift. After "Ekuma requested a fanfare from his father and mother in Europe, music resounded at Bokatola," wrote one.[114] The authors remembered Ekuma for bounty, distributing goods during the "large fêtes he organized," which lasted "for days on end." He offered drink, organized shooting and javelin-throwing tournaments, and encouraged wild dancing and sexual entertainment; the word *orgy* appears in one account.[115] Still, since war had ended, "our elders continued with rubber and selling chikwangue."[116] When Ekuma ended a fete, he would send people back to rubber collection.

This officer's capacity to make music created a stir, provoking suspicion and jealousy in his Coquilhatville superior, an officer nicknamed Polo.[117] His possession and use of the fanfare contributed to the impression that Ekuma wanted to make Bokatola a large, independent center. When "Commander Polo learned a brass band resonated in Bokatola," he sent Ekuma a letter ordering him to appear with the brass instruments, since he seemed to be seeking "to become another Commander" from Bokatola. Ekuma protested: "I did not receive it from their armed forces." He refused to go: "my father and my mother sent me from Europe. I refuse. I will not go there." Sensing "insubordination" in a man "looking to go to his village in Europe," the commander and his soldiers left Coquilhatville to seize the musical instruments,[118] approaching in one memory text by a fast boat with a rumbling sound. Many were assembled at Bokatola when they arrived. With the fanfare confiscated, Commander Polo returned to his headquarters. The seizure inflamed Ekuma. His father and mother entered the memory accounts again, as Ekuma informed them: "the Commander carried off the brass band they sent him." Boenga had his parents reprimanding from afar; "violently angry," they told their son he was wrong to have refused to deliver the fanfare to his commander. Ekuma's fury intensified. He vowed "never to go again to Europe,"[119] and began eating and drinking, before writing the letter that he left on the table. As the story was told, he called his servant and asked to be killed, but this "boy" refused. So Ekuma dressed himself in his most beautiful clothes, sat down, placed a gun under his chin, and pulled the trigger with a foot. Many heard the blast. Soon a bugle sounded, and soldiers assembled to see their dead commander through a window. As a crowd gathered, many cried, "Ekuma killed himself with a gunshot."[120]

That a fanfare suggests not only a brass band but also a clamorous display, ceremony, or stir is in keeping with these accounts.[121] Pro-Leopoldian propaganda books and brochures lauded technological developments in the Free State with images of railroads, bridges, and marching soldiers, as well as photographs of military and mission brass bands.[122] Modern fanfares and their brass instruments, still part of state parades, holiday celebrations, and funerals in a city like Kinshasa,[123] were vital to festive life and authority in early colonial Congo.

This intermingling of fanfares, festivity, and violence suggests parallels with other, larger histories and memories knotted in this book: those of childlessness, insurgency, and securitization, of motion, distraction, and emergent urbane sexual economies. Noteworthy is the way that, again and again, social and autobiographical memory returned to death. These Congolese writing memory texts in 1954, it seems, were drawn to bitter memories of terrible violence, as well as the enigma of a white man taking his life, veering toward sprightly musings about his newfangled, festive, musical instruments and their European origins in gift-giving parents who could scorn. Ekuma's fanfare produced in his time pandemonium as extravagant, uncanny festivity and as taut political and symbolic contest. But those remembering and writing were creatures of Equatuer's hedonistic 1950s, drawn to the antecedents of brass orchestras that had Coquins dancing giddily in their town's packed bars.

Conclusion

When Graham Greene spent time in 1950 Congo, he paused to wonder, "where in Europe does one hear so much laughter?"[124] The constant ribaldry seemed "a kind of cacophonous background music."[125] Gunshots occasionally pierced the air. Homicides occurred.[126]

If we consider a few more impressions of Equateur and Coquilhatville through Graham Greene's macabre imagination, his pictures confirm core arguments of this chapter. The medicalization of everyday life was full and thick. Imaginations ran wild and profuse in relation to affliction and harm, as well as in relation to the monstrous, the fanciful, and possible futures. Greene saw bicycles stacked up before dispensaries and discovered that *gonorrhea* was an everyday word. Pleasure came through gadgets and pictures, but also in partying, dancing, and exuberant bar life. While some of the images may seem superficial, madness and nervousness were powerfully present.

Greene strolled too, with irritation at times. He encountered the competitive fashions of women's associations and those debating venereal inspection protocols. Although he did not meet Bowane or Polycarpe, he developed a strong sense of difference between a hotel serving champagne and camembert and a Congolese bar. Kimbanguism arrived for a moment in his reflections, while the governor's deputy went on about the need for a religious mystique of some kind. Signs of Kitawala were absent from his Coquilhatville experience. But nervousness was intense.

Violent anticolonial rioting rocked Léopoldville on January 4, 1959, killing more than fifty. Nine days later, the government announced it was abandoning its idea of a long, gradual movement toward independence. It issued proposals for a speedy decolonizing process instead. When Greene landed on 31 January, he suggested decolonization had a global look, with Léopoldville's city streets "patrolled by tanks and lorries and black troops in single file reminiscent of the Indo-China war."[127] In Coq, newsflashes brought unsettling hints about how Congo's heated, tumultuous decolonization might unfold.

Nervousness had long stirred imperial imaginations in equatorial Africa and beyond. Now new hues of loss and abandonment entered in relation to this colony and pointed security decisions, like banning Lucienne Delyle's song with an insistent, edgy mood and a white man's house in flames. Banning the "Amalaouta" song suggests apprehension and a purpose: to keep such tonalities of colonial nervousness from entering Congo's dance halls and airwaves.

Ekuma and Bowane were *unlike* figures. Yet each represented a story that appealed to Congolese, while evoking dance, idleness, daydreaming, and bright futures. Motion had long stirred and enabled in Equateur, while security screening marked lives with fear and wariness. Some colonial nervousness was more visceral, some more material in its effects. From beginning to end in 1959, Congo's final colonial year, Europeans were on edge with suspicion, paranoia, insomnia, and nightmares all spiraling. An old priest told Greene of "his fear for Coq, of what the unemployed and *jeunesse* might start." At lunch one day, the novelist learned of a man who was "continually ringing up the Sûreté at night to say that there are Congolese outside his house who have come to murder him and his wife." When returning later after a drink in a Coq hotel, Greene "saw the lit windows" of this same "*fonctionnaire* who can't sleep at night for fear." Others had begun "sleeping with guns beside them" since they knew that their "chief danger is an incident provoked from fear."[128] By 1959, while the clamor of Coq's bars, dances, hotels, clinics, and women's associations surely continued, Europeans were shaken, fearing the aleatory more than ever.

Field Coda and Other Endings

This book began with a colonial state as a pair of guises. The heuristic yielded much about energies, expertise, persons, relations, and moods. Yet a singular—not doubled—nervous state emerged, fixated on xenophobia and childlessness. Nervousness also proved the stronger concept, though medicalizing processes never went away. Visceral energy fed campaigns against anticolonial rumors, therapeutic insurgencies, and infectious disease.

The nervous state was limited in its ability to understand, perceive, and control its colonial subjects. Well beyond the sight of territorial agents, however, uneasiness also surfaced within figures of healing and trembling trees. Nervousness opens much, therefore, especially when combined with showing how a colonial state came to be perceived through subaltern senses: as persons and forces with nicknames, habits, and needs.

Equateur's nervous doctors and territorials were mindful that plenty escaped their purview. Awareness came through dread and formal inquiry, while a doctor like Schwers dreamed of a better, more scientific laboratory. He was in a world of colonial experiments—from Songo to rolling out penicillin to penal colonies. If many were biopolitical, nervousness fed them all. Ekafera, a grim carceral trial, was in keeping with Balandier's conceptualization of the colony as a succession of crude sociological experiments.[1]

Today, when anthropologists investigate science and experimentality in Africa's present,[2] a history of a colonial regime confronting childlessness and defiance matters. Colonial medicine, Fanon taught, stirred ambivalence and anger.[3] In this history situated in a region with a long past of troubling violence and injury, colonial effacements of harm deepened resentment and suspicion, denial and guilt. Showing medical, demographic, even penal techniques at work is important, though colonial scientific practice alone would have been insufficient. When and how African therapeutics burst into visibility became a critical diagnostic as this wide history formed. Congolese emerged more than once as experts in creative, therapeutic experimentality. Attending to vernacular imaging and practices enabled glimpsing their reframing of this colonial milieu.

Vernacular ritual entailed dissent. It also suggested somatic—even biological—possibilities. At the same time, a colony-wide epidemiology of subversion developed. Some called the obsessive securitization in 1950s Belgian Congo paranoia. Much earlier, xenophobia became the key diagnostic category in policing aimed at interrogating, removing and containing. The same screening logic relegated the disorderly and politically contagious first to villages at a remove and from the 1940s into penal colonies.

Field Coda

Nervousness enabled this work's interpretation of *plasticity* within a brittle, twisted colonial situation, one embracing many spaces of experience from the 1900s. These spaces and memories of them also lingered in the postcolony, I learned. By 2002, the same southern Equateur region was enmeshed in a messy, twenty-first-century war of shadow networks, nasty sexual violence, and securitization.[4]

The first time I gleaned the meaning of "a nervous state" was during my own arrest and forced removal from remote Bolingo in former Ingende territory. I had just arrived after a two-day journey by canoe, involving much paddling and pushing up a narrow stream, heading north from the Busira's right bank. A small team of border police knocked on the hut door where I had just begun interviewing women. When the officers asked for me, they enunciated each of the three words of my legal name. Then, at the late hour of 10 P.M., they told me I must pack up and leave, despite darkness and all the stamps of approval in my passport received in Kinshasa and Mbandaka. So it was that I came to understand that someone nervous and at a very high level did not want an American woman up a remote stream, not far from a still contested boundary. This scrape with an insolvent, specially deputized security force of a shadow state at war also taught me much about pointed errands and patchy infrastructure.

Ethnography proper proved near impossible. But I continued to parachute—rather to be paddled—in. From that 2002 arrested expedition to Mbandaka, Ingende, and Bolingo, as well as during two 2007 journeys to Basankusu, Lingunda and up the Lomako, and also from Mbandaka to Maria N'koi's world, I learned much about women, their knowledge of medicines and myriad fish, their cackling amid laughter. Warm, kind, voluble, sometimes ribald, they are shrewd, brash, ever independent, easily riled. Men have similar temperaments, I learned, especially with the irate, welcoming, drunk Kitawala pastor I met when not far from the old Ekafera penal colony in a village along the Maringa. This journey was a double-canoe trip with members of an energetic, environmental NGO and its wildlife preservationist funders up the Lomako. It was designed to evaluate the promise of an ecotouristic research station among bonobo, while forging a peculiar, anti-bushmeat economy in this once violent Abir and Ekafera zone. Kitawala remain almost their own "tribe," defiant and refractory, some keen to discuss memories of Ekafera.

My most significant finding during my 2002 trip up the Ruki was the one-book library of a male nurse. I never learned whether I met barren women on that trip. Several suggested there were once many, pained by their circumstances, too. Rather, I went to Bolingo seeking traces of the planter Charles Lodewyckx and his campaigns to restore fertility by ending *lavement* practices. Soon after I arrived, the elderly, retired nurse appeared. He was keen to accompany me through his hamlet and beyond to long crumbled plantation buildings. Just as we were about to leave, he disappeared. I saw the nurse enter his house and come back out again with a big, fat book. When I spied this tome with black cover, I was sure he had fetched his Bible for prayers or protection as we walked. No, he told me. This hefty volume in French was his gynecology and obstetrics manual. Trained in Coquilhatville in the 1940s, he had specialized in this strongly promoted curricular option for Equateur nurses at the time. His cherished text allowed him to share how he had continued to specialize in venereology care, including among workers at this coffee plantation from the 1950s.

Yet another long journey in 2007 by canoe, up slender, vine-tangled streams beyond Bokatola had me, a Kinshasa history student, as well as the gifted journalist Charles Lonkama (translator of the 1954 memory texts) on a mission seeking traces of Maria N'koi. About the fourth day in, nerves frayed all around, an altercation erupted over dinner between the Kinois student and the sardonic Mongo Catholic intellectual able to mow down with words.

The evangelical affinities of the first had already met with derision.[5] Suddenly accusations exploded about Lonkama's mother having been sullied from marriage to a polygamist; this was enough for it to be heard that the God-fearing Kinois had proved himself righteous and tactless. With our research woven around infertility matters, Lonkama soon let tumble out intimate stories about his pair of mothers, designed to humiliate this Pentecostal parvenu from an arrogant city, never mind please the researcher in charge. His mother had not been his mother, so he began. Or, he had not learned or thought to ask which of his two mothers carried him in her womb. The one who he had been taught to call Mother showered him with maternal attention but had not given birth to him, he learned as a young man. The co-wife who carried the pregnancy was a maternal figure, too. Yet without polygamy and these practices of sharing, his social mother would not have preserved honor.[6] Such arrangements were ubiquitous at the time, he explained. So, in concluding, the dim Pentecostal from Kinshasa should take his high-handedness and head back to the big city.

Lonkama's indignant story suggested principled forms of ensuring belonging and inclusion within this shrunken milieu where infertility was rife. Polygamy, sharing, and fictive kin allowed many to save face, while barren women received a turn at mothering, pampering, nurturing, and raising babies and children.

Latitude in a Shrunken Milieu

Let's recall that Canguilhem defined health as "a certain latitude, a certain play." This book historicized latitude within an equatorial region reduced and harmed.[7] Motion, plasticity, and maneuvering enabled perceiving African forms of healing and distraction afresh, while not losing sight of this milieu as shrunken, marked by loss, coercion, and violence. Congolese trafficked in yearning, secrecy, artifice, and pleasure. The result yielded not simple narrative lines but unsettled, unresolved dynamics amid friction and reverie.

Milieu as concept allows framing a colonial situation as partially, sometimes profoundly shrunken. Balandier's sense of social pathology applies to a world where many were childless, and where many sought revenge against colonial masters, through their expulsion above all.[8] Many exercised ingenuity through insurgency and motion, some imaginary, some concrete. Some drew on the enchanted even when confronting captivity. Resourcefulness appeared again and again. Belgian colonials faced defiance, and often observed either charm destruction or human disappearance into marshy zones.

Grisly camps produced deadly violence, terror and flight in the 1900s.[9] The refugees, Songo among them, later became part of a grim pocket of reproductive disruption, of sterility set down within a "model colony." As the colonial regime became more biopolitical, it emphasized childlessness as spite, social suicide, and racialized degeneration. Schwers's study mission pointed to the ex-Abir zone along the Maringa as the most affected by pronounced infertility, while effacing references to history and violence. Colonial numeracy underlined a similar mapping of the problem. Not only doctors and missionaries, but Likili followers and budding journalists suggested the problem was profound and widespread.

Through healing, insurgency, and distraction, Congolese sidestepped colonial disaster logic through latitude. When in the 1930s, doctors fantasized catastrophe and extinction, Likili flourished before scattering under police pressure. Eviction reverie was pervasive: from Ikakota to Maria N'koi, from Likili to Kitawala. So too were practices of flight and concealment, with escapes from prison and an underground mail network. Among the myriad spaces beheld in this history,[10] the Befale infertility clinic and the Ekafera camp count as crucial. The penal colony was a world of sheer endurance and internal struggles, quite unlike the clinical space with women patients seeking prized futures through a gynecologist's apparatus.

Nganda endured. In these zones of refuge and respite, Congolese would have daydreamed about futures: their Belgian masters would be gone. In these marshy places deep in forest, people lingered to fish and collect copal, enabling an edge of independent wealth. Colonial authorities claimed nganda abnormal, a pathologization surely reactive to the autonomy afforded, since the colonial economy lost when many vanished into hiding. Congolese kept nganda alive, likely up until today by those who fish as well as by the region's remaining, fractious Kitawala.

Some spaces enabled rhythms of wonder in motion, like nganda, healing spots and dance bars. That today, in Lomongo as in Lingala, the word *nganda* means bar—a modern, urbane site of drinking, dance, and distraction— suggests a captivating historical channeling.[11] No easy, linear trajectory should be pictured. Distinctions among these spaces of experience—one ancient albeit transformed, one still novel and swinging—challenge any notion of a single colonial milieu. Nganda and bars relate to economies of pleasure, perhaps intimate forms of violence too. Either way, such distraction challenges the narrow historiographic box called "leisure."[12]

Other places provided special perches on pasts and futures, occasions to mend, expel, repair. Maria N'koi, special healer of Njondo spirits, soothed nervous conditions. In a trembling state when first losing her way, she surfaced in the roots of a *musenge* tree. Her miraculous vision may have erupted from her hitting a piece of wood against a tree, producing an immense thud that inspired crowds. Her therapeutic story suggests a variant to a regional template of healing psychic disturbance among women. Once tangled in trees, dances later helped rework selves and quieten cares.

Trees recurred, in history and event. Packed with medicines and meanings, foliage suggested much about healing patterns in a wide region. Trees and dancers became, more than once, history, event, and song. One tree split before a spectacular woman dancer, its medicines offering peace. So Jadot recorded in a poem containing traces of bloodied rubber and Ikakota. Trees went with loathing and expulsion, like the one felled across a warpath, blocking the arrival of colonial enemies near the Maringa in 1916. Yebola initiates hanging from trees were a common sight in the 1930s. Getting lost then found on a tree branch had become a sign of female spirit illness across the region. Trees and branches lingered, beyond Maria N'koi and Yebola into all kinds of medicines and song, while being basic to Likili origin stories.

Therapeutic practice produced spectacle and the festive, in Lianja and Ewewe processions, in Yebola too, especially as it turned toward the more urbane and recreational Zebola. Healing opened horizons, sweeping away calamity or urging for dance after long months of seclusion. Distraction[13] and healing blurred. Amid joy emerged a watching, participating, singing public.[14] Sometimes many formed a procession to cleanse a group of villages through an ancestral figure like Lianja's grandfather or *against* an intrusive colonial doctor like Charlier. The latter, sweeping out with flywhisks wielded by Likili, was more ambivalent than festive. This dancing procession knew aggression and anger, most of all.

Naming Disaster

Analysis was anchored not in places alone. The interpretation read figurations, suturing in,[15] and using nearness to perceive the aleatory and unsettled.[16] It sought less events with a causal force and less catastrophe than afterlives. In seeking the lived and navigated, materiality and imaginations came into view: within healing and harming, violence and festivity, and as colonial experts worked. Dreamlike material images[17] and the visceral enabled multiplying subject perception.

Anticipation and reverie pushed historical narration away from event-aftermath, away from situating subjects from the 1920s as irremediably under the imprint of terrible imperial violence. The focus was not a prurient imperial gaze or colonial sexualities. That doctors fantasized catastrophe and extinction suggests mounting guilt following the two world wars, with each war giving generations of Belgians—some individuals at least—a better appreciation of colonial harm and amputees. Regardless, Pierre Ryckmans was likely historically canny when choosing Songo for the first experiments in Befale territory.

The few clues on rape are compelling. The subject, absent from medical investigations, appeared in women's testimony before the King's Commission, a Bolenge life story, and a Jadot short story. Sexual violation also erupted as if in screen nightmares during Wangata's Likili struggles, and in a Loma wife's complaints of battering, suggesting Kitawala's darker edge. After the rapacious Free State years, harm and violation did not end.

Remembering

Who felt the weight of painful pasts? Congolese did not forget. Songs signaling awareness of an older rubber-working generation tell of memories remaining visible, noticed and heard. When Father Boelaert organized his 1954 essay contest, he was alert to likely memories. In this remarkable corpus of Lomongo texts,[18] Congolese wrote down stories some fifty years after violence made this region a grisly warzone.

In many senses, Boelaert asked late colonial subjects to invoke Blanchot, "to name . . . the disaster."[19] Some wrote about Ikakota power objects, or the suicidal Ekuma with *fanfare*, or baskets filled with human hands. Many wrote as if the past was legible, detailing battles, massacres, rape, and mutilation. Some regretted the reproductive troubles that arrived as if a Mongo consequence. Quite a few compared past and present, using the occasion to critique the colonial production of misery during the Second World War. That wartime return to rubber collection had been as bad, some accused, as what their grandparents endured during the gruesome first time of rubber.

If many were keen to write, others begged: Please don't ask us to remember.[20] Some mentioned irritation before the intrusive task. A few alluded to conversations with elders who pleaded against remembering, suggesting that recounting an abject past would endanger the living. Some told of grandfathers who cried that the past was too awful to commit to writing. While a few took frightful memories and almost pushed them aside, it is as if all shunned being slotted in as *aftermath*.

Many who narrated sought out the wry and the aleatory, the monstrous and abject. Some mused in a side-stepping move. Striking is the repetition. Writers echoed one another.[21] The cracks of wonder often suggest less ruins than wandering in reverie. Bachelard wrote of memory weighing down, while reverie is freeing as "vagabond thoughts . . . turn about an obsession" and "madnesses . . . multiply."[22] Memories were not singular: the monstrous, the wry, and the enchanting mingled. Some tell of war charms producing victories, enabling wonder amid death and cruelty. Others wrote of music and feasting during a time and space of violence. All was never broken, some texts suggest. Whether through insurgency, a white man's feasts, or music-making, much remembering kept catastrophic logic at bay.

This study tracked horizons and futures almost more than traces of pain, and not only because a surfeit of distress weighs down as trauma and social suffering.[23] Everyday privation fueled reverie. And a spectrum—violation to enchantment—returned more than once: in detached body parts suggesting the monstrous in ogre tales that enraptured, or in a stolen baby whose recovery in live theatrics produced joy.

We will never know exactly how sorrow combined with anger or spite, feeding compensations of diverse kinds. Some clues arrived through nervousness. Educating the body, learning dances of coiling and uncoiling with beating drums assisted entry into trancelike, possessed states. It did not always produce admiring audiences. But this kind of passage through nervous energy quieted, transforming selves through the spirits of Njondo, Yebola, likely Likili, too. With religious imaginations at work double-time, dance, song, and possession emerged as vital modes of being, even ends in themselves, though often spurred on by pregnancies that did not arrive.

Harm and Female Imaging

The range of images for women in these pages is wide. We observed women's lives from a time when many were locked up as hostages, a few were *ménagères*, and countless were raped, through decades when many entered healing places, colonial clinics, or associations linking ludic dance and fashion. Often, the imaging suggested fatigue, gauntness. Women did the bulk of porterage work and forced labor tasks. During the Free State years, rounded up within camp-like spaces, they met torture and sexual violations. We cannot determine whether rape prevented pregnancies or induced abortions. Yet it is plausible that pelvic inflammatory disease began, at that early date, to infect and damage reproductive tracts, producing difficulties in conception.

Forms of violence met therapeutics again and again: harming enemies while protecting and healing insiders. This theme is related to rape and the sexual violence engulfing Congo's warzones in the 1900s and again since 1996. This recent, urgent history is a reminder that war and rebellion in Congo and beyond have long involved poisonous medicines and protective, therapeutic objects, with medicinal technologies converging with those of war and safety.

Aggressive, caustic sexualities were part of the fallout of violent and less violent labor regimes in colonial Congo. While contemporary critics pointed to widespread death in Leopold's Congo, a few suggested reproductive consequences. Casement found the frightened and frail. The few births seemed related to weak bodies or women avoiding pregnancy during war. Hunger, starvation, loss of appetite also seemed responsible. Reproductive maladies likely first became rife during this time when violent sexual economies left many vulnerable. Some women's bodies were irremediably harmed.

This history wrestled against easy stereotypes for women, sexuality, and gender. In avoiding a tired focus on European fixations or black female sexuality, other aspects came into view. While many women sang, others revised healing repertoires. Ailing women danced within a process like Yebola that began with a malady like madness, suggesting a nervous state or, in missionary eyes, neurasthenia.

Signs of infertility fed nervous colonial knowledge. Clinicians' words about shock suggest awareness of alarm, distress, and brutality. Medical workers seem to have only dimly sensed the past of transgressive violence. If they knew clearly, their understanding went unrecorded. Schwers sought causal explanation in a profound, primitive shock undermining fecundity. His "shock" mixed the psychic and somatic, while historical sources for disturbance went unmentioned in his writing. He was among those who saw the Mongo as a degenerate race without vitality. Ryckmans fantasized about the likely extinction of those who seemed beleaguered yet often surfaced as feisty, refractory wage workers. In the postwar years, health and development became solutions to vexed security problems, ways of feeding an idea of progress among those deserving to be modern. Many Belgians aspired to make Congo a "model colony," and unspoken guilt likely fed choices about where to locate development projects. Songo chiefdom within the former Abir realm offered propinquity. It suggests a rueful, unconscious return to the word *Nsongo*, like viewed as such in exposé photographs taken decades before.

Hedonism and Sexual Economies

A Nervous State framed pleasure widely, aligning it with the festive and distraction. It also delinked sexuality from the stigmatizing notion of promiscuity, underlining that sexuality and reproduction were uncommonly *disjoined* in this situation. There is good reason to think more deeply and over a longer duration about Congolese forms of hedonism as latitude, as maneuvering within spaces and worlds.

Many women—not necessarily those without child or marked as sterile—sought out independent, urbane lives. Was there something special or homogeneous about a Kinshasa-Coquilhatville sexual urbanity? We glimpsed a women's society in 1931 and saw an explosion of fashion and dance associations in 1950s Coq. That a Yebola woman could be found crossing town in a special costume, when other town women arranged bar outings and fashioned fancy garments and coiffures, suggests parallel forms of aggrandizing self and body.

This work's approach to latitude gathered in bits about fanfares, high heels, and song; they tell about deflection and pleasure. Paying heed to fine scholarship suggesting a special character for hedonism in postcolonial Kinshasa (and its twin city, Brazzaville), this book suggests a wider spatial reach for the ludic and inspired. Interesting implications about urbanity, fashion, and bar life emerge from *not* seeing African sexuality as singular or promiscuous, not as moral deficits that caused or furthered the transmission of sexually transmitted disease. The history of hedonism in Belgian Africa may deserve more studies, anchored in different regions, tangled with other themes. Important is the simple fact that few who traveled in postwar Congo missed this colony's bars, their gaiety, *femmes libres*, and Rumba sounds. The well-traveled compared, remarking on how such places of dancing, beer, and social *métissage* were distinctive to the Belgian colonial zone.[24]

By using the word *urbane*, not urban or modern, I have tried to sidestep some old lexical frays. Urbanity was as old as umbrellas and fanfare music in this part of Congo. It was voluminous, moveable, neither applicable to space or place alone, but to persons and objects, language and music, dress and dance. Coquilhatville had stylish aspects. From this provincial capital on the Congo, urbanity bled to all industrial stopping places up the Ruki and Busira. Something similar occurred from Basankusu up the Maringa and later, via roads, from Befale.

Ekuma's fanfare was an early hint about hedonism, not bounded within any European milieu but bleeding into Congolese experience and memory.

Fun-loving Europeans encouraged Equateur bar life and frivolities from at least 1931, when a woman's association escaped from the pointing fingers of security police. Some dances imitated a latest craze. Others seemed European and arrived from Kinshasa.

A smattering of women likely long used their sexual capital to seek protection from a white man or soldier, while cloth and adventure may have come their way. Among the thin line of women who formed partnerships with white colonial men, many attained a special status within the interstices of mismatched colonial worlds. They knew a counterpart in women who sought gifts or cash. Some women ran away from marriages, fraught with fighting among co-wives; Maria N'koi was perhaps one. In many ways, sexual or romantic adventures, however servile, began over cloth, fashion, and style, with new forms of wealth motivating novel, emergent sexual economies. We saw wealthy cloth-buyers and bock-users in 1930s Ingende. A single métis woman had her home searched in 1931 Coq and likely helped organize a society called Amicale. Friendship marriages or sexual friendships were perceptible by the depression years too, usually as love adventures beside marriage, while a trickle of ménagère arrangements continued into the postwar years. Belgian authorities called such women *femmes libres*, usually imagining they were prostitutes. Promiscuity and polygamy also became wrapped up in colonial assumptions about venereal disease. But so were worker arrangements separating husbands and wives.

Congolese dances and stories provided a range of exquisite clues. Women used song for amusement, deep thinking, playful banter, and laughter. Song lifted. Sometimes singing brought solace or enabled hard, repetitive work. Some lyrics were salacious, some mocked. Women's songs suggested extramarital sexuality as a commonplace, one that mixed the erotic with showing off, counting lovers up to the number eight. Women sang of wanting love and struggling with men. Some specified not wanting one who would not last. While some sought the elegant, others wanted the type with books and papers. A man with a contagious disease suggested risk, as did lying traders. Jealous men who accused were trouble, while women who instigated adultery payments smelled of dirty underclothes. The risk of being caught out made some men hesitate before touching a cloth wrapper or commencing an affair. Sarcasm entered through soiled clothes, unwashed lovers, and lavements spied behind a house. A reheated, tinned dimension came with former lovers. Blemishes and sores signaled risk. Love was bafflement before possible dangers: of madness, sorrow, disease, payments, or blows.[25]

Whether women longed for lifelong partnerships with husbands or lovers is not clear. Divorce rates perhaps spiked in the 1930s. If the frequency of multiple, brief, love partnerships began growing at that time or was of a longer date is unclear. Still, a hedonistic economy developed, the more so as childlessness and overwork combined.[26] Urbanity moved along rivers and streams, far from towns, fashioning novel domestic and love arrangements in this world where sexuality and reproduction were often disengaged. Indeed, the emergence of Kinshasa's hedonistic, urbane culture of sexual competition and sarcastic humor may well have begun in Equateur, thus in the colony's most shrunken yet still quite exuberant milieu.

Reproductive Disappointment and Somatization

This study also wondered about the sorrows of infertility and reproductive disruption. Evidence on childless men and women is spare. Still, not only doctors and missionaries but Likili healers and their followers acted to suggest the problem was profound and widespread. Song lyrics show the pain and frenzied panic of a barren couple. The 1939 kidnapping of a baby told of an infertile couple of sorts, gone mad. Daughter and mother joined in a nervous state, bereft of child, yet willing to steal, feign, and cut to have a baby. However, we want to understand this theater of theft; it also staged childbirth with cutting, bleeding, and the panting sounds of pushing a baby into the world. This kind of twisted healing, a knowing about not knowing, came amid desperation.

We also know some men married additional wives, hoping one would become pregnant. Many households were not sterile, of course. A unique child had many a couple wishing for more. Men and women adapted to these one-child marriages in a myriad of ways. Bits of shame, mockery, despair, and accusation also came through in stories, proverbs, and song.[27] While humiliation often accompanied a lack of offspring, modifications and grace mattered. Just as there surely was more than one sexual economy,[28] there was more than one way of navigating and easing sadness and other symptoms. The clinical and pharmaceutical were among them, and the therapeutic knew the festive, idleness, and bodily practice.

Retel-Laurentin developed a subtle understanding of vernacular physiology among the Nzakara. This colonial doctor found out who was sick and who better, and with antibiotics she cured. As French ethnologist she also pursued the ethnographic while studying the low birth rate among these Ubangian people. She pursued venereal pathology, and she followed patients to diviners and oracles. She showed that miscarriage, prolonged childbirth labor, infant death, and adultery confessions were integral to the belly, a bodily site for diagnostic techniques, alimentary moods, and sorcery substances. Her emic physiology rested on oppositions between the well and ill fed, between digesting and expelling, eating and vomiting. Her knowing was anchored in metaphors of procreation, miscarriage, and eating. A full pregnant belly stood opposed to a womb expelling a tiny, malignant, bloody lizard. Her work on the symbolic logic of the reproductive—a womb—points toward practices ensuring health and flow, avoiding blockage or distortion. The same logic illuminates the significance of Equateur techniques, new and old, for sweeping out uterine tracts and birth canals and maintaining health as motion.[29]

Widespread infertility on Equateur's scale, in practice, went with *somatization*. Intentional is my inversion of conventional meanings for this psychiatric word, away from the somatic, idiomatic expression of psychic distress and toward pragmatic, meaningful attentions to an ailing self and body. We will never know precisely how the psychic and the somatic mediated each other. Yet practical somatization would have gone with objects and the techniques of women who flushed out alimentary and sorcery fluids and matter.

In Equateur, sterility went with an intensification of vernacular gynecology, of using forest-found and industrially manufactured lavement devices. In a context of much gonorrhea and genital ulcer disease, the douching and enemas may have spread sterilizing infection deeper within reproductive tracts. Such repetitive attending to the body likely complicated symptoms and somatic effects, with reproductive harm sometimes perceived as if a womb were carrying a distorted creature, a tiny ominous being in the making. This kind of body work via devices had women making meaning while rinsing out, trying to prevent blockage and achieve flow. Such practice was common in the wider region, in and outside of healing ritual. As vernacular healing intensified in the face of symptoms, new-fangled, imported irrigation devices arrived, supplementing, sometimes supplanting age-old clyster devices. The intensification of gynecological ritual as healing may have extended infection and sterility.

We are in a realm of epidemiological conjecture, of knowing about not knowing.[30] A key hunch resonates with a vital theme of this book: vernacular knowledge and practice *matter*. As women altered and shaped experience while seeking conception or ending a pregnancy, they drew on technologies of their day. In Equateur's forests from ancient times, such devices included found calabashes and twigs as irrigation syringes and abortifacients. From the 1930s, calabashes were still accessible and used, but manufactured irrigation devices with cords and bags for suspension purposes were available for sale. The plausibilities imply forms of inadvertent iatrogenesis through self-treatment and nervous repetition.

These were not the only devices in women's lives, of course. A few had lipstick. Many had fishing nets. Some more directly aimed at social and individual reproduction when they lay down under surgical lights, seeking help from reproductive technologies of the 1950s. Several hundred went to the rural infertility clinic at Befale, likely unique in Africa at the time. A few eagerly sought out the gynecologist's insufflation apparatus, hoping it might bring their infertility to an end. Some may have been categorized as femmes libres. Still, an important point is this: let us not oversexualize distraction nor equate sexualities of abandon with the city.

Harm and HIV Logics

The rubber decades involved rampant sexual violation. Perhaps among injured, some used long-standing ways to irrigate, soothe, or recommence bodily flow. Historians, epidemiologists, and virologists have been debating the factors that may have facilitated the emergence of HIV and AIDS in equatorial Africa.[31] Often they think in terms of prostitution, urbanization, and new technologies, such as injections and trains. It might be wiser to first think about the stark, grim imperial violence and the vernacular refusal of disaster that followed, despite living under ongoing, harsh labor regimes. This book has argued that human latitude followed as escape, distraction, reverie, and pleasure alongside new sexual economies privileging love, music, fashion, and fame.

That childlessness set in so publicly complicated this knot immeasurably. In part, it probably meant that in Equateur, patterns of therapeutic resort toward healing, with their ecological, prophetic and eviction logics, became especially intense and repetitive. They involved not only public, expressive healing, but intimate, expulsive logics of internal irrigation.

HIV may have appeared, faintly, without a name or recognition in this zone of riverain and urbane traffic, by the interwar period.[32] Yet would early AIDS have contributed to human infirmity from the 1930s on? Following the reasoning of Dr. Jaggard and Canguilhem, I have placed the burden for frailty rather with overwork, malnutrition, poor health, disease, and perhaps sorrow.

The relentlessness with which mass injections entered and spread has been signaled as a factor facilitating the spread of HIV. Urban sexualities and genital ulcer disease have been proposed as contributing factors as well. All of these seem plausible, though we need to be careful to not narrow the sexual into prostitution or sex work, while siting them in big Kinshasa alone.[33] A diagnostic vocabulary for genital ulcer disease was hardly present in interwar or postwar Equateur, at a time when doctors experimented with new sulfa drugs and antibiotics on a massive scale to end a perceived epidemic of gonorrhea and its counterpart, sterility.

This rolling out of penicillin amid the mass use of injections within a zone of intensifying medicalization is surely another dramatic example of highly efficient medical engineering in Belgian Congo. Still, this study cannot prove that injections or genital ulcer disease facilitated a spread of HIV in colonial Equateur, even if it was a milieu awash in the venereal. Shots did come into play against trypanosomiasis, yaws, and a host of sexually transmitted infections. That genital ulcer disease raged may have been significant for infertility, with ulcer sores prompting internal irrigation and assisting pelvic infection to disperse and harm.

Nor can this study determine whether a "sexual culture," like the one proposed for 1960 Kinshasa, favored the pandemic spread of HIV-1 M. Rather, the scholarly decision here to *not* reify sexuality as *culture* in Congo's towns, cities, and other places may set an example and have implications. First, the selection of a region with an epidemic in barrenness, situated among a historical knot of other factors, suggests great complexity. This milieu was also shrunken from harm and violence, occasioning sorrow, spite, and diverse compensations, all interlaced with medicalizing, securitizing, and insurgent dimensions. Were Equateur's bars, women's associations, and barren women part of a vortex of harm and latitude with wider central African beginnings? Surely. Is it important whether the AIDS pandemic, which only entered global and Congolese consciousness during the late 1980s, was one aspect of the venereal side of this vortex? Perhaps. What is important is this: that narrow, racialized epidemiological logic not dictate and taper reasoning, too narrowly *sexualizing* causality and in relation to a brittle delineation of city life. Concurrency—multiplying sexual partners—was common, for example. But we do not know whether concurrency within a slinking zone of urbanity extending into plantation worker camps differed from more ancient forms within nganda, village, and festive lives.

Southern Equateur was an important zone for junctions among injections, genital ulcers, and urbanity, but the trio of causes is reductive within the large panoply of elements presented here. This study's most striking contribution to current HIV debates relates to the way it advocates broadly *framing* matters of sexual economy, distraction, and pleasure, while never forgetting the history of harm and violence, therapeutic practices and insurgencies, and widespread childlessness.

Exit Time

This work suggests the importance of social and therapeutic logics about renewal and connection, through bodily flow and healing travels, split and trembling trees, therapeutic belonging, and expulsion techniques. It unearthed copious clues about ritualized and everyday health practices, entailing the moving of medicines and pollution in and out of bodies.

One ancestral hero was repeatedly worth burying again, collectively in interconnected villages, to expel the polluted. Ewewe was not a rescue figure swooping in and declaring a new day, like "Germani" or "Africa." Still, purging renewed. Such festive processions swept out the toxic that might make some ill and brought back to life the gestures of ancestors. The creation of new and better futures was suggested.

Expulsion was the crux not only of internal cleansing but of "xenophobic," eviction reverie. Central to the plasticity of making health—whether in bodily irrigation, flywhisk use, or imagining the eviction of colonial masters—was ousting, by moving out rotten persons and foods or destroying older charms.

The milieu was shrunken, though not catastrophically so. Its constraints and absurdities helped foster the forging of a fabulous urbane world of musical and erotic pleasures. Bowane led the way with brash, boisterous talk, and flamboyant dress. It was a world that was never all play or fun, never without wrangling and episodes of nasty, intimate violation. Yet it was a milieu shrunken by a series of punishing regimes, and by the dark shadows of an often unspeakable past with amputees and many raped women. Some injuries were starkly visible. Mutilations haunted colonial imaginations with guilt and fear, through magnification in lantern shows and through statistics about childless villages. The easy availability of young girls for mere coins emerged in this tropical world too, where a particular reading, a typing, knew repetition: Here women *did* "give."

Colonial nervousness morphed, growing in all directions. It knew diverse modalities, intellects, subjectivities—sometimes punitive as with Pierre Ryckmans, sometimes abject like Dr. Schwers, sometimes eroticized when penned by the literary Jadot. Colonial engineers had their "model colony" to build. So they did, combining nervous guilt with a vision of containing the colony's hardened religious rebels in a strict penal colony. In well-funded experimentalities, they tried to lift living standards, provide first-rate care, create a rural, middling class, and research the nuances of sterility in a tropical world. At night, in nervous Coquilhatville as in smaller towns, pleasure, fashion and desire ruled. When white, black, and Portuguese crossed in Congolese bars, they drank beer, danced to love songs among other Rumba tunes, and took in the femme libre garb, smooth and flashing.

Others may do the work of comparison offered up as possibility by this history moving across many tracks. Canguilhem's concept of a shrunken milieu is capacious enough to find differences within worlds colonial, enslaved, carceral, and medicalizing, zones of war or precarity too. That milieu goes with harm and latitude remains vital. Not all contexts or authors may equally push health towards poetic horizons, as in this Congolese bubbling up of dissident images and expression in musical pleasure.

In Equateur, at the colony's most troubled moment and with vitalist logic, the regime's officers became disturbed by the absence of joy. Part of the work of comparison needs to be about vitalisms, colonial and otherwise, stretching wide the medical and philosophical. Yet it should also be about latitude secured in relation to sound and dance, from trees in healing to the seedy glamour of bar life. This continuum—the therapeutic to the musical—does not reduce the richness of healing templates and stories. But it may widen our histories of modes and sites of diversion and distraction.

A persistent maneuver was to distract, sidetrack, divert, and disturb. The temperament may be as old as the seventeenth century in the wider region. It kept Congolese from Equateur *canny*—before the bleak. Whether facing postcolonial tyranny, terrible war, AIDS, or venalities yielding destitution, these skills read as latitude—as sizing up, navigating, manipulating the milieu. They suggest health. Some of the gift lies in the cognitive, mental, and spiritual, in a wondering imagination. This kind of health is *not* resilience. This fashionable, reductive, platitudinous word is a menace, born of neoliberal austerities. It misapprehends, underestimates. What is at work is not withstanding, weathering, or bearing up. No, it is the gift and capacity for activity, for motion. It often begins with skills in acute observation—without denial—and moves toward irony: bantering, jesting, deriding, daydreaming too. Mata, Munga, Bowane—each sized up inimitably, as did many a woman through biting song.

NOTES

ACKNOWLEDGMENTS

1. Charles Lodewyckx features in a few articles; see, for example, Nancy Hunt, "Bicycles, Birth Certificates, and Clysters," in *Commodification*; Nancy Hunt, "Colonial Medical Anthropology and the Making of the Central African Infertility Belt," in *Ordering Africa*; Nancy Hunt, "Rewriting the Soul in a Flemish Congo."

INTRODUCTION

1. During the Leopoldian period (1885–1908), Congo was called l'Etat Indépendant du Congo (Congo Free State); when the Belgian Parliament took over the colony in 1908, its name became Congo belge (Belgian Congo) until decolonization in 1960.

2. Joseph Conrad, *Heart of Darkness*, 139, 145; first published in 1902 as Conrad, *Youth*.

3. Gustaaf Hulstaert, *Chansons de danse mongo*.

4. Michel Foucault, "Nietzsche, Genealogy, History," in *The Foucault Reader*, 83.

5. William Steenkamp, *Is the South-West African Herero Committing Race Suicide?*

6. Arjun Appadurai, *Modernity at Large*.

7. On "latitude" and "shrunken milieu," see Georges Canguilhem, *Knowledge of Life*, 132; and Paula Marrati and Todd Meyers's insightful interpretation, "Forward: Life, as Such," in *Knowledge of Life*.

8. On ruination and duress, see Ann Stoler, "Introduction," in *Imperial Debris*; Stoler's powerful theorization inspired my reading of Leopoldian violence in Nancy Hunt, "An Acoustic Register," in *Imperial Debris*.

9. The bounds of official "Equateur" province and district shift over time, as will become clear; "northern Equateur" or Congo-Ubangi rarely are considered in *A Nervous State*.

10. This is the same extraordinary Irish Roger Casement who exposed exploitation in Congo, Putumayo, and Ireland before being executed for treason in 1916; see Séamus Síocháin, *Roger Casement*; and Colm Tóibín, "A Man of No Mind."

11. Conrad, *Heart of Darkness*, 7–8.

12. Adam Hochschild, *King Leopold's Ghost*.

13. I aim *not* to reproduce the spectral nor to haunt my readers, while *when* historical subjects *felt* haunted is always germane, of course.

14. Friedrich Nietzsche, "The Use and Abuse of History," in *The Untimely Meditations*, 101, 110, 132.

15. Edward Said, "Two Visions in *Heart of Darkness*," in *Culture and Imperialism*; Michael Taussig, "Culture of Terror—Space of Death"; and Hannah Arendt, *The Origins of Totalitarianism*, 130n16, 185n2. On imperial histories of genocide, see A. Dirk Moses, ed., *Empire, Colony, Genocide*; Samuel Totten and William Parsons, eds., *Centuries of Genocide*; Robert Gellately and Ben Kiernan, eds., *The Specter of Genocide*; Jürgen Zimmerer and Joachim Zeller, eds., *Genocide in German South-West Africa*; Volker Langbehn and Mohammad Salama, eds., *German Colonialism*; and even Hochschild, *King Leopold's Ghost*.

16. Nigel Thrift, "Space," 140. Emphasis added.

17. On trauma logic, *aftermath*, and *resilience*, see notably Allan Young, "Posttraumatic Stress Disorder of the Virtual Kind," in *Trauma and Memory*; also useful is Didier Fassin and Richard Rectman, *Empire of Trauma*.

18. Friedrich Nietzsche, *On the Advantage and Disadvantage of History for Life*, 14. On Nietzsche's concept, the "plastic power of life," see Nietzsche, "The Use and Abuse of History," 132.

19. Maurice Blanchot, *The Writing of the Disaster*, 1.

20. For example, Arthur Kleinman, Veena Das, and Margaret Lock, eds., *Social Suffering*; Pierre Bourdieu et al., *The Weight of the World*; and Dominick LaCapra, *Writing History, Writing Trauma*.

21. See Veena Das, *Life and Words*; Ann Stoler, ed., *Imperial Debris*; and Pamela Reynolds, *War in Worcester*.

22. Kleinman, Das, and Lock, eds., *Social Suffering*; João Biehl, *Vita: Life in a Zone of Social Abandonment*.

23. Louis Althusser, *Philosophy of the Encounter*, 264, 260, 260, 264, 265.

24. Reinhart Koselleck, *Futures Past*.

25. Such sensibilities are not new; on emotion, generation, and analytic versus source-embedded concepts, see Marc Bloch, *The Historian's Craft*. I also take inspiration from *histoire croisée*, though translating *croisement* as entanglement elides much. I seek rather *crossings* among scales, lives, categories, points of view. Michael Werner and Bénédicte Zimmermann, "Penser l'histoire croisée."

26. On "technique of nearness," see Walter Benjamin, *The Arcades Project*, 545.

27. Nietzsche, "The Use and Abuse of History," 132.

28. Nietzsche, "The Use and Abuse of History," 101, 110, 132.

29. Joseph Conrad, "An Outpost of Progress," in *Great Short Works of Joseph Conrad*, 17.

30. Joachim Radkau, *Max Weber*, 152, 471, 218, 333, 333.

31. Radkau, *Max Weber*, 60, 333. The idea of a "true nerve centre" continued; Karl Deutsch, *The Nerves of Government*.

32. Hugh Campbell, "The Influence of Civilization in the Production of Nervous Exhaustion," in *Nervous Exhaustion*, 1; and George Beard, *American Nervousness*. See Marijke Gijswijt-Hofstra and Roy Porter, eds., *Cultures of Neurasthenia from Beard to the First World War*; and David Schuster, *Neurasthenic Nation*.

33. For a colonial critique of the term as outdated, given the psychological turn toward anxiety, see Millais Culpin, "An Examination of Tropical Neurasthenia." See also A. Crozier, "What Was Tropical about Tropical Neurasthenia?"

34. An exception was the Italian doctor, later psychiatrist Marco Levi Bianchini; his medical texts from Congo suggest a fixation with psychiatric, nervous disorders during the same years when Free State agents faced scandal, scrutiny, and breakdowns. See Marco Levi Bianchini, "La psicologia della colonizzazione nell' Africa periequatoriale"; and Marianna Scarfone, "Les aventures de médecins italiens au Congo."

35. Usually nervousness went with a "cult of the will," aimed at overcoming neurasthenia; Michael Cowen, *Cult of the Will*; and Tom Lutz, *American Nervousness, 1903*. Inspiration for nervousness, nervous states, and neuropolitics in this book came from a wide spectrum, including Michael Taussig, *The Nervous System*; Michael Taussig, *Shamanism, Colonialism, and the Wild Man*; Andreas Killen, *Berlin Electropolis*; Homi Bhabha, "Anxious Nations, Nervous States," in *Supposing the Subject*; William Connolly, *Neuropolitics*; Retort, *Afflicted Powers*; and Nancy Scheper-Hughes, "Nervoso," in *Beyond the Body Proper*. See also Ulrike Linder et al., eds., *Hybrid Cultures—Nervous States*.

36. Frantz Fanon, "Medicine and Colonialism," in *A Dying Colonialism*, 121; emphasis added.

37. Stoler helped coin the notion of a "biopolitical state," while making Foucault critical for race, sexuality, and empire studies; see Ann Stoler, *Race and Education of Desire*. David Arnold brought Foucault into colonial medical history in *Colonizing the Body*.

38. See Michel Foucault, *The Birth of Biopolitics*; and Michel Foucault, *The History of Sexuality*, vol. 1.

39. Michel Foucault, *Society Must Be Defended*; and Michel Foucault, *Security, Territory, Population*.

40. Lynn Thomas, *Politics of the Womb*; Alison Bashford, *Imperial Hygiene*; Janice Boddy, *Civilizing Women*; Sarah Hodges, *Contraception, Colonialism and Commerce*; Margaret Lock and Vinh-Kim Nguyen, *An Anthropology of Biomedicine*; and Vinh-Kim Nguyen, *The Republic of Therapy*.

41. Walter Benjamin, "Critique of Violence," in *Selected Writings*, vol. 1; Walter Benjamin, "On the Concept of History," in *Selected Writings*, vol. 4; Giorgio Agamben, *State of Exception*; Giorgio Agamben, *Homo Sacer*; Giorgio Agamben, "What Is a Camp?" in *Means without End*.

42. Steven Feierman and John Janzen took the lead in historicizing the vernacular as health; see Nancy Hunt, "Health and Healing," in *Oxford Handbook of Modern African*

History. On reasons to reject Foucault for Africa, see Megan Vaughan, *Curing Their Ills*; and Frederick Cooper, "Conflict and Connection." On debates over biopower in Africa, see Thomas, *Politics of the Womb.*

43. Andrew Lakoff and Stephen Collier, eds., *Biosecurity Interventions.*

44. Albrecht Koschorke, "Figures/Figurations of the Third," accessed April 10, 2011, http://www.uni-konstanz.de/figur3/prg3.htm.

45. Kevin Grant, "Christian Critics of Empire." For Nsongo photograph captions, see E. D. Morel, *King Leopold's Rule in Africa*, facing 48 and 144.

46. The colonial archives in Brussels expanded vastly around 2000, when some seven kilometers of detailed territorial and police records in the Fonds GG, all from the Gouverneur Général offices in former Léopoldville, opened for research. Many historians previously relied on *metropolitan* colonial ministry records alone. Keyword searching (by locality, charm, movement, and the like) was also groundbreaking.

47. On the "argument of images," see James Fernandez, *Bwiti*, esp. 562–64.

48. On this methodological concept, see Werner and Zimmermann, "Penser l'histoire croisé."

49. See Jean-François Bayart, *The State in Africa*; Cooper, "Conflict and Connection"; Mahmood Mamdani, *Citizen and Subject*; Achille Mbembe, *On the Postcolony*; Frederick Cooper, *Africa since 1940*; Thomas, *Politics of the Womb*; James Ferguson, *Global Shadows*; Stephen Ellis, *Season of Rains*; and Jeffrey Herbst, *States and Power in Africa*. For work by Congo-Zaire specialists, see Michael Schatzberg, *Political Legitimacy in Middle Africa*; Georges Nzongola-Ntalaja, ed., *The Crisis in Zaire*; Crawford Young, *The African Colonial State in Comparative Perspective*; and Crawford Young, *The Postcolonial State in Africa.*

50. Edmond Boelaert, Honoré Vinck, and Charles Lonkama, eds. "Arrivée des blancs sur les bords des rivières équatoriales," *Annales Aequatoria* 16–17 (1995–96) (hereafter "Arrivée," *AAeq*). See too the insightful Osumaka Likaka, *Naming Colonialism.*

51. François Bontinck, "Les deux Bula Matari."

52. Thomas Hodgkin, *Nationalism in Colonial Africa*; Basil Davidson, *The African Awakening.*

53. On unintended consequences stemming from medical efficiency in Congo belge, see the important Jacques Pépin, *The Origins of AIDS*; the partly derivative Nuno Faria et al., "The Early Spread and Epidemic Ignition of HIV-1 in Human Populations"; and the strikingly original history of cross-colonial pharmaceutical fervor, Guillaume Lachenal, *Le médicament qui devait sauver l'Afrique.*

54. Rudolf Mrázek, *Engineers of Happy Land.*

55. Davidson, *The African Awakening*; Nancy Hunt, *A Colonial Lexicon*; and Bernard Toulier, Johan Lagae, and Marc Gemoets, *Kinshasa: Architecture et paysage urbains.*

56. Rik Ceyssens, "Mutumbula, mythe de l'opprimé"; Edouard Bustin, "Government Policy Toward African Cult Movements," in *African Dimensions*; Luise White, *Speaking with Vampires*; Hunt, *A Colonial Lexicon.*

57. Maryinez Lyons, *The Colonial Disease*; Hunt, *A Colonial Lexicon.*

58. Michel Foucault, *Surveiller et punir*.

59. Eric Hobsbawm, *Primitive Rebels*; resoundingly critiqued by Ranajit Guha, *Elementary Aspects of Peasant Insurgency in Colonial India*.

60. Ideas developed through studying the colonial literary oeuvre of Joseph-Marie Jadot and conversing with Andrew Cavin; see Andrew Cavin, "Encountering Others, Imagining Modernity" (Ph.D. diss., University of Michigan, 2014).

61. John Janzen, *The Quest for Therapy*; Julie Livingston, *Debility and the Moral Imagination in Botswana*.

62. Hunt, *A Colonial Lexicon*; and Stacey Langwick, *Bodies, Politics, and African Healing*. For references and discussion, see Hunt, "Health and Healing."

63. Last's context was Islamic northern Nigeria; Murray Last, "The Importance of Knowing about Not Knowing," in *On Knowing and Not Knowing in the Anthropology of Medicine*.

64. Georges Balandier, "Messianismes et nationalismes en Afrique noire"; Davidson, *The African Awakening*; and Hodgkin, *Nationalism in Colonial Africa*.

65. Karen Fields, *Revival and Rebellion in Colonial Central Africa*. See also, Terence Ranger, "Religious Movements and Politics in Sub-Saharan Africa."

66. Steven Feierman, "Healing as Social Criticism in the Time of Colonial Conquest," esp. 80. See also his "Colonizers, Scholars, and the Creation of Invisible Histories," in *Beyond the Cultural Turn*.

67. Willy De Craemer, Jan Vansina, and Renée Fox, "Religious Movements in Central Africa."

68. Steven Feierman, *The Shambaa Kingdom*; and Steven Feierman, *Peasant Intellectuals*.

69. Feierman, "Healing as Social Criticism." On public healing, see Neil Kodesh, *Beyond the Royal Gaze*; David Schoenbrun, "Conjuring the Modern in Africa."

70. Kasper Hoffman, "Militarised Bodies and Spirits of Resistance" (M.A. thesis, Roskilde University, 2007).

71. Catherine Coquery-Vidrovitch, Alain Forest, and Herbert Weiss, eds., *Rébellions-révolution au Zaire, 1963–1965*. Jonathan Shaw is doing important doctoral research on these issues now.

72. Agamben, *State of Exception*; Agamben, "What Is a Camp?"

73. Georges Dupré, *Un ordre et sa destruction*.

74. Pamela Feldman-Savelsberg, *Plundered Kitchens, Empty Wombs*.

75. Steven Feierman, "Struggles for Control."

76. The expression was perhaps first coined as such by Caldwell and Caldwell, though with important intellectual contributions by others, notably Romaniuk and Lorimer. Anatole Romaniuk, "Infertility in Tropical Africa," in *The Population of Tropical Africa*; Mark Belsey, "The Epidemiology of Infertility"; and John Caldwell and Pat Caldwell, "The Demographic Evidence for the Incidence and Cause of Abnormally Low Fertility in Tropical Africa," esp. 19. See too Frank Lorimer, "General Theory," in *Culture and Human Fertility*.

77. For example, Caldwell and Caldwell, "The Demographic Evidence."

78. See Steenkamp, *Is the South-West African Herero Committing Race Suicide?*

79. W. H. R. Rivers, "The Dying-Out of Native Races," part 2: 110, 110; part 1: 43; and part 2: 111, 109. See also W. H. R. Rivers, "The Psychological Factor," in *Essays in the Depopulation of Melanesia.*

80. Nancy Hunt, "Rewriting the Soul in a Flemish Congo"; Nancy Hunt, "Colonial Medical Anthropology and the Making of the Central African Infertility Belt," in *Ordering Africa.*

81. Nancy Hunt, "Fertility's Fires and Empty Wombs in Recent Africanist Writing."

82. On "ennui," see Nancy Hunt, "STDs, Suffering, and Their Derivatives in Congo-Zaire," in *Vivre et penser le sida en Afrique*; and Anne Retel-Laurentin, "Les soleils de l'ombre," in *La natte et le manguier.* On sorcery accusations, see Anne Retel-Laurentin, *Un pays à la dérive.*

83. Hunt, "Fertility's Fires."

84. Caroline Bledsoe, *Contingent Lives.*

85. John Janzen, *Lemba, 1650–1930*; John Thornton, *The Kongolese Saint Anthony.*

86. Hulstaert, *Chansons.*

87. Suzanne Comhaire-Sylvain opened key questions in *Food and Leisure among the African Youth of Leopoldville, Belgian Congo.* Hedonism, along with elegance, music, and masculinity, as well as darker, subterranean moods burst to the fore of Kinshasa-Brazzaville studies from the 1990s; Ch. Didier Gondola, "Dream and Drama"; Filip De Boeck and Marie-Françoise Plissart, *Kinshasa*; Bob White, *Rumba Rules*; Joe Trapido, "Love and Money in Kinois Popular Music"; Pedro Monaville, "Decolonizing the University" (Ph.D. diss., University of Michigan, 2013). See too Georges Balandier, *Sociologie des Brazzavilles noires*; J. D. Gandoulou, *Au coeur de la Sape*; Phyllis Martin, "Contesting Clothes in Colonial Brazzaville"; Janet MacGaffey and Rémy Bazenguissa-Ganga, *Congo-Paris*; Katrien Pype, "Fighting Boys, Strong Men and Gorillas"; Kristien Geenen, "'Sleep Occupies No Space.'"

88. Mary John and Janaki Nair, *A Question of Silence?: The Sexual Economies of Modern India.*

89. Georges Balandier, "The Colonial Situation," in *Social Change*; Canguilhem, *Knowledge of Life*, 132.

90. Hans Selye, "A Syndrome Produced by Diverse Nocuous Agents"; Rhodri Hayward, "Medicine and the Mind," in *The Oxford Handbook of the History of Medicine*; Young, "Posttraumatic Stress Disorder"; and Mark Jackson, *The Age of Stress.*

91. Kurt Goldstein, *The Organism*; Canguilhem, *Knowledge of Life*, 132.

92. Georges Canguilhem, "The Living and Its Milieu," in *Knowledge of Life.*

93. Georges Balandier, "La situation coloniale: approche théorique"; Balandier, "The Colonial Situation."

94. Balandier, "The Colonial Situation," 49, 37, 52, and 57.

95. Balandier, "The Colonial Situation," 43–44, 52; discussion esp. 56–57.

96. Balandier, "The Colonial Situation." There are exceptions: T. O. Beidelman, *Culture of Colonialism*, 286. Stoler and Cooper returned it to attention, and now it

circulates in imperial studies readers. Frederick Cooper and Ann Stoler, eds., *Tensions of Empire*; Stephen Howe, ed., *The New Imperial Histories Reader*.

97. Balandier, "The Colonial Situation," 37, 45, 49.

98. Balandier, "The Colonial Situation," 38, 52, 52.

99. Canguilhem, *Knowledge of Life*, 111, 113, 132–133; Balandier, "The Colonial Situation," 37.

100. Canguilhem, *Knowledge of Life*, 145.

101. Canguilhem, *Knowledge of Life*, 145–46. See Gaston Bachelard, *The Poetics of Reverie*; Gaston Bachelard, *On Poetic Imagination and Reverie*.

102. Nancy Hunt, "The Affective, the Intellectual, and Gender History."

103. J. A. Simpson and E. S. C. Weiner, eds., *Oxford English Dictionary*, 13:821.

104. Bachelard, *The Poetics of Reverie*, esp. 8.

105. Bachelard, *The Poetics of Reverie*.

106. On tonality, Gaston Bachelard, *The Poetics of Space*, 6.

107. Raymond Williams, "Structures of Feeling," in *Marxism and Literature*; Raymond Williams, "Dominant, Residual, and Emergent," in *Marxism and Literature*.

108. Paolo Virno, *A Grammar of the Multitude*.

109. Bachelard, *The Poetics of Reverie*.

110. On idleness and distraction, see Walter Benjamin's convolutes, esp. "Idleness," in *The Arcades Project*. See also Georg Simmel, "The Metropolis and Mental Life," in *On Individuality and Social Forms*; and Siegfried Kracauer, *The Mass Ornament*.

111. Hunt, "An Acoustic Register"; Hunt, *A Colonial Lexicon*.

112. Reinhart Koselleck, "Space of Experience and Horizon of Expectation," in *Futures Past*. On assymetry, see Reinhart Koselleck, "The Historical-Political Semantics of Asymmetric Counterconcepts," in *Futures Past*.

113. Benjamin, *The Arcades Project*, 545.

114. Gustaaf Hulstaert, *Contes d'ogres mongo*; Gustaaf Hulstaert, *Poèmes mongo modernes*; Hulstaert, *Chansons*.

115. Balandier, "The Colonial Situation."

116. Nancy Hunt, *Suturing New Medical Histories of Africa*.

117. Veena Das, *Critical Events*.

118. Hobsbawm, *Primitive Rebels*.

119. Pierre Vanderlinden, *Pierre Ryckmans, 1891–1959*; Pierre Vanderlinden, *Main d'oeuvre, église, capital et administration dans le Congo des années trente*.

CHAPTER 1: REGISTERS OF VIOLENCE

*Map 1.1 sources: DIVA-GIS, *Digital Chart of the World*, map data set (1992), "Download data by country," accessed 5 September 2014, http://diva-gis.org/gdata; Robert Harms, "The End of Red Rubber"; Samuel Nelson, "Inner Congo Basin Showing Concession Zones and Missions, c. 1902," in *Colonialism in the Congo Basin, 1880–1940*, 88, fig. 6 (map: ca. 0.75 in = 100 mi).

**Map 1.2 sources: *Natural Earth*, version 2.0, map data set (North American Cartographic Information Society, 2012), accessed 18 June 2013, http://www.naturalearthdata .com; Samuel Nelson, "Congo Basin Showing Areas Influenced by the Atlantic Slave Trade and Zanzibari Traders," in *Colonialism in the Congo Basin, 1880–1940*, 47, fig. 4 (map, scale not given); David Van Reybrouck, "Central Africa in the Mid-nineteenth Century," in *Congo*, 28, fig. 3 (map; ca. 34 mm = 1000 km).

1. S. L. Clemens to Dr. Barbour, New York, 8 January 1906, F4/19, E. D. Morel Papers, London School of Economics Archives (hereafter LSE); and Mark Twain, *King Leopold's Soliloquy*.

2. Frederick Starr, *The Truth about the Congo*, 126.

3. Adam Hochschild, *King Leopold's Ghost*, 116–17.

4. Kevin Grant, "Christian Critics of Empire."

5. Riley Brothers, Ltd., "Lantern Lecture on the Congo Atrocities," in *Red Rubber*, verso.

6. Roland Barthes, "Shock-Photos," in *The Eiffel Tower and Other Mythologies*; Marina Warner, *Phantasmagoria*, 353, 202. Also see Kevin Grant, *A Civilised Savagery*; Sharon Sliwinski, "The Childhood of Human Rights"; Isabelle de Rezende, "Visuality and Colonialism in the Congo" (Ph.D. diss., University of Michigan, 2012).

7. Cathy Caruth, *Unclaimed Experience*, 3.

8. Hochschild, *King Leopold's Ghost*. On Hochschild's inflated death numbers and Holocaust allusions, see Philippe Marechal, "La controverse sur Léopold II et le Congo dans la littérature et les médias," in *La Mémoire du Congo*; Jean-Luc Vellut, "Introduction," in *La Mémoire du Congo*; and Jean-Luc Vellut, ed., *Selection of Exhibition Texts: Memory of the Congo*.

9. As in Hochschild, *King Leopold's Ghost*; or Ch. Didier Gondola, *The History of Congo*; Nan Woodruff, *American Congo*, 229n1; and Sven Lindqvist, *"Exterminate All the Brutes."* Yet see Jean-Luc Vellut, "La violence armée dans L'Etat Indépendant du Congo"; Aldwin Roes, "Towards a History of Mass Violence in the Etat Indépendant du Congo, 1885–1908"; and Jean-Luc Vellut, "Réseaux transnationaux dans l'économie politique du Congo léopoldien, c. 1885–1910," in *Afrikanische Beziehungen, Netzwerke und Räume*.

10. Hochschild, *King Leopold's Ghost*, 5.

11. When I traveled the Maringa and Lomako in 2007, human emptiness along riverbanks sobered. "African voices" as method has been widely debated, leading to subtlety in combining text, image, and words. Voices, just dropped in, suggest a "native slot" still, whereas critique of the fashion for textualities is overdue. See Nancy Hunt, "Letter-Writing, Nursing Men, and Bicycles in the Belgian Congo," in *Paths toward the Past*; Luise White, Stephan Miescher, and David Cohen, eds., *African Words, African Voices*; Karin Barber, ed., *Africa's Hidden Histories*; and Nancy Hunt, "Between Fiction and History."

12. Edmond Boelaert, Honoré Vinck, and Charles Lonkama, "Arrivée," *AAeq* 16–17 (1995–96). The commissioners considered concessionary abuses, depopulation, "abandoned" children; "Rapport au Roi-Souverain," *Bulletin Officiel de l'Etat Indépendant du Congo*.

13. Privileging sources by skin color ("African voices") has meant eliding hermeneutic work on rich sources about, not produced by, Africans.

14. See Robert Harms, "The World Abir Made." On *Arabisé* incursions, beautiful Basankusu, and Abir-Nsongo confrontations, see E. Boelaert, "L'Abir," 6/1/1, and on allegations about Abir director Delvaux as syphilitic pederast, see Veulemans to Procureur, 30 April 1905, 6/1/4, both in Papiers Maurice De Ryck, MS 131, Memorial Library, University of Wisconsin-Madison. For maps of Arabisé posts and Tetela arrivals, see "Note sur la pénétration des Arabisés," 1937, Papiers Frantz Cornet, Musée Royal de l'Afrique Centrale, Tervuren (hereafter MRAC).

15. Sliwinski, "The Childhood of Human Rights," 355.

16. Barthes, "Shock-Photos."

17. Seeking "perceptibility," Benjamin sought a "technique of nearness"; Walter Benjamin, *The Arcades Project*, 545.

18. Vigdis Broch-Due, "Violence and Belonging," in *Violence and Belonging*.

19. Naming Leopold's Congo as the "red rubber" period (after Morel) is a historiographical commonplace; E. D. Morel, *Red Rubber*; Robert Harms, "The End of Red Rubber."

20. See the stunning new edition, Séamas Síocháin and Michael Sullivan, eds., *The Eyes of Another Race*.

21. Síocháin and Sullivan, *The Eyes of Another Race*, 61, 84, 69.

22. On "houses" as big man–centered, domestic networks and trading firms, see Jan Vansina, *Paths in the Rainforests*; Robert Harms, *River of Wealth, River of Sorrow*.

23. Bogumil Jewsiewicki and Mumbanza Mwa Bawele, "The Social Context of Slavery in Equatorial Africa during the 19th and 20th Centuries," in *The Ideology of Slavery in Africa*. On Wangata, see Daniel Vangroenweghe, "Le journal de Charles Lemaire à l'Equateur, 1891–1893," *AAeq*; Honoré Vinck, "Résistance et collaboration au début de la colonisation à Mbandaka (1883–1893)," in *Forschungen in Zaïre*. On Basankusu, see Viscount Mountmorres, *The Congo Independent State*, 128; Emile Vandervelde, *Les dernier Jours de l'Etat du Congo*.

24. Excellent on these basics in African history is Steven Feierman, "A Century of Ironies in East Africa (c. 1780–1890)," in *African History*.

25. Síocháin and Sullivan, *The Eyes of Another Race*.

26. Síocháin and Sullivan, *The Eyes of Another Race*, 156, 84, 155–56, 149.

27. Síocháin and Sullivan, *The Eyes of Another Race*, 147, 69, 158, 95, 98, 114, 68, 112; emphasis added.

28. Síocháin and Sullivan, *The Eyes of Another Race* (Bikela) 149; (Sekolo) 151.

29. Antoine-Marcus Boyoto, memory text in "Arrivée," *AAeq* 17:143–45 (hereafter memory texts to be cited per author and in *AAeq* 16 or 17).

30. Françis Dhanis, large Abir Journal, 21 April–11 September 1904, 380 pp., Papiers Françis Dhanis, MRAC (hereafter Abir Journal). Daniel Vangroenweghe used this invaluable source in *Du sang sur les lianes*.

31. Harms, "The World Abir Made."

32. Michael Taussig, *Shamanism, Colonialism and the Wild Man*, 10.

33. Dhanis, Abir Journal.

34. Dhanis, Abir Journal (swollen finger: 122). See too Françis Dhanis, "1904 Abir," Small Journal, Dhanis letters, 19 June–19 September 1904, Papiers Françis Dhanis, MRAC. Compare the thirty some letters of Abir agent R. De Grez, 1903–5, from Baringa, Mompono, Brussels; he remarked on "la faiblesse de cette race," De Grez to Morel, 17 February 1905, E. D. Morel Papers F81/36 and M473, LSE. Less evocative are the papers of an Abir agent: Papiers Clément Huet, 1901–5, MRAC. On faint traces and duress, see Ann Stoler, "Introduction," in *Imperial Debris*.

35. E. J. Glave, *Six Years of Adventure in Congo-land*, 202, 191.

36. Glave, *Six Years of Adventure in Congo-land*, 188–206, esp. 189. Stanley introduced Glave's book, justifying the Free State on humanitarian grounds. Those living along the Maringa and Ikelemba seemed vulnerable to raiding, and Glave "redeemed" several for his crew; Glave, *Six Years of Adventure in Congo-land*, 192–93, 202–3.

37. Harms, "The World Abir Made."

38. Stanley became Leopold's collaborator. Without Tippu Tip, the powerful Zanzibari with Lualaba raiding bases, Stanley's journey of 1876–77 would have failed; Henry Stanley, *Through the Dark Continent*. On pioneers in Equateur, see Camille Coquilhat, *Sur le Haut-Congo*; Alexandre Delcommune, *Vingt années de vie africaine*; Vangroenweghe, "Le journal de Charles Lemaire"; and Gustaaf Hulstaert, "Le voyage au Congo d'un officier danois."

39. In German East Africa, Sangu removed hands from dead rebels, delivering them either to chiefs or German authorities; James Giblin, "The Victimization of Women in Late Precolonial and Early Colonial Warfare in Tanzania," in *Sexual Violence in Conflict Zones*, esp. 94. On Ngoni ruga-ruga as mercenary plunderers, see Aylard Shorter, "Nyungu-Ya-Mawa and the 'Empire of the Ruga-Rugas.'"

40. François Bombute in *AAeq* 16:54–58.

41. Joseph Imome (16:51–52) and Bombute (16:54–58), both in *AAeq*.

42. Vangroenweghe, *Du sang sur les lianes*. The Force Publique recruited Zanzibari, Tetela, even Hausa, and also made soldiers out of "liberated" captives; Vellut, "La violence armée."

43. On "composing" wealth, see Jane Guyer and Samuel M. Eno Belinga, "Wealth in People as Wealth in Knowledge."

44. Harms, *River of Wealth*.

45. J. L. Grootaers and Ineke Eisenburger, eds., *Forms of Wonderment*, 1:168.

46. Coquilhat spoke of Equateur people as "un peu dégénér," with poor diets and "lascivious" dances; Coquilhat, *Sur le Haut-Congo*, 155–56.

47. Dhanis, Abir Journal, 245–47.

48. Dhanis, Abir Journal, 114.

49. Síocháin and Sullivan, eds., *The Eyes of Another Race*, 170.

50. Donna Goldstein, *Laughter Out of Place*.

51. Síocháin and Sullivan, eds., *The Eyes of Another Race*, 158.

52. "Congo cartoons," E. D. Morel Papers F1/8/13, LSE.

53. Dhanis, Abir Journal, 211.

54. Charles Baudelaire, "L'essence du rire et généralement du comique dans les arts plastiques," in *Oeuvres complètes de Baudelaire*.

55. Georges Bataille, "Writings on Laughter, Sacrifice, Nietzsche, Unknowing," 90, 90, 70, 70. On laughter, derision, and excess in central Africa see Achille Mbembe, *On the Postcolony*; Nancy Hunt, "Tintin and the Interruptions of Congolese Comics," in *Images and Empires*. During the Atlantic trade, a discussion of slave "supply" from the central African coast described "Congolese as great mockers," "mimes who amusingly imitate," with an "inclination for pleasure" making them "unsuitable for hard work." Jean-Baptiste-Pierre Le Romain, "Negroes," in *The Encyclopedia of Diderot and d'Alembert, Collaborative Translation Project*, accessed 15 July 2014, http://hdl.handle.net/2027/spo.did2222.0000.029.

56. Ann Stoler, "Reframing Dissent and Duress," in *Along the Archival Grain*.

57. The laugh was neither cackling or carnivalesque; see M. M. Bakhtin, *Rabelais and His World*.

58. Síocháin and Sullivan, eds., *The Eyes of Another Race*, 76.

59. Dhanis, Abir Journal, 59, 62, 71.

60. He wrote, "Mais eut l'air de tout tourner en ridicule"; Dhanis, Abir Journal, 71.

61. Dhanis, Abir Journal, 101–2.

62. Hochschild, *King Leopold's Ghost*, 234, 166.

63. As historical modeling suggested; David Voas, "Subfertility and Disruption in the Congo Basin," in *African Historical Demography*, vol. 2.

64. Riley Brothers, Ltd., "Lantern Lecture," verso.

65. Congo Reform Association, *The Indictment against the Congo Government*, in E. D. Morel Papers F13/3/2, LSE. Compare reporting in "Rapport au Roi-Souverain," 224; with E. D. Morel, *King Leopold's Rule in Africa*; Morel, *Red Rubber*.

66. "Murderland! New Series of Congo Articles by E. D. Morel," *The Penny Pictorial* 34 (31 August 1907): 51, with caption about "The woman Boaji [*sic*]," in E. D. Morel Papers F13/1/6, LSE.

67. Twain, *King Leopold's Soliloquy*.

68. Joseph Conrad, *Heart of Darkness*, 132, 139, 145.

69. On repetition in Kabila's Congo, see Nancy Hunt, "An Acoustic Register," in *Imperial Debris*.

70. Hochschild, *King Leopold's Ghost*.

71. Peter Bate, *Congo: White King, Red Rubber, Black Death*, video recording.

72. Few historians have used these, yet see Jules Marchal, *E. D. Morel contre Léopold II*; A. M. Delathuy, *De geheime documentatie van de Onderzoekcommissie in de Kongostaat*; and in a minor, poignant way, Hochschild, *King Leopold's Ghost*.

73. Five dossiers name those who testified; that depositions are in French suggests processes of mediation; AE 528 (349), Campagne anti-congolaise, Commission d'enquete, liasse 1, Archives Africaines, Brussels (hereafter AA). See Congo Reform Association, *Evidence Laid before the Congo Commission of Inquiry*.

74. Boali of Ekolongo, Deposition 172, at Baringa, 12 December 1904, AE 528 (349).

75. In Casement's words; Síocháin and Sullivan, eds., *The Eyes of Another Race*, 126.

76. Síocháin and Sullivan, eds., *The Eyes of Another Race*, 163.

77. Síocháin and Sullivan, eds., *The Eyes of Another Race*, 141.

78. Congo Reform Association, *Treatment of Women and Children in the Congo State, 1895–1904.* "Hostages" were significant; "Rapport au Roi-Souverain."

79. Síocháin and Sullivan, eds., *The Eyes of Another Race*, 153.

80. For "delight in," see Síocháin and Sullivan, eds., *The Eyes of Another Race*; Arthur Conan Doyle, *The Crime of the Congo*, 21; E. J. Glave, "New Conditions in Central Africa," 913.

81. Mingo of Ilua, Deposition 267, at Bonginda, 2 January 1905, AE 528 (349).

82. Broch-Due, "Violence and Belonging," 25; Mingo of Ilua, Deposition 267, at Bonginda, January 2, 1905, AE 528 (349).

83. Kapinga of Bene–Kapindi, Deposition 358, 4 February 1905, AE 528 (349).

84. Tema, Lokoka's wife of Bofungi, Deposition 242, 28 December 1904, AE 528 (349).

85. Mausato, Deposition 147, at Bokotola, 4 December 1904, AE 528 (349).

86. Amandine Lauro, *Coloniaux, ménagères et prostituées au Congo belge, 1885–1930.*

87. Eva May Dye, "Ikengo," in "Life Sketches of the Women who have asked to become Christians since July '04," Royal Dye Papers, Disciples of Christ Historical Society, Nashville (hereafter DCHS).

88. Dhanis, Abir Journal, 58 (also on Sheldon, 25, 55–74, 86, 102, 126, and 223–24). Dhanis became angry when Harris rushed to seek the celebrity visitor's sympathy; Dhanis, Abir Journal. Sheldon's alliances were plain; she arrived by Abir boat and afterward, defended Leopold and his state ("Anti-Congo Calumnies"; "The Congo State, To the Editor of the Times," 1905, in "Writings"); sought out King Albert and Stanley's widow; and publicized the Belgian colony into the 1930s. Her time at Abir is sparsely documented ("Passports, oversize"; "Notes, Africa," Box 2), while her scribbling about "memories," "distortions," "reputations," "falsehoods," "histories concocted" ("Notes, Misc.," n.d., Box 3) suggests this professional writer may have destroyed quite a bit. Mary French Sheldon Papers, Manuscript Division, Library of Congress, Washington, DC. See Tracey Boisseau, *White Queen*, though it misses nuances of Sheldon's Congo travels.

89. Another scholar might decode these script entries; Dhanis, Abir Journal.

90. Dhanis, Abir Journal, 102.

91. Dhanis, Abir Journal, 74.

92. Dhanis, Abir Journal, 73–74.

93. Dhanis, "en tournant la chose en plaisanterie." Dhanis, Abir Journal, 101–2.

94. Dhanis, Abir Journal, 206, 229–30.

95. Síocháin and Sullivan, eds., *The Eyes of Another Race*, 249, 144, 130, 132.

96. Hochschild, *King Leopold's Ghost.*

97. Harms, "The End of Red Rubber."

98. Corvées were by product and village; food villages had an easier time than rubber ones. On refugees, see Roger Anstey, "The Congo Rubber Atrocities"; and Harms, "The End of Red Rubber," 85–86. On Congolese *as* guerilla, see the important Michel Merlier, *Le Congo de la colonisation belge à l'indépendance.*

99. Mountmorres, *The Congo Independent State*, 45–47; emphasis added.

100. Yet on another sexual violation, genital removal among "men slain," see Síocháin and Sullivan, eds., *The Eyes of Another Race*, 125.

101. Síocháin and Sullivan, eds., *The Eyes of Another Race*, 321n43. The Ottoman harem reference is not elaborated. On Casement's missionary source for rape by "native State soldiers," see Séamus Síocháin, *Roger Casement*, 114.

102. Hochschild, *King Leopold's Ghost*, 175, 162.

103. Síocháin and Sullivan, eds., *The Eyes of Another Race*, 152.

104. An unparalleled source, available in French thanks to indefatigable work by Charles Lonkoma and Honoré Vinck, who also compiled a list of author names and origins or locations; see "Arrivée," *AAeq* 16 (1996): 14–21.

105. Joseph Ilanga in *AAeq* 16:81–83.

106. Jean Lokwa (17:165–66); Arsène Pambi (16:68–71); Joseph Ekuku (16:62–65); Louis Efonge (16:65–68); Pambi (16:68–71); and Joseph Eukola (16:47–49) in *AAeq*.

107. Antoine Boongo (16:36–38); and Paul Yampala (16:39) in *AAeq*.

108. Hochschild, *King Leopold's Ghost*, 166. On Tswambe, see Efonge in *AAeq* 16:66, 68.

109. Jean-Ambroise Yolo in *AAeq* 16:108–10.

110. *Bote*; Gustaaf Hulstaert, *Dictionnaire Lomóngo-français*, 334.

111. Petelo Wenga in *AAeq* 17:42.

112. Paul Impote in *AAeq* 16:84–87.

113. Paul Bofumbo in *AAeq* 16:91–94.

114. Jean Bolampunga in *AAeq* 16:95–102.

115. Is'ey'Oongo Ilondo in *AAeq* 16:75–76.

116. Antoine Boleja in *AAeq* 17:60–63.

117. Chief Ingonju in *AAeq* 17:88–90.

118. On nicknames, see Osumaka Likaka, *Naming Colonialism*.

119. Ilanga in *AAeq* 16:82–83, 83.

120. Impote in *AAeq* 16:86.

121. Wenga in *AAeq* 17:41–43.

122. Impote in *AAeq* 16:86.

123. *Bosise*; Hulstaert, *Dictionnaire Lomóngo-français*, 317–18.

124. Impote in *AAeq* 16:84–87.

125. For a prohibitions list, see Pambi in *AAeq* 16:68–71.

126. Impote in *AAeq* 16:84–87.

127. Bofumbo in *AAeq* 16:91–94.

128. The powerful Societé Anonyme Belge pour le Commerce du Haut Congo (SAB) formed in 1888 as a merger of trading companies; its African headquarters were at Wangata.

129. Ingonju in *AAeq* 17:88–90.

130. A Wangata *féticheur* displayed a "ferocious" keenness to chase out whites; Ch. Liebrichts, *Congo: Leopoldville, Bolobo, Equateur (1883–1889)*, 152–54, esp. 152.

131. Antoine Boyoto in *AAeq* 17:211.

132. See Vangroenweghe, *Du sang sur les lianes*, 134, for an instance near Boende.

133. Joseph Bolongo in *AAeq* 17:240–42.

134. Gaston Bachelard, *The Poetics of Reverie*.

135. Victor de Bellefroid, Liège, to De Ryck, 10 January 1954 in 42.15, "Miscellaneous local matters in Equateur district: statements and correspondence (1904–1907)," Papiers Maurice De Ryck, Reel 2, pt. 25, sub-pt. 7, Memorial Library, University of Wisconsin-Madison.

136. Edmond Boelaert, Honoré Vinck, and Charles Lonkama, "Noms des blancs," in "Arrivée," *AAeq* 17:372.

137. Edmond Boelaert, "Liwenthal (Charles)," in *Biographie Coloniale Belge*, vol. 5, col. 561–62 (hereafter BCB or its successor, BBOM).

138. Jean Boenga in *AAeq* 17:24–35; received *"très bien"* from Boelaert.

139. François Bompuku in *AAeq* 16:105–6.

140. From Papiers Maurice De Ryck 25/1, Memorial Library, University of Wisconsin-Madison; published as S. Veys, "Territoire d'Ingende," Annexe 3 in "Arrivée," *AAeq* 16:127–34.

141. A food staple, fermented cassava wrapped in banana leaves.

142. Louis Ikilinganya in *AAeq* 16:110–12.

143. Ikilinganya in *AAeq* 16:110–12.

144. Ikilinganya in *AAeq* 16:110–12.

145. François Robert Bosulu in *AAeq* 17:15–17.

146. Victor Imbamba in *AAeq* 16:73–74.

147. Jean Esona in *AAeq* 17:20–22.

148. Papiers Maurice De Ryck 25/1, Memorial Library, University of Wisconsin-Madison; published as S. Veys, "Territoire d'Ingende," *AAeq* 16:127–34.

149. Bompuku in *AAeq* 16:105–6.

150. Boenga in *AAeq* 17:24–35.

151. Lomboto in S. Veys, "Territoire D'Ingende," *AAeq* 16:132. After Ekuma's suicide, Lomboto seemed an Arab *seigneur*, "robbing and killing" until relegated to Léopoldville; Edmond Boelaert, "Bokatola," Annexe 2 in "Arrivée," *AAeq* 16:126–27.

152. Engels, "Costermans (Paul-Marie-Adolphe)," in BCB, vol. 1, col. 268–71. On "brulé la cervelle," see R. De Grez to E. D. Morel, Brussels, 25 March 1905, E. D. Morel Papers M473, LSE.

153. M. Coosemans, "Shanu (Herzekiah-André)," in BCB, vol. 4, col. 838–39; Françoise Morimont, "H. A. Shanu," in *La Mémoire du Congo*, 213–17. Shanu's letters touched on British subjects in Congo; Van Calcken's farcical indigency certificate; his own photographs; see E. D. Morel Papers M473, LSE. The photographer became "spy" in many eyes; see André Van Iseghem, *Au Congo belge en 1896*, 48–49. For another suicide, see Frederick Starr Papers, Box 9, f. 7, Special Collections, University of Chicago.

154. Dhanis, Abir Journal, 15–21, 29.

155. Dhanis, Abir Journal, 94.

156. *Nganda*; Hulstaert, *Dictionnaire Lomóngo-français*, 1406.

157. Jon May and Nigel Thrift, eds., *TimeSpace*; Doreen Massey, "Space-Time, 'Science' and the Relationship between Physical Geography and Human Geography."

158. Commandant Coursez, Opération de police, Rapport, Territoire de Bokote, 15 October 1916, GG 13.744, AA. (There is no biography for Coursez in the BCB.)

159. Coursez, Rapport, GG 13.744.

160. Coursez, Rapport, GG 13.744.

161. Contrast the King Commission's report, which reported on "depression" and depopulation, linked to sleeping sickness, corvée avoidance, armed expedition "anxiety," aborting to enable flight, and the blow to wealth that came with the end of slaving, with trading vanishing from riverbanks; "Rapport au Roi-Souverain," 236–41, esp. 237.

162. Coursez, Rapport, GG 13.744.

163. Recently displayed at Rivington Place London, "Congo Dialogues: Alice Seeley Harris and Sammy Baloji," accessed 26 March 2015, http://autograph-abp.co.uk /exhibitions/congo-dialogues; and the International Slavery Museum in Liverpool, "Brutal Exposure: The Congo," accessed 26 March 2015, http://autograph-abp.co.uk /exhibitions/brutal-exposure.

164. Voas, "Subfertility and Disruption."

CHAPTER2: MARIA N'KOI

*Map 2.1 sources: DIVA-GIS, *Digital Chart of the World,* map data set (1992), "Download data by country," accessed 5 September 2014, http://diva-gis.org/gdata; *Natural Earth,* version 2.0, map data set (North American Cartographic Information Society, 2012), accessed 18 June 2013, http://www.naturalearthdata.com; *Map of Franco-British Conquest of German Cameroon 1916,* map (The New Society for the Diffusion of Knowledge).

**Map 2.1 inset sources: *Natural Earth,* version 2.0, map data set (North American Cartographic Information Society, 2012), accessed June 18, 2013, http://www.natural earthdata.com; "Africa Prior to WWI, 1914," in *The Outline of History,* by H. G. Wells, 986 (map, scale not given), Maps ETC, accessed November 18, 2014, http://etc.usf.edu /maps/pages/3600/3689/3689.htm.

1. Interview with Antoine Sonzolo Efoloko, 18 May 2007, Mbandaka.

2. Joseph-Marie Jadot, "Marie aux léopards," in *Sous les manguiers en fleurs*; Armand Collignon, *La véritable histoire de Marie aux léopards.*

3. Bogumil Jewsiewicki, "La contestation sociale et la naissance du prolétariat au Zaïre au cours de la première moitié du XXe siècle"; Jean-Luc Vellut, "Résistances et espaces de liberté dans l'histoire coloniale du Zaïre," in *Rébellions-révolution au Zaïre, 1963–1965,* vol. 1. See too David Van Reybrouck, *Congo,* 137–38.

4. An alleged "treasure trove" of Jadot papers (Sabine Cornelis, personal communication, 11 February 2008, with much gratitude) has apparently still not opened for research in Tournai or Brussels.

5. Formal and informal interviews during this journey, 7–19 May 2007, in Besefe, Ikanga, Bokatola, and Mbandaka.

6. Ancestral spirits; on *bokali* (sg.), see Gustaaf Hulstaert, *Dictionnaire Lomóngo-français,* 155; Gustaaf Hulstaert, "Les idées religieuses des Nkundo"; and E. Possoz, "Essai d'interprétation des épreuves superstitieuses dans l'Equateur," 2, 12. *Bekali* warn

not to neglect them through dreams or an owl's cries; Brunhilde Biebuyck, "Nkundo Mongo Tales" (Ph.D. diss., Indiana University, 1980), 26–27.

7. The term is Steven Feierman's; see his "Colonizers, Scholars, and the Creation of Invisible Histories," in *Beyond the Cultural Turn*.

8. On Batswa, see Paul Schebesta, *Vollblutneger und Halbzwerge*; A. Wauters, "Magiciens et écoles de magiciens chez les Batswa de l'Equateur." On Ekonda, see Georges Célis, "Fondeurs et forgerons Ekonda"; and Joseph Iyandza-Lopoloko, *Bobongo, danse renommée des Ekonda du Lac Léopold II*.

9. Agent often abbreviated as *territorial*. See, Marie-Benedicte Dembour, *Recalling the Belgian Congo*. On this territorial, see Collignon, Armand François, 1914–15, SPA 14702 (K 2431), AA.

10. AT A. Collignon to CDD, 17 June 1915, Relégations, no. 47, "Sombe dite Maria Nkoie," GG 16.105, AA. On political tensions in his territory at the time, see Collignon, *La véritable histoire*. On copal in Tshuapa, see Samuel Nelson, *Colonialism in the Congo Basin, 1880–1940*, 113–51.

11. Sleeping sickness campaigns deeply disturbed; Maryinez Lyons, *The Colonial Disease*. See also Deborah Neill, *Networks in Tropical Medicine*; Mari Webel, "Medical Auxiliaries, Colonial Fieldwork, and Sleeping Sickness Research in the Lake Victoria and Lake Tanganyika Basins before 1914," in *Citizens, Courtrooms, Crossings*.

12. Collignon to CDD, 17 June 1915; and A. Collignon to CDD, 25 July 1915; in Relégations, no. 47, GG 16.105.

13. Collignon to CDD, 25 July 1915, Relégations, no. 47, GG 16.105.

On Bokatola's political situation, Besefe, and Chief Pia, see Mission Cornet, Registre de la situation politique de Bokatola, 1908–13, Papiers Frantz Cornet, 59.31.1, MRAC.

14. Collignon, *La véritable histoire*. Collignon later suggested he knew an arrest was coming, and the visit was a way to test out and not fail the day of arrest; Collignon to CDD, 25 July 1915, Relégations, no. 47, GG 16.105.

15. Collignon to CDD, 25 July 1915, Relégations, no. 47, GG 16.105.

16. Collignon to CDD, 25 July 1915, Relégations, no. 47, GG 16.105; see Collignon, *La véritable histoire*.

17. Collignon to CDD, 25 July 1915, Relégations, no. 47, GG 16.105.

18. M. Durbecq and AT De Laveleye, "Rapport sur la reconnaissance opérée du 14 juillet au 5 août," District Lac Léopold II, Kiri Territory, 6 August 1915, Relégations, no. 47, GG 16.105.

19. The Great War has been little studied for Congo; see Bryant P. Shaw, "Force Publique, Force Unique" (Ph.D. diss., University of Wisconsin, 1984); and Guy Vanthemsche, *Le Congo belge pendant la Première Guerre mondiale*. British officials read Congolese as "cannibals" and avoided recruiting them as soldiers in the East African campaign; Hew Strachan, *The First World War in Africa*.

20. Durbecq and De Laveleye, "Rapport," Relégations, no. 47, GG 16.105.

21. On the organization of the Belgian war campaign in and from Congo, see Louis Habran, *Le Congo belge dans la guerre mondiale*; Ch. Tombeur, *Campagnes des troupes coloniales belges en Afrique Centrale, 1914–1917*; *The War of 1914–1916: The Belgian*

Campaigns in the Cameroons and in German East Africa; and Belgium, *Éphémérides des campagnes belges en Afrique (1914–1917)*.

22. CDD Inongo to GG, 26 July 1915, Relégations, no. 47, GG 16.105. The upgrading never happened; CDD Inongo to GG, 24 December 1915, Relégations, no. 47, GG 16.105. In 1915, there were nine military and twenty police operations; Shaw, "Force Publique, Force Unique," 177.

23. Durbecq and de Laveleye, "Rapport," Relégations, no. 47, GG 16.105.

24. This "cassava bread," fermented staple made from soaked cassava, has been common in the region since the time of Atlantic slavery; Jan Vansina, *The Tio Kingdom of Middle Congo, 1880–1892*.

25. Durbecq and de Laveleye, "Rapport," Relégations, no. 47, GG 16.105.

26. "Poisoned stakes" were still in use in the 1920s; Shaw, "Force Publique, Force Unique," 171–72.

27. Durbecq and de Laveleye, "Rapport," Relégations, no. 47, GG 16.105.

28. Durbecq and de Laveleye, "Rapport," Relégations, no. 47, GG 16.105.

29. We know too little about hemp or cannabis as crops with commercial, ritual, medicinal, or recreational uses. See Johannes Fabian, "Charisma, Cannabis, and Crossing Africa," in *Out of Our Minds*; and Ann Laudati, "Out of the Shadows," in *Drugs in Africa*.

30. AT Henry, Bokatola, to M. le CDD, 12 May 1917, "Operation de polize à Bokatola, 1917–18," GG 13.546, AA.

31. Durbecq and de Laveleye, "Rapport," Relégations, no. 47, GG 16.105.

32. Henry to CDD, 12 May 1917; and maps in "Operation de polize à Bokatola, 1917–18" in GG 13.546.

33. Durbecq and de Laveleye, "Rapport," Relégations, no. 47, GG 16.105.

34. Durbecq and de Laveleye, "Rapport," Relégations, no. 47, GG 16.105; see too Collignon to CDD, 25 July 1915, Relégations, no. 47, GG 16.105

35. Collignon to CDD, 25 July 1915, Relégations, no. 47, GG 16.105.

36. For the GG, "Ordre de relégation," Boma, 16 December 1915, Relégations, no. 47, GG 16.105.

37. Octave Louwers, *Codes et lois du Congo belge*, 439–41, 765–70, esp. 441, 767. For the 1903 circular, see Léon Strouvens and Pierre Piron, *Codes et lois du Congo belge*, 559–60.

38. "Copie de rapport de AT A. de Laveleye de Kiri," ca. 4 July 1915, Relégations, no. 47, GG 16.105. On *kisi*, Hulstaert, *Dictionnaire Lomóngo-français*, 1000.

39. "Interrogatoire du nommé Loniamela de Dongo," ca. 10 September 2015, Relégations, no. 47, GG 16.105.

40. John Weeks, "Anthropological Notes on the Bangala of the Upper Congo River," part 3, 394.

41. W. Holman Bentley, *Pioneering on the Congo*, 2:176 and n1.

42. Harry Johnston, *George Grenfell and the Congo*, 2:813. See Weeks, "Anthropological Notes on the Bangala," part 1, 105.

43. Johnston, *George Grenfell and the Congo*, 2:813.

44. On copal exports and history, see Edgar van der Straeten, *L'agriculture et les industries agricoles au Congo belge*, 33, 59, 65, and 346; L. Pynaert, "Le copal et son exploitation au Congo belge"; Gaston Gelissen, "Note sur le copal"; Jean-Philippe Peemans, *Le Congo-Zaire au gré du XXe siècle*; Julia Siebert, "More Continuity than Change?," in *Humanitarian Intervention and Changing Labor Relations*; Thaddeus Sunseri, "The Political Ecology of the Copal Trade in the Tanzanian Coastal Hinterland, c. 1820–1905." On Congo copal as a binding medium in British gloss paints and international demand, see "Movements and the War"; Harry Collin, "The Revival of Belgian International Trade"; Harriet Standeven, "The Development of Decorative Gloss Paints in Britain and the United States, c. 1910–1960." On British designer Terence Conran (b. 1931) accompanying his gum-copal dealer father to London's docks as a child to watch freighters unload Belgian Congo copal, see Terence Conran, "Introduction," in *Bermondsey Riverside*, accessed 10 April 2015, http://www.lddc-history.org.uk/bermondsey/index.html; Nick Barrett, "Terence Conran."

45. Henry Stanley, *The Congo and the Founding of Its Free State*, 2:353.

46. The King's Commission deemed copal unproblematic, even though children collected it; compensation for it attracted collectors, and the gulf in purchase prices between Congo and Europe seemed unsurprising; "Rapport au Roi-Souverain," *Bulletin Officiel de l'Etat Independant du Congo*, 190.

47. Séamas Síocháin and Michael Sullivan, eds., *The Eyes of Another Race*, 67–68.

48. Jadot, "Marie aux Léopards."

49. Rules in 1910–12 allowed selling directly to traders; taxes were still often paid in "food supplies or products" because there was "no coined money in a large part of the colony"; Frederick Starr, "The Congo Free State and Congo Belge," 394. On typical imports, see Richard Rathbone, "World War I and Africa," 7–8.

50. A 1910 decree gave chiefs salaries, though some could still receive tribute payments; Edouard Bustin, *Lunda under Belgian Rule*, 51.

51. Durbecq and De Laveleye, "Rapport," Relégations, no. 47, GG 16.105.

52. Coercion in copal labor varied. When war began, the recently introduced regime of Congolese commercial liberty seemed dangerous. Quite cut off from the occupied metropole, colonial imports shrank. While prices dropped, copal exports nearly doubled in 1915–16. Wartime encouraged the sale of depreciated goods, which may have stimulated Congolese copal production; "Le commerce du Congo belge."

53. "La gomme-copal au Congo"; and "Le commerce du Congo belge."

54. On stereotypes and campaigns against small traders see Jean-Luc Vellut, "La présence portugaise au Congo du XVe siècle à la Deuxième Guerre mondiale," esp. 44–47. On "petit commerçant" figurations, see Jadot, "Marie aux Léopards," 219 and 221.

55. Alexandre Delcommune, *L'avenir du Congo belge menacé*.

56. Jadot, "Marie aux Léopards"; Collignon, *La véritable histoire*.

57. "La gomme-copal au Congo."

58. Collignon, *La véritable histoire*.

59. For photographs of chiefs, see Georges Van der Kerken, *L'Ethnie mongo*, vol. 1, pl. 15, no. 66 (1911) and pl. 20, no. 87 (1929).

60. On ivory, see CDD Inongo to CDD Coq, 4 August 1915, Relégations, no. 47, GG 16.105. On hens and much else, see Collignon to CDD, 25 July 1915; CDD Inongo to GG, 4 August 1915; AT de 1ére classe, Congo belge, Enquête administrative, Affaire Maria N'Koie, "Interrogatoire de Maria N'koi," ca. 9 August 2015; Deposition, R. P. Van Houtte, Supérieur, Mission Ibeke Gemboi (Kiri), Ibeke, 28 August 1915; in Relégations, no. 47, GG 16.105.

61. "Interrogatoire du nommé Loniamela de Dongo," ca. 10 September 1915, Relégations, no. 47, GG 16.105.

62. "Interrogatoire de Maria N'koi de Bokatola," ca. 9 August 2015, Relégations, no. 47, GG 16.105.

63. "History of the UAC. Materials for B. Lunn's History. Notes by S. Edkins, 28.01.1937," United Africa Company Archives, Blackfriars, London; notes taken by J. L. Vellut, 1983, with much gratitude.

64. "Interrogatoire de Maria N'koi de Bokatola," ca. 9 August 2015, Relégations, no. 47, GG 16.105.

65. Durbecq and de Laveleye, "Rapport," Relégations, no. 47, GG 16.105.

66. His second letter recast his first as "urgent." Collignon to CDD, 25 July 1915, Relégations, no. 47, GG 16.105.

67. CDD Inongo to GG, 4 August 1915, Relégations, no. 47, GG 16.105.

68. CDD Inongo to GG, 4 August 1915; and Durbecq and de Laveleye, "Rapport," Relégations, no. 47, GG 16.105. Collignon, Armand François, 1914–15, SPA 14702 (K 2431); Collignon, Armand François, 1918, SPA 23163 (K 3865), AA. On political tensions in his territory at the time, see Collignon, *La véritable histoire*.

69. Collignon, *La véritable histoire*.

70. Durbecq and De Laveleye, "Rapport," Relégations, no. 47, GG 16.105.

71. Edmond Boelaert, "Liwenthal (Charles)" in *BCB*, vol. 5, col. 561–62; Edmond Boelaert, Honoré Vinck, and Charles Lonkama, "Arrivée," *AAeq* 16–17 (1995–96).

72. Like Ekuma or Liwenthal. Collignon, *La véritable histoire*. On self-representations of territorials for later periods, see Dembour, *Recalling the Belgian Congo*.

73. Jadot, "Marie aux léopards"; and Collignon, *La véritable histoire*.

74. Collignon, *La véritable histoire*.

75. Jadot, "Marie aux Léopards."

76. "Les magistrats congolais" mocks gentlemen who arrived knowing little, then acquitted Congolese, condemned whites, while always demanding another inquiry. Others mock a colonial "inconvenience": *mulâtres*; P. Hubin, Alexandre Leclercq, and Léon Pirsoul, *Chansons congolaises par trois moustiquaires*, 16–18, 44–45. Some clarify colonial ranks and categories.

77. Suggested in songs about African lovers: "La négresse" and "Viens près de moi ma p'tite Yaya" in Hubin, Leclercq, and Pirsoul, *Chansons congolaises*, 32–34, 87–89. "Congo Côte d'Azur" suggests a new fashion: Belgian wives and children arriving along with cinema, dancing, electricity, and a "paradise" of amusements; "La Femme blanche au Congo," Hubin, Leclercq, and Pirsoul, *Chansons congolaises*, 21–24, 82–83.

78. Born to a doctor in 1886, educated at Namur, Jadot shifted from priestly aspirations to law at Louvain, graduating in 1910 already a published poet. At twenty-four, he chose to be a colonial prosecutor, increasingly fashioning himself as man of colonial letters, with "a pride a bit naïve"; A. Gérard, "Jadot (Joseph-Marie Camille)," in *BBOM*, vol. 8, col. 191–97. Also: Jean Leyder, "Jadot (Joseph-Marie)," in *Le graphisme et l'expression graphique au Congo belge*, 47. Key works include Joseph-Marie Jadot, *Sous les manguiers en fleurs*; Joseph-Marie Jadot, *Nous—en Afrique*; and Joseph-Marie Jadot, *Apéritifs*.

79. Gérard, "Jadot"; L. Lejeune, "Joseph-Marie Jadot," in *La femme noire vue par les écrivains africanistes*. See Silvia Riva, "L'épanouissement de cette fleur de culture par nos soins de bons jardiniers," in *Figures et paradoxes de l'histoire au Burundi, au Congo et au Rwanda*; Lissia Jeurissen, *Quand le métis s'appelait "mulâtre"*; "Mulâtres, Avant 1940," AI 14 (4874), AA; Gustaaf Hulstaert, "Le Problème des mulâtres," parts 1 and 2; and Joseph-Marie Jadot, "Le droit de métis au Congo Belge," in *Congrès International pour l'étude des problèmes résultant du mélange des races*, 45–49, 121–22.

80. Jeurissen, *Quand le métis*.

81. See Pierre Halen, "A propos de Gaston-Genys Périer et de la notion d'art vivant"; Jean-Luc Vellut, "Colonial Kitsch," in *An Anthology of African Art*.

82. Joseph-Marie Jadot, *Trois contes de l'Afrique en guerre*.

83. See Leyder, "Jadot (Joseph-Marie)"; Gérard, "Jadot"; Riva, "L'épanouissement de cette fleur"; Jeurissen, *Quand le métis*.

84. On imperial nervosité in literary and medical registers, see Joseph Conrad, *Heart of Darkness*; and David Kerr Cross, *Health in Africa*.

85. A *bagne* is a tropical penal colony. French examples dating to the eighteenth century include Biribiri; Peter Redfield, *Space in the Tropics*. (A factual penal colony is a subject in chapter 5.)

86. Joseph-Marie Jadot, "Le Campement," in *Sous les manguiers en fleurs*.

87. The loathing was partly tropical (ecological), partly racialized (more visceral); see, Nancy Stepan, *Picturing Tropical Nature*.

88. In Jadot's writing; also in the relegation archive.

89. Jeurissen, *Quand le métis*.

90. Gérard, "Jadot," col. 191–97.

91. Joseph-Marie Jadot, *Poèmes d'ici et de là-bas*; Riva, "L'épanouissement de cette fleur."

92. Joseph-Marie Jadot, "La Charge (Mambamu)," in *Sous les manguiers en fleurs*.

93. Durbecq and De Laveleye, "Rapport," Relégations, no. 47, GG 16.105. On clay funerary figures, see Biebuyck, "Nkundo Mongo Tales," 24. There is no parallel with Wangata anthropomorphic coffins (bearing a Bobangi influence); see Gustaaf Hulstaert, "La fabrication des cercueils anthropomorphes."

94. Little is known about the size or avidity of Jadot's readership.

95. Jadot, "Marie aux Léopards."

96. Durbecq and De Laveleye, "Rapport," Relégations, no. 47, GG 16.105.

97. On ambivalence, see Habran, *Le Congo belge dans la guerre mondiale*, 10–11.

98. "Déclarations complementaires de Bonkali, Chef investi des Banga, et de Lubaka Thomas, de Banga," ca. 10 September 1915; Interrogatoire de Biko femme de Bomba, Chef investi de Dyembe," ca. 10 September 1915; in Relégations, no. 47, GG 16.105.

99. Collignon to CDD, 25 July 1915; "Interrogatoire de Maria N'koi de Bokatola," ca. 9 August 1915, Relégations, no. 47, GG 16.105. In some three years, villages near Coquilhatville lost about three quarters of their populations to sleeping sickness. Atoxyl was in use by hospitals; Fritz Van der Kinden, *Le Congo, les noirs et nous*, 72.

100. Armstrong wrote of Nkema, a "bright Christian" who became agitated, a "ferocious creature" near Boginda. By 1908, the state "placed him on an island"; W. D. Armstrong Papers, 26/6, 30 August 1905–30 July 1908, Regions Beyond Missionary Union Archive, University of Edinburgh, Edinburgh. In July 1914, the Ekwayolo territorial Charles Lodewyckx began trypanosomiasis duties, as district doctor Russo left with half a sanitary brigade and bush-clearing equipment; "Lodewyckx, Charles," SPA (4482), AA. Official investigation meant travel with soldiers, lumbar punctures, and medication; Lyons, *The Colonial Disease*.

101. Interview with Antoine Sonzolo Efoloko, 18 May 2007, Mbandaka; also on pregnancy and travel, Durbecq and De Laveleye, "Rapport," Relégations, no. 47, GG 16.105.

102. On the cluster of words and meanings surrounding infertility, sterility, and aridity, see Hulstaert, *Dictionnaire Lomóngo-français*, 259, 422, 520, 979.

103. "Interrogatoire de Biko; femme de Bomba, Chef investi de Dyembe," ca. 10 September 1915, Relégations, no. 47, GG 16.105.

104. Jadot, "Marie aux léopards."

105. A fascinating exception is Riva, "L'épanouissement de cette fleur." Pierre Halen kindly advised me: "Littérairement, l'écriture de Jadot était déjà un peu démodée . . . en son temps" (personal communication, 14 August 2006). Halen at first set Jadot aside. Compare: Pierre Halen, *"Le petit Belge avait vu grand"*; with Catherine Gravet and Pierre Halen, "Littératures viatique et coloniale," in *Littératures belges de langue française*, 538.

106. Jadot, "Marie aux Léopards."

107. For Equateur photographic scenes in a romanticized register, see Joseph-Marie Jadot, "La Province de l'Equateur," in *Le miroir du Congo belge*, vol. 1.

108. Gérard, "Jadot." Female porterage remained an issue into the 1930s.

109. Alexandre Paris, *Leçons de psychiatrie*, cited in Jadot, "Marie aux Léopards," 208.

110. Edmond Boelaert, "Yebola"; Gustaaf Hulstaert, "Marie aux léopards (quelques souvenirs historiques)."

111. Durbecq and De Laveleye, "Rapport," Relégations, no. 47, GG 16.105.

112. "Interrogatoire de Maria N'koi de Bokatola," ca. 9 August 1915; "Déclarations complémentares de Bokolo, vieux notable de Banga, Kiri," 10 September 1915; "Interrogatoire de Biko; femme de Bomba, Chef investi de Dyembe," ca. 10 September 1915; in Relégations, no. 47, GG 16.105.

113. Tape recorded interviews in 2007, with groups and individuals gathered in Besefe (population four thousand) on 13 May, including Mboto Y'Ofaya, David Ikeke,

and Thomas Ndio; in Ikanga (population one thousand) on 13 May, including Dieu-donné Bosembu, Nzampenda Lokamba, Bekolo Lokombo, Booto, and Eloliin Ikanga; and Bokatola (population five thousand) on 14–15 May, with visits to the school and Ekuma's gravesite.

114. In 2007, in Besefe and Ikanga, some said she saw Jesus in the forest or "angels during the birth of Christ."

115. At Besefe in 2007 a group interview erupted when Thomas Ndio announced her husband had been caught out with a beautiful Batswa. As news of the affair spread, the ashamed, angry Maria N'koi fled, entering the forest for her visions. Some accused Ndio of lying; sexual relations with Batswa are anathema. Ndio insisted nothing was wrong with sharing his version. His reasoning—disgrace producing flight, illness, visions—seemed plausible to all. Others suggested she was pregnant and went to be with her mother.

116. Her malady partly stemmed from marital troubles, Jadot's story tells: After she took a lover in Ikanga, rivalries ensued, and Ikanga's Chief Monkeka connived to steer her messages and control her gifts before betraying her to the "Commandant." Jadot, "Marie aux léopards." Collignon spurned Jadot's plot as fiction; Collignon, *La véritable histoire*.

117. Perhaps such transgressions were everyday. In 2007, many described Maître Bozi, a Bandundu painter who lived among them in 2006–7, painting war and other scenes on their houses in return for cannabis: he took a Batswa lover and this transgression forced his departure.

118. She had seven grandchildren, two daughters, and two sons; her last, Pierre Efokolo, fathered Sonzolo. Her Nkundo parents of Ikanga farmed, trapped, and fished. She and her Ekonda husband resided in Besefe, where Batswa tended to live at the edges of the village.

119. Commissaire General to Gov., Province de l'Equateur, 18 February 1926; Gov. Duchesne, Coq to Gov., Province Orientale, 1 October 1926; Gov. Duchesne to GG, 28 September 1929; for the GG to Gov., Province de l'Equateur, 14 October 1929; Secr. Gen. for GG, Boma, ordonannce, 14 October 1929; in Relégations, no. 47, GG 16.105.

120. Hulstaert, "Marie aux Léopard."

121. Interview with Antoine Sonzolo Efoloko, 18 May 2007, Mbandaka. Tax receipts were dated 1961–70. Research on Congo-Zaire's postcolonial medical history is needed; this evidence of a healer certification program tells of Mobutu's patrimonial state incorporating healing into its *authenticité* remit. For hints, see Gilles Bibeau, "New Legal Rules for an Old Art of Healing"; Gilles Bibeau, Rashim Ajluwalia, and Bernard Méchin, *Traditional Medicine in Zaire*. Compare with the wonderful Stacy Langwick, *Bodies, Politics, and African Healing*.

122. One man instead told of her meeting God who gave her healing powers just when Yebola was born. Others insisted that Yebola (featured again in chapter 3) and Njondo not be confused; Yebola was usually practiced further afield and emphasized spectacle more.

123. For *njondo* as anvil, with photograph, see Hulstaert, *Dictionnaire Lomóngo-français*, 1447.

124. An Ekonda short sword, University of Michigan Museum of Art, 1998/1.68, accessed 27 March 2015, http://quod.lib.umich.edu/m/musart/x-1998-sl-1.68/1998_1.68 ___jpg#.

125. Iyandza-Lopoloko, *Bobongo*; René Tonnoir, "Bobongo ou l'art choréographique chez les Ekonda, Yembe et Tumba du Lac Léopold II"; Yoka Lye Mudaba, "Bobongo"; Van der Kerken, *L'Ethnie mongo*.

126. Célis, "Fondeurs et forgerons"; Eugenia Herbert, *Iron, Gender, and Power*.

127. In the 1990s, the best Njondo healers were Batswa; Misago Kanimba and Charles Lonkama, "Un chant njondo des environs de Bokuma," *AAeq* 16 (1995).

128. Kanimba and Lonkama, "Un chant njondo," 177–78.

129. Piet Korse, Lokonga Mondjulu, and Bonje wa Mpay Bongondo, *Jebola*; Constantine Petrides, "A Figure for *Cibola*." In Bokatola, some said Njondo and Yebola differed by symptoms; each had healers living nearby. Yet Pentecostalism had produced change: "prayers are there and people go to church." Many in Besefe and Ikanga called Maria N'koi the founder of Njondo.

130. Unlike in Yebola or the pleasures of sitting with a drink near a radio's dance sounds, where "If you wish to sing, you only have to sing." Sonzolo also suggested instantaneous distraction came with radio possession: "Today, if you want to listen to a Koffi song, you only have to put the tape in the cassette radio." His grandmother did not sing Zebola or do healing ending with a spectacle as in Yebola; the latter morphed into Zebola healing and commercial, entertaining Zebola songs from at least the 1970s. Yebola knew raphia skirts, smeared bodies, collapsing from possession, patients found in trees, dancing, treating with medicines, and applying the colors of spectacle; interview with Antoine Sonzolo Efoloko, 18 May 2007, Mbandaka. On urban Zebola in 1970s Kinshasa, see the invaluable work on healing and individuation by Ellen Corin, notably "A Possession Psychotherapy in an Urban Setting"; Ellen Corin and Kintenda Ki Mata Ndombasi, *Zebola: possession et thérapie au Zaïre*, video recording; Ellen Corin, "Refiguring the Person," in *Bodies and Persons*. From the 2010s, YouTube became a rich source for Zebola as popular, Kinois dance music and spectacle.

131. Interview with Antoine Sonzolo Efoloko, 18 May 2007, Mbandaka.

132. Joseph-Marie Jadot, "La légende d'Inongo," in *Poèmes d'ici et de là-bas*, 111–15.

133. Gaston-Dénys Périer, *Notes de littérature coloniale*.

134. Sarah Nuttall, "Introduction: Rethinking Beauty," in *Beautiful/Ugly*, 10; Petrine Archer-Straw, *Negrophilia*; Elizabeth Ezra, *The Colonial Unconscious*; and Nancy Hunt, "Tintin and the Interruptions of Congolese Comics," in *Images and Empires*.

135. Habran, *Le Congo belge dans la guerre mondiale*, 10–11; emphasis added.

136. Tombeur, *Campagnes des troupes coloniales belges en Afrique centrale, 1914–1917*, 31. See also *The War of 1914–1916: The Belgian Campaigns in the Cameroons and in German East Africa*; Belgium, *Éphémérides des campagnes belges en Afrique (1914–1917)*; Pierre Daye, *Trois ans de victoires belges en Afrique*; Joseph Gauderique Aymérich, *La conquête de Cameroun*.

137. The Great War's impact on imaginations, emotions, and practice in Africa has been little studied, though see Gregory Mann, *Native Sons*. For a useful bibliography,

see Strachan, *The First World War in Africa*; for the still fine framing of questions, see Rathbone, "World War I and Africa."

138. As in colonial relegation and penal colonies; see Peter Redfield, "Foucault in the Tropics," in *Anthropologies of Modernity*, 59.

139. On "aleatory encounters," see Louis Althusser, *Philosophy of the Encounter*. Feierman argues that "healing cults," like descent groups, "had their own historicities"; Steven Feierman, *Peasant Intellectuals*, 29.

140. See related work on sexuality and empire; Amandine Lauro, *Coloniaux, ménagères et prostituées au Congo belge, 1885–1930*; Ann Stoler, *Carnal Knowledge and Imperial Power*.

141. Paolo Virno, *A Grammar of the Multitude*.

142. Hulstaert, "Marie aux léopards," 433–35, esp. 435.

143. Steven Feierman, "Healing as Social Criticism in the Time of Colonial Conquest," 87.

144. Jacqueline Rose, *States of Fantasy*.

145. Gaston Bachelard, *The Poetics of Reverie*; Gaston Bachelard, *On Poetic Imagination and Reverie*.

CHAPTER 3: EMERGENCY TIME

1. Schebesta (1887–1967) of Congregation of the Divine Word (and Wilhelm Schmidt's Anthropos Institute, near Vienna) spent a brief part of 1930 in Equateur with Batswa and their Nkundo neighbors. Paul Schebesta, *Vollblutneger und Halbzwerge*; Paul Schebesta, *My Pygmy and Negro Hosts*.

2. Schebesta, *Vollblutneger*, 223 (translated by Marti Lybeck, August 2006, with much gratitude).

3. Schebesta, *Vollblutneger*, 224–25.

4. Since 1911, this Lever Brothers affiliate was establishing large palm oil plantations in Belgian Congo; from 1930, HCB, part of the multinational Unilever, was the most well financed concern in this part of Equateur. See Charles Wilson, *History of Unilever*; Pierre Vanderlinden, *Pierre Ryckmans, 1891–1959*; and Jules Marchal, *Lord Leverhulme's Ghosts*. HCB's Flandria zone warrants more research; in 2008, the Unilever archives (Port Sunlight, UK) advised me they had no Congo material.

5. Pierre Daye, *L'Empire colonial belge*, 207, 210.

6. Daye, *L'Empire colonial belge*, 218–26, esp. 207, 210.

7. Daye, *L'Empire colonial belge*, 230–35, esp. 230, 231.

8. Daye, *L'Empire colonial belge*, 230–35, esp. 233; "Enseignements d'une révolte des indigènes au Congo belge," *Notre Colonie* (16 December 1924).

9. On Kimbangu, see Jean-Luc Vellut, *Simon Kimbangu, 1921*; Jean-Luc Vellut, "Episodes anticommunistes dans l'ordre colonial belge (1924–1932)," in *La Peur du rouge*. For Equateur, see "Communisme, Affaire Esukula," Dossier secret, Sectes, Service des renseignements, Coquilhatville, GG 8005, AA.

10. "Enseignements d'une révolte," esp. 252.

11. Dr. Louis Jaggard to R. A. Doan, 9 August 1917, Louis Jaggard Papers, DCHS.

12. "Enseignements d'une révolte," 252.

13. R. Mouchet, "Note pour Monsieur le Médecin en Chef," 6 March 1931, GG 12.266, AA. The towering Mottoulle was architect of welfare capitalism, notably family health care in Katanga; see Nancy Hunt, "'Le bébé en brousse,'" 417, 419, 420. For two prominent British travelers' perceptions of this Belgian doctor figure, see Margery Perham, *African Apprenticeship*, 215–24 ("Dr. Mottone"); and Basil Davidson, *The African Awakening*, 109–11, 166–67, 170.

14. Léopold Mottoulle, *Le problème de la main-d'oeuvre au Congo belge*. In the 1900s, territorials sided with chiefs and elders against wives fleeing to Catholic missions near Coquilhatville; "Mission trappiste," 1899–1907, M 74 (576), AA.

15. Dr. L. Strada, Médecin Provincial, "Objet: Contrôle démographique," to Messieurs les Médecins de District, Province de l'Equateur, 26 October 1932, GG 12.266.

16. Mottoulle, *Le problème*, 30–31.

17. Mouchet, "Note," 6 March 1931, GG 12.266.

18. Mottoulle, *Le problème*.

19. G. Schwers, 20 August 1934; Dratz to Schwers, 14 September 1934; Armani to Schwers, 5 October 1934; in GG 12.266.

20. Mottoulle, *Le problème*.

21. Mottoulle, *Le problème*.

22. Mouchet, "Note," 6 March 1931, GG 12.266.

23. Mouchet, "Note," 6 March 1931, GG 12.266. See also Dratz, "Rapport annuel 1932 concernant le fonctionnement du SAMI," Bokote, 3 January 1933, GG 12.266.

24. Michael Worboys, "Unsexing Gonorrhoea."

25. See Roger Davidson, *Dangerous Liaisons*; and Annet Mooij, *Out of Otherness*.

26. Dratz, "Territoire des Kundu. Chefferie des Wangata-Tumba," 15 February 1933, GG 12.266.

27. Bonura, "Rencensement médical," GG 12.266.

28. Bonura, "Rencensement médical," GG 12.266.

29. Dratz, "Territoire des Kundu. Chefferie des Wangata-Tumba," 15 February 1933, GG 12.266.

30. Dratz, "Rapport annuel 1932 concernant le fonctionnement du SAMI," Bokote, 3 January 1933, GG 12.266.

31. Mouchet, "Note," 6 March 1931, GG 12.266. Nicolas Favre (now lymphogranuloma venereum, caused by a *Chlamydia trachomatis* subtype) is a genital ulcerative disease (GUD) that may contribute to infertility. In the 1970s, another *Chlamydia* subtype was found to cause highly sterilizing pelvic inflammatory disease; J. D. Oriel and G. L. Ridgeway, *Genital Infection by Chlamydia trachomatis*, 61–64. On the implications for historians of the early spread of HIV-1 group M in early twentieth-century central Africa, see Tamara Giles-Vernick et al., "Social History, Biology, and the Emergence of HIV in Colonial Africa." Nicolas Favre among GUDs facilitated Congo's early human HIV transmission; see João de Sousa et al., "High GUD Incidence in the Early Twentieth Century Created a Particularly Permissive Time Window for the Origin and Initial Spread of Epidemic HIV Strains." On medical efficiency, injections, sexual commod-

ification, and prostitution in Belgian colonial towns, notably Léopoldville-Kinshasa, see Jacques Pépin, *The Origins of AIDS*; and Nuno Faria et al., "The Early Spread and Epidemic Ignition of HIV-1 in Human Populations." *A Nervous State* critiques the mechanical causalities suggested by this literature, in part by showing the relevance of upriver towns and worker camps. It also demonstrates that sexual economies were complex and manifold, interlinked with bodily practices like irrigation (enemas and douching), infertility dynamics, and hedonism.

32. Dratz, "Rapport annuel 1932 concernant le fonctionnement du SAMI," Bokote, 3 January 1933, GG 12.266.

33. Dratz, "Territoire des Kundu. Chefferie des Wangata-Tumba," 15 February 1933, GG 12.266.

34. Mouchet, "Note," 6 March 1931, GG 12.266. Irate patient refusal of gynecological examination by speculum has long been a feature of feminist histories; see Judith Walkowitz, *Prostitution and Victorian Society*.

35. Dratz, "Sous-secteur de la Lulonga Ikelemba," Basankusu, 3 June 1935, GG 12.266.

36. V. Barthélémi, "Étude sur la syphilis au Congo belge" (Examen B, no. 16a, Institut de la Médecine Tropicale, Antwerp, 1921).

37. Jaggard to Schwers, 19 January 1935, GG 12.266.

38. Dratz, "Territoire des Kundu. Chefferie des Wangata-Tumba," 15 February 1933, GG 12.266.

39. Van Reeth to AT, 3 August 1931; "Huilever Flandria," Rapport by Commissaire Général Jorissen after trip (29 January–6 February), 1932 (Flandria director Feuillien complains about low Wangata production and listless territorials; predicts revolt); AT Brumagne to Gouverneur, 28 January 1932 (attempts to increase cutter production); in Equateur, "Dossiers divers," GG 11.347, AA.

40. R. Vereecken to Governor, 20 March 1932; Vereecken to GG, 21 March 1932; Duchesne to GG, 2 April 1932; in GG 11.347.

41. Bogumil Jewsiewicki, "Le colonat agricole européen au Congo belge, 1910–1960."

42. A married agent had to cover costs for two households when on journeys, which could last two weeks; from 1925, Unatra boats, not a cheaper company, were required. Duchesne to GG, 19 May 1932, GG 11.347.

43. GG Tilkens to M. le Gouverneur, 8 January 1932, GG 11.347.

44. Duchesne to Tilkens, 12 January 1932; F. Requilé to Gouverneur, 12 January 1932, "Coût de la vie au 31/12/1931"; in GG 11.347.

45. On first-term agent losses, devotion to "the native 'thing,'" temperaments mattering more than backgrounds, and "the Colony itself" as the best school, see Duchesne to GG, 11 May 1932, GG 11.347.

46. CDD Van Reeth to M l'AT, Boende, 5 August 1931, GG 11.347.

47. AT Brumagne, Bokatola, to Gouverneur, 28 January 1932, in Equateur, "Dossiers divers," GG 11.347.

48. Daye, *L'Empire colonial belge*; Vellut, "Épisodes anticommunistes."

49. The Dengese and Pende rebellions coincided with economic depression in 1931; they shocked with their murders of Europeans. On Dengese, see "Les révoltes du

Sankuru et des Dekese," *XXème siécle*, 14 April 1932 in GG 11.347; "Dengese," GG 11.347; Martin Thomas, *Violence and Colonial Order*. HCB abuse underlay the Pende revolt, but it was ignited by outrage over the sexual possession of chiefly daughters by two state agents; Louis-François Vanderstraeten, *La répression de la révolte des Pende du Kwango en 1931*. On Pende, see Siketele Gize, "Les racines de la révolte Pende de 1931"; Zoe Strother, *Inventing Masks*; Marchal, *Lord Leverhulme's Ghosts*. More attention to sexual violations as insults causing colonial rebellions is in order.

50. AT Brumagne to M. le Gouverneur, Bokatola, 28 January 1932, GG 11.347.

51. AT Brumagne to M. le Gouverneur, 28 January 1932, GG 11.347.

52. AT Brumagne to M. le Gouverneur, 28 January 1932, GG 11.347.

53. AT Brumagne to M. le Gouverneur, 28 January 1932, GG 11.347. See too Schebesta, *Vollblutneger*, 231–32.

54. Schebesta, *Vollblutneger*.

55. On "technique of nearness," see Walter Benjamin, *The Arcades Project*, 545; also Nancy Hunt, *Suturing New Medical Histories of Africa*.

56. *Boseka*; Gustaaf Hulstaert, *Dictionnaire lomóngo-français*, 309.

57. CDD-Adjoint Bourton to AT de Boende, 1 December 1930, "Menaces de troubles. Propagande communiste," Dossier secret. Sectes, Service des reseignements, Coquilhat-ville, no. 2/6, GG 8005.

58. Gov. Jorissen to GG, 7 March 1931, "Menaces de troubles. Propagande commu-niste," GG 8005.

59. Commissariat de Police, Rapport, 18 December 1930, "Menaces de troubles. Propagande communiste," GG 8005.

60. P-V, no. 1799. Pro-Justitia, 18 December 1930, "Menaces de troubles. Propagande communiste," GG 8005.

61. P-V, no. 1799. Pro-Justitia, 18 December 1930, "Menaces de troubles. Propagande communiste," GG 8005.

62. P-V, no. 1799. Pro-Justitia, 18 December 1930, "Menaces de troubles. Propagande communiste," GG 8005.

63. P-V, no. 1799. Pro-Justitia, 18 December 1930, "Menaces de troubles. Propagande communiste," GG 8005.

64. P-V, no. 1799. Pro-Justitia, 18 December 1930, "Menaces de troubles. Propagande communiste," GG 8005.

65. P-V, no. 1800. Procés-Verbal, 19 December 1930, "Menaces de troubles. Propa-gande communiste," GG 8005. *Basendji*, Swahili for "savage or uncivilized," wended its way into other Congolese languages, like Lingala.

66. P-V, no. 1800. Procés-Verbal, 19 December 1930, "Menaces de troubles. Propa-gande communiste," GG 8005.

67. P-V, no. 1801. Procés-Verbal, 19 December 1930, "Menaces de troubles. Propa-gande communiste," GG 8005.

68. Procés-Verbal de saisie de prevenus, 19 December 1930, "Menaces de troubles. Propagande communiste," GG 8005.

69. Secrétaire Marée to Gouverneur, 20 December 1930, "Menaces de troubles. Propagande communiste," GG 8005.

70. Marée to Procureur du Roi, 22 December 1930, "Communisme, Affaire Esukula," GG 8005.

71. Procureur du Roi E. Mendiaux, 22 December 1930, "Communisme, Affaire Esukula," GG 8005.

72. Lissia Jeurissen, "Colonisation et 'question des mulâtres' au Congo belge," in *Figures et paradoxes de l'histoire au Burundi, au Congo et au Rwanda.*

73. "Dossier secret, Sectes, Service des renseignements, Couilhatville," "Communisme, Affaire Esukula," GG 8005. "Communisme, Affaire Esukula," GG 8005.

74. De Bisschop to AT Principal, 22 December 1930, "Communisme, Affaire Esukula," GG 8005.

75. President Jorissen, Secrétaire Marée, rapport, 24 December 1930, "Communisme, Affaire Esukula," GG 8005.

76. J. Jorissen and C. Marée, Rapport, 8 January 1931, "Dossier secret, Sectes, Service des renseignements, Coquilhatville," "Communisme, Affaire Esukula," GG 8005.

77. Jorissen and Marée, Rapport, 8 January 1931, "Communisme, Affaire Esukula," GG 8005. "Communisme, Affaire Esukula," GG 8005.

78. "Abandon de la colonie aux Américains," Dossier secret, Sectes, Service des renseignements, Coquilhatville, no. 4, GG 8005.

79. J. Jorissen and C. Marée, Rapport, 8 January 1931, "Communisme, Affaire Esukula," GG 8005. Regarding Compagnie Maritime Belge shipments between Matadi and Antwerp, see Vellut, "Épisodes anticommunistes," 186.

80. On Marcus Garvey, Bolshevik propaganda, and the need to purify colonial cadres, within metropolitan colonial archives, see "Mouvements anti-européens. Mouvement pan-nègre"; "Congrès Pan-Africain"; "Coupures de presse. Communisme. Kibangisme [*sic*]," 1924, 1930–31, 1934 (especially "Les menées bolchevistes dans notre empire africain, Le Gouverneur Duchesne a repris la direction de la province de l'Equateur," *XXème siècle*, 18 April 1931); and "Mouvement communiste et anti-impérialiste, 1925–36," AI 1405, AA. On Garveyism in Congo, see also Jean-Luc Vellut, "Résistances et espaces de liberté dans l'histoire coloniale du Zaïre," in *Rébellions-révolution au Zaïre, 1963–1965,* 1:34–35. For southern Africa, see Robert Vinson, *The Americans Are Coming!* See Robert Hill and Gregory Pirio, "Africa for the Africans," in *Politics of Race, Class and Nationalism in Twentieth-Century South Africa*; and Michael West, "Seeds Are Sown."

81. "Communisme, Affaire Esukula," GG 8005.

82. "Communisme, Affaire Esukula," GG 8005.

83. Mottoulle, *Le problème*, 63–64.

84. Provincial Commissioner to GG, August 1934, GG 12.266.

85. Armani, "Rapport sur la dénatalité indigène," Boende, 26 January 1935, GG 12.266. Schwers implied shock but did not say "psychic traumatism" as early as 1934. Shock was not part of Darwin's vocabulary; Charles Darwin, *The Descent of Man*, 2nd ed. It became ubiquitous during the Great War with "shell-shock," then within neurology and endocrinology, before *stress* came to the fore; see Mark Jackson, *The Age of Stress.* For a critique of colonial effects on "native zest" by the anthropologist, psychiatrist, and neurologist key to shell shock research, see W. H. R. Rivers, "The Dying-

Out of Native Races," parts 1 and 2; W. H. R. Rivers, ed., *Essays on the Depopulation of Melanesia.*

86. Italics added. Armani, "Rapport sur la dénatalité indigène," Boende, 26 January 1935, GG 12.266.

87. Mouchet, "Note," 6 March 1931, GG 12.266. Jaggard to Bro Dean, 26 September 1917. Jaggard wrote home about elephant hunting for Christmas dinner into the 1930s; Louis Jaggard Papers, DCHS. Ryckmans hunted elephants during war campaigns up the Sangha; Vanderlinden, *Pierre Ryckmans, 1891–1959.* An Itoko territorial showed off his "private museum of elephant skeletons"; Mary Sue Havens, *Mary Sue's Diary*, 23.

88. Jaggard to Schwers, 19 January 1935, GG 12.266.

89. Jaggard to Schwers, 19 January 1935, GG 12.266.

90. Jaggard to Schwers, 19 January 1935, GG 12.266.

91. P. Bonura, "Recensement médical de la chefferie des Mongandanga, de l'agglération chrétienne de la mission catholique de Bokote et de la chefferie des Bokala," 15 July 1931, GG 12.266.

92. Bonura, "Recensement médical," 15 July 1931, GG 12.266.

93. Samuel Nelson, *Colonialism in the Congo Basin, 1880–1940*, 113–51. Congo resin was fossilized; production rose from 20 to 23,000 tons between 1900 and 1936. "Hard Resins," accessed 11 June 2010, www.fao.org/docrep/v9236e/V9236e07.htm.

94. Bonura, "Recensement médical," GG 12.266.

95. Compare: "Documentation sur les pêcheries au Congo belge," parts 1 and 2.

96. Bonura, "Recensement médical," GG 12.266. Armani, "Rapport sur la dénatalité indigène," Boende, 26 January 1935, GG 12.266.

97. P. de Briey to GG, 24 August 1934, GG 12.266.

98. "Copal-Equateur-1924," 1919–24, GG 16.812, AA.

99. "Enseignements d'une révolte."

100. Bonura, "Recensement médical," GG 12.266. See "Copal-Equateur-1924," GG 16.812.

101. Armani, "Rapport sur la dénatalité indigène," Boende, 26 January 1935, GG 12.266.

102. de Briey to GG, 24 August 1934, GG 12.266.

103. Samuel Nelson, "Colonialism, Capitalism, and Work in the Congo Basin" (Ph.D. diss., Stanford University, 1986).

104. The effort to drive out Portuguese buyers intensified. In 1932, six Portuguese firms near Bokala complained about dwindling amounts of copal for sale; the state was privileging Belgian companies, with most moving into palm. "Equateur," Dossiers divers, C–Cabinet 1932, GG 11.347. Some had argued for driving out Portuguese competition from 1921; Joseph-Marie Jadot, *La Province equatoriale du Congo belge*; Alexandre Delcommune, *L'avenir du Congo belge menacé.*

105. Nelson, "Colonialism, Capitalism, and Work," 349. Industrial hygiene dossiers suggest more attentive scrutiny; "Hygiène industrielle, dossiers individuels, firmes divers," GG 9552, AA.

106. Mouchet, "Note," 6 March 1931, GG 12.266; "Politique contre mouvements subversifs, 1946–64," GG 6076.

107. Mouchet, "Note," 6 March 1931, GG 12.266.

108. Edmond Boelaert, "Yebola," 16–17. See also, Edmond Boelaert, "Visscherij in mijn negerij."

109. Boelaert, "Yebola," 17–18.

110. Boelaert, "Yebola," 18–19.

111. Boelaert, "Yebola," 16.

112. Gustaaf Hulstaert, *Le mariage des Nkundo*, 341, 344–47 (the favorite wife or *nkonde* was revered and celebrated at length).

113. Boelaert, "Yebola"; Hulstaert, *Dictionnaire Lomóngo-français*, 1918–20.

114. George Beard, *American Nervousness*.

115. *Yebola*; Hulstaert, *Dictionnaire Lomóngo-français*, 1918–20; and Gustaaf Hulstaert, "Notes sur la Yébola," in *Petit lexique des croyances magiques mongo*.

116. Boelaert, "Yebola," 19.

117. Mottoulle, *Le problème*, 73, 69.

118. Mottoulle, *Le problème*; Edmond Boelaert, "De bons amis." See also Edmond Boelaert, "Halewijn," 1480.

119. Mottoulle, *Le problème*.

120. On Ekonda dance, Joseph Iyandza-Lopoloko, *Bobongo*. On Lianja, Edmond Boelaert, "Nsong'a Lianja: Het Groote Epos der Nkundo-Mongo"; Edmond Boelaert, "Nsong'a Lianja. L'épopée nationale des Nkundo"; and Edmond Boelaert, "La procession de Lianja."

121. Schebesta, *Vollblutneger*, 229–46, esp. 231, 247.

122. Boelaert, "Nsong'a Lianja: Het Groote Epos." On fifty-six versions, see Stephen Belcher, *Epic Traditions of Africa*, 29, 31–38. On Flemish missionary identifications, see Nancy Hunt, "Rewriting the Soul in a Flemish Congo." Precious is Luc de Heusch, "Myth and Epic in Central Africa," in *Religion in Africa*.

123. Boelaert, "Nsong'a Lianja: Het Groote Epos."

124. Boelaert, "Nsong'a Lianja: Het Groote Epos."

125. Belcher, *Epic Traditions of Africa*, 33, 37.

126. Boelaert, "Nsong'a Lianja: Het Groote Epos."

127. To use Schebesta's term; Schebesta, *Vollblutneger*. See Boelaert, "Nsong'a Lianja. L'épopée nationale des Nkundo.

128. Boelaert, "Nsong'a Lianja. L'épopée nationale des Nkundo."

129. Gustaaf Hulstaert, *Berceuses mongio et formules de numeration*, 22–23, 27, 37, 44, 49; Gustaaf Hulstaert, *Le jeu des parties du corps*. For actual counterparts, see Brunhilde Biebuyck, "Nkundo Mongo Tales" (PhD diss., Indiana University, 1980).

130. Biebuyck, "Nkundo Mongo Tales," esp. 6–47, 145, 151, 156, 197. Gustaaf Hulstaert, *Contes d'ogres mongo*.

131. Proverb 13 (*Bote nk'asi ntacweka nkasa*) in Edward Ruskin, *Mongo Fables and Proverbs*.

132. With resonances suggesting sterility, dryness, and ruin, a salient theme in Africa, see the important essay, Françoise Héritier, "Stérilite, aridité, sécheresse," in *Le sens du mal*.

133. See Gustaaf Hulstaert, *Poèmes mongo modernes*.

134. Schebesta, *Vollblutneger*, 222, 224.

135. Schebesta, *Vollblutneger*, 232. On elima and procreation, see also Gustaaf Hulstaert, *Petit lexique des croyances magiques mongo*.

136. Edmond Boelaert, "Uit mijn negerij: De elima's."

137. David Doris, *Vigilant Things*.

138. Edmond Boelaert, "Les épouvantails-amulettes."

139. Boelaert, "Les épouvantails-amulettes."

140. Biebuyck,"Nkundo Mongo Tales," 198, 200.

141. Boelaert, "Les épouvantails-amulettes."

142. Jean Robert Bofuky, "Comme au temps du Roi Salomon," in *Le Coq chante* 4 (1 February 1939), 11–12.

143. Procureur du Roi E. Mendiaux, 22 December 1930, "Communisme, Affaire Esukula," GG 8005.

144. Lingala risked overtaking Lonkundo, as in Belgium, where French long dominated Flemish; Boelaert, "De bons amis"; or Edmond Boelaert, "Beste vrienden of mijneerste Congoroman"; see Hunt, "Rewriting."

145. Interviews with two Charles Lodewyckx family members in Belgium, as well as Congolese associates and friends who knew him in Kinshasa, Brussels, Mbandaka, and Bolingo, 2000–2001. For an initial, partial interpretation of this threshold figure, see Hunt, "Rewriting."

146. On European attitudes and policies see Peter Baldwin, *Contagion and the State in Europe, 1830–1930*.

147. Maria Quine, *Population Politics in Twentieth-Century Europe*, 23. *Bock* means bottle in French; a *bock à lavement* is often translated as *enema bag* in English.

148. Dratz, "Territoire des Kundu. Chefferie des Wangata-Tumba," 15 February 1933, GG 12.266.

149. Dratz, "Territoire des Kundu. Chefferie des Wangata-Tumba," 15 February 1933, GG 12.266.

150. Gustaaf Hulstaert, *Chansons de danse mongo*.

151. Hulstaert did not use the words "friendship marriage" but keenly discussed kinds of sexual arrangements and liaisons. Hulstaert, *Le mariage des Nkundo*.

152. Hulstaert, *Chansons*, 46, 44, 59, 50, 57, 49, 48, 50, 53.

153. Hulstaert, *Chansons*, 61, 48–49, 61, 53, 57, 58.

154. Hulstaert, *Chansons*, 57, 48–49, 56, 51, 49, 52.

155. Hulstaert, *Chansons*, 52, 54, 55, 48, 46, 59.

156. Gustaaf Hulstaert, "Le problème des mulâtres," parts 1 and 2.

157. Boelaert, "De bons amis"; or Boelaert, "Beste vrienden of mijneerste Congoroman."

158. A subject disdained in Charles Lodewyckx, "Encore la dénatalité."

159. Dratz, "Rapport annuel 1932 concernant le fonctionnement du SAMI," Bokote, 3 January 1933, GG 12.266.

160. Jaggard to Schwers, 19 January 1935, GG 12.266. On the veracity of his ideas into the postcolonial period, see Ulla Larssen, "Primary and Secondary Infertility in Sub-Saharan Africa."

161. See Nancy Hunt, "Colonial Medical Anthropology and the Making of the

Central African Infertility Belt," in *Ordering Africa*; Nancy Hunt, "STDs, Suffering, and Their Derivatives in Congo-Zaire," in *Vivre et penser le sida en Afrique*.

162. For example, Lewis Gaines, "Mental Disturbances and Syphilis," 474–78, esp. 476; and Georges Luys, *A Text-Book on Gonorrhea and Its Complications*, 84.

163. Jean LaFontaine, "The Free Women of Kinshasha," in *Choice and Change*.

CHAPTER 4: SHOCK TALK AND FLYWHISKS

1. Edmond Boelaert, "La procession de Lianja," 2.

2. Boelaert, "La procession de Lianja."

3. Edmond Boelaert, "Nsong'a Lianja: Het Groote Epos der Nkundo-Mongo"; Edmond Boelaert, "Nsong'a Lianja. L'épopée nationale des Nkundo"; and Boelaert, "La procession de Lianja." On Lianja within Africanist epic scholarship, a useful beginning is Stephen Belcher, *Epic Traditions of Africa*.

4. Equateur province became resized as Coquilhatville province, from 1935–47, with three districts: Congo-Ubangi (Lisala), Equateur (Coquilhatville), and Tshuapa (Boende). Lac Léopold II (Inongo) became part of Léopoldville. L. De Saint Moulin, "Histoire de l'organisation administrative du Zaïre." I continue to use the word *Equateur* for the entire southern terrain (always excluding northern Congo-Ubangi), embracing Basankusu, Boende, Coquilhatville, and Bokatola.

5. The subject is absent as story in missionary sources. Fathers Boelaert and Hulstaert wrote in alarmist, demographic terms. Congo Balolo and Disciples of Christ Protestants did not write intimate vignettes about an issue touching lives and marriages.

6. Chef du Service de l'Hygiene Van Hoof to Méd. Prov. Schwers, 16 March 37, GG 12.266 AA, quoting Ryckmans.

7. Belgian missionaries were largely Flemish; most functionaries and territorials were francophone; Nancy Hunt, "Rewriting the Soul in a Flemish Congo."

8. *Flamingant* suggests promoter of a Flemish nation, with language as romantic soul, *not* Flemish separatist from Belgium. They increasingly used *Mongo* to embrace Nkundo, Ekonda, Songo, and many more, using linguistic and Lianja evidence to do so. *Nkundo* hyphenated into Nkundo-Mongo, then dropped away in their publications; Hunt, "Rewriting."

9. "Losilo jwa bonanga bokiso," reprinted as "Une région qui se meurt," *La page chrétienne* (June 1937), Périodiques locaux, microfiche 6, Archives Aequatoria Microfiche Collection. See Edmond Boelaert, "Koloniale krabbels," 8; Edmond Boelaert, *La situation démographique des Nkundo-Mongo*.

10. "Une région qui se meurt."

11. "Une région qui se meurt."

12. "Losilo," *Le Coq chante* (15 August 1937): n.p. For letters see Boniface Bakutu Jr., "Losilo," *Le Coq chante* 3 (15 September 1937): 25; Benoît Bolanjabe, "Losilo," *Le Coq chante* 4 (1 April 1939): 4; Benoît Bolanjabe, "Losilo," *Le Coq chante* 4 (15 April 1939): 4; Boniface Bongonda, "Losilo," *Le Coq chante* 4 (15 April 1939): 4; Boloko Bernard Besau, "Losilo," *Le Coq chante* 4 (15 July 1939): 3.

13. Pour le GG absent, le VGG P. Ermens to Chef de Province, Coq, 19 February 1937, GG 12.266.

14. Another distinguished colonial career that began during the Great War. M. Kivits, "Hoof (Van) (Lucien-Marie-Joseph-Jean)," in BBOM, vol. 6, col. 503–6.

15. For GG (absent) to Chef de Province, Coq, 19 February 1937, GG 12.266.

16. For GG (absent) to Chef de Province, 19 February 1937, GG 12.266.

17. Van Hoof to Schwers, 16 March 1937, GG 12.266.

18. Van Hoof to Schwers, 16 March 1937; see also Ryckmans to Chef de Province, Coquilhatville, 18 March 1937; in GG 12.266.

19. Van Hoof to Schwers, 16 March 1937, GG 12.266. Van Hoof included mutilating venereal diseases: chancroid, Nicolas Favre, granuloma venereum.

20. Van Hoof to Schwers, 16 March 1937, GG 12.266; and many letters in GG 12.266.

21. Tableau, Munji Territoire, 1933, GG 12.266.

22. Charles Flood and William Sherman, "Medical Care in Belgian Congo."

23. H. Lermusieaux, Bokungu to Schwers, 4 May 37; Agent sanitaire du Bus Bloc, Iwela to Schwers, 7 May 1937; both with other letters in GG 12.266.

24. R. Charlier to Méd. Prov. Schwers, 16 March 1937, GG 12.266.

25. Dewame, Gérant de la plantation, Likete, SAB to Schwers de passage à Bekili, 29 April 1937; Plantations Lievin Mombeek manager ("route"), Lonoli-Lez-Wema, to Schwers, 29 April 1937; in GG 12.266.

26. G. Schwers, "La dépopulation dans le district de la Tshuapa. Rapport préliminaire," n.d., GG 12.266.

27. Jean Robert Bofuky, "Comme au temps du Roi Salomon," in *Le Coq chante* 4 (1 February 1939), 11–12.

28. On Ryckmans, see Pierre Vanderlinden, *Pierre Ryckmans, 1891–1959*. On Tshuapa, see Van Hoof to Schwers, 16 March 1937, GG 12.266.

29. In Van Hoof to Schwers, 16 March 1937, GG 12.266.

30. Van Hoof to Schwers, 16 March 1937, GG 12.266. On the Pacific see Richard Lee, "The Extinction of Races"; and Patrick Brantlinger, *Dark Vanishings*.

31. Schwers, "La dépopulation. Rapport préliminaire," 6, GG 12.266.

32. On "therapeutic citizenship," see the wonderful Vinh-Kim Nguyen, *The Republic of Therapy*.

33. AT Brebant, Bolenge to AT, Ingende, 10 May 1936, GG 16.702, AA.

34. All quotations in P. Ekonyo, "Bote wa Likili." On owls, see Brunhilde Biebuyck, "Nkundo Mongo Tales" (Ph.D. diss., Indiana University, 1980), esp. 26–27.

35. Ekonyo, "Bote wa Likili."

36. Charles Lodewyckx, "Est-il possible de relever la natalité Nkundo?," 3, mentions the burning of wooden beds, mattresses, blankets, mosquito nets, and clothes.

37. See "Bofomela," 1927–46, GG 8052, AA, including the disappearance of young Louise Kongo; Sectes secrètes: "Secte Bofomela," Monkoto, 1947, GG 14.014, AA.

38. Ekonyo, "Bote wa Likili."

39. AT Brebant, Bolenge to AT, Ingende, 10 May 1936, GG 16.702.

40. AT Brebant, Bolenge to AT, Ingende, 10 May 1936, GG 16.702.

41. Likili perhaps derived from the French *recrue* (recruit), suggesting new, "newly arrived," or "new measure bringing back life"; Gustaaf Hulstaert, note in Dutch, in "Bote wa Likili," by P. Ekonyo, 69n5.

42. *Bonsaswa* (*bensasawa*, pl.), flywhisk suggests "minor authority." Hulstaert, note in "Bote wa Likili," 69n7.

43. CDD Vanderhallen, Ingende to Chef de la Province, Coq, 14 March 1937; AT G. De Brier, Ingende to CDD de la Tshuapa, 14 March 1937; in GG 14.014.

44. Brebant to AT Ingende, 10 May 1936, GG 16.702; see also De Brier, Boangi, Bokala to CDD Boende, 11 May 1937, GG 14.014.

45. CDD Vanderhallen to Chef de Province, Coq, 14 March 1937, GG 16.702; see also Procès-Verbal, 9 March 1937, Ingende, GG 14.014.

46. Vanderhallen to Chef de Province, 14 March 1937, GG 16.702.

47. AT G. De Brier, Ingende, "Note sur la secte 'Likili,'" n.d., in CDD J. Vanderhallen to Chef de Province Coq, 12 June 1937, GG 14.014.

48. Ekonyo, "Bote wa Likili."

49. De Brier to CDD Tshuapa, 14 March 1937, GG 14.014.

50. Vanderhallen to Chef de Province, 14 March 1937, GG 14.014.

51. Quotations from Ekonyo, "Bote wa Likili," except Hulstaert's footnote (in Dutch) to the same.

52. Charlier to Schwers, 16 March 37, GG 12.266.

53. Van Hoof searched Léopoldville; he found Noël Fiessinger, *Endocrinologie*; and Raymond Rivoire, *Les acquisitions nouvelles de l'endocrinologie*. Van Hoof to Schwers, 12 May 1937, and other letters in GG 12.266.

54. Schwers, "La dépopulation. Rapport préliminaire," GG 12.266.

55. Schwers, "La dépopulation. Rapport préliminaire," GG 12.266.

56. Schwers, "La dépopulation. Rapport préliminaire," GG 12.266.

57. Schwers, "La dépopulation. Rapport préliminaire"; also Rodhain in "1937"; in GG 12.266.

58. Daniel Pick, *Faces of Degeneration*, 41.

59. On shell shock, see Fiona Reid, *Broken Men*; Paul Lerner, *Hysterical Men*; Anton Kaes, *Shell Shock Cinema*. On neurasthenia, see Marijke Gijswijt-Hofstra and Roy Porter, eds., *Cultures of Neurasthenia from Beard to the First World War*; David Schuster, *Neurasthenic Nation*. On nervous breakdowns before the war, see Janet Oppenheim, *Shattered Nerves*. On Selye's experiments with distress, exhaustion, and adaptation, see Hans Selye, "A Syndrome Produced by Diverse Nocuous Agents," 32; Hans Selye, *The Stress of Life*. First to describe bodily stress in terms of the hypothalamic-pituitary-adrenal axis, Selye elaborated glandular states such as "alarm," "resistance," and "exhaustion"; Mark Jackson, *The Age of Stress*.

60. Pick, *Faces of Degeneration*. The historiography on endocrinology has been dominated by the reproductive, with little attention to racial attitudes and primitivism in the study of nonreproductive endocrine glands; David Serlin, *Replaceable You*, 118–37. Contrast Victor Medvei, *The History of Clinical Endocrinology*.

61. Schwers, "Rapport dénatalité Tshuapa," March–August 1937, Fonds Hulstaert 7.4, Centre Aequatoria, Bamanya.

62. Schwers, "La dépopulation. Rapport préliminaire," 6, GG 12.266; G. A. Schwers, "Les facteurs de la Dénatalité au Congo belge." On Rivers, and the "'shock' of life under colonialism" and shell shock parallels, see Nancy Hunt, "Colonial Medical Anthropology and the Making of the Central African Infertility Belt," in *Ordering Africa*; Hunt "Rewriting," 208.

63. A primitivist discourse of long date; see Brantlinger, *Dark Vanishings*.

64. Ekonyo, "Bote wa Likili," 69. See G. De Brier, "Note sur la secte 'Likili,'" ca. 12 June 1937, GG 14.014.

65. Ekonyo, "Bote wa Likili," 69. See too De Brier, "Note," GG 14.014.

66. Sécretaire-greffier Tshoambe, Bompanga, to AT Adjoint, 14 March 1938, GG 8005.

67. Ekonyo, "Bote wa Likili," 68; and Hulstaert, note in "Bote wa Likili," 68n3.

68. Ekonyo, "Bote wa Likili," 68. See too De Brier, "Note," GG 14.014.

69. Ekonyo, "Bote wa Likili," 68–70.

70. Hunt, "Rewriting."

71. VGG to Ministre des Colonies, 3 November 1937, GG 12.266.

72. VGG to Ministre, 3 November 1937, GG 12.266.

73. VGG to Ministre, 3 November 1937, GG 12.266.

74. Conseil Supérieur d'Hygiène Coloniale, Commission pour l'étude du problème de la dénatalité dans le district de la Tshuapa, minutes, 21 December 1937, GG 12.266.

75. Conseil Supérieur d'Hygiène Coloniale, Commission, minutes, 21 December 1937, GG 12.266.

76. Schwers to Van Hoof, 7 October 1937; Schwers, "Note," 10 December 1937, in GG 12.266. Vital on sterility and its measurement in contemporary Africa is Ulla Larssen, "Primary and Secondary Infertility in Sub-Saharan Africa."

77. Schwers to Van Hoof, 7 October 1937, GG 12.266.

78. Henry to Ryckmans, 30 March 1937, GG 12.266.

79. Ermens to Chef de Province, 10 November 1937, GG 12.266.

80. Schwers, "Note," 10 December 1937, GG 12.266.

81. Schwers, "Note," 10 December 1937, GG 12.266.

82. Van Hoof to Schwers, December 18, 1937; Van Hoof to Schwers, February 10, 1938, GG 12.266.

83. Schwers, "Note," 10 December 1937, GG 12.266.

84. Eva May Dye, "Life Sketches of the Women who have asked to become Christians since July '04," ca. 1907, Royal Dye Papers, DCHS.

85. Royal Dye Papers; Louis Jaggard Papers; and Gervase Barger Papers, DCHS.

86. A discrepancy between narrative and historical time; Gérard Genette, *Narrative Discourse*. On anachrony as concept and method, see Nancy Hunt, "Between Fiction and History"; and Nancy Hunt, *Suturing New Medical Histories of Africa*.

87. Sigmund Freud, *The Uncanny*, 152.

88. Myrtle Lee Smith, "Three Babies in Congo," *World Call* (December 1931), 28–29,

in Jaggard Papers, DCHS. On another red rubber story coming to life in the 1930s, see Lillian Profrock Johnston, "'Bring Out Your Rubber,'" *World Call* (January 1935), 28.

89. Gustaaf Hulstaert, *Le mariage des Nkundo*.

90. Hulstaert, note in "Bote wa Likili," 70–71n8. *Likili*; Gustaaf Hulstaert, *Dictionnaire Lomóngo-français*, 1150.

91. Hulstaert, note in "Bote wa Likili," 70–71n8.

92. Hulstaert, note in "Bote wa Likili," 70–71n8.

93. Ekonyo, "Bote wa Likili," 69, 70.

94. Ekonyo, "Bote wa Likili," 69.

95. Gustaaf Hulstaert, *Petit lexique des croyances magiques mongo*, 52.

96. Tshoambe to AT Adjoint, Bompanga village, 5 April 1938, with "Rapport sur le secte Likili," Chefferie des Tomba, 5 April 1938, GG 8005.

97. AT Brebant, Bolenge to AT, Ingende, 10 May 1936, GG 16.702.

98. If the Ingende archive had contained *chefferie*-produced documents, Likili there might suggest less unanimity and harmony.

99. Tshoambe to AT Adjoint, Bompanga village, 5 April 1938, GG 8005, AA.

100. Tshoambe to AT Adjoint, Bompanga village, 5 April 1938; Judgment no. 45, Eale Paul of Bokala contre Ifenge Pierre of Boangi, 11 April 1938, Wangata, signed E. B[ongese], GG 8005.

101. Tshoambe to AT Adjoint, Bompanga village, 5 April 1938, GG 8005.

102. E. Bongese was likely kin to Chief Bongese of flag-raising rumors, see chapter 3. Judgment no. 45, 11 April 1938; see too Judgment no. 44, Wangata, 27 May 1938; in GG 8005.

103. Judgment no. 45, 11 April 1938, GG 8005.

104. *Talisman*, common colonial translation for *bote*, was almost interchangeable with *sect*. That a charm and its network were one and the same is in keeping with therapeutic associations throughout central Africa.

105. Judgment no. 45, 11 April 1938, GG 8005.

106. Judgment no. 45, 11 April 1938.

107. Judgment no. 45, 11 April 1938; emphasis added.

108. Judgment no. 45, 11 April 1938.

109. Judgment no. 45, 11 April 1938.

110. Tshoambe to AT Adjoint, 5 April 1938; E. B[ongese], Chef investi des Tomba to AT Adjoint, 11 April 1938; Judgment no. 45, 11 April 1938, GG 8005.

111. Sigmund Freud, "Screen Memories," in *The Uncanny*.

112. Judgment no. 45, 11 April 1938, GG 8005.

113. Schwers to Van Hoof, 7 October 1937; Schwers, "Note," 10 December 1937, both in GG 12.266.

114. Schwers, "La dépopulation. Rapport préliminaire," 11, GG 12.266.

115. *Annexites*: inflammation of uterine appendages. Gynecologists today specify oophoritis (ovaries) or salpingitis (fallopian tubes), whereas adnexectomy stands in for surgical salpingo-oophorectomy.

116. Schwers, "La dépopulation. Rapport préliminaire," 22, 28, GG 12.266.

117. See Michael Worobey et al., "Direct Evidence of Extensive Diversity of HIV-1 in Kinshasa by 1960"; B. Korber et al., "Timing the Ancestor of the HIV-1 Pandemic Strains." See the recent consensus overview of a large group of epidemiologists seeking causal vectors in medical and transport technologies and sex (including the talented Jacques Pépin and João de Sousa, one of the few to delve into Equateur's archive). See Faria et al. forgo the more subtle causal logics of historians and anthropologists Giles-Vernick, Lachenal, Gondola, and Schneider, who suggest that by de-centering HIV pathogens and vectors, inquiry may be stretched and thickened. Contrast Nino Faria et al. "The Early Spread and Epidemic Ignition of HIV-1 in Human Populations"; and Tamara Giles-Vernick et al., "Social History, Biology and the Emergence of HIV in Colonial Africa."

118. Van Hoof to Schwers, 16 March 1937, GG 12.266.

119. Maria Quine, *Population Politics in Twentieth-Century Europe*, 23.

120. Elisha Renne, "'Cleaning the Inside' and Regulation of Menstruation in Southwestern Nigeria," in *Regulating Menstruation*; the entire volume is of interest.

121. Lodewyckx, "Est-il possible de relever la natalité Nkundo?"; Charles Lodewyckx, "Encore la dénatalité."

122. Paul Schebesta, *Vollblutneger und Halbzwerge*; Renaat Devisch, *Weaving the Threads of Life*.

123. The key critic of the dangers of enema use was the planter Charles Lodewyckx; see Nancy Hunt, "Bicycles, Birth Certificates, and Clysters," in *Commodification*; Hunt, "Rewriting"; and Hunt, "Colonial Medical Anthropology."

124. The very best on such symbolic thought remains Françoise Héritier, "Stérilité, aridité, sécheresse," *Le sens du mal*.

125. Frantz Fanon, "Medicine and Colonialism," in *A Dying Colonialism*.

126. See especially, Devisch, *Weaving the Threads of Life*. Also see a review by Nancy Hunt, "Fertility's Fires and Empty Wombs in Recent Africanist Writing"; and Hunt, "Bicycles."

127. On the use of soldiers in Belgian colonial medicine, Flood and Sherman, "Medical Care in Belgian Congo."

128. Steven Feierman, *The Shambaa Kingdom*; Steven Feierman, *Peasant Intellectuals*.

129. Devisch, *Weaving the Threads of Life*, is groundbreaking, essential, and rich on such intricate bodily dimensions.

130. To return to Louis Althusser's expression in *Philosophy of the Encounter*.

131. Van Hoof to Schwers (and discussing Ryckmans), 16 March 1937, GG 12.266. Nothing suggests Bwaka *were* ever so recruited.

CHAPTER 5: A PENAL COLONY, AN INFERTILITY CLINIC

*Map 5.1 sources; DIVA-GIS, *Digital Chart of the World*, map data set (1992), "Download data by country," accessed 5 September 2014, http://diva-gis.org/gdata; Robert Harms, "The End of Red Rubber"; J. Flamme and Fr. Menger, Untitled map of the

Belgian Congo, drawn from documents of the Service cartographique du Ministère des Colonies (1:5,000,000) [ca. 1935]; Institut Géographique du Congo belge, *Carte administrative et politique de la Province de l'Equateur* (map: 1:1,000,000), édition provisoire (1955); FBEI, "F.B.I.'s Areas of Intensive Action" and "F.B.I.'s Action in the Medico-Social Sphere," in *A Work of Co-operation in Development* (maps, no scales given), facing 32 and facing 96.

**Map 5.2 sources: *Natural Earth*, version 2.0, map data set (North American Cartographic Information Society, 2012), accessed 18 June 2013, http://www.naturalearthdata .com; L. De Saint Moulin, "Histoire de l'organisation administrative du Zaïre."

1. Pistor studied another Congolese region; Dominic Pistor, "Developmental Colonialism and Kitawala Policy in 1950s Belgian Congo" (M.A. thesis, Simon Fraser University, 2012).

2. Basil Davidson, *The African Awakening*.

3. Excellent on Kitawala are Mwene-Batende, *Mouvements messianiques et protestation sociale*; John Higginson, *A Working Class in the Making*. Also Daniel Biebuyck, "La société kumu face au Kitawala"; Jacques Gérard, *Les fondements syncrétiques du Kitawala*. On Mwana Lesa and Watch Tower, see Terence Ranger, "The Mwana Lesa Movement of 1925," in *Themes in the Christian History of Central Africa*; and Karen Fields, *Revival and Rebellion in Colonial Central Africa*. On Kimbangu, see the important Jean-Luc Vellut, *Simon Kimbangu, 1921*. On Mpadi see Mbasani Mbambi, "Simon-Pierre Mpadi, étude biographique."

4. Margery Perham, *African Apprenticeship*, 226–27.

5. The Bushiri trial concluded in 1945 with the public hanging of Bushiri and his assistant Alleluya; Yogolelo Tambwe ya Kasimba and Hangi Shamamba, "Bushiri Lungundu, c. 1911–1945, Kitawala," in *Encyclopedia Africana Dictionary of African Biography*.

6. Davidson, *The African Awakening*.

7. Repressive decree of 25 August 1937, in Jean Comhaire, "Sociétés secrètes et mouvements prophétiques au Congo belge."

8. "Colonie Agricole pour Relégués Dangereux," GG 10.062, AA.

9. *Belgian Congo at War*; Jean Stengers and Jean-Jacques Synoens, eds., *Le Congo belge durant la Seconde Guerre mondiale*; Lufungula Lewono, "Execution des mesures prises contre les sujets ennemis pendant la Second Guerre mondiale dans le région de l'Equateur."

10. Boelaert, critic of colonial complicity with finance capital, was suspected of pro-German leanings; Honoré Vinck, "La guerre de 1940–45 vécue à Coquilhatville." The suspicion influenced 1950s publication decisions of Belgium's Royal Colonial Institute, which rejected a Boelaert historical essay, based on memories collected and critical of the Free State; Honoré Vinck, personal communication, Bamanya, 1989.

11. Jaggard to C. M. Yocum, 1 June 1940. The Jaggard children, from American orphanages and foster homes, became acutely estranged. A daughter bristled about her parents' neglect and also their black servants. Louis Jaggard Papers, DCHS Archives, Nashville.

12. Pierre Ryckmans, *Allo! Congo! Chroniques radiophoniques*; Pierre Ryckmans, "Effort de guerre: Production agricole."

13. Painful memories investigated by Boelaert: Edmond Boelaert, "Ntange," parts 1 and 2.

14. Martha Bateman, "Two Hundred Miles via Bicycle."

15. Nancy Hunt, *A Colonial Lexicon*.

16. Equateur, "Hygiène industrielle," GG 9952, AA.

17. Van Hoof to Schwers, 12 December 1940; Note du Médecin Provincial, 16 December 1940, "Etudes démographiques—dénatalité Tshuapa," GG 12.266, AA.

18. G. A. Schwers, "Les facteurs de la dénatalité au Congo Belge."

19. S. F. W. Fox, South African Institute for Medical Research, to H. Dratz, 11 November 1940, GG 12.266.

20. Dratz to GG, 24 November 1940; Dratz, "Intoxications provoques par une alimentation composée trop uniformement de manioc," 18 November 1940, GG 12.266. Others did research: D. H. Baker, "Etude concernant la situation sanitaire et démographique de quelques villages du district de la Tshuapa"; H. Ledent and D. H. Baker, "La dépopulation chez les Nkundo."

21. Van Hoof to Schwers, 21 January 1939, GG 12.266. Many Dratz studies are in GG 12.266.

22. In 1941–42, two-thirds had left Bongandanga: 391 men and 1,491 women. Bellefontaine, Bongandanga, to Méd. Prov., 17 February 1943, GG 12.267, AA.

23. Equateur, "Hygiène industrielle," GG 9952.

24. G. Schwers, "Route Coquilhatville-Boende, Rapport d'inspection du Médecin Provincial, 22 août–11 septembre 1945," Centre Aequatoria, Bamanya.

25. Dr. Bellefontaine, Bongandanga to Méd. Prov., 17 February 1943, GG 12.267.

26. Letter from Gustaaf Hulstaert to Placide Tempels, 4 October 1945; François Bontinck, ed., *Aux origines de la philosophie bantoue*, 83–84. On Tempels see V. Y. Mudimbe, *Tales of Faith*.

27. Belgium, *Rapport annuel sur l'activité de la colonie du Congo belge pendant l'année 1934* (hereafter *Rapport annuel*).

28. "Colonie Agricole pour des Relégués Dangeureux d'Ekafera" (hereafter "CARD d'Ekafera"), 1937–48, GG 10.062. On Mpadi, see Mbambi, "Simon-Pierre Mpadi."

29. Mpadi escaped more than once and spent years in prison. Many of his followers ended up in Ekafera. In 1970, Mpadi had some fifteen thousand supporters; Mbambi, "Simon-Pierre Mpadi."

30. Most letters came from Oshwe, on the Lukenie, a relegation destination and then CARD, mostly for Kimbanguists from Bas Congo; "Divers," 1939–44, GG 6076, AA.

31. "Divers," 1939–44, GG 6076.

32. Van Campenhout to Grandry, "Lokongo" affair, 21 August 1941, GG 6076.

33. "Divers," 1939–44, GG 6076. Laxity with colonial prisoners fed legends about sly criminals; Paul Cornil, *Réflexions sur la justice pénale au Congo Belge*, 36.

34. "Divers," 1939–44, GG 6076.

35. "Mouvement 1942," 1942–45, GG 6076. On Inongo, age-based associations in Tshuapa; Samuel Nelson, *Colonialism in the Congo Basin, 1880–1940*, esp. 109–11.

36. "Politique contre mouvements subversifs, 1946–54," GG 6076.

37. Van Campenhout to CDD, 2 February 1943, in "Mouvement 1942," 1942–45, GG 6076.

38. Van Campenhout to CDD, 3 December 1942, "Mouvement 1942," 1942–45, GG 6076.

39. Van Campenhout to CDD, 5 September 1944, "Mouvement 1944," 1944–46, GG 6076; and Dr. E. R. Wide, Baringa, to AT Chef Territoire du Befale 2 October 1944, in "Mission des Noirs," GG 6076

40. Ryckmans to Gouverneur, 21 August 1942, "CARD d'Ekafera," 1937–48, GG 10.062. On 1942 plan, see GG 12.735. Congolese prisoners often worked in striped jerseys under slight discipline, guarded by a detainee turned overseer; Cornil, *Réflexions sur la justice pénale au Congo belge*, 18, 21.

41. Van Campenhout to CDD, 23 February 1946, "Fin 1945," 1945–46, GG 6076.

42. For a superb treatment, which compares colonial carceral techniques of exile (relegation) to penal colonies; Peter Redfield, "Foucault in the Tropics," in *Anthropologies of Modernity*.

43. "Fin 1945," GG 6076.

44. On the Harris photographs and the word Nsongo, see reprinted versions in E. D. Morel, *King Leopold's Rule in Africa*; captions read "of the Nsongo District" (facing 48) and "of Wala in the Nsongo District" (facing 144).

45. Gouverneur to GG, 10 May 1944, in Procès-Verbal, Commission provinciale de la dénatalité, 30 July 1945, GG 10.102, AA.

46. Gouverneur to GG, 10 May 1944, in P-V, 30 July 1945, GG 10.102.

47. Ryckmans to Gouverneur, 23 August 1945, GG 8211, AA.

48. Ryckmans to Gouverneur, 23 August 1945, GG 8211.

49. GG to Gouverneur, 17 March 1945, in P-V, 30 July 1945, GG 10.102.

50. GG to Gouverneur, 17 March 1945, in P-V, 30 July 1945, GG 10.102.

51. P-V, 30 July 1945, GG 10.102.

52. P-V, 30 July 1945, GG 10.102.

53. P-V, 30 July 1945, GG 10.102.

54. P-V, 30 July 1945; and P-V, 22 April 1947, GG 10.102.

55. P-V, 8 April 1947; on Cuperus, see 30 July 1945; in GG 10.102.

56. P-V, 8 April 1947, GG 10.102.

57. W. Rousseau, "Rapport Songo," 3–4, 29 May 1946, GG 9450, AA; see too P-V, 10 April 1946, GG 10.102; and W. Rousseau, "Rapport Songo," 19 May 1946, GG 9450.

58. Procureur du Roi L. Dewaersegger, "Mémoire sur la dénatalité dans la Tshuapa," received AIMO, 29 June 1946, in Documentation, 1943–46, GG 10.102. See too his opinions in P-Vs: 30 July 1945; 8 April 196; 2 July 1946; and 14 November 1947; in GG 10.102.

59. P-V, 22 April 1947; Dewaersegger, "Mémoire sur la dénatalité"; in GG 10.102.

60. Dewaersegger, "Mémoire sur la dénatalité," GG 10.102.

61. P-V, 22 April 1947, GG 10.102.

62. De Bisscop, "Rapport de la mission médicale en chefferie Nsongo," 31 December 1946, GG 9450.

63. P-V, 14 November 1947; Dewaersegger, "Mémoire sur la dénatalité"; in GG 10.102.

64. P-V, 14 November 1947, GG 10.102.

65. In Ingende territory, Lodewyckx's subsidized natalist campaign received praise for improving the birth rate and "psychological climate." FBEI, *Rapport de gestion et comptes de l'exercice de 1950* (hereafter *Rapport de gestion* . . .), 28, 45. On Lodewyckx, see GG 10.102, notably "Correspondances diverses, 1945–48," and "Dossier Lodewyckx," 1948.

66. Compare his mission report of 1937 with his 1944 article: G. Schwers, "La dépopulation dans le district de la Tshuapa. Rapport préliminaire," n.d., GG 12.266; G. A. Schwers, "Les facteurs de la dénatalité au Congo belge."

67. Mark Jackson, *The Age of Stress*; and David Cantor and Edmund Ramsden, eds., *Stress, Shock, and Adaptation in the Twentieth Century*.

68. Helen Tilley, *Africa as a Living Laboratory*.

69. On *paysannats*, see Osumaka Likaka, *Rural Society and Cotton in Colonial Zaire*.

70. De Bisscop, "Rapport de la mission médicale en chefferie Nsongo," 31 December 1946, GG 9450.

71. Van Campenhout, Befale, "Expérience Songo. Possibilités d'application. FBEI. Propositions," 14 September 1948, GG 8275, AA.

72. Van Campenhout, "Expérience Songo," GG 8275.

73. "Songo," 1945–48, GG 8211.

74. Arguments also made in Pistor, "Developmental Colonialism."

75. The words *extinction* and *shock* faded too. "Race suicide," an old American generationist refrain, surfaced in South West Africa after the Herero genocide: William Steenkamp, *Is the South-West African Herero Committing Race Suicide?* On extinction anxieties, see Patrick Brantlinger, *Dark Vanishings*. Rivers critiqued colonial distress and depopulation: W. H. R. Rivers, "The Psychological Factor," in *Essays on the Depopulation of Melanesia*; and Georges Van der Kerken, *L'Ethnie Mongo*, 797–800.

76. "Mouvement 1942," 1942–45, GG 6076.

77. Relegation could be lifted when a return was unproblematic; relégués were to be aided in establishing their forced residences; Léon Strouvens and Pierre Piron, *Codes et lois du Congo belge*, 559–60. A 1903 circular expected *relégué* registers; Léon Strouvens and Pierre Piron, *Codes et lois du Congo belge*, 559–60. A 1906 decree specified relegation for infringements of order, and instructed on movements and kin; Octave Louwers, *Codes et lois du Congo belge*, 439–41, 765–70, esp. 441, 767.

78. Belgium, *Rapport annuel . . . 1936*, 17.

79. Kimbanguism was more nationalist ("Congo for Congolese"); Jean-Pierre Paulus, "Le Kitawala au Congo Belge."

80. Belgium, *Rapport annuel . . . 1936*, 17.

81. Issued by AIMO; Strouvens and Piron, *Codes et lois du Congo belge*, 559–60.

82. "CARD d'Ekafera," 1942–48, GG 10.062.

83. Emphasis added. "CARD d'Ekafera," 1942–48, GG 10.062.

84. Higginson, *A Working Class in the Making*, 173–74.

85. "CARD d'Ekafera," 1937–48, GG 10.062.

86. On colonial prisons and criminality, see Daniel Branch, "Imprisonment and Colonialism in Kenya, c. 1930–1952"; Florence Bernault, ed., *A History of Prison and Confinement in Africa*; Vicente Rafael, ed., *Figures of Criminality in Indonesia, the Philippines, and Colonial Vietnam*. In 1922, Equateur's 2,992 detainees were mostly in mud houses; Belgium, *Rapport annuel . . . 1922*, 47–48. When a 1934 ordinance forbade the chain, a 23 percent increase in escapes was reported; Belgium, *Rapport annuel . . . 1935*. Prisoners rose in number (from 77,830 in 1934 to 100,518 in 1935); Belgium, *Rapport annuel . . . 1935*. By 1953, there was overcrowding with the mentally ill in chains. Many were jailed for tax or crop labor evasion; Cornil, *Réflexions sur la justice pénale au Congo belge*, 21–24. When reforms began, one prison color-coded by stripe, boasted a library, chapel, and game room, and encouraged art, song, and a serial publication; G. Mus, *L'établissement pénitentiaire de Jadotville*.

87. Katanga, Just AIMO, 1937–51, GG 5487, AA.

88. Katanga, Just AIMO, 1937–51, GG 5487.

89. Katanga, Just AIMO, 1937–51, GG 5487. The Swahili letters are worthy of careful study.

90. Yogolelo Tambwe ya Kasimba and Shamamba, "Bushiri Lungundu."

91. "CARD d'Ekafera," 1942–48, GG 10.062.

92. On plans, see GG 12.735.

93. "CARD d'Ekafera," 1942–48, GG 10.062.

94. Règlement d'ordre intérieur, 12 July 1943, GG 8164, AA.

95. Ekafera, penal colonies, and the carceral are deserving of more research. I was not granted access to many Ekafera dossiers at the African Archives in Brussels; the nervous state continues, we might say, through the postcolonial closure of archives. That Sureté archives are usually closed ensured that most Kitawala and many Ekafera archives were unavailable to me.

96. "CARD d'Ekafera," 1942–48, GG 10.062.

97. Annet Mooij, *Out of Otherness*.

98. On penicillin-resistant gonnorhea, C. R. Amies, "Development of Resistance of Gonococci to Penicillin." See too the valuable Anatole Romaniuk, *L'aspect démographique de la stérilité des femmes congolaises*.

99. Méd. Prov. to Méd., 14 September 1948, GG 19.389, AA.

100. Karen Jochelson, *The Colour of Disease*; Bryan Callahan, "Syphilis and Civilization" (Ph.D. diss., Johns Hopkins University, 2002); Megan Vaughan, "Syphilis in Colonial East and Central Africa," in *Epidemics and Ideas*.

101. For example, 8 December 1934, Schwers to Méd. en Chef; 16 January 1935, Van Hoof to Schwers, 21 January 1935, Schwers to Médicins de la Province; and 22 October 1937, Méd. Prov. Guerin to Medecins sous-secteur Bumba; in GG 19.389.

102. Dr. Goldman, Gandu to Schwers, 22 March 1939, GG 19.389. See Mooij, *Out of Otherness*; and Phillippa Levine, *Prostitution, Race and Politics*, 76, 149, on irrigation techniques like Janet's *grand lavages* treatment.

103. Dr. E. R. Wide, Baringa to Méd. Prov., 12 June 1941, GG 19.389.

104. Equateur, Laboratoire de bacteriologie, 1939–47, GG 19.385, AA.

105. Dr. David, Stanleyville to Medecin en Chef, 7 July 1944, GG 19.389.

106. Equateur, "Hygiène industrielle," GG 9952.

107. Dr. Simon of Banzyville to Schwers, 16 October 1945, GG 19.389.

108. Among letters: Simon to Schwers, 16 October 1945; Schwers to Méd., Gemena, 21 March 1946, GG 19.389.

109. Méd. Dir. Borger to Méd. Prov., 7 October 1947, GG 19.389.

110. Schwers to Méd. at Baya, 25 February 1947; Schwers to Rev. Soeur, Dispensaire, Missions nationales, Bokote, 17 June 1947, GG 19.389.

111. Schwers to Méd., Bumba, 13 September 1947, GG 19.389.

112. Equateur, "Hygiène industrielle," GG 9952.

113. Equateur, "Hygiène industrielle," GG 9952.

114. Van Laethem, Ingende to Méd. Prov., 17 July 1948, GG 19.389.

115. Bellfontaine, Basankusu to Méd. Prov., 7 October 1948, GG 19.389.

116. Borgers, Hôpital des Noirs, Coq, to Méd. Prov., 28 October 1948, GG 19.389.

117. De Bisscop, Befale to Méd. Prov., 28 September 1948, GG 19.389.

118. Schwers to Méd. agrée, Baringa, 30 June 1949, GG 19.389.

119. G. Schwers, "Note pour Messieurs les Médecins," 7 August 1948, GG 19.389.

120. Schwers to Méd., Lolo, 7 February 1949; Méd., Banzyville to Méd. Prov., 20 August 1948; in GG 19.389.

121. Schwers to Méd. Dir. Des Hôpitaux, Libenge, 8 December 1949, GG 19.389.

122. Schwers to AT Bumba, 11 March 1949, GG 19.389.

123. Schwers to Méd., Bwamanda, 25 September 1948; Méd., Gemena to Méd. Prov., 7 March 1946; in GG 19.389; Equateur, "Hygiene industrielle," GG 9952.

124. Geerts, Méd., Colonie Bumba, 27 August 1947, GG 19.389.

125. Schwers to Sécr. Prov., 23 September 1948, GG 19.389.

126. Dr. De Bisscop, Befale to Méd. Prov., 28 September 1948, GG 19.389.

127. On sexual concurrency in Africa, see Helen Epstein, *The Invisible Cure*.

128. Schwers to Rev. Soeur, Dispensaire, Bokote, 17 June 1947, GG 19.389.

129. Schwers to Méd., 5 October 1948, GG 19.389.

130. C. Van Ackere, Befale to Méd. Prov., 13 May 1949, GG 19.389.

131. Schwers to Méd. Dir. des Hôpitaux, Libenge, 8 December 1949, GG 19.389.

132. Schwers to Méd., Lolo, 7 February 1949; Dr. Breyne, Méd., Lolo, to Méd. Prov., 21 February 1949, GG 19.389.

133. Faria et al. hypothesize that Congolese transmission of HIV-1 (group M) increased due to unsterilized injections in urban venereal clinics after the second world war; Faria et al. "The Early Spread and Epidemic Ignition of HIV-1 in Human Populations." It is not clear that money-based sexual transactions in Equateur changed as a result of the rural antivenereal campaign, though the campaign may have fostered greater

individualized discretion, secrecy, and camouflage. It is important also to interrogate less commercial forms of sexual transactions, including those suggested in this study (marriage, sexual friendships, and the like).

134. On the request to remove Kaiva Mashimpi, see Delobbe, CDD Tshuapa, "Rapport d'inspection effectuée du 29.12.45 au 2.1.46," CARD Ekafera, GG 8164. On this mutiny, see Jean-Luc Vellut, "Le Katanga industriel en 1944," in *Le Congo Belge durant la Seconde Guerre mondiale*.

135. Delobbe, CDD Tshuapa, "Rapport d'inspection," 1945–46, GG 8164.

136. "CARD d'Ekafera," 1937–48, GG 10.062.

137. "1947" file, GG 6076.

138. Delobbe, CDD Tshuapa, "Rapport d'inspection," 1945–46, GG 8164; see too "CARD d'Ekafera," 1937–48, GG 10.062.

139. Van Hoeck to GG 14 October 1937, among many Boyela documents in "CARD d'Ekafera," 1937–48, GG 10.062.

140. "CARD d'Ekafera," 1937–48, GG 10.062.

141. "CARD d'Ekafera," 1937–48, GG 10.062.

142. "Mouvement 1944," 1944–46, GG 6076.

143. On the AIMO law, see "CARD d'Ekafera," 1937–48, GG 10.062.

144. CDD Triest, "Rapport de visite," 21–22 December 1950, GG 10.062.

145. Rapport, 26–29 March 1957, GG 8164.

146. Patrice Lumumba, "Speech on June 30, 1960, Independence Day," in *Teacher's Guide*.

147. Delobbe, CDD Tshuapa, "Rapport d'inspection," 1945–46, GG 8164.

148. Corporal punishment often meant whipping, as popular paintings tell; see Bogumil Jewsiewicki, *Cheri Samba*; and Johannes Fabian, *Remembering the Present*. While prisoners long circulated in chains, by 1953 colonial claims asserted shackles had largely disappeared, while whipping as penitentiary discipline could not exceed four blows. One of 60 (200,000 of 11–12 million) Congolese subjects entered prison a year, often for a month alone; Cornil, *Réflexions sur la justice pénale au Congo Belge*, 18.

149. "Divers," 1947–49, GG 6076.

150. Lumumba, "Speech on June 30, 1960."

151. "Divers confidentiel," 1950–56, GG 6076.

152. "Divers confidentiel," 1950–56.

153. A history of the carceral in Belgian Africa is long overdue, and others may well encounter a wider, more accessible archive in Brussels than I did. Global thematics are beginning; see Mary Gibson, "Global Perspectives on the Birth of the Prison."

154. "CARD à Ekafera," [ca. 1952–54], GG 8243.

155. CDD Asst. E. Pien, 23–25 February 1954, GG 8164. On perceptions of flights of grandeur, see Eugène Grégoire, "Les maladies mentales des indigènes," *Le Courrier d'Afrique*, 5 February 1940, 5–6.

156. CDD Asst. Godefroid, 14–15 March 1955, GG 8164.

157. FBEI, *A Work of Co-operation in Development*, esp. 31–32; important on budgets are FBEI reports, such as *Rapport de gestion et comtes de l'exercice 1949*. On postwar

colonial development planning, see Pierre Wigny, *A Ten Year Plan for the Economic and Social Development of the Belgian Congo*; Guy Vanthemsche, *Genèse et porté du "Plan décennal du Congo belge" (1949-1959)*; and a critique: Pistor, "Developmental Colonialism."

158. FBEI, *Rapport de gestion . . . 1952*.

159. On colonial medical utopias, see the excellent Guillaume Lachenal, *Le médicament qui devait sauver l'Afrique*.

160. FBEI, *A Work of Co-operation*, 95–96.

161. J. P. Bouckaert and R. Ruel, *Contribution à l'étude de la population du district de la Tshuapa*. See too Joseph Van Riel and R. Allard, *Contribution à l'étude de la dénatalité dans l'ethnie mongo*. Van Riel and Allard began their research in the late 1940s.

162. FBEI, *A Work of Co-operation*.

163. H 4520, II A.05.07, 1948–49; Van Riel and Allard, *Contribution à l'étude de la dénatalité*, 6.

164. FBEI, *Rapport de gestion . . . 1949*; FBEI, *Rapport de gestion . . . 1951*.

165. FBEI, *Rapport de gestion . . . 1952*.

166. FBEI, *A Work of Co-operation*, 95–96; Joseph Van Riel and R. Allard, *Contribution à l'étude de la dénatalité dans l'ethnie mongo*.

167. Joseph Van Riel and R. Allard, *Contribution à l'étude de la dénatalité* 38–39. R. Allard, "Essai d'évaluation des facteurs de stérilité chez les Mongo de Befale" (Examen B, 242, Institute of Tropical Medicine, Antwerp, 1956); R. Allard, "Contribution gynécologique à l'étude de la stérilité chez les Mongo de Befale."

168. Van Riel and Allard, *Contribution à l'étude de la dénatalité*.

169. Van Riel and Allard, *Contribution à l'étude de la dénatalité*. This valuable work came earlier than the colony-wide Romaniuk census of 1955–57; Anatole Romaniuk, *La fécondité des populations congolaises*.

170. Allard, "Essai d'évaluation des facteurs de stérilité," 73.

171. Allard, "Essai d'évaluation des facteurs de stérilité."

172. Bolela, "Conseil de Province de l'Equateur. Discours de M. le Gouverneur Schmit (suite du no. 13). Situation démographique," *Mbandaka*, 7 April 1956, 3.

173. André Ombredane, *L'exploration de la mentalité des Noirs congolais au moyen d'une épreuve projective: le Congo T. A. T*. On American "psy" perspectives in American gynecology at the time, see I. C. Fisher, "Psychogenic Aspects of Sterility"; E. S. Ford et al. "A Psychodynamic Approach to the Study of Infertility"; T. Benedek, "Infertility as Psychosomatic Defense"; B. B. Rubenstein, "An Emotional Factor in Infertility: A Psychosomatic Approach"; and M. Heiman, "Psychoanalytic Evaluation of the Problem of One-Child Sterility."

174. Allard, "Essai d'évaluation des facteurs de stérilité," 55–56.

175. I. C. Rubin, *Uterotubal Insufflation*; Samuel Siegler, "The Tubal Factor," in *Fertility in Women*. On "uterotubal spasm," see Rubin, *Uterotubal Insufflation*, 219–25. For a kymographic tracing showing spasm, see Samuel Siegler, *Fertility in Women*, 257 (fig. 126).

176. American and British gynecologists reported on some women conceiving

after insufflation; Rubin, *Uterotubal Insufflation*, table 33, 391–412; Siegler, *Fertility in Women*, 261–62; Naomi Pfeffer, *The Stork and the Syringe*, 64–65, 135.

177. Allard, "Essai d'évaluation des facteurs de stérilité," 49–50.

178. R. Allard, "Contribution gynécologique à l'étude de la stérilité chez les mongo de Befale." Allard cited the work of the key American expert I. C. Rubin, "Uterotubal Insufflation: Value in the Treatment of Tubal Obstruction to Ovular Migations."

179. Allard, "Essai d'évaluation des facteurs de stérilité."

180. For important and enduring analyses, see Thomas Hodgkin, *Nationalism in Colonial Africa*; and Basil Davidson, *African Nationalism and the Problems of Nation-Building*.

181. Michael Crowder, *The Flogging of Phinehas McIntosh*.

182. Ekafera's sinister side continued under the postcolony. From 1974, Mobutu used Ekafera to punish political prisoners with extreme isolation. Most arrived by foot. With high rates of mortality and depression, there were three to four hundred in solitary cells, more in a communal section, and most slept on the ground in Zaire's "most notorious detention camp"; Amnesty International, *Human Rights Violations in Zaire, an Amnesty International Report*, 16–18, map on 17; Peter Rosenblum, *Prison Conditions in Zaire*, 41. Michael Chambers found Ekafera empty and "sinister" in the 1980s, though with "solid attractive buildings set in what must have been a well-kept park." His guides spoke of Kitawala (Pierre Ilombo) once kept in solitary; Michael Chambers, "Basankusu to Ekafera," in "Lomako: A Zairian Journey," 50–74, esp. 72.

183. As Songo project reports suggested; see "Songo," 1945–48, GG 8211.

184. Equateur, Befale, "Divers," 1946, GG 6020, AA.

185. Raymond Williams, "Structures of Feeling."

186. Edmond Boelaert, Honoré Vinck, and Charles Lonkama, "Arrivée," *AAeq* 16–17 (1995–96).

187. Romaniuk arrived in 1953 Léopoldville after receiving wartime refugee status and a doctorate in Belgium. His Congo census received a reputation as Africa's best. He also battled to ensure Congolese did the delicate fieldwork. At Princeton in the 1960s, Africanist demographers nicknamed him the "sterility man." Interview with Anatole Romaniuk, Ottawa, 18 August 2004. See Congo Belge, AIMO *Enquêtes démographiques. District de la Tshuapa*; Congo Belge, *Equateur*. Territorial data was divided into rural, urban, and mixed (plantation) zones. Coquilhatville and Basankusu had the most women; Congo Belge, *Equateur*, 90–91. In Equateur district, 40 percent were without a child; sterility percentages were 54, 48, and 30 in Coquilhatville, Basankusu, and Ingende territories. Such anomalously high sterility rates only knew a parallel among the Zande; Anatole Romaniuk, *La fécondité des populations congolaises*; Romaniuk, *L'aspect démographique de la stérilité des femmes congolaises*. On Africa census fears and deception, see Elisha Renne, *Population and Progress in a Yoruba Town*; Lynn Thomas, *Politics of the Womb*.

188. Allard contended that new modern women were avoiding maternity, a theme in global circulation and notably among American sterility experts too; Margaret Marsh and Wanda Ronner, *The Empty Cradle: Infertility in America from Colonial Times to the*

Present. Abortifacient use was a Catholic theme; see A. Verbeeck, "Anticonceptionele Middelen."

CHAPTER 6: MOTION

1. Jacques Rancière, *Althusser's Lesson.*
2. On Parisian flânerie, see Walter Benjamin, *Charles Baudelaire*; Walter Benjamin, *The Arcades Project.*
3. Walter Benjamin, "The Flâneur" and "Idleness," in *The Arcades Project.*
4. Walter Benjamin, "Idleness," in *The Arcades Project.* Compare Georg Simmel, "The Metropolis and Mental Life," in *On Individuality and Social Forms*; Siegfried Kracauer, *The Mass Ornament.* On distraction, see Siegfried Kracauer, *The Salaried Masses.*
5. Frantz Fanon, *The Wretched of the Earth*, 15, 84; Nancy Hunt, *A Colonial Lexicon*; and "Ethnographies of the Road," Special issue, *Africa* 83, no. 3 (2013).
6. Reinhart Koselleck, *Futures Past.*
7. Hunt, *A Colonial Lexicon.*
8. On social pathologies, see Georges Balandier, "The Colonial Situation."
9. The literature on sapeurs is long and rich; see J. D. Gandoulou, *Au coeur de la Sape*; Ch. Didier Gondola, "Dream and Drama"; and Katrien Pype, "Fighting Boys, Strong Men and Gorillas."
10. "Fin 1945," ca. 1945–46, GG 6076, AA. For name lists of hundreds of the "infected" in Songo and Loma *chefferies*, "1947," GG 6076.
11. François Poffé to Befale AT, 3 April 1948, "Divers, 1947–49," GG 6076.
12. "Divers, 1947–49," GG 6076.
13. "Divers, 1947–49," GG 6076.
14. "Divers, 1947–49," GG 6076.
15. "Divers, 1947–49," GG 6076.
16. "Divers, 1947–49," GG 6076.
17. "Divers, 1947–49," GG 6076.
18. "Divers, 1947–49," GG 6076.
19. "Divers, 1947–49," GG 6076.
20. "Divers, 1947–49," GG 6076.
21. "Divers, 1947–49," GG 6076.
22. Fanon, *The Wretched of the Earth*, 15, 84.
23. Robert Vinson, *The Americans Are Coming!*
24. Walter Benjamin, "Dream Kitsch," in *Selected Writings*, vol. 2, part 1, 3.
25. "Mouvement 1942," 1942–45, GG 6076.
26. Fanon, *The Wretched of the Earth*, 39, 52, 56, 56, 55, 71, 56, 56, and 58.
27. Fanon, *The Wretched of the Earth*, 56, 71.
28. "Généralités," 1945–50, GG 6076.
29. On Lucienne Delyle, see René Baudelaire, *La chanson réaliste.*
30. "Généralités," 1945–50, GG 6076.
31. Joseph Conrad, *Heart of Darkness.*

32. See Alain Ruscio, *Que la France était belle au temps des colonies. Anthologie de chansons coloniales et exotiques françaises*; and Maryse J. Bray and Agnes Calatayud, "La chanson populaire en France au temps des colonies," accessed 15 November 2014, http://westminsterresearch.wmin.ac.uk/140/1/Bray_2002_final.pdf.

33. "Amalaouta" is available on iTunes; Isabelle de Rezende kindly transcribed and translated the French. On the Lucienne Delyle CD, "Mon amant de Saint-Jean," the song is cut 12. An Aimé Barelli, Jacques Larue, and Lucienne Delyle production, first released in Paris in 1946, its alternative name was "Embrasse-moi." Other cultural products banned by Belgian colonial authorities included "Arbre" in *Récits de la cabane abandonnée (Tales of an Empty Cabin)* by Grey Owl (1888–1938), a popular conservationist who celebrated native Canadians while pointing to the violence of conquest. Available in libraries for Congolese, one passage (238–40) seemed able to produce "a hostile mentality towards the work of civilization"; Governor to AT Befale, 7 November 1950, "Divers confidentiel, 1950," GG 6076. See Jane Onyanga-Omara, "Grey Owl: Canada's Great Conservationist and Imposter," accessed 14 July 2014, http://www.bbc.com /news/uk-england-sussex-24127514.

34. "Une Congolaise à Lisbonne," *Mbandaka*, 8 January 1955, 3.

35. "Quand les Congolais voyagent par avion," *Mbandaka*, 8 January 1955, 3.

36. C. C. De Backer, "Les femmes congolaises ont fait un grand voyage d'études merveilleux," *Mbandaka*, 13 July 1957, 7.

37. J. M. Bomboko, "Lorsque les Congolais découvrent la Belgique. Impressions générales," *Mbandaka*, 18 June 1955, 3. Bomboko impressed Mobutu, Belgium, and Larry Devlin of CIA fame, who recalled, "wild card for dinner parties. . . . one of the most charming and intelligent men I have ever met, full of stories—humorous or serious—always ready to comment on political developments . . . great source of information on tribalism. . . . notorious ladies' man about town." Larry Devlin, *Chief of Station, Congo*, 142–43. See Emizet François Kisangani and F. Scott Bobb, "Bomboko Lokumba Is Elenge, Justin-Marie (1928–)," in *Historical Dictionary of the Democratic Republic of the Congo*, 57.

38. "A propos de l'accès des Congolais dans les établissements publics," *Mbandaka*, 18 June 1955, 3.

39. Graham Greene, *In Search of a Character*, 3, 26.

40. Greene, *In Search of a Character*, 64. See Michel Lechat, "Diary."

41. Greene, *In Search of a Character*, 3, 5, 16, 64, 54, 11–12, 50.

42. "Distribution d'eau potable à Coq II," *Mbandaka*, 23 April 1955, 4.

43. *Mbandaka*, 5 February 1955, 1; J. M. Bomboko, "Nos femmes et le Foyer Social," *Mbandaka*, 10 December 1955, 1 and 3; and "Notre reportage photographique sur la dernière exposition organisée au Foyer Social de Coquilhatville," *Mbandaka*, 24 December 1955, 4–5.

44. "Quelles sont les préférences des Congolais en ce qui concerne la musique," *Mbandaka*, 8 January 1955, 3.

45. Equateur, Rapport AIMO, 1947, 86–87, RA/CB (221) 22, AA.

46. Equateur, Rapport AIMO, 1948, 74, RA/CB (221) 23.

47. Equateur, Rapport AIMO, 1949, 85–86, RA/CB (91) 1.

48. Equateur, Rapport AIMO, 1950, 86, RA/CB (221) 24.

49. Equateur, Rapport AIMO, 1953, 91, RA/CB (91) 2.

50. Equateur, Rapport AIMO, 1948, 74, RA/CB (221) 23.

51. Greene, *In Search of a Character*, 16–17; on "consumer" colonialism, see Fanon, *The Wretched of the Earth*, 26.

52. "Divers confidentiel, 1950," GG 6076.

53. "Divers confidentiel" [1950–56], GG 6076.

54. *Mbandaka*, 2 July 1955, 8.

55. Greene, *In Search of a Character*, 16–17.

56. Greene, *In Search of a Character*, 17.

57. R. Ilanga, "Les 'Coquins' sont-ils contents de leurs bars?," *Mbandaka*, 9 October 1954, 3.

58. Georges-Roger Nkana, "Autour des associations féminines à Coq," *Mbandaka*, 1 February 1958, 1 and 3; Georges-Roger Nkana, "Les bars du C.E.C. Coq," *Mbandaka*, 14 December 1957, 6; Observateur [J. M. Boboko], "Associations de femmes congolaises au C.E.C. de Coquilhatville," *Mbandaka*, 11 September 1954, 2. Another subject was medicine: "Tarifs de soins médicaux et des frais d'hospitalisation pour Congolais dans les formations sanitaires de la colonie," *Mbandaka*, 14 July 1956, 4; "Communiqués du Service Médical," *Mbandaka*, 21 December 1957, 3–5; and "Les maladies vénériennes," *Mbandaka*, 9 February 1957, 1.

59. "Un peuple qui meurt: Les Mongos," *Le Progrès*, 25 June 1948, 1.

60. Joseph Lazarite Esser, "Terres sans people," *Courrier d'Afrique*, 18 April 1945, 1.

61. A. O. Bolela, "Conseil de Province de l'Equateur. Discours de M. le Gouverneur Schmit. Situation démographique," *Mbandaka*, 31 March 1956, 3 and 6, and 7 April 1956, 1 and 3; J. Van Wing, "Démographie congolaise," *Courrier d'Afrique*, 19 May 1945, 1; "Le problème démographique au Congo Belge," *Courrier d'Afrique*, 26 August 1945, 1; "Polygamie et dénatalité," *Courrier d'Afrique*, 16 October 1945, n.p.; "Causerie sur la natalité par M. Ch. Lodewyckx," *Mbandaka*, 2 June 1951, 2.

62. Fermin Molifa, "A Stanleyville: Primes de natalité," *Le Progrès*, 12 May 1949, 2.

63. Eugène N'djoku, "Grave plaie de l'Equateur: le dépeuplement des Mongo."

64. J. M. Bomboko, "La réorganisation des cours à l'école des infirmiers de Coquilhatville," *Mbandaka*, 9 January 1954, 1–2.

65. "Programme pro-natal," *Mbandaka*, 24 September 1949, 3; "Conférence sur la dénatalité," *Mbandaka*, 5 November 1949, 2; "Propagande pro-natale," *Mbandaka*, 26 November 1949, 2.

66. *Mbandaka*, 23 December 1950, 1.

67. *Mbandaka*, 6 May 1950, 2; *Mbandaka*, 17 June 1950, 2; *Mbandaka*, 24 June 1950, 2. See also Regine, "Conseils à une jeune maman," *Mbandaka*, 29 June 1957, 7.

68. "Nouvelles de Coquilhatville," *Mbandaka*, 13 January 1951, 1; *Mbandaka*, 26 January 1957, 1; "Au Service Médical," *Mbandaka*, 7 February 1957, 3; and "Avis: Ecole des Infirmiers de Coquilhatville," *Mbandaka*, 18 May 1957, 3.

69. *Mbandaka*, 24 February 1951, 1.

70. "Donneurs de sang," *Mbandaka*, 12 November 1955, 4–5; "Avis au public," *Mbandaka*, 11 August 1951, 1.

71. Bomboko, "La réorganisation des cours à l'école des infirmiers de Coquilhatville"; J. M. Bomboko, "Expérience Songo en Territoire de Befale serait une réussite complète," *Mbandaka*, 21 August 1954, 1; J. M. B[omboko], "Activité du Fonds du Bien-Etre Indigène dans le territoire de Befale," *Mbandaka*, 9 October 1954, 1–2. See too Nina, "Propagande pronatale de M. Charles Lodewyckx," *Mbandaka*, 5 October 1952, 1.

72. A. M. Mobe, "Pour la garde de nos maladies à l'hôpital," *Mbandaka*, 20 June 1953, 3.

73. Greene, *In Search of a Character*, 4, 6–7, 23, 59, 59, 56.

74. Greene, *In Search of a Character*, 29, 22.

75. Greene, *In Search of a Character*, 23, 56–57.

76. Greene, *In Search of a Character*, 58, 56.

77. Ferdinand Wassa, "Liberté de la femme noire et prostitution," 71–72.

78. Nancy Hunt, "Noise over Camouflaged Polygamy, Colonial Morality Taxation, and a Woman-Naming Crisis in Belgian Africa."

79. Abbé Jean Sumuwe, "Crise de mariage. Concubinage perpétuel," 282–85.

80. Ntefo, "La polygamie camouflée au centre extra-coutumier," *Mbandaka*, 26 May 1956, 1 and 3.

81. "L'erreur des pseudo-évolués: le Tape-à-l'Oeil," *Mbandaka*, 26 May 1956, 1 and 3.

82. AT Adjoint Legraie, Bomongiri, to AT Monkoto, GG 8052, AA.

83. Nkana, "Autour des associations féminines," 1 and 3.

84. "Taxe pour les femmes célibataires," *Mbandaka*, 10 December 1955, 1.

85. A. O. Bolela, "Moyens d'existence de la femme indigène dans les centres extra-coutumiers," *Mbandaka*, 27 October 1956, 1 and 3.

86. Nkana, "Les bars du C.E.C. Coq," 6.

87. Observateur [J. M. Boboko], "Associations de femmes congolaises," 2.

88. N.d.l.R., "Le point de vue de nos abonnés. A propos des associations de femmes," *Mbandaka*, 11 December 1954, 4.

89. *Mbandaka*, 25 December 1954, 1.

90. Observateur, "Associations de femmes congolaises," 2; see also, Hunt, "Noise over Camouflaged Polygamy."

91. "L'action médicale dans la province de l'Equateur," *Mbandaka*, 27 August 1949, 1.

92. J. M. Bomboko, "Lutte contre les maladies vénériennes: Une réforme qui s'impose," *Mbandaka*, 15 October 1954, 1 and 3.

93. Testis, "Le point de vue de nos abonnés: Recensement médical au centre extra-coutumier de Coquilhatville," *Mbandaka*, 23 October 1954, 4.

94. "Départ de M. Le Docteur Schwers, Médecin Provincial," *Mbandaka*, 31 December 1949, 2.

95. Testis, "Le point de vue de nos abonnés: Recensement," *Mbandaka*, 23 October 1954, 4; Sébastien Lomboto, "Territoire de Bomongo: Carence du service médical," *Mbandaka*, 23 October 1954, 6.

96. Nuno Faria et al., "The Early Spread and Epidemic Ignition of HIV-1 in Human Populations"; and compare Tamara Giles-Vernick et al., "Social History, Biology, and the Emergence of HIV in Colonial Africa."

97. "Divers, 1947–49," GG 6076. The sheets confiscated were not in the dossier.

98. "Divers, 1947–49," GG 6076.

99. "Divers, 1947–49," GG 6076.

100. Commissioner Warnant to AT Befale, September 11, 1950, "Divers confidentiel, 1950," GG 6076.

101. Warnant to AT Befale, 11 September 1950, "Divers confidentiel, 1950" GG 6076.

102. AT Befale to Warnant, 19 September 1950, "Divers confidentiel, 1950," GG 6076.

103. On postwar social psychologists, see Nancy Hunt, "Colonial Medical Anthropology and the Making of the Central African Infertility Belt," in *Ordering Africa*; for example, Robert Mastriaux, *La Femme et le destin de l'Afrique*.

104. "Divers, 1947–49," GG 6076.

105. "Divers, 1947–49," GG 6076. See the longhand written document with more about Maliani, dances, songs, phonographs.

106. "Divers, 1947–49," GG 6076. On Henri Bowane, recording-studio owner Nicolas Jeronimidis, and the early years of Congolese rumba, see Gary Stewart, *Rumba on the River*; and Bob White, "Congolese Rumba and Other Cosmopolitanisms." For the later years, see Bob White, *Rumba Rules*.

107. "Divers" (1939–44), GG 6076.

108. "Divers" (1939–44), GG 6076. See the longhand interrogation.

109. Louisa's lovers were in a struggle with her father over modern marriage, with car and guitars as ammunition: "Tell me where is Louisa. . . . I'll wait for you tomorrow at your father's house. . . . Your father refused to let us marry / You and me, we love each other / We'll get married, Mama Louisa. . . . Your father told me to think about it / He insulted me really in a clever way. . . . Feel like a child, Louisa / I won't marry anyone else / The father insults me because of Louisa / You don't know that Bowane is your father / Where are you Louisa? . . . Wendo you're wasting your breath / We have a car / We have our own guitars / We have our own? / We'll run away with her on the road to Kingabwa." Bob White, "Congolese Rumba and Other Cosmopolitanisms," 674.

110. Edmond Boelaert, Honoré Vinck, and Charles Lonkama, "Arrivée," *AAeq* 16–17 (1995–96).

111. François Robert Bosulu in *AAeq* 17:15–17; and Louis Ikilinganya in *AAeq* 16:110–12; François Bompuku in *AAeq* 16:105–6.

112. Bompuku in *AAeq* 16:105–6.

113. Jean Boenga in *AAeq* 17:24–35.

114. Boenga in *AAeq* 17:24–35.

115. Lomboto, account collected by S. Veys, "Territoire d'Ingende," Annexe 3 in "Arrivée," *AAeq* 16:131.

116. Boenga in *AAeq* 17:24–35.

117. On nicknames, see Osumaka Likaka, *Naming Colonialism*; in memory texts see

"Arrivée," *AAeq* 17:362–87. Polo, sometimes "Molo" or "Paul," was identified as Commissaire Guillaume De Bauw; *AAeq* 17:382, 384.

118. Boenga in *AAeq* 17:24–35.

119. Boenga in *AAeq* 17:24–35.

120. Boenga in *AAeq* 17:24–35; Bompuku in *AAeq* 16:105–6; and Lomboto in "Arrivée," *AAeq* 16:132.

121. The French word *fanfare* is in the Lomongo accounts; Boenga in *AAeq* 17:24–35; Pierre Damien Lowango in *AAeq* 17:191–92; Joseph Mbile in *AAeq* 16:89–90.

122. See L'Exposition universelle et internationale de Liège, *Notice sur L'État Indépendant du Congo*; Demetrius Boulger, *The Congo State.*

123. At some stage, fanfares became integral to funerals in Congo's major towns. In 2007 Kinshasa, many funerals had a marching fanfare. The keen eye could spot makeshift signs renting fanfares, with the instruments and musicians usually rented as a unit. Just as it would be interesting to know much more about Bowane, a history of fanfares would be a fine addition to Congolese music studies.

124. Greene, *In Search of a Character*, 15.

125. Greene, *In Search of a Character*, 17.

126. "L'assassin de la sentinelle de M. Lemos est condamné à mort," *Mbandaka*, 8 January 1955, 1.

127. Greene, *In Search of a Character*, 4. Narratives of Congo's decolonization are legion; for a detailed 1965 version, see Crawford Young, *Politics in the Congo*. On Greene in Equateur, see Michael Meeuwis, "Tiny Bouts of Contentment. Rare Film Footage Of Graham Greene in the Belgian Congo, March 1959," accessed 15 October 2014, http://rozenbergquarterly.com/tiny-bouts-of-contentment-rare-film-footage-of-graham-greene-in-the-belgian-congo-march-1959/.

128. Greene, *In Search of a Character*, 22, 16, 22, 16.

CONCLUSION: FIELD CODA AND OTHER ENDINGS

1. Georges Balandier, "The Colonial Situation," in *Social Change.*

2. Vinh-Kim Nguyen, "Government-by-Exception"; Richard Rottenburg, "Social and Public Experiments and New Figurations of Science and Politics in Postcolonial Africa"; and P. Wenzel Geissler and Catherine Molyneux, eds., *Evidence, Ethos and Experiment.*

3. Frantz Fanon, "Medicine and Colonialism," in *A Dying Colonialism.*

4. For a beautiful, literary history of these wars, their implications and antecedents from the 1870s to the 2000s, with rich human detail, see David Van Reybrouck, *Congo: The Epic History of a People.*

5. Lonkama knew that I had been studying how Pentecostalisms had virtually eliminated Kinshasa's Zebola; see Ellen Corin, "Refiguring the Person," in *Bodies and Persons.*

6. See also Anne Retel-Laurentin, *Un pays à la derive.*

7. On "latitude" and "shrunken milieu," see Georges Canguilhem, *Knowledge of Life*, 132; and Paula Marrati and Todd Meyers's insightful interpretation, "Forward: Life, as Such" in *Knowledge of Life.*

8. Canguilhem, *Knowledge of Life*, 132 ("shrunken milieu"); Balandier, "The Colonial Situation."

9. Giorgio Agamben, "What Is a Camp?" in *Means without End*.

10. Reinhart Koselleck, "Space of Experience and Horizons of Expectations."

11. In 1935 *nganda* meant "fishing hut," whereas in 2004 *nganda* could mean "fishing village," and *nganda ya massanga* "a bar, a night club"; Malcolm Guthrie, ed., *Lingala Grammar and Dictionary*, 186; Eyamba Georges Bokamba and Molingo Virginie Bokama, *Tósololo na Lingála*, 407, 398.

12. Distraction has worked best as a historiographic category amid other themes, as in Terence Ranger, *Dance and Society in Eastern Africa, 1890–1970*; Charles van Onselen, *Studies in the Social and Economic History of Witwatersrand, 1886–1914*. Compare Emmanuel Akyeampong and Charles Ambler, "Leisure in African History: An Introduction."

13. On distraction, see Walter Benjamin's convolutes, esp. "Idleness," in *The Arcades Project*; Siegfried Kracauer, *The Mass Ornament*; and Siegfried Kracauer, *The Salaried Masses*.

14. Carine Plancke, "On Dancing and Fishing."

15. Nancy Hunt, *Suturing New Medical Histories of Africa*.

16. On "technique of nearness," see Walter Benjamin, *The Arcades Project*, 545.

17. As in Bachelard's sense of the poetic images of material things within reverie; Gaston Bachelard, *The Poetics of Reverie*; Gaston Bachelard, *On Poetic Imagination and Reverie*.

18. Edmond Boelaert, Honoré Vinck, and Charles Lonkama, "Arrivée des blancs sur les bords des rivières équatoriales," *AAeq* 16–17 (1995–96). See also Nancy Hunt, "Espace, temporalité et rêverie: Ecrire l'histoire des futurs au Congo belge."

19. Maurice Blanchot, *The Writing of the Disaster*, 4.

20. See Pierre Damien Lowango, *AAeq* 17:192 and Joseph Bolakofo *AAeq* 17:207.

21. Gilles Deleuze, *Difference and Repetition*.

22. Bachelard, *The Poetics of Reverie*, 51.

23. Allan Young, "Posttraumatic Stress Disorder of the Virtual Kind," in *Trauma and Memory*.

24. Basil Davidson, *The African Awakening*; Georges Balandier, *Sociologie actuelle de l'Afrique noire*; Georges Balandier, *Afrique ambiguë*; Georges Balandier, *Sociologie des Brazzaville noires*; Suzanne Comhaire-Sylvain, *Food and Leisure among the African Youth of Leopoldville, Belgian Congo*.

25. Gustaaf Hulstaert, *Chansons de danse mongo*.

26. On sexual arrangements and liaisons, see Gustaaf Hulstaert, *Le mariage des Nkundo*; Hulstaert, *Chansons*.

27. See also Nancy Hunt, "Fertility's Fires and Empty Wombs in Recent African-ist Writing"; Anne Retel-Laurentin, *Un pays à la dérive*; Karina Kielmann, "Barren Ground," in *Pragmatic Women and Body Politics*; and Maria Inhorn and Frank Balen, eds., *Infertility around the Globe*.

28. Mary John and Janaki Nair, *A Question of Silence?: The Sexual Economies of Modern India*.

29. See especially Anne Retel-Laurentin, *Sorcellerie et ordalies.*

30. Murray Last, "The Importance of Knowing about Not Knowing," in *On Knowing and Not Knowing in the Anthropology of Medicine.*

31. On studying not origins but the emergence of HIV/AIDS, see Tamara Giles-Vernick et al., "Social History, Biology, and the Emergence of HIV in Colonial Africa."

32. Timing derives from genetic age estimates; for recent estimates see Nuno Faria et al., "The Early Spread and Epidemic Ignition of HIV-1 in Human Populations." See also Michael Worobey et al., "Direct Evidence of Extensive Diversity of HIV-1 in Kinshasa by 1960."

33. On Belgian injection efficiency, sexual commodification in Léopoldville, and railroads, see Jacques Pépin, *The Origins of AIDS.* On genital ulcers facilitating Congo's early human spread, see João de Sousa et al., "High GUD Incidence in the Early Twentieth Century Created a Particularly Permissive Time Window for the Origin and Initial Spread of Epidemic HIV Strains." On reservations, see Faria et al., "The Early Spread and Epidemic Ignition of HIV-1 in Human Populations."

BIBLIOGRAPHY

ARCHIVES AND MANUSCRIPTS

Belgium
Archives Africaines, Brussels
AE 528 (349)
AI 14 (4874); 1405
GG 5487; 6020; 6076; 8005; 8052; 8164; 8211; 8243; 8275; 9450; 9552; 9952; 10.062;
10.102; 11.347; 12.266; 12.267; 12.735; 13.546; 13.744; 14.014; 16.105; 16.702; 16.812;
19.385; 19.389
H 4520, II A.05.07, 1948–49
M 74 (576)
RA/CB (91); (221)
SPA (4482); 14702 (K 2431); 23163 (K 3865)
Musée Royal de l'Afrique Centrale, Tervuren, Belgium
Papiers Frantz Cornet
Papiers Françis Dhanis
Papiers Clément Huet

Democratic Republic of Congo
Centre Aequatoria, Bamanya
Fonds Hulstaert

United Kingdom
London School of Economics, Archives, London
E. D. Morel Papers
Regions Beyond Missionary Union Archive, University of Edinburgh, Edinburgh

Regions Beyond Missionary Union Manuscripts and Publications
W. D. Armstrong Papers

United States

Disciples of Christ Historical Society, Congo Mission Collection, Nashville
    Gervase Barger Papers
    Royal Dye Papers
    Louis Jaggard Papers
Library of Congress, Manuscript Division, Washington, DC
    Mary French Sheldon Papers
University of Chicago Special Collections, Chicago
    Frederick Starr Papers
University of Wisconsin-Madison Memorial Library, Special Collections, Madison
    Papers Maurice De Ryck

FORMAL INTERVIEWS

Canada

Anatole Romaniuk, 18 August 2004, Ottawa

Democratic Republic of the Congo

Group interview, including Mboto Y'Ofaya, David Ikeke, and Thomas Ndio, 13 May
    2007, Besefe
Group interview, including Dieudonné Bosembu, Nzampenda Lokamba, Bekolo
    Lokombo, Booto, and Eloliin Ikanga, 13 May 2007, Ikanga
Antoine Sonzolo Efoloko, 18 May 2007, Mbandaka

OTHER SOURCES

"Africa Prior to WWI, 1914." Map. Scale not given. In *The Outline of History*, ed. H. G.
    Wells, 986. New York: Macmillan, 1921. Available at Maps ETC. Accessed 18 Novem-
    ber 2014. http://etc.usf.edu/maps/pages/3600/3689/3689.htm.
Agamben, Giorgio. *Homo Sacer: Sovereign Power and Bare Life*. Trans. Daniel Heller-
    Roazen. Stanford, CA: Stanford University Press, 1998.
Agamben, Giorgio. *State of Exception*. Trans. Kevin Attell. Chicago: University of Chi-
    cago Press, 2005.
Agamben, Giorgio. "What Is a Camp?" In *Means without End: Notes on Politics*, 36–44.
    Trans. Vincenzo Binetti and Cesare Casarino. Minneapolis: University of Minnesota
    Press, 2000.
Akyeampong, Emmanuel, and Charles Ambler. "Leisure in African History: An Intro-
    duction." *International Journal of African Historical Studies* 35, no. 1 (2002): 1–16.
Allard, Robert. "Contribution gynécologique à l'étude de la stérilité chez les Mongo de
    Befale." *Annales de la Société Belge de Médecine Tropicale* 35 (1955): 631–48.
Allard, Robert. "Essai d'évaluation des facteurs de stérilité chez les Mongo de Befale."
    Examen B 242. Institut de la Médecine Tropicale, Antwerp, 1956.

Althusser, Louis. *Philosophy of the Encounter: Later Writings, 1978–87.* Trans. G. M. Goshgarian. London: Verso, 2006.

Amies, C. R. "Development of Resistance of Gonococci to Penicillin: An Eight-Year Study." *Canadian Medical Association Journal* 96 (7 January 1967): 33–35.

Amnesty International. *Human Rights Violations in Zaire, an Amnesty International Report.* London: Amnesty International Publications, 1980.

Annuaire des importateurs, exportateurs, entreprises commerciales, industrielles, minières et agricoles opérant au Congo belge, 1934. Brussels, 1934. Distributed free of charge in Congo by the Ministère des Colonies and in Belgium by the Compagnie Belge de Propagande Coloniale.

Anstey, Roger. "The Congo Rubber Atrocities—A Case Study." *African Historical Studies* 4, no. 1 (1971): 59–76.

Appadurai, Arjun. *Modernity at Large: Cultural Dimensions of Globalization.* Minneapolis: University of Minnesota Press, 1996.

"A propos de l'accès des Congolais dans les établissements publics." *Mbandaka,* 18 June 1955, 3.

Archer-Straw, Petrine. *Negrophilia: Avant-Garde Paris and Black Culture in the 1920s.* New York: Thames and Hudson, 2000.

Arendt, Hannah. *The Origins of Totalitarianism.* New ed. with added prefaces. San Diego: Harcourt, 1976.

Arnold, David. *Colonizing the Body: State Medicine and Epidemic Disease in Nineteenth-Century India.* Berkeley: University of California Press, 1993.

"Au service médical." *Mbandaka,* 7 February 1957, 3.

"Avis: Ecole des Infirmiers de Coquilhatville." *Mbandaka,* 18 May 1957, 3.

"Avis au public." *Mbandaka,* 11 August 1951, 1.

Aymérich, Joseph Gauderique. *La Conquête du Cameroun: 1er août 1914–20 février 1916.* Paris: Payot, 1933.

Bachelard, Gaston. *On Poetic Imagination and Reverie: Selections from Gaston Bachelard.* Rev. ed. Trans. Colette Gaudin. Dallas: Spring Publications, 1987.

Bachelard, Gaston. *The Poetics of Reverie: Childhood, Language, and the Cosmos.* Trans. Daniel Russell. Boston: Beacon Press, 1971.

Bachelard, Gaston. *The Poetics of Space.* Trans. Maria Jolas. Boston: Beacon Press, 1994.

Baker, D. H. "Etude concernant la situation sanitaire et démographique de quelques villages du district de la Tshuapa (pathologie—dénatalité)." *Recueil de Travaux de Science Médicales au Congo belge,* no. 2 (January 1944): 141–50.

Bakhtin, M. M. *Rabelais and His World.* Trans. Helene Iswolsky. Cambridge, MA: MIT Press, 1968.

Bakutu, Boniface, Jr. "Losilo." *Le Coq chante* 3 (15 September 1937): 25.

Balandier, Georges. *Afrique ambiguë.* Paris: Plon, 1957.

Balandier, Georges. "The Colonial Situation: A Theoretical Approach." In *Social Change: The Colonial Situation,* ed. Immanuel Wallerstein, 34–61. New York: John Wiley, 1966.

Balandier, Georges. "La situation coloniale: Approche théorique." *Cahiers Internationaux de Sociologie* 11 (1951): 44–79.

Balandier, Georges. "Messianismes et nationalismes en Afrique noire." *Cahiers Internationaux de Sociologie* 14 (1953): 41–65.

Balandier, Georges. *Sociologie actuelle de l'Afrique noire: Dynamique sociale en Afrique centrale.* 2nd ed. Paris: Presses Universitaires de France, 1963.

Balandier, Georges. *Sociologie des Brazzavilles noires.* 2nd ed., rev. and augm. Paris: Presses de la fondation nationale politique, 1985.

Baldwin, Peter. *Contagion and the State in Europe, 1830–1930.* Cambridge: Cambridge University Press, 1999.

Barber, Karin, ed. *Africa's Hidden Histories: Everyday Literacy and Making the Self.* Bloomington: Indiana University Press, 2006.

Barrett, Nick. "Terence Conran." *Telegraph,* 3 March 2007.

Barthélémi, V. "Étude sur la syphilis au Congo belge." Examen B, No. 16a. Institut de la Médecine Tropicale, Antwerp, 1921.

Barthes, Roland. "Shock-Photos." In *The Eiffel Tower and Other Mythologies,* trans. Richard Howard. New York: Hill and Wang, 1979.

Bashford, Alison. *Imperial Hygiene: A Critical History of Colonialism, Nationalism and Public Health.* Houndsmills, UK: Palgrave Macmillan, 2004.

Bataille, Georges. "Writings on Laughter, Sacrifice, Nietzsche, Unknowing." *October* 36 (1986).

Bate, Peter. *Congo: White King, Red Rubber, Black Death.* Video recording produced by Periscope Productions in coproduction with the BBC. New York: ArtMattan Productions, 2004.

Bateman, Martha. "Two Hundred Miles via Bicycle." *World Call* 19 (February 1942): 26.

Baudelaire, Charles. "L'essence du rire et généralement du comique dans les arts plastiques." In *Oeuvres complètes de Baudelaire,* ed. Claude Pichois, 975–93. Paris: Gallimard, 1961.

Baudelaire, René. *La chanson réaliste.* Paris: L'Harmattan, 1996.

Bayart, Jean-François. *The State in Africa: The Politics of the Belly.* New York: Longman, 1993.

Beard, George. *American Nervousness: Its Causes and Consequences: A Supplement to Nervous Exhaustion (Neurasthenia).* New York: G. P. Putnam's Sons, 1881.

Beidelman, T. O. *Culture of Colonialism.* Bloomington: Indiana University Press, 2012.

Belcher, Stephen. *Epic Traditions of Africa.* Bloomington: Indiana University Press, 1999.

Belgian Congo at War. New York: Belgian Information Center, 1942.

Belgium. *Éphémérides des campagnes belges en Afrique (1914–1917).* Le Havre: Bureau documentaire belge, 1918.

Belgium. *Rapport annuel sur l'activité de la colonie du Congo belge pendant l'année 1922.* Brussels: F. Van Gompel, 1924.

Belgium. *Rapport annuel sur l'administration de la colonie du Congo belge pendant l'année 1934.* Brussels: Van Gompel, 1935.

Belgium. *Rapport annuel sur l'administration de la colonie du Congo belge pendant l'année 1935*. Brussels: Van Gompel, 1936.

Belgium. *Rapport annuel sur l'administration de la colonie du Congo belge pendant l'année 1936*. Brussels: Van Gompel, 1937.

Belsey, Mark. "The Epidemiology of Infertility: A Review with Particular Reference to Sub-Saharan Africa." *Bulletin of the World Health Organization* 54 (1976): 319–41.

Benedek, T. "Infertility as Psychosomatic Defense." *Fertility and Sterility* 3, no. 6 (1952): 537–41.

Benjamin, Walter. *The Arcades Project*. Trans. Howard Eiland and Kevin McLaughlin. Cambridge, MA: Belknap Press, 1999.

Benjamin, Walter. *Charles Baudelaire: A Lyric Poet in the Era of High Capitalism*. Trans. H. Zohn. London: Verso, 1983.

Benjamin, Walter. "Critique of Violence." In *Selected Writings*, vol. 1, 1913–1926, ed. Marcus Bullock and Michael Jennings, 236–52. Cambridge, MA: Belknap Press, 1996.

Benjamin, Walter. "Dream Kitsch: Gloss on Surrealism." In *Selected Writings*, vol. 2, part 1, 1927–1930, ed. Michael Jennings, Howard Eiland, and Gary Smith, 3–5. Cambridge, MA: Belknap Press, 1999.

Benjamin, Walter. "The Flâneur." In *The Arcades Project*, trans. H. Eiland and K. McLaughlin, 416–55. Cambridge, MA: Belknap Press, 1999.

Benjamin, Walter. "Idleness." In *The Arcades Project*, trans. H. Eiland and K. McLaughlin, 800–806. Cambridge, MA: Belknap Press, 1999.

Benjamin, Walter. "On the Concept of History." In *Selected Writings*, vol. 4, 1938–1940, ed. Howard Eiland and Michael Jennings, 389–400. Cambridge, MA: Belknap Press, 2003.

Bentley, W. Holman. *Pioneering on the Congo*. Vol. 2. London: Religious Tract Society, 1900.

Bernault, Florence, ed. *A History of Prison and Confinement in Africa*. Portsmouth, UK: Heinemann, 2002.

Besau, Boloko Bernard. "Losilo." *Le Coq chante* 4 (15 July 1939): 3.

Bhabha, Homi. "Anxious Nations, Nervous States." In *Supposing the Subject*, ed. Joan Copjec, 201–17. London: Verso, 1994.

Bianchini, Marco Levi. "La psicologia della colonizzazione nell' Africa periequatoriale." *Rivista di psicologia applicata alla pedagogia ed alla psicopatologia* 2 (1906): 395–403.

Bibeau, Gilles. "New Legal Rules for an Old Art of Healing: The Case of Zairian Healers' Associations." *Social Science and Medicine* 16 (1982): 1843–49.

Bibeau, Gilles, Rashim Ajluwalia, and Bernard Méchin. *Traditional Medicine in Zaire: Present and Potential Contribution to the Health Services*. Ottawa: International Development Research Centre, 1980.

Biebuyck, Brunhilde. "Nkundo Mongo Tales: Analysis of Form and Content." Ph.D. diss., Indiana University, 1980.

Biebuyck, Daniel. "La société kumu face au Kitawala," *Zaïre* 11, no. 1 (January 1957): 7–40.

Biehl, João. *Vita: Life in a Zone of Social Abandonment*. Berkeley: University of California, 2005.

Blanchot, Maurice. *The Writing of the Disaster*. New ed. Trans. Ann Smock. Lincoln: University of Nebraska Press, 1995.

Bledsoe, Caroline. *Contingent Lives: Fertility, Time, and Aging in West Africa*. Chicago: University of Chicago Press, 2002.

Bloch, Marc. *The Historian's Craft*. Trans. Peter Putnam. New York: Knopf, 1953.

Boddy, Janice. *Civilizing Women: British Crusades in Colonial Sudan*. Princeton, NJ: Princeton University Press, 2007.

Boelaert, Edmond. "Beste vrienden of mijn eerste Congoroman." *Almanak* (Bogerhout) 39 (1933): 34–46.

Boelaert, Edmond. "Bokatola." Annexe 2 in "Arrivée des blancs sur les bords des rivières équatoriales," by Edmond Boelaert, Honoré Vinck, and Charles Lonkama. *Annales Aequatoria* 16 (1995): 122–27.

Boelaert, Edmond. "De bons amis, ou ma première aventure au Congo." *Annales de Notre-Dame du Sacré-Coeur* 44 (1933).

Boelaert, Edmond. "Halewijn." *Hooger Leven, Averbode* 8, no. 47 (1934): 1480.

Boelaert, Edmond. "Koloniale krabbels: Sterft Kongo uit?" *Nieuw Vlaanderen* 5, no. 28 (15 July 1939): 8.

Boelaert, Edmond. "La procession de Lianja." *Aequatoria* 25, no. 1 (1962): 1–9.

Boelaert, Edmond. *La situation démographique des Nkundo-Mongo*. Elisabethville, DRC: Centre d'Etude des Problèmes Sociaux Indigènes, 1946.

Boelaert, Edmond. "Les épouvantails-amulettes." *Congo* 17, no. 1 (1936): 677–79.

Boelaert, Edmond. "Liwenthal (Charles)." In *Biographie coloniale belge*. Vol. 5, col. 561–62. Brussels: Falk van Campenhout, 1958.

Boelaert, Edmond. "Nsong'a Lianja: Het Groote Epos der Nkundo-Mongo." *Congo* 15 (1934): 49–71; 197–216.

Boelaert, Edmond. "Nsong'a Lianja. L'épopée nationale des Nkundo." *Aequatoria* 12 (1949): 1–76.

Boelaert, Edmond. "Ntange." Parts 1 and 2. *Aequatoria* 15, no. 2 (1952): 58–63; 15, no. 3 (1952): 96–100.

Boelaert, Edmond. "Uit mijn negerij: De elima's." *Hooger Leven, Averbode* 9, no. 2 (1935): 60–61.

Boelaert, Edmond. "Visscherij in mijn negerij." *Congo* 14, no. 2 (December 1933): 705–24.

Boelaert, Edmond. "Yebola." *Kongo-Overzee* 1, no. 1 (1934–35): 16–19.

Boelaert, Edmond, Honoré Vinck, and Charles Lonkama. "Arrivée des blancs sur les bords des rivières équatoriales." Parts 1 and 2. *Annales Aequatoria* 16 (1995): 11–134; 17 (1996): 7–416.

Boelaert, Edmond, Honoré Vinck, and Charles Lonkama. "Noms des blancs." In "Arrivée des blancs sur les bords des rivières équatoriales." *Annales Aequatoria* 17 (1996): 362–87.

Bofuky, Jean Robert. "Comme au temps du Roi Salomon: Une histoire vécue par l'auteur oú on parle d'un enfant perdu et retrouvé." *Le Coq chante* 4 (1 February 1939): 11–12.

Boisseau, Tracey. *White Queen: May French Sheldon and the Imperial Origins of American Feminist Identity*. Bloomington: Indiana University Press, 2004.

Bokamba, Eyamba Georges, and Molingo Virginie Bokama. *Tósololo na Lingála: A Multidimensional Approach to the Teaching and Learning of Lingála as a Foreign Language*. Madison, WI: NALRC Press, 2004.

Bolanjabe, Benoît. "Losilo." *Le Coq chante* 4 (1 April 1939): 4.

Bolanjabe, Benoît. "Losilo." *Le Coq chante* 4 (15 April 1939): 4.

Bolela, A. O. "Conseil de Province de l'Equateur: Discours de M. le Gouverneur Schmit (suite du no. 13). Situation démographique." *Mbandaka*, 31 March 1956, 3 and 6.

Bolela, A. O. "Conseil de Province de l'Equateur: Discours de M. le Gouverneur Schmit (suite du no. 13). Situation démographique." *Mbandaka*, 7 April 1956, 1 and 3.

Bolela, A. O. "Moyens d'existence de la femme indigène dans les Centres Extra-Coutumiers." *Mbandaka*, 27 October 1956, 1, 3.

B[omboko], J. M. "Activité du Fonds du Bien-Etre Indigène dans le territoire de Befale." *Mbandaka*, 9 October 1954, 1–2.

Bomboko, J. M. "Expérience Songo en territoire de Befale serait une réussite complete." *Mbandaka*, 21 August 1954, 1.

Bomboko, J. M. "La réorganisation des cours à l'Ecole des infirmiers de Coquilhatville." *Mbandaka*, 9 January 1954, 1–2.

Bomboko, J. M. "Lorsque les Congolais découvrent la Belgique. Impressions générales." *Mbandaka*, 18 June 1955, 3.

Bomboko, J. M. "Lutte contre les maladies vénériennes: Une reforme qui s'impose." *Mbandaka*, 15 October 1954, 1, 3.

Bomboko, J. M. "Nos femmes et le Foyer Social." *Mbandaka*, 10 December 1955, 1, 3.

Bongonda, Boniface. "Losilo." *Le Coq chante* 4 (15 April 1939): 4.

Bontinck, François. *Aux origines de la philosophie bantoue: La correspondance Tempels-Hulstaert, 1944–1948*. Kinshasa: Faculté de Théologie Catholique, 1985.

Bontinck, François. "Les deux Bula Matari." *Etudes Congolaises* 12, no. 3 (July–September 1969): 83–97.

Bouckaert, J. P., and R. Ruel. *Contribution à l'étude de la population du district de la Tshuapa*. Brussels: Institut Royal du Congo belge, 1952.

Boulger, Demetrius. *The Congo State: Or the Growth of Civilisation in Central Africa*. London: W. Thacker and Co., 1898.

Bourdieu, Pierre, et al. *The Weight of the World: Social Suffering in Contemporary Society*. Trans. Priscilla Ferguson, Susan Emanuel, Joe Johnson, and Shoggy Waryn. Stanford, CA: Stanford University Press, 1999.

Branch, Daniel. "Imprisonment and Colonialism in Kenya, c. 1930–1952: Escaping the Carceral Archipelago." *International Journal of African Historical Studies* 38, no. 2 (2005): 239–65.

Brantlinger, Patrick. *Dark Vanishings: Discourse on the Extinction of Primitive Races, 1800–1930*. Ithaca, NY: Cornell University Press, 2003.

Bray, Maryse J., and Agnes Calatayud. "La chanson populaire en France au temps des colonies: De l'insouciance à la contestation." Accessed 15 November 2014. http:// westminsterresearch.wmin.ac.uk/140/1/Bray_2002_final.pdf.

Broch-Due, Vigdis. "Violence and Belonging: Analytical Reflections." In *Violence and Belonging: The Quest for Identity in Post-Colonial Africa*, ed. Vigdis Broch-Due, 1–40. London: Routledge, 2005.

"Brutal Exposure: The Congo." Exhibition at the International Slavery Museum, Liverpool. Accessed 26 March 2015. http://autograph-abp.co.uk/exhibitions/brutal-exposure.

Bustin, Edouard. "Government Policy toward African Cult Movements: A Case Study from Katanga." In *African Dimensions: Essays in Honor of William O. Brown*, ed. Mark Karp, 113–36. New York: Africana/Holmes and Meier, 1975.

Bustin, Edouard. *Lunda under Belgian Rule: The Politics of Ethnicity*. Cambridge, MA: Harvard University Press, 1975.

Caldwell, John, and Pat Caldwell. "The Demographic Evidence for the Incidence and Cause of Abnormally Low Fertility in Tropical Africa." *World Health Statistics Quarterly* 36, no. 1 (1983): 2–34.

Callahan, Bryan. "Syphilis and Civilization: A Social and Cultural History of Sexually Transmitted Disease in Colonial Zambia and Zimbabwe, 1890–1960." Ph.D. diss., Johns Hopkins University, 2002.

Campbell, Hugh. "The Influence of Civilization in the Production of Nervous Exhaustion." In *Nervous Exhaustion and The Diseases Induced by It. . . .* London: Longmans, Green, Reader, and Dyer, 1873.

Canguilhem, Georges. *Knowledge of Life*. Trans. Stefanos Geroulanos and Daniela Ginsburg. New York: Fordham University Press, 2008.

Canguilhem, Georges. "The Living and Its Milieu." In *Knowledge of Life*. Trans. Stefanos Geroulanos and Daniela Ginsburg, 98–120. New York: Fordham University Press, 2008.

Cantor, David, and Edmund Ramsden, eds. *Stress, Shock, and Adaptation in the Twentieth Century*. Rochester, NY: University of Rochester Press, 2014.

Caruth, Cathy. *Unclaimed Experience: Trauma, Narrative, and History*. Baltimore: Johns Hopkins University Press, 1996.

"Causerie sur la natalité par M. Ch. Lodewyckx." *Mbandaka*, 2 June 1951, 2.

Cavin, Andrew. "Encountering Others, Imagining Modernity: Primitivism in German Ethnology, Art, and Theory." Ph.D. diss., University of Michigan, 2014.

Célis, Georges. "Fondeurs et forgerons Ekonda (Equateur, Zaïre)." *Anthropos* 82 (1987): 109–34.

Ceyssens, Rik. "Mutumbula, mythe de l'opprimé." *Cultures et Développement* 7 (1975): 483–550.

Chambers, Michael Margrave. "Basankusu to Ekafera." In "Lomako: A Zairian Journey," 50–74. Spiral bound document, produced by author, Montreal.

Collignon, Armand. *La véritable histoire de Marie aux Léopards*. Paris: Naert, 1933.

Collin, Harry. "The Revival of Belgian International Trade." *Annals of the American Academy* 94 (March 1921): 20–24.

Comhaire, Jean. "Sociétés secrètes et mouvements prophétiques au Congo Belge." *Africa* 25, no. 1 (1955): 54–59.

Comhaire-Sylvain, Suzanne. *Food and Leisure among the African Youth of Leopoldville, Belgian Congo*. Rondebosch: University of Cape Town, 1950.

"Communiqués du Service médical." *Mbandaka*, 21 December 1957, 3–5.

"Conférence sur la dénatalité." *Mbandaka*, 5 November 1949, 2.

Congo Belge, Affaires Economiques, Direction de la Statistique. *Résultats des enquêtes démographiques. Population indigène de la Province de l'Equateur* (August 1959).

Congo Belge, AIMO *Enquêtes Démographiques. District de la Tshuapa*, no. 5 (January 1958).

"Congo Dialogues: Alice Seeley Harris and Sammy Baloji." Exhibition at Rivington Place, London. Accessed 26 March 2015. http://autograph-abp.co.uk/exhibitions /congo-dialogues.

Congo Reform Association. *Evidence Laid before the Congo Commission of Inquiry*. Liverpool: J. Richardson and Sons, 1905.

Congo Reform Association. *The Indictment against the Congo Government*. Boston: Congo Reform Association, [1906].

Congo Reform Association. *Treatment of Women and Children in the Congo State, 1895–1904: An Appeal to the Women of the United States of America*. Boston: Congo Reform Association, 1904.

"Congo Scenes." *Regions Beyond* 29, no. 6 (June 1908): facing 118.

Connolly, William. *Neuropolitics: Thinking, Culture, Speed*. Minneapolis: University of Minnesota Press, 2002.

Conrad, Joseph. *Heart of Darkness*. 3rd ed. New York: Penguin Books, 1999. Originally published in *Youth: A Narrative, and Two Other Stories*, 45–162. London: William Blackwood, 1902.

Conrad, Joseph. "An Outpost of Progress." In *Great Short Works of Joseph Conrad*. New York: Harper and Roe, 1967.

Conran, Terence. "Introduction." In *Bermondsey Riverside: A Brief History to Mark the LDDC's Completion of Its Regeneration Remit*. London: London Docklands Development Corporation, 1997. Accessed 10 April 2015. http://www.lddc-history.org.uk /bermondsey/index.html.

Cooper, Frederick. *Africa since 1940: The Past of the Present*. Cambridge: Cambridge University Press, 2002.

Cooper, Frederick. "Conflict and Connection: Rethinking Colonial African History." *American Historical Review* 99, no. 5 (1994): 1516–45.

Cooper, Frederick, and Ann Stoler, eds. *Tensions of Empire: Colonial Cultures in a Bourgeois World*. Berkeley: University of California Press, 1997.

Coosemans, M. "Shanu (Herzekiah-André)." In *Biographie Coloniale Belge*. Vol. 4, col. 838–39. Brussels: Falk van Campenhout, 1955.

Coquery-Vidrovitch, Catherine, Alain Forest, and Herbert Weiss, eds. *Rébellions-révolution au Zaïre, 1963–1965*. Paris: l'Harmattan, 1987.

Coquilhat, Camille. *Sur le Haut-Congo*. Paris: J. Lebegue, 1888.

Corin, Ellen. "A Possession Psychotherapy in an Urban Setting: Zebola in Kinshasa." *Social Science and Medicine* 13B, no. 4 (1979): 327–38.

Corin, Ellen. "Refiguring the Person: The Dynamics of Affects and Symbols in an African Spirit Possession Cult." In *Bodies and Persons: Comparative Perspectives from Africa and Melanesia*, ed. Michael Lambek and Andrew Strathern, 80–102. Cambridge: Cambridge University Press, 1998.

Corin, Ellen, and Kintenda Ki Mata Ndombasi. *Zebola: Possession et thérapie au Zaïre.* Video recording. Régie nationale des productions éducatives et culturelles, DRC; Centre de recherches pour le développement international, Canada; Institut de recherche scientifique, DRC. 1978.

Cornil, Paul. *Réflexions sur la justice pénale au Congo Belge.* Conference du Jeune Barreau de Bruxelles, 28 February 1953. Nivelles, Belgium: Imprimerie pénitentiaire, 1953.

Cowen, Michael. *Cult of the Will: Nervousness and German Modernity.* University Park: Pennsylvania State University Press, 2008.

Cross, David Kerr. *Health in Africa; a medical handbook for European travellers and residents, embracing a study of malarial fever as it is found in British Central Africa.* London: Nisbet, 1897.

Crowder, Michael. *The Flogging of Phinehas McIntosh: A Tale of Colonial Folly and Injustice: Bechuanaland 1933.* New Haven, CT: Yale University Press, 1988.

Crozier, A. "What Was Tropical about Tropical Neurasthenia? The Utility of the Diagnosis in the Management of British East Africa." *Journal for the History of Medicine and Allied Sciences* 64, no. 4 (2009): 518–48.

Culpin, Millais. "An Examination of Tropical Neurasthenia." *Proceedings of the Royal Society of Medicine* 26, no. 7 (1933): 911–22.

Darwin, Charles. *The Descent of Man.* 2nd ed. London: J. Murray, 1890.

Das, Veena. *Critical Events: An Anthropological Perspective on Contemporary India.* Oxford: Oxford University Press, 1995.

Das, Veena. *Life and Words: Violence and Descent into the Ordinary.* Berkeley: University of California Press, 2007.

Davidson, Basil. *The African Awakening.* London: Jonathan Cape, 1955.

Davidson, Basil. *African Nationalism and the Problems of Nation-Building.* Lagos: Nigerian Institute of International Affairs, 1987.

Davidson, Roger. *Dangerous Liaisons: A Social History of Venereal Disease in Twentieth-Century Scotland.* Amsterdam: Rodopi, 2000.

Daye, Pierre. *L'Empire colonial belge.* Brussels: Editions du "Soir," 1923.

Daye, Pierre. *Trois ans de victoires belges en Afrique.* Brussels: G. Van Oest, 1920.

Daye, Pierre, et al. *Le miroir du Congo belge.* Vol. 1. Brussels: Editions N.E.A., 1929.

De Backer, C. C. "Les femmes congolaises ont fait un grand voyage d'études merveilleux." *Mbandaka*, 13 July 1957, 7.

De Boeck, Filip, and Marie-Françoise Plissart, photographer. *Kinshasa: Tales of the Invisible City.* Tuveren: Musée Royal de l'Afrique Centrale, 2004.

De Craemer, Willy, Jan Vansina, and Renée Fox. "Religious Movements in Central

Africa: A Theoretical Study." *Comparative Studies in Society and History* 18, no. 4 (1976): 458–75.

de Heusch, Luc. "Myth and Epic in Central Africa." In *Religion in Africa: Experience and Expression*, ed. Thomas Blakely, Walter van Beek, and Dennis Thomson, 229–38. London: Heinemann, 1994.

Delathuy, A. M. [Jules Marchal]. *De geheime documentatie van de Onderzoekcommissie in de Kongostaat*. Berchem, Belgium: EPO, 1988.

Delcommune, Alexandre. *L'avenir du Congo belge menacé; Bilan des dix premières années (1909–1918) d'administration coloniale gouvernementale, Le mal—le remède*. 2nd ed. 2 vols. Brussels: Lebègue, 1921.

Delcommune, Alexandre. *Vingt années de vie africaine: récits de voyages, d'aventures et d'exploration au Congo belge, 1874–1893*. 2 vols. Brussels: Larcier, 1922.

Deleuze, Gilles. *Difference and Repetition*. New York: Columbia University Press, 1994.

Deleuze, Gilles. *The Fold: Leibniz and the Baroque*. Trans. Tom Conley. Minneapolis: University of Minnesota Press, 1993.

Dembour, Marie-Benedicte. *Recalling the Belgian Congo: Conversations and Introspection*. New York: Berghahn Books, 2000.

"Départ de M. le docteur Schwers, Médecin provincial." *Mbandaka*, 31 December 1949, 2.

de Rezende, Isabelle. "Visuality and Colonialism in the Congo: From the 'Arab War' to Patrice Lumumba, 1880s to 1961." Ph.D. diss., University of Michigan, 2012.

De Saint Moulin, L. "Histoire de l'organisation administrative du Zaïre." *Zaïre-Afrique*, no. 261 (1992): 29–54.

de Sousa, João, Viktor Müller, Philippe Lemey, and Anne-Mieke Vandamme. "High GUD Incidence in the Early Twentieth Century Created a Particularly Permissive Time Window for the Origin and Initial Spread of Epidemic HIV Strains." *PloS One* 5, no. 4 (2010): e9936.

Deutsch, Karl. *The Nerves of Government: Models of Political Communication and Control*. New York: Free Press, 1966.

Devisch, Renaat. *Weaving the Threads of Life: The Khita Gyn-Eco-Logical Healing Cult among the Yaka*. Chicago: University of Chicago Press, 1993.

Devlin, Larry. *Chief of Station, Congo: Fighting the Cold War in a Hot Zone*. New York: Public Affairs, 2007.

"Distribution d'eau potable à Coq II." *Mbandaka*, 23 April 1955, 4.

DIVA-GIS. *Digital Chart of the World*. Map data set. DIVA-GIS, 1992. "Download data by country." Accessed 5 September 2014. http://diva-gis.org/gdata.

"Documentation sur les pêcheries au Congo belge." Parts 1 and 2. *Bulletin Agricole du Congo Belge* 20, no. 3 (1929): 306–51; 20, no. 4 (1929): 501–30.

"Donneurs de sang." *Mbandaka*, 12 November 1955, 4–5.

Doris, David. *Vigilant Things: On Thieves, Yoruba Anti-aesthetics, and the Strange Fates of Ordinary Objects in Nigeria*. Seattle: University of Washington Press, 2011.

Doyle, Arthur Conan. *The Crime of the Congo*. 4th ed. London: Hutchinson and Co., 1909.

Dupré, Georges. *Un ordre et sa destruction*. Paris: ORSTOM, 1982.

Ekonyo, P. "Bote wa Likili." Trans. and ed. Gustaaf Hulstaert. *Aequatoria* 2, no. 6 (June 1939): 66–71.

Ellis, Stephen. *Season of Rains: Africa in the World*. London: Hurst and Co., 2011.

Engels. "Costermans (Paul-Marie-Adolphe)." In *Biographie coloniale belge*. Vol. 1, col. 268–71. Brussels: Falk van Campenhout, 1948.

"Enseignements d'une révolte des indigènes au Congo belge." *Notre Colonie* 5, no. 17 (16 December 1924): 249–52.

Epstein, Helen. *The Invisible Cure: Africa, the West, and the Fight against AIDS*. New York: Farrar Straus Giroux, 2007.

Esser, Joseph Lazarite. "Terres sans peuple." *Courrier d'Afrique*, 18 April 1945, 1.

"Ethnographies of the Road." Special issue of *Africa* 83, no. 3 (August 2013).

Ezra, Elizabeth. *The Colonial Unconscious: Race and Culture in Interwar France*. Ithaca, NY: Cornell University Press, 2000.

Fabian, Johannes. "Charisma, Cannabis, and Crossing Africa." In *Out of Our Minds: Reason and Madness in the Exploration of Central Africa*, 151–79. Berkeley: University of California Press, 2000.

Fabian, Johannes. *Remembering the Present: Painting and Popular History in Zaire*. Berkeley: University of California Press, 1996.

Fanon, Frantz. "Medicine and Colonialism." In *A Dying Colonialism*, 121–45. New York: Grove Press, 1967.

Fanon, Frantz. *The Wretched of the Earth*. New York: Grove Press, 1965.

Faria, Nuno, et al. "The Early Spread and Epidemic Ignition of HIV-1 in Human Populations." *Science* 346, no. 6205 (2014): 56–61.

Fassin, Didier, and Richard Rectman. *Empire of Trauma*. Trans. Rachel Gomme. Princeton, NJ: Princeton University Press, 2009.

FBEI. "F.B.I.'s Action in the Medico-Social Sphere." Map. No scale given. In *A Work of Co-operation in Development: Fifteen Years' Operation by the Native Welfare Fund in the Congo, Rwanda and Burundi, 1948–1963*, facing 96. Brussels: FBEI, 1964.

FBEI. "F.B.I.'s Areas of Intensive Action." Map. No scale given. In *A Work of Co-operation in Development: Fifteen Years' Operation by the Native Welfare Fund in the Congo, Rwanda and Burundi, 1948–1963*, facing 32. Brussels: FBEI, 1964.

FBEI. *Rapport de gestion et comptes de l'exercice 1949*. Brussels: FBEI, [1950].

FBEI. *Rapport de gestion et comptes de l'exercice de 1950*. Brussels: FBEI, [1951].

FBEI. *Rapport de gestion et comptes de l'exercice 1951*. Brussels: FBEI, [1952].

FBEI. *Rapport de gestion et comptes de l'exercice 1952*. Brussels: FBEI, [1953].

FBEI. *A Work of Co-operation in Development: Fifteen Years' Operation by the Native Welfare Fund in the Congo, Rwanda and Burundi, 1948–1963*. Brussels: FBEI, 1964.

Feierman, Steven. "A Century of Ironies in East Africa (c. 1780–1890)." In *African History: From Earliest Times to Independence*, ed. Philip Curtin, Steven Feierman, Leonard Thompson, and Jan Vansina, 2nd ed., 352–76. Harlow, UK: Longman, 1995.

Feierman, Steven. "Colonizers, Scholars, and the Creation of Invisible Histories." In *Beyond the Cultural Turn: New Directions in the Study of Society and Culture*, ed. Victoria Bonnell and Lynn Hunt, 182–216. Berkeley: University of California Press, 1999.

Feierman, Steven. "Healing as Social Criticism in the Time of Colonial Conquest." *African Studies* 54, no. 1 (1995): 73–88.

Feierman, Steven. *Peasant Intellectuals: Anthropology and History in Tanzania*. Madison: University of Wisconsin Press, 1990.

Feierman, Steven. *The Shambaa Kingdom: A History*. Madison: University of Wisconsin Press, 1974.

Feierman, Steven. "Struggles for Control: The Social Roots of Health and Healing in Modern Africa." *African Studies Review* 28, nos. 2–3 (1985): 73–147.

Feldman-Savelsberg, Pamela. *Plundered Kitchens, Empty Wombs: Threatened Reproduction and Identity in the Cameroon Grassfields*. Ann Arbor: University of Michigan Press, 1999.

Ferguson, James. *Global Shadows: Africa in the Neoliberal World Order*. Durham, NC: Duke University Press, 2006.

Fernandez, James. *Bwiti: An Ethnography of the Religious Imagination in Africa*. Princeton, NJ: Princeton University Press, 1982.

Fields, Karen. *Revival and Rebellion in Colonial Central Africa*. Princeton, NJ: Princeton University Press, 1985.

Fiessinger, Noël. *Endocrinologie*. Paris: Masson et cie, 1935.

Fisher, I. C. "Psychogenic Aspects of Sterility." *Fertility and Sterility* 4, no. 6 (1953): 466–71.

Flamme, J., and Fr. Menger. Untitled map of the Belgian Congo, drawn from documents of the Service cartographique du Ministère des Colonies. 1:5,000,000 [ca. 1935].

Flood, Charles, and William Sherman. "Medical Care in Belgian Congo." *American Journal of Tropical Medicine* 24 (July 1944): 267–71.

Ford, E. S., I. Foreman, J. R. Willson, W. Char, W. T. Mixson, and C. Scholz. "A Psychodynamic Approach to the Study of Infertility." *Fertility and Sterility* 4, no. 6 (1953): 456–65.

Foucault, Michel. *The Birth of Biopolitics: Lectures at the Collège de France, 1978–1979*. Ed. Michel Senellart. Trans. Graham Burchell. Houndsmills, UK: Palgrave Macmillan, 2008.

Foucault, Michel. *The History of Sexuality*. Vol. 1: *The Will to Knowledge*. London: Penguin, 2008.

Foucault, Michel. "Nietzsche, Genealogy, History." In *The Foucault Reader*, ed. Paul Rabinow, 76–100. London: Penguin, 1991.

Foucault, Michel. *Security, Territory, Population: Lectures at the Collège de France 1977–1978*. Trans. Graham Burchell. New York: Picador, 2007.

Foucault, Michel. *Society Must Be Defended: Lectures at the Collège de France 1975–1976*. Trans. David Macey. New York: Picador, 2003.

Foucault, Michel. *Surveiller et punir: Naissance de la prison*. Paris: Gallimard, 1975.

Freud, Sigmund. "Screen Memories." In *The Uncanny*. Trans. David McLintock, 1–22. New York: Penguin, 2003.

Freud, Sigmund. *The Uncanny*. Trans. David McLintock. New York: Penguin Books, 2003.

Gaines, Lewis. "Mental Disturbances and Syphilis." *American Journal of Syphilis, Gonorrhea, and Venereal Diseases* 2 (1918): 474–78.

Gandoulou, J. D. *Au coeur de la Sape: Moeurs et aventures des Congolais à Paris.* Paris: l'Harmattan, 1989.

Geenen, Kristien. "'Sleep Occupies No Space': The Use of Public Space by Street Gangs in Kinshasa." *Africa* 79, no. 3 (2009): 347–68.

Geissler, P. Wenzel, and Catherine Molyneux, eds., *Evidence, Ethos and Experiment: The Anthropology and History of Medical Research in Africa.* Oxford: Berghahn Books, 2011.

Gelissen, Gaston. "Note sur le copal." *Congo* 21 (1940): 273–83.

Gellately, Robert, and Ben Kiernan, eds. *The Specter of Genocide: Mass Murder in Historical Perspective.* Cambridge: Cambridge University Press, 2003.

Genette, Gérard. *Narrative Discourse: An Essay in Method.* Trans. Jane Lewin. Oxford: Basil Blackwell, 1980.

Gérard, A. "Jadot (Joseph-Marie Camille)." In *Biographie belge d'Outre-Mer.* Vol. 8, col. 191–97. Brussels: Académie Royale des Sciences d'Outre-Mer, 1998.

Gérard, Jacques. *Les fondements syncrétiques du Kitawala.* Brussels: CRISP, 1969.

Giblin, James. "The Victimization of Women in Late Precolonial and Early Colonial Warfare in Tanzania." In *Sexual Violence in Conflict Zones: From the Ancient World to the Era of Human Rights,* ed. Elizabeth Heineman, 89–102. Philadelphia: University of Pennsylvania Press, 2011.

Gibson, Mary. "Global Perspectives on the Birth of the Prison." *American Historical Review* 116, no. 4 (October 2011): 1040–63.

Gijswijt-Hofstra, Marijke, and Roy Porter, eds. *Cultures of Neurasthenia from Beard to the First World War.* New York: Rodopi, 2001.

Giles-Vernick, Tamara, Ch. Didier Gondola, Guillaume Lachenal, and William Schneider. "Social History, Biology, and the Emergence of HIV in Colonial Africa." *Journal of African History* 54, no. 1 (2013): 11–30.

Gize, Siketele. "Les racines de la révolte Pende de 1931." *Etudes d'histoire africaine* 5 (1973): 99–153.

Glave, E. J. "New Conditions in Central Africa." *Century Illustrated Monthly Magazine* 53 (April 1897): 900–915.

Glave, E. J. *Six Years of Adventure in Congo-land.* London: Sampson Low, Marston, and Co., 1893.

Goldstein, Donna. *Laughter Out of Place: Race, Class, Violence, and Sexuality in a Rio Shantytown.* Berkeley: University of California Press, 2003.

Goldstein, Kurt. *The Organism: A Holistic Approach to Biology Derived from Pathological Data in Man.* New York: Zone Books, 1995.

Gondola, Ch. Didier. "Dream and Drama: The Search for Elegance among Congolese Youth." *African Studies Review* 42, no. 1 (April 1999): 23–48.

Gondola, Ch. Didier. *The History of Congo.* Westport, CT: Greenwood Press, 2002.

Grant, Kevin. "Christian Critics of Empire: Missionaries, Lantern Lectures, and the Congo Reform Campaign in Britain." *Journal of Imperial and Commonwealth History* 29, no. 2 (2001): 27–58.

Grant, Kevin. *A Civilised Savagery: Britain and the New Slaveries in Africa, 1884–1926*. New York: Routledge, 2005.

Gravet, Catherine, and Pierre Halen. "Littératures viatique et coloniale." In *Littératures belges de langue française: Histoire et perspectives (1830–2000)*, ed. C. Berg and P. Halen, 515–42. Brussels: Le Cri, 2000.

Greene, Graham. *In Search of a Character: Two African Journals*. New York: Viking, 1962.

Grégoire, Eugene. "Les maladies mentales des indigènes." *Le Courrier d'Afrique*, 5 February 1940, 5–6.

Grey Owl. "Arbre." In *Récits de la Cabane Abandonnée (Tales of an Empty Cabin)*. Trans. Jeanne Roche-Mazon, 209–53. Paris: Boivin, 1939.

Grootaers, J. L., and Ineke Eisenburger, eds. *Forms of Wonderment: The History and Collections of the Afrika Museum, Berg en Dal*. Vol. 1. Berg en Dal, Netherlands: Afrika Museum, 2002.

Guha, Ranajit. *Elementary Aspects of Peasant Insurgency in Colonial India*. Delhi: Oxford, 1983.

Guthrie, Malcome, ed. *Lingala Grammar and Dictionary*. [Léopoldville-oest]: Conseil Protestant du Congo, [1935]. (Missing title and copyright pages.)

Guyer, Jane, and Samuel M. Eno Belinga. "Wealth in People as Wealth in Knowledge: Accumulation and Composition in Equatorial Africa." *Journal of African History* 36, no. 1 (1995): 91–120.

Habran, Louis. *Le Congo belge dans la guerre mondiale*. Brussels: Librarie Falk Fils, 1919.

Halen, Pierre. "A propos de Gaston-Genys Périer et de la notion d'art vivant." *Textyles*, no. 20 (2001): 46–56.

Halen, Pierre. *"Le petit Belge avait vu grand": Une littérature coloniale*. Brussels: Labor, 1993.

"Hard Resins." Accessed 11 June 2010. www.fao.org/docrep/v9236e/V9236e07.htm.

Harms, Robert. "The End of Red Rubber: A Reassessment." *Journal of African History* 16 (1975): 125–39.

Harms, Robert. *River of Wealth, River of Sorrow: The Central Zaire Basin in the Era of the Slave and Ivory Trade*. New Haven, CT: Yale University Press, 1981.

Harms, Robert. "The World Abir Made: The Maringa-Lopori Basin, 1885–1903." *African Economic History* 12 (1983): 125–39.

Harris, John. *Dawn in Darkest Africa*. New York: E. P. Dutton, 1912.

Havens, Mary Sue. *Mary Sue's Diary: The Informal Account of Two Weeks' Trail through the Congo Jungle*. Cincinnati, OH: Powell and White, 1927.

Hayward, Rhodri. "Medicine and the Mind." In *The Oxford Handbook of the History of Medicine*, ed. Mark Jackson, 524–42. Oxford: Oxford University Press, 2011.

Heiman, M. "Psychoanalytic Evaluation of the Problem of One-Child Sterility." *Fertility and Sterility* 6, no. 5 (1955): 405–14.

Herbert, Eugenia. *Iron, Gender, and Power: Rituals of Transformation in African Societies*. Bloomington: Indiana University Press, 1993.

Herbst, Jeffrey. *States and Power in Africa: Comparative Lessons in Authority and Control*. Princeton, NJ: Princeton University Press, 2000.

Héritier, Françoise. "Stérilité, aridité, sécheresse: quelques invariants de la pensée symbolique." In *Le sens du mal: Anthropologie, histoire, sociologie de la maladie*, ed. Marc Augé and Claudine Herzlich, 123–54. Paris: Editions des Archives Contemporaines, 1984.

Higginson, John. *A Working Class in the Making: Belgian Colonial Labor Policy, Private Enterprise, and the African Mineworker, 1907–1951*. Madison: University of Wisconsin Press, 1989.

Hill, Robert, and Gregory Pirio. "Africa for the Africans: The Garvey Movement in South Africa, 1920–1940." In *Politics of Race, Class and Nationalism in Twentieth-Century South Africa*, ed. Shula Marks and Stanley Trapido, 209–53. New York: Longman, 1987.

Hobsbawm, Eric. *Primitive Rebels: Studies in Archaic Forms of Social Movement in the 19th and 20th Centuries*. New York: W. W. Norton, 1959.

Hochschild, Adam. *King Leopold's Ghost: A Story of Greed, Terror, and Heroism in Colonial Africa*. Boston: Houghton Mifflin, 1998.

Hodges, Sarah. *Contraception, Colonialism and Commerce*. Aldershot, UK: Ashgate, 2008.

Hodgkin, Thomas. *Nationalism in Colonial Africa*. New York: New York University Press, 1957.

Hoffman, Kasper. "Militarised Bodies and Spirits of Resistance. Armed Governmentalities and the Formation of Militarised Subjectivities in South Kivu/DR Congo: The Case of the Maï-Maï Group of General Padiri." M.A. thesis, Roskilde University, 2007.

Howe, Stephen, ed. *The New Imperial Histories Reader*. London: Routledge, 2009.

Hubin, P., Alexandre Leclercq, and Léon Pirsoul. *Chansons congolaises par trois moustiquaires, dessins de P. R. De Meyer*. Brussels: Eugène Denis, 1922.

Hulstaert, Gustaaf. *Berceuses mongo et formules de numération*. Bandundu: Centre d'Etudes Ethnologiques de Bandundu, 1977.

Hulstaert, Gustaaf. *Chansons de danse mongo*. Bandundu: Centre d'Etudes Ethnologiques de Bandundu, 1982.

Hulstaert, Gustaaf. *Contes d'ogres mongo*. Brussels: Académie Royale des Sciences d'Outre-Mer, 1971.

Hulstaert, Gustaaf. *Dictionnaire Lomóngo-français*. Tervuren: Musée Royal de l'Afrique Centrale, 1957.

Hulstaert, Gustaaf. "La fabrication des cercueils anthropomorphes." Académie Royale des Sciences d'Outre-Mer, *Bulletin des séances* 18, no. 4 (1972): 492–505.

Hulstaert, Gustaaf. *Le jeu des parties du corps: Textes mongo traduits et commentés*. Tervuren: Annales du Royal Museum of Central Africa, 1971.

Hulstaert, Gustaaf. *Le mariage des Nkundo*. Brussels: Falk, Van Campenhout, 1938.

Hulstaert, Gustaaf. "Le problème des mulâtres." Parts 1 and 2. *Africa* 15 (1945): 129–44; 16 (1946): 39–44.

Hulstaert, Gustaaf. "Les idées religieuses des Nkundo." *Congo* 17, no. 2 (1936): 668–76.

Hulstaert, Gustaaf. "Le voyage au Congo d'un officier danois: Notes et commentaires sur le séjour à l'Equateur de Knud Jespersen (1898–1908)." *Enquêtes et Documents d'histoire africaine* 4 (1980).

Hulstaert, Gustaaf. "Marie aux Léopards (quelques souvenirs historiques)." *Annales Aequatoria* 11 (1990): 433–35.

Hulstaert, Gustaaf. Notes in Dutch. In "Bote wa Likili," by P. Ekonyo. *Aequatoria* 2, no. 6 (June 1939): 68–71.

Hulstaert, Gustaaf. "Notes sur la Ybola." Annex in *Petit lexique des croyances magiques Mongo*, 91–124. Bandundu: Centre d'Etudes Ethnologiques de Bandundu Publications, 1981.

Hulstaert, Gustaaf. *Petit lexique des croyances magiques Mongo*. Bandundu: Centre d'études ethnologiques de Bandundu Publications, 1981.

Hulstaert, Gustaaf. *Poèmes mongo modernes: recueillis, traduits et annotés*. Brussels: Académie Royale des Sciences d'Outre-Mer, 1972.

Hunt, Nancy. "An Acoustic Register: Rape and Repetition in Congo." In *Imperial Debris: On Ruins and Ruination*, ed. Ann Stoler, 39–66. Durham, NC: Duke University Press, 2013.

Hunt, Nancy. "The Affective, the Intellectual, and Gender History," *Journal of African History* 55 (2014): 331–45.

Hunt, Nancy. "Between Fiction and History: Modes of Writing Abortion in Africa." *Cahiers d'Etudes Africaines* 47, no. 186 (June 2007): 277–312.

Hunt, Nancy. "Bicycles, Birth Certificates, and Clysters: Colonial Objects as Reproductive Debris in Mobutu's Zaire." In *Commodification: Things, Agency, and Identities*, ed. Wim van Binsbergen and Peter Geschiere, 123–42. Münster: Lit Verlag, 2005.

Hunt, Nancy. *A Colonial Lexicon: Of Birth Ritual, Medicalization, and Mobility in Colonial Congo*. Durham, NC: Duke University Press, 1999.

Hunt, Nancy. "Colonial Medical Anthropology and the Making of the Central African Infertility Belt." In *Ordering Africa: Anthropology, European Imperialism, and the Politics of Knowledge*, ed. Helen Tilley with Robert Gordon, 252–81. Manchester, UK: Manchester University Press, 2007.

Hunt, Nancy. "Espace, temporalité et rêverie: Ecrire l'histoire des futurs au Congo belge." *Politique africaine*, no. 135 (October 2014): 115–36.

Hunt, Nancy. "Fertility's Fires and Empty Wombs in Recent Africanist Writing." *Africa* 75, no. 3 (2005): 421–35.

Hunt, Nancy. "Health and Healing." In *Oxford Handbook of Modern African History*, ed. John Parker and Richard Reid, 378–95. Oxford: Oxford University Press, 2013.

Hunt, Nancy. "'Le bébé en brousse': European Women, African Birth Spacing and Colonial Intervention in Breast Feeding in the Belgian Congo." *International Journal of African Historical Studies* 21, no. 3 (1988): 401–32.

Hunt, Nancy. "Letter-Writing, Nursing Men, and Bicycles in the Belgian Congo: Notes towards the Social Identity of a Colonial Category." In *Paths toward the Past: African Historical Essays in Honor of Jan Vansina*, ed. Robert Harms, Joseph Miller, David Newbury, and Michele Wagner, 187–210. Atlanta: African Studies Association Press, 1994.

Hunt, Nancy. "Noise over Camouflaged Polygamy, Colonial Morality Taxation, and a Woman-Naming Crisis in Belgian Africa." *Journal of African History* 32, no. 3 (1991): 471–94.

Hunt, Nancy. "Rewriting the Soul in a Flemish Congo." *Past and Present*, no. 198 (February 2008): 185–215.

Hunt, Nancy. "STDs, Suffering, and Their Derivatives in Congo-Zaire: Notes towards an Historical Ethnography of Disease." In *Vivre et penser le sida en Afrique/ Experiencing and Understanding AIDS in Africa*, ed. Charles Becker, Jean-Pierre Dozon, Christine Obbo, and Moriba Touré, 111–31. Paris: Karthala, 1999.

Hunt, Nancy. *Suturing New Medical Histories of Africa*. Carl Schlettwein Lectures, no. 7. Zurich: Lit Verlag, 2013.

Hunt, Nancy. "Tintin and the Interruptions of Congolese Comics." In *Images and Empires: Visuality in Colonial and Postcolonial Africa*, ed. Paul S. Landau and Deborah Kaspin, 90–123. Berkeley: University of California Press, 2002.

Hutchinson, Walter, ed. *Customs of the World*. Vol. 1. London: Hutchinson and Co., 1913.

Ilanga, R. "Les 'Coquins' sont-ils contents de leurs bars?" *Mbandaka*, 9 October 1954, 3.

Inhorn, Maria, and Frank Balen, eds. *Infertility around the Globe: New Thinking on Childlessness, Gender, and Reproductive Technologies*. Berkeley: University of California Press, 2002.

Institut Géographique du Congo Belge. *Carte administrative et politique de la Province de l'Equateur*. Map. 1:1,000,000. Edition provisoire. Institut Géographique du Congo belge, 1955.

Iyandza-Lopoloko, Joseph. *Bobongo, danse renommée des Ekonda du Lac Léopold II, une institution parascolaire*. Tervuren: Musee Royal de l'Afrique Centrale, 1961.

Jackson, Mark. *The Age of Stress: Science and the Search for Stability*. Oxford: Oxford University Press, 2013.

Jadot, Joseph-Marie. *Apéritifs*. Brussels: Expansion Coloniale, 1934.

Jadot, Joseph-Marie. "La Charge (Mambamu)." In *Sous les manguiers en fleurs: Histoires des Bantous*, 57–65. Paris: Editions de Belles Lettres, 1922.

Jadot, Joseph-Marie. "La légende d'Inongo." In *Poèmes d'ici et de là-bas*, 111–15. Namur: Godenne, 1914.

Jadot, Joseph-Marie. "La Province de L'Equateur." In *Le Miroir du Congo belge*, ed. Pierre Daye et al., vol. 1, 53–120. Brussels: Editions N.E.A., 1929.

Jadot, Joseph-Marie. *La Province Equatoriale du Congo belge*. Conférence donnée aux étudiants de l'Université Coloniale d'Anvers le 3 mai 1926. Brussels: L'Essor Colonial et Maritime, [ca. 1926].

Jadot, Joseph-Marie. "Le Campement." In *Sous les manguiers en fleurs: Histoires des Bantous*, 107–51. Paris: Editions de Belles Lettres, 1922.

Jadot, Joseph-Marie. "Le droit de métis au Congo Belge." In *Congrès International pour l'Etude des problèmes résultant du mélange des races. 11 et 12 octobre 1935*, 45–49, 121–22. Brussels: Exposition internationale et universelle de Bruxelles, 1935.

Jadot, Joseph-Marie. "Marie aux Léopards." In *Sous les manguiers en fleurs: Histoires des Bantous*, 177–224. Paris: Editions de Belles Lettres, 1922.

Jadot, Joseph-Marie. *Nous—en Afrique*. Brussels: Revue Sincère, 1926.

Jadot, Joseph-Marie. *Poèmes d'ici et de là-bas*. Namur: Godenne, 1914.

Jadot, Joseph-Marie. *Sous les manguiers en fleurs: Histoires des Bantous*. Paris: Editions de Belles Lettres, 1922.

Jadot, Joseph-Marie. *Trois contes de l'Afrique en guerre*. Brazzaville: Imprimerie française, 1916.

Janzen, John. *Lemba, 1650–1930: A Drum of Affliction in Africa and the New World*. New York: Garland Publishing, 1982.

Janzen, John. *The Quest for Therapy: Medical Pluralism in Lower Zaire*. Berkeley: University of California Press, 1982.

Jeurissen, Lissia. "Colonisation et 'question des mulâtres' au Congo Belge. Joseph-Marie Jadot (1886–1967)." In *Figures et paradoxes de l'histoire au Burundi, au Congo et au Rwanda*, ed. Marc Quaghebeur, Jean-Claude Kangomba, and Amélie Schmitz, 82–104. Paris: l'Harmattan, 2002.

Jeurissen, Lissia. *Quand le métis s'appelait "mulâtre": Société, droit et pouvoir coloniaux face à la descendance des couples eurafricains dans l'ancien Congo belge*. Louvain-la-Neuve: Academia Bruylant, 2003.

Jewsiewicki, Bogumil. *Cheri Samba: The Hybridity of Art*. Quebec: Galerie Amrad African Art Publications, 1995.

Jewsiewicki, Bogumil. "La contestation sociale et la naissance du prolétariat au Zaïre au cours de la première moitié du XXe siècle." *Canadian Journal of African Studies* 10 (1976): 47–71.

Jewsiewicki, Bogumil. "Le colonat agricole européen au Congo belge, 1910–1960." *Journal of African History* 20, no. 4 (1979): 559–71.

Jewsiewicki, Bogumil, and Mumbanza Mwa Bawele. "The Social Context of Slavery in Equatorial Africa during the 19th and 20th Centuries." In *The Ideology of Slavery in Africa*, ed. Paul Lovejoy, 73–98. Beverly Hills, CA: Sage, 1981.

Jochelson, Karen. *The Colour of Disease: Syphilis and Racism in South Africa, 1880–1950*. New York: Palgrave, 2001.

John, Mary, and Janaki Nair, eds. *A Question of Silence?: The Sexual Economies of Modern India*. London: Zed Books, 2000.

Johnston, Harry. *George Grenfell and the Congo*. Vol. 2. London: Hutchinson and Co., 1908.

Johnston, Lillian. "Bring Out Your Rubber." *World Call* (January 1935): 28.

Kaes, Anton. *Shell Shock Cinema: Weimar Culture and the Wounds of War*. Princeton, NJ: Princeton University Press, 2009.

Kanimba, Misago, and Charles Lonkama. "Un chant njondo des environs de Bokuma." *Annales Aequatoria* 16 (1995): 175–81.

Kielmann, Karina. "Barren Ground: Contesting Identities of Infertile Women in Pemba, Tanzania," in *Pragmatic Women and Body Politics*, ed. Margaret Lock and Patricia Kaufert, 127–63. Cambridge: Cambridge University Press, 1998.

Killen, Andreas. *Berlin Electropolis: Shock, Nerves, and German Modernity.* Berkeley: University of California Press, 2006.

Kisangani, Emizet François, and F. Scott Bobb. "Bomboko Lokumba Is Elenge, Justin-Marie (1928–)." In *Historical Dictionary of the Democratic Republic of the Congo,* 3rd ed., 57. Lanham, MD: Scarecrow Press, 2010.

Kivits, M. "Hoof (Van) (Lucien-Marie-Joseph-Jean)." In *Biographie belge d'Outre-Mer.* Vol. 6, col. 503–6. Brussels: Académie Royale des Sciences d'Outre-Mer, 1968.

Kleinman, Arthur, Veena Das, and Margaret Lock, eds. *Social Suffering.* Berkeley: University of California Press, 1997.

Kodesh, Neil. *Beyond the Royal Gaze: Clanship and Public Healing in Buganda.* Charlottesville: University of Virginia Press, 2010.

Korber, B., et al. "Timing the Ancestor of the HIV-1 Pandemic Strains." *Science* 288, no. 547 (9 July 2000): 1789–96.

Korse, Piet, Lokonga Mondjulu, and Bonje wa Mpay Bongondo. *Jebola: Textes, rites et signification: Thérapie traditionnelle mongo.* Bamanya: Centre Aequatoria, 1990.

Koschorke, Albrecht. "Figures/Figurations of the Third." Accessed 10 April 2011. http://www.uni-konstanz.de/figur3/prg3.htm.

Koselleck, Reinhart. *Futures Past: On the Semantics of Historical Time.* Trans. Keith Tribe. New York: Columbia University Press, 2004.

Koselleck, Reinhart. "The Historical-Political Semantics of Asymmetric Counterconcepts." In *Futures Past: On the Semantics of Historical Time.* Trans. Keith Tribe, 155–91. New York: Columbia University Press, 2004.

Koselleck, Reinhart. "Space of Experience and Horizon of Expectation: Two Historical Categories." In *Futures Past: On the Semantics of Historical Time.* Trans. Keith Tribe, 255–76. New York: Columbia University Press, 2004.

Kracauer, Siegfried. *The Mass Ornament: Weimar Essays.* Cambridge, MA: Harvard University Press, 1995.

Kracauer, Siegfried. *The Salaried Masses: Duty and Distraction in Weimar Germany.* Trans. Quintin Hoare. London: Verso, 1998.

LaCapra, Dominick. *Writing History, Writing Trauma.* Baltimore: Johns Hopkins University Press, 2001.

Lachenal, Guillaume. *Le médicament qui devait sauver l'Afrique.* Paris: La découverte, 2014.

"L'action médicale dans la province de l'Equateur." *Mbandaka,* 27 August 1949, 1.

LaFontaine, Jean. "The Free Women of Kinshasa: Prostitution in a City in Zaire." In *Choice and Change: Essays in Honor of Lucy Mair,* ed. J. Davis, 89–113. London: Althlone, 1974.

"La gomme-copal au Congo." *Mouvement Géographique,* 26 October 1911, col. 612.

Lakoff, Andrew, and Stephen Collier, eds. *Biosecurity Interventions: Global Health and Security in Question.* New York: Columbia University Press, 2008.

Langbehn, Volker, and Mohammad Salama, eds. *German Colonialism: Race, the Holocaust, and Postwar Germany.* New York: Columbia University Press, 2011.

Langwick, Stacey. *Bodies, Politics, and African Healing: The Matter of Maladies in Tanzania.* Bloomington: Indiana University Press, 2011.

Larssen, Ulla. "Primary and Secondary Infertility in Sub-Saharan Africa." *International Journal of Epidemiology* 29, no. 2 (2000): 285–91.

"L'assassin de la sentinelle de M. Lemos est condamné à mort." *Mbandaka*, 8 January 1955, 1.

Last, Murray. "The Importance of Knowing about Not Knowing." In *On Knowing and Not Knowing in the Anthropology of Medicine*, ed. Ronald Littlewood, 1–17. Walnut Creek, CA: Left Coast Press, 2007.

Laudati, Ann. "Out of the Shadows: Negotiations and Networks in the Cannabis Trade in Eastern Democratic Republic of Congo." In *Drugs in Africa: Histories and Ethnographies of Use, Trade, and Control*, ed. Gernot Klantschnig, Neil Carrier, and Charles Ambler, 161–82. New York: Palgrave Macmillan, 2014.

Lauro, Amandine. *Coloniaux, ménagères et prostituées au Congo belge, 1885–1930*. Loverval: Labor, 2005.

Lechat, Michel. "Diary." *London Review of Books* 29, no. 15 (2 August 2007): 34–35.

"Le commerce du Congo belge." *Mouvement géographique*, 2 February 1919, cols. 50–52.

Ledent, H., and D. H. Baker, "La dépopulation chez les Nkundo," *Recueil de Travaux de science médicales au Congo belge*, no. 2 (January 1944): 130–41.

Lee, Richard. "The Extinction of Races." *Journal of the Anthropological Society of London* 2 (1964): xcv–xcix.

Lejeune, L. "Joseph-Marie Jadot," in *La femme noire vue par les écrivains africanistes*. Brussels: Académie Royale des Sciences d'Outre-Mer, 1967.

"Le problème démographique au Congo belge." *Courrier d'Afrique*, 26 August 1945, 1.

Lerner, Paul. *Hysterical Men: War, Psychiatry, and the Politics of Trauma in Germany, 1890–1930*. Ithaca, NY: Cornell University Press, 2003.

Le Romain, Jean-Baptiste-Pierre. "Negroes." In *The Encyclopedia of Diderot and d'Alembert Collaborative Translation Project*, trans. Pamela Cheek, n.p. Ann Arbor: MPublishing, University of Michigan Library, 2003. Accessed 15 July 2014. http://hdl.handle.net/2027/spo.did2222.0000.029. Originally published as "Nègres," *Encyclopédie ou dictionnaire raisonné des sciences, des arts et des métiers* 11 (1765): 80–83.

"L'erreur des pseudo-évolués: Le tape-à-l'oeil," *Mbandaka*, 26 May 1956, 1 and 3.

"Les maladies véneriennes." *Mbandaka*, 9 February 1957, 1.

Levine, Phillippa. *Prostitution, Race and Politics: Policing Venereal Disease in the British Empire*. New York: Routledge, 2003.

Lewono, Lufungula. "Execution des mesures prises contre les sujets ennemis pendant la second guerre mondiale dans le région de l'Equateur." *Annales Aequatoria* 9 (1988): 219–31.

L'Exposition universelle et internationale de Liège. *Notice sur L'Etat Indépendant du Congo*. Brussels: Imprimerie veuve Monnom, 1905.

Leyder, Jean. "Jadot (Joseph-Marie)." In *Le graphisme et l'expression graphique au Congo belge*, 47. Brussels: Société royale belge de géographie, 1950.

Liebrichts, Ch. *Congo: Léopoldville, Bolobo, Equateur (1883–1889)*. Brussels: J. Lebèque, 1909.

Likaka, Osumaka. *Naming Colonialism: History and Collective Memory in the Congo, 1870–1960*. Madison: University of Wisconsin Press, 2009.

Likaka, Osumaka. *Rural Society and Cotton in Colonial Zaire*. Madison: University of Wisconsin Press, 1997.

Linder, Ulrike, et al., eds. *Hybrid Cultures—Nervous States: Britain and Germany in a (Post)colonial World*. Amsterdam: Rodopi, 2010.

Lindqvist, Sven. *"Exterminate All the Brutes."* Trans. Jean Tate. New York: New Press, 1996.

Livingston, Julie. *Debility and the Moral Imagination in Botswana*. Bloomington: Indiana University Press, 2005.

Lock, Margaret, and Vinh-Kim Nguyen. *An Anthropology of Biomedicine*. Chichester, UK: Wiley-Blackwell, 2010.

Lodewyckx, Charles. "Encore la dénatalité." *Aequatoria* 14 (1951): 131–35.

Lodewyckx, Charles. "Est-il possible de relever la natalité nkundo?" *Aequatoria* 11 (1948): 1–5.

Lomboto, Sébastien. "Territoire de Bomongo: Carence du service médical." *Mbandaka*, 23 October 1954, 6.

Lorimer, Frank. "General Theory." Part 1 in *Culture and Human Fertility: A Study of the Relation of Cultural Conditions to Fertility in Non-Industrial and Transitional Societies*, 13–251. Paris: UNESCO, 1954.

"Losilo." *Le Coq chante* (15 August 1937): n.p.

Louwers, Octave. *Codes et Lois du Congo belge*. Brussels: M. Weissenbruch, 1914.

Lumumba, Patrice. "Speech on June 30, 1960, Independence Day." In *Teacher's Guide: A Congo Chronicle: Patrice Lumumba in Urban Art*, by Nathanial Johnson and Dana Elmquist with Bogumil Jewsiewicki, 29–32. New York: Museum for African Art, 2008.

Lutz, Tom. *American Nervousness, 1903: An Anecdotal History*. Ithaca, NY: Cornell University Press, 1991.

Luys, Georges. *A Text-Book on Gonorrhea and Its Complications*. New York: William Wood, 1913.

Lyons, Maryinez. *The Colonial Disease: A Social History of Sleeping Sickness in Northern Zaire, 1900–1940*. Cambridge: Cambridge University Press, 1992.

MacGaffey, Janet, and Rémy Bazenguissa-Ganga. *Congo-Paris: Transnational Traders on the Margins of the Law*. Bloomington: Indiana University Press, 2000.

Mamdani, Mahmood. *Citizen and Subject: Contemporary Africa and the Legacy of Late Colonialism*. Princeton, NJ: Princeton University, 1996.

Mann, Gregory. *Native Sons: West African Veterans and France in the Twentieth Century*. Durham, NC: Duke University Press, 2006.

Map of Franco-British Conquest of German Cameroon 1916. Map. The New Society for the Diffusion of Knowledge.

Marchal, Jules. *E. D. Morel contre Léopold II*. Paris: l'Harmattan, 1996.

Marchal, Jules. *Lord Leverhulme's Ghosts: Colonial Exploitation in the Congo*. Trans. Martin Thom. London: Verso, 2008.

Marechal, Philippe. "La controverse sur Léopold II et le Congo dans la littérature et les médias: Réflexions critiques." In *La Mémoire du Congo: Le temps colonial*, ed. Jean-Luc Vellut, 43–50. Ghent: Editions Snoeck, 2005.

Marrati, Paula, and Todd Meyers. "Forward: Life, as Such." In *Knowledge of Life*, ed. Georges Canguilhem, vii–xii. New York: Fordham University Press, 2008.

Marsh, Margaret, and Wanda Ronner. *The Empty Cradle: Infertility in America from Colonial Times to the Present*. Baltimore: Johns Hopkins University Press, 1996.

Martin, Phyllis. "Contesting Clothes in Colonial Brazzaville." *Journal of African History* 35, no. 3 (1994): 423–26.

Massey, Doreen. "Space-Time, 'Science' and the Relationship between Physical Geography and Human Geography." *Transactions of the Institute of British Geographers* 24, no. 3 (1999): 261–76.

Mastriaux, Robert. *La Femme et le destin de l'Afrique: les sources psychologiques de la mentalité dite "primitive."* Elisabethville: Centre d'Etude des Problèmes Sociaux Indigènes, 1964.

May, Jon, and Nigel Thrift, eds. *TimeSpace: Geographies of Temporality*. New York: Routledge, 2001.

Mbambi, Mbasani. "Simon-Pierre Mpadi-Etude biographique." *Cahiers des religions africaines* 15, no. 29 (January 1981): 103–25.

Mbembe, Achille. *On the Postcolony*. Berkeley: University of California Press, 2001.

Medvei, Victor. *The History of Clinical Endocrinology: A Comprehensive Account of Endocrinology from Earliest Times to the Present Day*. Carnforth, UK: Parthenon, 1993.

Meeuwis, Michael. "Tiny Bouts of Contentment: Rare Film Footage of Graham Greene in the Belgian Congo, March 1959." *Rosenberg Quarterly*, 8 December 2013. Accessed 17 May 2015. http://rozenbergquarterly.com/tiny-bouts-of-contentment-rare-film-footage-of-graham-greene-in-the-belgian-congo-march-1959/.

Merlier, Michel [Auguste Maurel]. *Le Congo de la colonisation belge à l'indépendance*. Paris: Maspero, 1962.

Mobe, A. M. "Pour la garde de nos maladies à l'hôpital." *Mbandaka*, 20 June 1953, 3.

Molifa, Fermin. "A Stanleyville: Primes de natalité." *Le Progrès*, 12 May 1949, 2.

Monaville, Pedro. "Decolonizing the University: Postal Politics, the Student Movement, and Global 1968 in the Congo." Ph.D. diss., University of Michigan, 2013.

Mooij, Annet. *Out of Otherness: Characters and Narrators in the Dutch Venereal Disease Debates, 1850–1990*. Trans. Beverley Jackson. Amsterdam: Rodopi, 1998.

Morel, E. D. *King Leopold's Rule in Africa*. London: William Heinemann, 1904.

Morel, E. D. *Red Rubber: The Story of the Rubber Slave Trade Flourishing on the Congo in the Year of Grace 1907*. 4th ed., 5th impression. London: T. Fisher Unwin, 1907.

Morimont, Françoise. "H. A. Shanu: photographe, agent de l'Etat et commerçant africain (1858–1905)." In *La Mémoire du Congo* in *La Mémoire du Congo: le temps colonial*, ed. Jean-Luc Vellut, 213–17. Ghent: Editions Snoeck, 2005.

Moses, A. Dirk, ed. *Empire, Colony, Genocide: Conquest, Occupation, and Subaltern Resistance in World History*. New York: Berghahn Books, 2008.

Mottoulle, Léopold. *Le problème de la main-d'oeuvre au Congo belge: rapport de la Commission de la main-d'oeuvre indigène 1930–1931: Province de l'Equateur.* Brussels: A. Lesigne, 1931.

Mountmorres, Viscount. *The Congo Independent State: A Report on a Voyage of Enquiry.* London: Williams and Norgate, 1906.

"Movements and the War." *Geographical Review* 1 (March 1916): 209–10.

Mrázek, Rudolf. *Engineers of Happy Land: Technology and Nationalism in a Colony.* Princeton, NJ: Princeton University Press, 2002.

Mudaba, Yoka Lye. "Bobongo: La danse sacrée et la libération." *Cahiers des religions africaines* 16, nos. 31–32 (1982): 277–91.

Mudimbe, V. Y. *Tales of Faith: Religion as Political Performance in Central Africa.* London: Athlone Press, 1997.

Mus, G. *L'établissement pénitentiaire de Jadotville.* Jadotville: L'établissement pénitentiaire, 1954.

Mwene-Batende. *Mouvements messianiques et protestation sociale. Le cas du Kitawala chez les Kumu du Zaïre.* Kinshasa: Faculté de Théologie Catholique, 1982.

Natural Earth. Version 2.0. Map data set. North American Cartographic Information Society, 2012. Accessed 18 June 2013. http://www.naturalearthdata.com.

N'Djoku, Eugène. "Grave plaie de l'Equateur: le dépeuplement des Mongo." *La Voix du Congolais* x, no. 1 (January 1954): 244–54.

N.d.l.R. "Le point de vue de nos abonnés. A propos des associations de femmes." *Mbandaka,* 11 December 1954, 4.

Neill, Deborah. *Networks in Tropical Medicine: Internationalism, Colonialism, and the Rise of a Medical Specialty, 1890–1930.* Stanford, CA: Stanford University Press, 2012.

Nelson, Samuel. "Colonialism, Capitalism, and Work in the Congo Basin: A History of Social Change in the Tshuapa Region, 1880s to 1940." Ph.D. diss., Stanford University, 1986.

Nelson, Samuel. *Colonialism in the Congo Basin, 1880–1940.* Athens: Ohio University Center for International Studies, 1994.

Nelson, Samuel. "Congo Basin Showing Areas Influenced by the Atlantic Slave Trade and Zanzibari Traders." Map. No scale given. In *Colonialism in the Congo Basin, 1880–1940,* 47, fig. 4. Athens: Ohio University Center for International Studies, 1994.

Nelson, Samuel. "Inner Congo Basin Showing Concession Zones, c. 1902." Map (ca. 0.75 in = 100 mi). In *Colonialism in the Congo Basin, 1880–1940,* 88, fig. 6. Athens: Ohio University Center for International Studies, 1994.

Nguyen, Vinh-Kim. "Government-by-Exception: Enrolment and Experimentality in Mass HIV Treatment Programmes in Africa." *Social Theory and Health* 7 (2009): 196–217.

Nguyen, Vinh-Kim. *The Republic of Therapy: Triage and Sovereignty in West Africa's Time of AIDS.* Durham, NC: Duke University Press, 2010.

Nietzsche, Friedrich. *On the Advantage and Disadvantage of History for Life: Part II of Thoughts out of Season.* Trans. Peter Preuss. Indianapolis: Hackett, 1980.

Nietzsche, Friedrich. "The Use and Abuse of History." In *The Untimely Meditations*

(Thoughts out of Season Parts I and II), trans. Anthony Ludovici and Adrian Collins, 96–134. [New York]: Digireads, 2009.

Nina. "Propagande pronatale de M. Charles Lodewyckx." *Mbandaka*, 5 October 1952, 1.

Nkana, Georges-Roger. "Autour des associations féminines à Coq." *Mbandaka*, 1 February 1958, 1, 3.

Nkana, Georges-Roger. "Les bars du C.E.C. Coq." *Mbandaka*, 14 December 1957, 6.

"Notre reportage photographique sur la dernière exposition organisée au Foyer Social de Coquilhatville." *Mbandaka*, 24 December 1955, 4–5.

"Nouvelles de Coquilhatville." *Mbandaka*, 13 January 1951, 1.

Ntefo. "La polygamie camouflée au Centre Extra-Coutumier." *Mbandaka*, 26 May 1956, 1, 3.

Nuttall, Sarah. "Introduction: Rethinking Beauty." In *Beautiful/Ugly: African and Diaspora Aesthetics*, ed. Sarah Nuttall, 6–29. Durham, NC: Duke University Press, 2006.

Nzongola-Ntalaja, Georges, ed., *The Crisis in Zaire: Myths and Realities*. Trenton, NJ: World Africa Press, 1986.

Observateur [J. M. Bomboko]. "Associations de femmes congolaises au C.E.C. de Coquilhatville." *Mbandaka*, 11 September 1954, 2.

Onyanga-Omara, Jane. "Grey Owl: Canada's Great Conservationist and Imposter." BBC News, 9 September 2013. Accessed 14 July 2014. http://www.bbc.com/news/uk-england-sussex-24127514.

Oppenheim, Janet. *Shattered Nerves: Doctors, Patients, and Depression in Victorian England*. New York: Oxford University Press, 1991.

Oriel, J. D., and G. L. Ridgeway. *Genital Infection by Chlamydia trachomatis*. New York: Elsevier Biomedical, 1983.

Paris, Alexandre. *Leçons de psychiatrie, caractères de dégénérescence et aliénations mentales*. Paris: Maloine, 1909. [Cited in Jadot, "Marie aux Léopards," 208.]

Paulus, Jean-Pierre. "Le Kitawala au Congo belge." *Revue de l'Institut de Sociologie*, nos. 2–3 (1956).

Peemans, Jean-Philippe. *Le Congo-Zaire au gré du XXe siècle: Etat, économie, société, 1880–1990*. Paris: l'Harmattan, 1997.

Pépin, Jacques. *The Origins of AIDS*. Cambridge: Cambridge University Press, 2011.

Perham, Margery. *African Apprenticeship: An Autobiographical Journey*. New York: Africana Publishing Company, 1974.

Périer, Gaston-Denys. *Notes de littérature coloniale*. Brussels: A. Dewit, 1930.

Petrides, Constantine. "A Figure for *Cibola*: Art, Politics, and Aesthetics among the Luluwa People of the Democratic Republic of the Congo." *Metropolitan Museum Journal* 36 (2001): 235–58.

Pfeffer, Naomi. *The Stork and the Syringe: A Political History of Reproductive Medicine*. Cambridge: Polity Press, 1993.

Pick, Daniel. *Faces of Degeneration: A European Disorder, c. 1848–c. 1918*. Cambridge: Cambridge University Press, 1989.

Pistor, Dominic. "Developmental Colonialism and Kitawala Policy in 1950s Belgian Congo." M.A. thesis, Simon Fraser University, 2012.

Plancke, Carine. "On Dancing and Fishing: Joy and Celebration of Fertility among the Puna of Congo-Brazzaville." *Africa* 80, no. 4 (November 2010): 620–41.

"Polygamie et dénatalité." *Courrier d'Afrique*, 16 October 1945, n.p.

Possoz, E. "Essai d'interprétation des épreuves superstitieuses dans l'Equateur." *Aequatoria* 1, no. 5 (1938).

"Programme pro-natale." *Mbandaka*, 24 September 1949, 3.

"Propagande pro-natale." *Mbandaka*, 26 November 1949, 2.

Pynaert, L. "Le copal et son exploitation au Congo belge." *Bulletin Agricole du Congo Belge* 15, no. 2 (1924): 334–59.

Pype, Katrien. "Fighting Boys, Strong Men and Gorillas: Notes on the Imagination of Masculinities in Kinshasa." *Africa* 77, no. 2 (2007): 264–66.

"Quand les Congolais voyagent par avion." *Mbandaka*, 8 January 1955, 3.

"Quelles sont les preférénces des Congolais en ce qui concerne la musique." *Mbandaka*, 8 January 1955, 3.

Quine, Maria. *Population Politics in Twentieth-Century Europe: Fascist Dictatorships and Liberal Democracies*. London: Routledge, 1996.

Radkau, Joachim. *Max Weber: A Biography*. Trans. Patrick Camiller. Cambridge, UK: Polity Press, 2009.

Rafael, Vicente, ed. *Figures of Criminality in Indonesia, the Philippines, and Colonial Vietnam*. Ithaca, NY: Cornell Southeast Asia Program, 1999.

Rancière, Jacques. *Althusser's Lesson*. Trans. Emiliano Battista. London: Continuum, 2011.

Ranger, Terence. *Dance and Society in Eastern Africa, 1890–1970: The Beni Ngoma*. Berkeley: University of California Press, 1975.

Ranger, Terence. "The Mwana Lesa Movement of 1925." In *Themes in the Christian History of Central Africa*, ed. T. O. Ranger and John Weller, 45–75. Berkeley: University of California Press, 1975.

Ranger, Terence. "Religious Movements and Politics in Sub-Saharan Africa." *African Studies Review* 29, no. 2 (June 1986): 1–70.

"Rapport au Roi-Souverain." *Bulletin Officiel de l'Etat Indépendant du Congo* 21, nos. 9–10 (September–October 1905): 133–285.

Rathbone, Richard. "World War I and Africa: Introduction." *Journal of African History* 19 (1978): 1–9.

Redfield, Peter. "Foucault in the Tropics: Displacing the Panopticon." In *Anthropologies of Modernity: Foucault, Governmentality, and Life Politics*, ed. Jonathan Inda, 50–82. Malden, MA: Blackwell, 2005.

Redfield, Peter. *Space in the Tropics: Convicts to Rockets in French Guiana*. Berkeley: University of California Press, 2000.

Regine. "Conseils à une jeune maman." *Mbandaka*, 29 June 1957, 7.

Reid, Fiona. *Broken Men: Shell Shock, Treatment and Recovery in Britain, 1914–1930*. London: Continuum, 2010.

Renne, Elisha. "'Cleaning the Inside' and Regulation of Menstruation in Southwestern Nigeria." In *Regulating Menstruation: Beliefs, Practices, Interpretations*, ed. Etienne van de Walle and Elisha Renne, 187–201. Chicago: University of Chicago Press, 2001.

Renne, Elisha. *Population and Progress in a Yoruba Town*. Ann Arbor: University of Michigan Press, 2003.

Retel-Laurentin, Anne. "Les soleils de l'ombre." In *La natte et le manguier*, ed. Colette Le Cour Grandmasson, Anne Retel-Laurentin, and Ariane Deluize, 85–183. Paris: Mercure de France, 1978.

Retel-Laurentin, Anne. *Sorcellerie et ordalies. L'epreuve du poison en Afrique noire, essai sur le concept de négritude*. Paris: Editions Anthropos, 1974.

Retel-Laurentin, Anne. *Un pays à la dérive. Une société en régression démographique. Les Nzakara de l'Est centrafricain*. Paris: Jean-Pierre Delarge, 1979.

Retort. *Afflicted Powers: Capital and Spectacle in a New Age of War*. London: Verso, 2005.

Reynolds, Pamela. *War in Worcester: Youth and the Apartheid State*. New York: Fordham University Press, 2013.

Riley Brothers, Ltd. "Lantern Lecture on the Congo Atrocities." Advertisement in *Red Rubber: The Story of the Rubber Slave Trade Flourishing on the Congo in the Year of Grace 1907*, 4th ed., 5th impression, by E. D. Morel, verso. London: T. Fisher Unwin, 1907.

Riva, Silvia. "L'épanouissement de cette fleur de culture par nos soins de bons jardiniers. Ou Joseph-Marie Jadot et les écrivains africains du Congo belge et du Ruanda-Urundi." In *Figures et paradoxes de l'histoire au Burundi, au Congo et au Rwanda*, ed. Marc Quaghebeur, Jean-Claude Kangomba, and Amélie Schmitz, 105–19. Paris: l'Harmattan, 2002.

Rivers, W. H. R. "The Dying-Out of Native Races." Parts 1 and 2. *Lancet* (3 January 1920): 42–44; (10 January 1920): 109–11.

Rivers, W. H. R., ed. *Essays on the Depopulation of Melanesia*. Cambridge: Cambridge University Press, 1922.

Rivers, W. H. R. "The Psychological Factor." In *Essays in the Depopulation of Melanesia*, ed. W. H. R. Rivers, 84–113. Cambridge: Cambridge University Press, 1922.

Rivoire, Raymond. *Les acquisitions nouvelles de l'endocrinologie*. 2nd ed. Paris: Masson et Cie, 1935.

Roes, Aldwin. "*Towards a History of Mass Violence in the Etat Indépendant du Congo, 1885–1908*." *South African Historical Journal* 62, no. 4 (2010): 634–70.

Romaniuk, Anatole. "Infertility in Tropical Africa." In *The Population of Tropical Africa*, ed. John Caldwell and Chukuka Okonjo, 214–24. London: Longmans, 1968.

Romaniuk, Anatole. *La fécondité des populations congolaises*. Paris: Mouton, 1967.

Romaniuk, Anatole. *L'aspect démographique de la stérilité des femmes congolaises*. Léopoldville: Editions de l'Université, 1963.

Rose, Jacqueline. *States of Fantasy*. New York: Oxford University Press, 1996.

Rosenblum, Peter. *Prison Conditions in Zaire*. New York: Human Rights Watch, 1993.

Rottenburg, Richard. "Social and Public Experiments and New Figurations of Science and Politics in Postcolonial Africa." *Postcolonial Studies* 12 (2009): 423–40.

Rubenstein, B. B. "An Emotional Factor in Infertility: A Psychosomatic Approach." *Fertility and Sterility* 2, no. 1 (1951): 80–86.

Rubin, I. C. *Uterotubal Insufflation: A Clinical Diagnostic Method of Determining the*

Tubal Factor in Sterility including Therapeutic Aspects and Comparative Notes on Hysterosalpingography. St. Louis, MO: C. V. Mosby, 1947.

Rubin, I. C. "Uterotubal Insufflation: Value in the Treatment of Tubal Obstruction to Ovular Migations." *Fertility and Sterility* 5, no. 4 (1954): 311–24.

Ruscio, Alain. *Que la France était belle au temps des colonies: Anthologie de chansons coloniales et exotiques françaises.* Paris: Maisonneuve et Larose, 2001.

Ruskin, Edward. *Mongo Fables and Proverbs.* Bongandanga: Congo Balolo Mission Press, 1921.

Ryckmans, Pierre. *Allo! Congo! Coroniques radiophoniques: Le Congo vous parle.* Brussels: Edition Universelle, 1935.

Ryckmans, Pierre. "Effort de guerre: Production agricole." No. 5666 Agri. Léo, 22 April 1942. Léopoldville: Gouvernement Général, 1942.

Said, Edward. "Two Visions in *Heart of Darkness.*" In *Culture and Imperialism,* 19–30. New York: Knopf, 1993.

Scarfone, Marianna. "Les aventures de médecins italiens au Congo." Paper presented at the conference entitled "Des Italiens au Congo aux Italien du Congo: images, écrits, oeuvres d'une Italie glocale," Université de Lorraine, 16–18 October 2014, Nancy, France.

Schatzberg, Michael. *Political Legitimacy in Middle Africa: Father, Family, Food.* Bloomington: Indiana University Press, 2001.

Schebesta, Paul. *My Pygmy and Negro Hosts.* Trans. Gerald Griffin. London: Hutchinson and Co., 1936.

Schebesta, Paul. *Vollblutneger und Halbzwerge: forschungen unter waldnegern und halbpygmäen am Ituri in Beigisch Kongo.* Salzburg-Leipzig: Anton Pustet, 1934.

Scheper-Hughes, Nancy. "Nervoso." In *Beyond the Body Proper: Reading the Anthropology of Material Life,* ed. Margaret Lock and Judith Farquhar, 459–67. Durham, NC: Duke University Press, 2007.

Schoenbrun, David. "Conjuring the Modern in Africa: Durability and Rupture in Histories of Public Healing Between the Great Lakes of East Africa." *American Historical Review* 111, no. 5 (December 2006): 1403–39.

Schuster, David. *Neurasthenic Nation: America's Search of Health, Happiness, and Comfort, 1869–1920.* New Brunswick, NJ: Rutgers University Press, 2011.

Schwers, G. A. "Les facteurs de la dénatalité au Congo Belge." *Recueil de Travaux de sciences médicales au Congo belge* 3 (1945): 43–55.

Selye, Hans. *The Stress of Life: A New Theory of Disease.* New York: McGraw-Hill, 1956.

Selye, Hans. "A Syndrome Produced by Diverse Nocuous Agents." *Nature* 138 (4 July 1936).

Serlin, David. *Replaceable You: Engineering the Body of Postwar America.* Chicago: University of Chicago Press, 2004.

Shaw, Bryant P. "Force Publique, Force Unique: The Military in the Belgian Congo 1914–1939." Ph.D. diss., University of Wisconsin, 1984.

Shorter, Aylard. "Nyungu-Ya-Mawa and the 'Empire of the Ruga-Rugas.'" *Journal of African History* 9, no. 2 (1968).

Siebert, Julia. "More Continuity than Change? New Forms of Unfree Labor in the Belgian Congo, 1908–1930." In *Humanitarian Intervention and Changing Labor Relations: The Long-Term Consequences of the Abolition of the Slave Trade*, ed. Marcel van der Linden, 369–86. Leiden: Brill, 2011.

Siegler, Samuel. *Fertility in Women: Causes, Diagnosis and Treatment of Impaired Fertility*. Philadephia: J. P. Lippincott, 1944.

Siegler, Samuel. "The Tubal Factor." In *Fertility in Women: Causes, Diagnosis and Treatment of Impaired Fertility*. Philadephia: J. P. Lippincott, 1944.

Simmel, Georg. "The Metropolis and Mental Life." In *On Individuality and Social Forms: Selected Writings*, ed. Donald Levine, 324–39. Chicago: University of Chicago Press, 1971.

Simpson, J. A., and E. S. C. Weiner, eds. *Oxford English Dictionary*. 2nd ed. Vol. 13, 821. Oxford: Clarendon Press, 1989.

Síocháin, Séamus. *Roger Casement: Imperialist, Rebel, Revolutionary*. Dublin: Lilliput, 2008.

Síocháin, Séamas, and Michael Sullivan, eds. *The Eyes of Another Race: Roger Casement's Congo Report and 1903 Diary*. Dublin: University College Dublin Press, 2003.

Sliwinski, Sharon. "The Childhood of Human Rights: The Kodak on the Congo." *Visual Culture* 5, no. 3 (2006): 333–63.

Smith, Myrtle. "Three Babies in Congo." *World Call* (December 1931): 28–29.

Standeven, Harriet. "The Development of Decorative Gloss Paints in Britain and the United States, c. 1910–1960." *Journal of the American Institute for Conservation of Historic and Artistic Works* 26 (2006): 51–65.

Stanley, Henry. *The Congo and the Founding of Its Free State: A Story of Work and Exploration*. Vol. 2. London: Sampson Low, 1885.

Stanley, Henry. *Through the Dark Continent*. 2 vols. New York: Harper, 1878.

Starr, Frederick. "The Congo Free State and Congo Belge." *Journal of Race Development* 1, no. 4 (1911): 383–99.

Starr, Frederick. *The Truth about the Congo: The Chicago Tribune Articles*. Chicago: Forbes and Co., 1907.

Steenkamp, William. *Is the South-West African Herero Committing Race Suicide?* Cape Town: Unievolkspers Bkp., printer, 1944.

Stengers, Jean, and Jean-Jacques Synoens, eds. *Le Congo belge durant la Seconde Guerre mondiale*. Brussels: Académie Royale des Sciences d'Outre-Mer, 1983.

Stepan, Nancy. *Picturing Tropical Nature*. Ithaca, NY: Cornell University Press, 2001.

Stewart, Gary. *Rumba on the River: A History of the Popular Music of the Two Congos*. London: Verso, 2000.

Stoler, Ann. *Carnal Knowledge and Imperial Power: Race and the Intimate in Colonial Rule*. Berkeley: University of California Press, 2002.

Stoler, Ann, ed. *Imperial Debris: On Ruins and Ruination*. Durham, NC: Duke University Press, 2013.

Stoler, Ann. "Introduction: 'The Rot Remains': From Ruins to Ruination." In *Imperial*

Debris: On Ruins and Ruination, ed. Ann Stoler, 1–37. Durham, NC: Duke University Press, 2013.

Stoler, Ann. *Race and Education of Desire: Foucault's History of Sexuality and the Colonial Order of Things*. Durham, NC: Duke University Press, 1995.

Stoler, Ann. "Reframing Dissent and Duress." In *Along the Archival Grain: Epistemic Anxieties and Colonial Common Sense*, ed. Ann Stoler, 111–14. Princeton, NJ: Princeton University Press, 2010.

Strachan, Hew. *The First World War in Africa*. Oxford: Oxford University Press, 2004.

Strother, Zoe. *Inventing Masks: Agency and History in the Art of the Central Pende*. Chicago: University of Chicago Press, 1998.

Strouvens, Léon, and Pierre Piron. *Codes et lois du Congo belge*. Léopoldville: Edition de Guerre des Codes Louwers, 1943.

Sumuwe, Abbé Jean. "Crise de mariage. Concubinage perpetual." *La Voix du Congolais* 6, no. 50 (May 1950): 282–85.

Sunseri, Thaddeus. "The Political Ecology of the Copal Trade in the Tanzanian Coastal Hinterland, c. 1820–1905." *Journal of African History* 48, no. 2 (2007): 201–20.

"Tarifs de soins médicaux et des frais d'hospitalisation pour Congolais dans les formations sanitaires de la colonie." *Mbandaka*, 14 July 1956, 4.

Taussig, Michael. "Culture of Terror—Space of Death: Roger Casement's Putumayo Report and the Explanation of Torture." *Comparative Studies in Society and History* 26, no. 3 (July 1984): 467–97.

Taussig, Michael. *The Nervous System*. New York: Routledge, 1992.

Taussig, Michael. *Shamanism, Colonialism, and the Wild Man: A Study in Terror and Healing*. Chicago: Chicago University Press, 1987.

"Taxe pour les femmes célibataires." *Mbandaka*, 10 December 1955, 1.

Testis. "Le point de vue de nos abonnés: Recensement médical au centre extra-coutumier de Coquilhatville." *Mbandaka*, 23 October 1954, 4.

Thomas, Lynn. *Politics of the Womb: Women, Reproduction, and the State in Kenya*. Berkeley: University of California Press, 2003.

Thomas, Martin. *Violence and Colonial Order: Police, Workers and Protest in the European Colonial Empires, 1918–1940*. Cambridge: Cambridge University Press, 2012.

Thornton, John. *The Kongolese Saint Anthony: Dona Beatriz Kimpa Vita and the Antonian Movement, 1684–1706*. Cambridge: Cambridge University Press, 1998.

Thrift, Nigel. "Space." *Theory, Culture and Society* 23, nos. 2–3 (May 2006): 139–46.

Tilley, Helen. *Africa as a Living Laboratory: Empire, Development, and the Problem of Scientific Knowledge, 1870–1950*. Chicago: University of Chicago Press, 2011.

Tóibín, Colm. "A Man of No Mind," *London Review of Books* 34, no. 17 (13 September 2012): 15–16.

Tombeur, Ch. *Campagnes des troupes coloniales belges en Afrique centrale, 1914–1917*. Brussels: Notre colonie, 1918.

Tonnoir, René. "Bobongo ou l'art choréographique chez les Ekonda, Yembe et Tumba du Lac Léopold II." *Problèmes d'Afrique centrale* (Brussels), no. 20 (1953): 87–109.

Totten, Samuel, and William Parsons, eds. *Centuries of Genocide: Essays and Eyewitness Accounts*. 4th ed. New York: Routledge, 2013.

Toulier, Bernard, Johan Lagae, and Marc Gemoets. *Kinshasa: Architecture et paysage urbains*. Paris: Somogy, 2010.

Trapido, Joe. "Love and Money in Kinois Popular Music." *Journal of African Cultural Studies* 22, no. 2 (2010): 121–44.

Twain, Mark [Samuel Clements]. *King Leopold's Soliloquy: A Defense of His Congo Rule*. Boston: P. R. Warren Co., 1905.

"Une Congolaise à Lisbonne." *Mbandaka*, 8 January 1955, 3.

"Une région qui se meurt." *La page chrétienne* (June 1937). Périodiques locaux, microfiche 6, Archives Aequatoria Microfiche Collection.

University of Michigan Museum of Art. Ekonda short sword, accession number 1998/1.68. Accessed 27 March 2015. http://quod.lib.umich.edu/m/musart /x-1998-sl-1.68/1998_1.68_jpg#.

"Un peuple qui meurt: Les Mongos." *Le Progrès*, 25 June 1948, 1.

Van der Kerken, Georges. *L'Ethnie Mongo*. Vol. 1: *Première partie: Histoire, groupements, sous-groupments, origines*. Brussels: Van Campenhout, 1944.

Van der Kinden, Fritz. *Le Congo, les Noirs et nous*. Paris: Challemel, 1910.

Vanderlinden, Pierre. *Main d'oeuvre, église, capital et administration dans le Congo des années trent*. Vol. 1. Brussels: Académie Royale des Sciences d'Outre-Mer, 2007.

Vanderlinden, Pierre. *Pierre Ryckmans, 1891–1959: Coloniser dans l'honneur*. Brussels: De Boeck, 1994.

van der Straeten, Edgar. *L'agriculture et les industries agricoles au Congo Belge*. Brussels: L. Cuypers, 1945.

Vanderstraeten, Louis-François. *La répression de la révolte des Pende du Kwango en 1931*. Brussels: Académie Royale des Sciences d'Outre-Mer, 2001.

Vandervelde, Emile. *Les derniers Jours de l'Etat du Congo, journal de voyage (juillet–octobre 1908)*. Paris: La Société Nouvelle, 1909.

Vangroenweghe, Daniel. *Du sang sur les lianes: Léopold II et son Congo*. Brussels: Didier Hatier, 1986.

Vangroenweghe, Daniel. "Le journal de Charles Lemaire à l'Equateur, 1891–1893." *Annales Aequatoria* 7 (1996): 7–73.

Van Iseghem, André. *Au Congo belge en 1896*. Brussels: Dewit, 1935.

van Onselen, Charles. *Studies in the Social and Economic History of Witwatersrand, 1886–1914*. 2 vols. New York: Longman, 1982.

Van Reybrouck, David. "Central Africa in the Mid-nineteenth Century." Map (ca. 34 mm = 1000 km). In *Congo: The Epic History of a People*. Trans. Sam Garrett, 28, fig. 3. New York: Ecco, 2014.

Van Reybrouck, David. *Congo: The Epic History of a People*. Trans. Sam Garrett. New York: Ecco, 2014.

Van Riel, Joseph, and R. Allard. *Contribution à l'étude de la dénatalité dans l'ethnie mongo*. Brussels: Institut Royal du Congo belge, 1953.

Vansina, Jan. *Paths in the Rainforests: Toward a History of Political Tradition in Equatorial Africa*. Madison: University of Wisconsin Press, 1990.

Vansina, Jan. *The Tio Kingdom of Middle Congo, 1880–1892*. London: Oxford University Press 1973.

Vanthemsche, Guy. *Genèse et porte du "Plan décennal du Congo belge" (1949–1959)*. Brussels: Académie Royale des Sciences d'Outre-Mer, 1994.

Vanthemsche, Guy. *Le Congo belge pendant la Première Guerre mondiale: les rapports du ministre des Colonies Jules Renkin au roi Albert Ier, 1914–1918*. Brussels: Palais des Académies, 2009.

Van Wing, J. "Démographie congolaise." *Courrier d'Afrique*, 19 May 1945, 1.

Vaughan, Megan. *Curing Their Ills: Colonial Power and African Illness*. Stanford, CA: Stanford University Press, 1991.

Vaughan, Megan. "Syphilis in Colonial East and Central Africa: The Social Construction of an Epidemic." In *Epidemics and Ideas: Essays on the Historical Perception of Pestilence*, ed. Terence Ranger and Paul Slack, 269–302. Cambridge: Cambridge University Press, 1992.

Vellut, Jean-Luc. "Colonial Kitsch." In *An Anthology of African Art: The Twentieth Century*, ed. N'Goné Fall and Jean Loup Pivin, 160–63. New York: DAP, 2002.

Vellut, Jean-Luc. "Episodes anticommunistes dans l'ordre colonial belge (1924–1932)." In *La Peur du rouge*, ed. P. Dewit and J. Gotovitch, 183–89. Brussels: Editions de l'Université de Bruxelles, 1996.

Vellut, Jean-Luc. "Introduction: Regards sur le temps colonial." In *La Mémoire du Congo: le temps colonial*, ed. Jean-Luc Vellut, 11–21. Gand: Editions Snoeck, 2005.

Vellut, Jean-Luc. "La présence portugaise au Congo du XVe siècle à la Deuxième Guerre mondiale." *La Revue Générale*, no. 8–9 (1991).

Vellut, Jean-Luc. "La violence armée dans L'Etat Indépendant du Congo: Ténébres et clartés d'un état conquérant." *Cultures et développement* 16, nos. 3–4 (1984): 671–707.

Vellut, Jean-Luc. "Le Katanga industriel en 1944: Malaises et anxiétés dans la société coloniale." In *Le Congo Belge durant la Seconde Guerre Mondiale: Recueil d'études*, ed. Jean Stengers and Jean-Jacques Synoens, 495–523. Brussels: Académie Royale des Sciences d'Outre-Mer, 1983.

Vellut, Jean-Luc. "Reseaux transnationaux dans l'economie politique du Congo leopoldien, c. 1885–1910." In *Afrikanische Beziehungen, Netzwerke und Räume*, ed. Laurence Marfaing and Brigitte Reinwald, 131–46. Hamburg: Lit Verlag, 2001.

Vellut, Jean-Luc. "Résistances et espaces de liberté dans l'histoire coloniale du Zaïre: Avant la marche à l'indépendance, ca. 1876–1945." In *Rébellions-révolution au Zaïre, 1963–1965*, ed. C. Coquery-Vidrovitch, A. Forest, and H. Weiss, vol. 1, 24–73. Paris: l'Harmattan, 1987.

Vellut, Jean-Luc, ed. *Selection of Exhibition Texts: Memory of the Congo: The Colonial Era*. Tevuren: Musée Royal de l'Afrique Centrale, 205.

Vellut, Jean-Luc. *Simon Kimbangu, 1921: De la prédication à la déportation*. Parts 1 and 2. Brussels: Académie Royale des Sciences d'Outre-Mer, 2005–10.

Verbeeck, A. "Anticonceptionele Middelen." *Aequatoria* 14, no. 1 (1951): 26–28.

Vertenten, Petrus. Block print of man with cap and cigarette. *Le Coq chante* 4 (1 September 1939): 14.

Veys, S. "Territoire d'Ingende. Renseignements historiques fournis par Lomboto, capita du village de Bokatola." Annexe 3 in "Arrivée des blancs sur les bords des rivières équatoriales," by Edmond Boelaert, Honoré Vinck, and Charles Lonkama. *Annales Aequatoria* 16 (1995): 127–34.

Vinck, Honoré. "La guerre de 1940–45 vécue à Coquilhatville." *Annales Aequatoria* 22 (2001): 21–101.

Vinck, Honoré. "Résistance et collaboration au début de la colonisation à Mbandaka (1883–1893)." In *Forschungen in Zaïre: In memoriam Erika Sulzmann (7.1.1911–17.6.1989)*, ed. Ernst Müller and Anna-Maria Brandstetter, 481–508. Münster: Lit Verlag, 1992.

Vinson, Robert. *The Americans Are Coming! Dreams of African American Liberation in Segregationist South Africa*. Athens: Ohio University Press, 2012.

Virno, Paolo. *A Grammar of the Multitude: For an Analysis of Contemporary Forms of Life*. Trans. Isabella Bertoletti, James Cascaito, and Andrea Casson. Cambridge, MA: Semiotext (e), 2003.

Voas, David. "Subfertility and Disruption in the Congo Basin." In *African Historical Demography*, vol. 2, 777–802. Proceedings of a seminar held in the Centre of African Studies, University of Edinburgh, 24–25 April 1981. Edinburgh: Centre of African Studies, University of Edinburgh, 1981.

Walkowitz, Judith. *Prostitution and Victorian Society: Women, Class, and the State*. Cambridge, UK: Cambridge University Press, 1980.

Warner, Marina. *Phantasmagoria: Spirit Visions, Metaphors, and Media in the Twenty-first Century*. Oxford: Oxford University Press, 2006.

The War of 1914–1916: The Belgian Campaigns in the Cameroons and in German East Africa. London: Sir Joseph Causton and Sons, 1917.

Wassa, Ferdinand. "Liberté de la femme noire et prostitution." *La Voix du Congolais* 4, no. 15 (February 1948): 71–72.

Wauters, A. "Magiciens et écoles de magiciens chez les Batswa de l'Equateur." *Annales Aequatoria* 1, no. 2 (1980).

Webel, Mari. "Medical Auxiliaries, Colonial Fieldwork, and Sleeping Sickness Research in the Lake Victoria and Lake Tanganyika Basins before 1914." In *Citizens, Courtrooms, Crossings*, ed. Astri Andresen et al., 169–87. Bergen: Stein Rokkan Centre, 2008.

Weeks, John. "Anthropological Notes on the Bangala of the Upper Congo River." Parts 1 and 3. *Journal of the Royal Anthropological Institute of Great Britain and Ireland* 39, no. 1 (1909): 97–136; 40, no. 2 (1910): 360–427.

Werner, Michael, and Bénédicte Zimmermann, "Penser l'histoire croisée: entre empirie et réflexivité." *Annales. Historie, Sciences Sociales* 58, no. 1 (2003): 7–36.

West, Michael. "Seeds Are Sown: The Garvey Movement in Zimbabwe in the Interwar Years." *International Journal of African Historical Studies* 35, nos. 2–3 (2003): 335–62.

White, Bob. "Congolese Rumba and Other Cosmopolitanisms." *Cahiers d'études africaines* 42, no. 4 (2002): 663–86.

White, Bob. *Rumba Rules: The Politics of Dance Music in Mobutu's Zaire*. Durham, NC: Duke University Press, 2008.

White, Luise. *Speaking with Vampires: Rumor and History in Colonial Africa*. Berkeley: University of California Press, 2000.

White, Luise, Stephan Miescher, and David Cohen, eds. *African Words, African Voices: Critical Practices in Oral History*. Bloomington: Indiana University Press, 2001.

Wigny, Pierre. *A Ten Year Plan for the Economic and Social Development of the Belgian Congo*. New York: Belgian Government Information Center, 1950.

Williams, Raymond. "Dominant, Residual, and Emergent." In *Marxism and Literature*, 121–27. Oxford: Oxford University Press, 1977.

Williams, Raymond. *Marxism and Literature*. Oxford: Oxford University Press, 1977.

Williams, Raymond. "Structures of Feeling." In *Marxism and Literature*, 128–35. Oxford: Oxford University Press, 1977.

Wilson, Charles. *History of Unilever: A Study in Economic Growth and Social Change*. New York: Praeger, 1968.

Woodruff, Nan. *American Congo: The African American Freedom Struggle in the Delta*. Cambridge, MA: Harvard University Press, 2003.

Worboys, Michael. "Unsexing Gonorrhoea: Bacteriologist, Gynaecologists, and Suffragists in Britain, 1860–1920." *Social History of Medicine* 17, no. 1 (2004): 41–59.

Worobey, Michael, et al. "Direct Evidence of Extensive Diversity of HIV-1 in Kinshasa by 1960." *Nature* 455, no. 7213 (2 October 2008): 661–64.

Yogolelo Tambwe ya Kasimba and Hangi Shamamba. "Bushiri Lungundu, c. 1911–1945, Kitawala." In *Encyclopedia Africana Dictionary of African Biography*, ed. L. H. Ofosu-Appiah. Vol. 2, Sierra Leone-Zaire. New York: Reference Publications, 1979. Accessed 11 August 2010. http://www.dacb.org/stories/demrepcongo/bushiri_lungundu.html.

Young, Allan. "Posttraumatic Stress Disorder of the Virtual Kind: Trauma and Resilience in Post-9/11 America." In *Trauma and Memory: Reading, Healing, and Making Law*, ed. Austin Sarat, Nadav Davidovitch, and Michal Alberstein, 21–48. Stanford, CA: Stanford University Press, 2007.

Young, Crawford. *The African Colonial State in Comparative Perspective*. New Haven, CT: Yale University Press, 1994.

Young, Crawford. *Politics in the Congo: Decolonization and Independence*. Princeton, NJ: Princeton University Press, 1965.

Young, Crawford. *The Postcolonial State in Africa: Fifty Years of Independence, 1960–2010*. Madison: University of Wisconsin Press, 2012.

Zimmerer, Jürgen, and Joachim Zeller, eds. *Genocide in German South-West Africa: The Colonial War (1904–1908) in Namibia and Its Aftermath*. Trans. Edward Neather. Monmouth, Wales: Merlin Press, 2008.

INDEX

Harms, Robert, 38

Harris, Alice, photographs, 8, 28, 36, 41, 59, 73*f*

Harris, John, photographs, 73*f*

HCB. *See* Huileries du Congo Belge

healing: associations, 14, 136; distraction and, 21, 116, 240–41, 242; harming and, 164, 166, 212, 242; historicities, 278n139; patrimonial state and, 276n121; public, 12, 19, 63, 132, 250; secrecy and, 19; therapeutic insurgency, 7, 9, 11–12, 18, 21, 22, 25, 241; through trees, 85–86, 91, 93, 118, 242, 253; vernacular, 7, 9, 11–12, 18, 21, 72, 164–65, 249; Yebola, 116–20, 132, 245; Zebola, 118. *See also* Likili; Maria N'koi

Heart of Darkness (Conrad), 3, 32

hedonism, 15, 225, 233, 246–48, 260n87

hemp trade, 69–70

Hennaert (warden), 192

Herero, 13

HIV/AIDS, 10, 163, 225, 250–51, 297–98n133

Hobsbawm, Eric, 11

Hochschild, Adam, 3, 28, 29–30, 41, 48

Hodgkin, Thomas, 11–12

hospitals, 154–55, 154–55*f*; biopolitics and, 153; as a camp, 55; culture of, 221; in Katanga, 169; Kitawala in, 213–14; mission, 97, 152, 182, 199; refuge in, 213–14; rural economy and, 198; sleeping sickness and, 275n99; sulfa, use of, 189; surveillance and, 110, 133; venereal control in, 189. *See also* clinics; dispensaries

hostage houses, 43, 59

Huileries du Congo Belge (HCB), 96, 99–101, 103, 116, 278n4, 281n49

Hulstaert, Gustaaf, 87–88, 124–25, 128, 137, 141, 145, 149, 156–57, 173

Ieli-Ininga (chief), 70

ikaie charm, 97

Ikakota charm, 49–53, 459

Ikenga (chief), 69

Ilanga, Joseph, 51

imaginations, 2, 3, 6, 18; Congolese territories and, 82; economic slump and, 119–20; in Ewewe, 136; immediacy and, 31; Likili and, 157, 158; materiality and, 20, 242; mutilations in, 252; nervousness and, 234; religious, 66*f*, 110, 196, 244; reverie and, 19, 22, 110; violence and, 94, 165

Imome, Joseph, 37

independent women. *See femme libres*

infertility, 12–14, 22; causes, 112, 136–37, 251; clinic, 8, 167–69, 199, 205, 241, 250; device, 201–3, 202*f*, 205; Likili and, 137, 157–58, 162, 165; nervousness and, 158, 245; rape and, 161, 163; widespread, 131, 165, 240, 249. *See also* sterility

Ingonda, Phillipe, 212

interrogations. *See* security: interrogations

irrigation, internal. See *lavement* practices

ivory trade, 36

Jadot, Joseph-Marie, 79*f*; Collignon critique of, 62, 72, 74, 77–78; Equateur image, 120*f*; fiction by, 62, 68, 72, 74, 76–80, 81, 83–85, 93–94, 243, 252; on Maria N'koi, 79–80, 81, 83–85, 87, 91–92, 111, 152; poem by, 91–92, 242; on primitivism, 78, 91–92

Jaggard, Louis, 97, 100, 112–13, 130, 131, 152, 171, 250

Janzen, John, 11

Kamerun, 23, 63, 64*f*, 67, 80, 92

Katanga, 59, 98, 110, 169–71, 186–88, 192, 195, 196

Kemba, Jean, 107

Kimbangu, Simon, 11–12, 17, 97, 119, 132, 169, 196, 218

Kimbanguism, 169, 173–74, 203, 208

kimpassi (healing associations), 14

King Leopold's Ghost (Hochschild), 3, 28

King Leopold's Soliloquy (Twain), 27, 41

Kinshasa. *See* Léopoldville (Kinshasa)

Kiri territory, 67–72, 68f, 75, 82, 86, 92–93
Kitawala, 169–71, 175–76, 203, 207, 220, 239, 243; Boyela and, 192–95; as disruptive, 185–87, 204, 212, 241; dreamwork of, 205, 210, 213–14; in hospitals, 213–14; as illegal, 194; Kimbanguism and, 208; Loma chiefdom and, 210–13, 225; punishment of, 195–96
Koselleck, Reinhart, 21

Lancet, The (journal), 184
"Lantern Lecture on the Congo Atrocities," 28
Last, Murray, 11
latitude, 2, 16–18, 240–42, 246, 253
laughter, nervous, 39–41, 59, 60
lavement practices, 128–29, 131, 161, 163, 239, 249, 280n31
Lechat, Michel, 218, 222
leopards (*n'koi*), 61, 62, 66f, 94
Leopold II, King of the Belgians, 1, 2, 27, 42
Léopoldville (Kinshasa), 17, 128, 218, 233–34, 240, 246–48, 251, 306n123
Lesa, Mwana, 170
Levy, Macha Simba, 196
Lianja, 19, 21, 56, 121–25, 130, 149, 242
Likili, 136, 220, 241; flywhisks, 22, 143, 144f, 151–52, 158, 163–64; infertility and, 141–43, 157–58, 161, 162, 165; nervous chiefdom and, 157–59; origin stories, 147–48; police arrests, 145; power of, 137
Lintombe, Jean, 212–13
Liwenthal, Charles (Ekuma), 53–54, 77, 77f, 231–35, 246–47
Lodewyckx, Charles, 239, 275n100
Lokongo, David, 174
Lokuli, Marc, 212
Loma chiefdom, 210–13
Lomboto, Joseph, 224
Lomongo language, 21–22, 38, 48–49, 137–38
Lompoko (chief), 67
Lonkama, Charles, 239–40

Lonkundo (language), 21
Lopombo (chief), 46–47
Losilo (magazine), 138
Losilo pamphlet, 137–38
low birth rates: depopulation and, 147, 172, 177; examinations for, 100; investigation of causes, 96–97, 98, 110–13, 136–41, 146–47, 150–51, 177–85, 248–49; Likili and, 157–58; nervous states and, 7, 96, 171, 201, 221, 237; psychosomatic factors, 13, 199–201, 295n65; rape and, 59, 244; recovery from, 199–200, 295n65; shock and, 16; Songo experiment, 177–85
Lubuka, Thomas, 82
Lumumba, Patrice, 3, 195, 196

Mabille, Marie, 125
Maï-Maï combatants, 12
Maison Patou ("Auditorium"), 229
makango. See *femme libres*
Malengreau, Dr., 149
Maliani, Henri (Bowane), 225–26, 228–31, 230f, 234–35, 252
Mangi, old men of, *56f*
Manono insurrection (1941), 186, 195
Marée, C., 106, 108
Maria N'koi, 60–63; betrayal of, 86–88; charm and words (*n'Kissi*), 72, 93; Collignon and, 65–67, 70–72, 75–76, 77–78; colonial milieu of, 63, 64f, 115f; on copal, 63, 72–75; on copal labor, 74; death, 88; De Laveleye and, 67–70, 75, 80–81; eviction reverie, 61, 68, 82, 94; family, 276n118; figurations of, 62, 63, 93–94; Germani and, 61, 63, 81–82; as healer, 23, 61–63, 82, 86–87, 88–91, 93, 241–42, 276n122; husband's affair, 276nn115–16; identity card, 89f; Jadot on, 79–80, 81, 83–85, 87, 91–94, 111, 152; leopards (*n'koi*) and, 62, 66f, 93; as nerve-wracking, 92–93, 165–66; Njondo and, 89–90, 118, 241–42, 277n129; relegation of, 62, 63, 70–72, 170f, 176, 185; on sleeping

sickness, 82–83; tax rebellion, 23, 63, 65, 71; trees and, 85–86, 91, 93, 242; on white hens, 75–76; white hens story, 75–76

"Marie-Louisa" (Maliani-Bowane song), 230

Mata, David, 225–27

Mbandaka (newspaper), 219, 220, 221

medicalization: biopolitics and, 25, 132; harm and, 234; intensified, 145, 191, 234, 251; medical passports, 208, 224; nurse figures, 230–31; security and, 7, 110, 133, 213; women's examinations, 100, 161–62, 224–25

Melanesia, 13

memory accounts (1954–55), 30, 48–49, 50*f*, 52–54, 59, 231, 233, 243–44

ménagères (housekeepers-mistresses), 45

messianism, 11–12

milieu, concept, 240. *See also* shrunken milieu

miscarriage, 98, 99–100, 113, 132, 183, 248–49

Mission des Noirs, 169, 174–75, 185, 192, 196

mission stations, 55

modernization, 219

modes of presence, 7–8, 25

Mongo, 14, 19, 38–39, 48, 59, 81*f*, 140, 157, 177–78, 286n8. *See also* Lomongo (language)

Morel, E. D., 3, 27, 29, 30, 43, 47

motion, 2; distraction and, 20, 208, 229, 233; Likili and, 136–37; reverie and, 20–21, 169

Mottoulle, Léopold, 98, 110–11, 120–21, 130

Mouchet, R., 98–99, 100, 114, 116, 149

Mountmorres, Viscount, 47–48, 55, 59

Mpadi, Simon, 110, 169, 173–75, 196

Mpadisme, 110

Muleliste rebels, 12

multitudes, 7, 20, 60, 93

Munga, Maurice, 225, 227–28, 231

mutilation: photographs, 2–3, 20, 27–28, 30, 41–42, 42*f*, 154–55*f*, 156, 177, 203–4; practices as old, 36; remembering and, 20, 31, 49, 243–44, 252; report on, 32, 42; severed hands and feet, 20, 33, 40, 41–42, 42*f*, 49, 154–55*f*, 177, 252, 264n39; by sentries, 36–39, 41, 49, 52–53; venereal disease and, 139

Native Welfare Fund. *See* Fonds du Bien Etre Indigène (FBEI)

Ndio, Thomas, 276nn115–16

nearness: Casement report, 32–34; techniques of (Walter Benjamin concept), 5, 21, 31, 59, 242; security interrogations and, 104

Negro World (Garvey), 96

nervousness, 5–7, 18; colonial, 20–21, 205, 210, 215–16, 225, 234–35, 252; decolonization and, 21, 25, 168, 171, 204–5, 207, 210, 214, 234; diagnostics and, 143–45; infertility and, 158, 245; about interracial sexuality, 100; laughter, 39–41, 59, 60; Likili and, 157–59; past present of, 21; plasticity and, 238; security and, 193, 238; various types of, 96; violence and, 5–6, 20. *See also* neurasthenia

nervous states: biopolitics and, 8, 25; low birth rates and, 7, 96, 171, 201, 221, 237; on Maria N'koi, 63; postcolonial, 296n95; security and, 92, 168–69, 173–77, 193–94, 213, 215–18, 227, 234–35, 238; subalternity and, 237; xenophobia and, 8–9, 12, 137, 143–45, 165, 237, 238

neurasthenia, 6, 116–20, 130, 132, 245, 257n35

nganda, 56, 57, 114*f*, 114–16, 241, 307n11

Niamanene (chief), 69–70

Nicolas Favre (lymphogranuloma venereum), 99

Nietzsche, Friedrich, 3, 4, 5

subjectivity: collective, 20, nervousness and, 252; women's, 132

subversive movements, 87, 175–76, 185–86, 193, 195, 203, 226, 229

Sudanic region, 36

sulfa drugs, 188, 189

surveillance, 10, 96, 102, 105, 174–75, 182, 185–86, 192, 194, 208, 215, 228. *See also* security

syphilis, 100, 131–32, 139, 181

Taussig, Michael, 3

taxes, 58; in coin, 49, 55; evasion, 103, 115, 209–10, 296n86; in kind, 73, 74–75, 272n49; rebellion against, 23, 63, 65, 71, 83–84; reduction for births, 221; rubber, 1, 40; for single women, 223; work to pay, 58

therapeutic insurgency, 7, 9, 11–12, 18, 21, 22, 25, 241

Thrift, Nigel, 3–4

Tippu Tip, 36

tonality, 8, 9, 19, 39–40, 167

traders, 58, 74, 79, 96, 97, 100, 116, 181

trading networks, 37*f*

trees, 85–86, 91, 93, 242, 253

Trolli, Dr., 149, 150

Tshoambe, 158–60

Tshuapa, 138, 141, 149, 151, 174, 175, 177–78, 183, 193–94

Twain, Mark, 3, 27, 41

Ubangi region, 36

Unilever, 101, 278n4. *See also* Huileries du Congo Belge

Union Minière, 98

urbanity, 15, 17, 20, 188, 218–20, 225

Van Ackere, Cécile, 191, 199, 227, 228

Van Calcken, Raoul, 40–41, 46–47

Van Campenhout, Falk, 174–76, 184, 194, 198

Van Den Eeden, Dr., 221

Vanderhallen, J., 143–45

Van Goethem, E., 128

Van Hoeck, 179–80, 182

Van Hoof, Lucien, 138, 141, 146, 151, 155, 156, 163, 164, 172

Van Riel (FBEI advisor), 198, 199–200

Vansina, Jan, 12

venereal disease. *See* sexually transmitted disease

Vereecken, Richard, 101–2

vernacular healing. *See* healing: vernacular

violence: to bodies, 2, 27–31, 32–33, 36, 40, 52–53, 59, 164–65, 210; genocidal, 3, 13; nervousness and, 5–6, 20; predatory, 36; rubber extraction and, 28–29, 47–48, 94; sexual, 41–44, 49, 52–53, 59, 124–25, 244, 250; spectacular, 3, 4; torture, 195–97. *See also* mutilation

Virno, Paolo, 20

visual economies, 41–47

vitalism, 13–14, 122, 138, 148, 156–57, 178, 180, 183–84, 200, 244, 253

Voas, David, 59

"voices" as historical method, 29–30

voyeurism, 27–28, 44, 45–46

Wala massacre (1904), 40

Wangata, 32, 49

wartime duress, WWII, 171–73

Weber, Max, 6

white-black relations, 96–97

white trash, 97, 100, 130

Williams, Raymond, 19–20

women: associations, 125–28, 223, 246, 247; *femme libres*, 118, 119, 126–28, 130, 209, 221, 224, 246, 247, 272, 292; images of, 244–45; immorality charges, 98–99; *lavement* practices, 128–29, 131, 161, 163, 239, 249, 280n31; medical examinations, 100, 161–62, 224–25; porterage work,

110–13, 244; single, taxes for, 223; sociality, 222–23; stereotypes, 245; temperaments, 239

Writing of the Disaster, The (Blanchot), 4

xenophobia, 8, 12, 97, 137, 143–45, 165, 169, 203, 237, 238, 252

Yebola, 116–20, 130, 132, 242, 244, 245, 276n122, 277nn129–30

Yolo, Jean-Ambroise, 49–50

Zebola, 118, 242, 277n130, 306n5

zest, 13, 149, 157, 179, 180

Zilani, Jérome, 174–75, 193